Martin Heidegger
and the Problem of
Historical Meaning

Martin Heidegger and the Problem of Historical Meaning

Revised and Expanded Edition

<small>JEFFREY ANDREW BARASH</small>

FORDHAM UNIVERSITY PRESS
New York
2003

Perspectives in Continental Philosophy, no. 31
ISSN 1089–3938

Library of Congress Cataloging-in-Publication Data

Barash, Jeffrey Andrew.
    Martin Heidegger and the problem of historical meaning/Jeffrey Andrew Barash.—2nd rev. ed.
        p. cm.—(Perspectives in continental philosophy)
Includes bibliographical references and index.
    ISBN 0-8232-2264-0 (pbk. : alk. paper)
    1. Heidegger, Martin, 1889–1976. 2. History—Philosophy. I. Title. II. Series.
B3279.H49B273   2003
901—dc21   2003011499

Printed in the United States of America
07 06 05 04 03   5 4 3 2 1
First edition

To the memory of my mother and father

CONTENTS

Foreword by Paul Ricœur   vii

Introduction   xvii

Part I   Toward an Ontology of History: 1912–1927

1   The Emergence of the Problem of Historical Meaning
    in Nineteenth-Century German Thought   1

2   Metaphysics and Historical Meaning in Heidegger's
    Early Writings   64

3   Existence and History: Heidegger's Radical Turning
    Point between 1918 and 1923   98

4   The Theological Roots of Heidegger's Interpretation
    of Historical Meaning   132

5   Historical Meaning in the Fundamental Ontology of
    Being and Time   157

Part II   Toward a History of Being: 1927–1964

6   Anthropology, Metaphysics, and the Problem of Historical
    Meaning in Heidegger's Interpretation of the *Kehre*   191

Conclusion   255

Selected Bibliography   259

Index   281

FOREWORD

On the basis of rare texts and of unpublished correspondence, *Martin Heidegger and the Problem of Historical Meaning* proposes to interpret Heidegger by reconstructing the philosophical landscape at the beginning of the twentieth century and between the two World Wars. Standing out in the foreground of this landscape are the two mountains of Heidegger's *Sein und Zeit* (Being and time; 1927) and his work following the reversal (*Kehre*) in his thinking in the thirties and forties. Jeffrey Andrew Barash's reconstruction establishes subterranean continuities between Heidegger's work and his intellectual environment, drawing on the contrast between them to make that work more intelligible.

To appreciate the consequences of continuity as well as of discontinuity, Barash has raised the perdurable touchstone question of historical meaning and summoned to address it all the protagonists, including Heidegger himself, of an intellectual debate dating back nearly a hundred years. By "historical meaning," he refers to the stubborn question most closely approximated by the term "coherence" as it applies to history. Almost from the outset, he returns again and again to this key term and to the touchstone question it signals. Such an emphasis seems strange considering the variety of meanings of history the author explores even as he seeks to evaluate its coherence: from the events of the past taken as a whole (the course of history), to the discourse centered on these events (historiography), to the historical condition of the being that we are (historicity), to Being itself in its epochal manifestations.

Barash's fortunate discovery is precisely this: as vast as the space of variation covered by the term "history" might be, one question constantly arises: what makes it "hold together [*zusammenhängen*]"— whether this concerns phases in the course of history, conditions of possibility in the critique of historical understanding, ontological components of historicity, or epochs of a history of Being? Barash devotes his work to situating Heidegger in the space of variations opened by answers to this penetrating question. In this space, Heidegger appears at once consonant with the question of coherence, identifiable in its new guises, and dissonant with all responses to it. This accounts for the strange impression one receives from reading Barash's book: Heidegger appears at times infinitely more integrated within his period than one might suspect, say, from reading *Being and Time* deliberately out of context, yet also more refractory to categorization under a generic philosophical designation such as existentialism, relativism, or irrationalism—or indeed to any categorization in progressive or reactionary terms. And yet, it is the coherence of history—in whatever way one takes this term—that makes Heidegger and his times hold together.

Readers will first discover a remarkably articulated investigation of the great debate centered in Germany, before and after World War I, on the problem of the sense of history. They will take the measure of Heidegger's proximity to this debate—a proximity that often leads us to underestimate his brief discussions, even the silence of *Being and Time* on the epistemology of historical knowledge. At the same time, they will be prepared for a consideration of the "history of Being" during the forties and fifties as an unexpected resurgence of the question underlying the controversies dating from the beginning of the century.

This book attempts nothing less than to reconnect the thread between the beginning and the end of a life work that never ceased moving away from itself. But before turning to the question of the "history of Being," to which the entire second part of the book is devoted, we should consider in the first part the author's patient *mise en place* of the theme of the historicity of *Dasein* (finite human existence) in *Being and Time.** This familiar theme assumes a new shape once we recognize the philosophical standpoint to which it offers a resolutely discordant reply, without ever abandoning a certain common field of questioning.

Firmly holding the thread of his investigation, Barash concentrates on identifying a dilemma encountered by the critical philosophy of history at the beginning of the century, a dilemma this philosophy exacerbated by its very efforts to resolve it, and one assumed by the question of meaning in history once one has abandoned hope of distilling immutable metaphysical truths from the historical flux. If all is historical, how could truth itself not be so? In this regard, the destiny of the term "historicism" is eloquent: on the one hand, it celebrates the triumph of a vision of the world that establishes the history of culture as the matrix of all conceptions, norms, and values; on the other, it stigmatizes the relativism that seems a heavy tribute to pay for this glorious discovery. Truth should be historical. Where, then, is the difficulty? Precisely in the possibility of continuing to conceive of something like a coherence of history, without which nothing could be signified by the term "history" itself.

Barash begins his main text with a highly detailed study of the diverse forms that this dilemma assumed in the work of thinkers as different as Hermann Cohen and Paul Natorp of the Marburg School and, above all, Wilhelm Windelband and Heinrich Rickert of the Baden School, who were more directly concerned with the problem of criteria of validity for historical judgment. We are familiar with the struggle engaged in by these thinkers for the autonomy of historical knowledge in relation to the natural sciences. Barash clearly illuminates the connection between two, usually misunderstood questions: the role of historical comprehension in the so-called human disciplines and the coherence of normative truth, given the diversity of its historical expressions. The more the specificity of historical comprehension was emphasized as the method appropriate to the human sciences, the more urgent it became to establish universal criteria of coherence transcending historical individuality and the diversity of cultural perspectives. Although Barash focuses our attention on Rickert's attempt to guarantee the systematic stability and the coherence of normative values beyond the diversity of empirical contexts, it is Wilhelm Dilthey and Edmund Husserl, responding to the neo-Kantianism of Cohen, Natorp, Windelband, and Rickert, that Heidegger confronts in *Being and Time*. For these two important thinkers, the possibility of normative criteria of truth in the face of truth's historicity remained the pivotal theme of analysis. In this regard, Husserl's *Logos* article "Philosophy as Rigorous Science," his refutation of historicism, assumes a decisive significance. The principle of coherence was no longer sought in suprahistorical norms, but in the structures of a consciousness that were as much prehistorical as prenatural. Indeed, as Heidegger might have insisted, Husserl never took historical themes seriously into account. The role of Dilthey appears more complex: it is he who elaborated the problem of a concatenation (*Zusammenhang*), and thus a coherence, inherent to manifestations of human life. The topic of a coherence of life was even adopted by Heidegger himself for

a while, under the related term "life experience [*Lebenserfahrung*]";
one can thus legitimately see in the historicity of *Dasein* a theme of
analysis substituted for Dilthey's concept. What remains difficult to
fathom in Dilthey's own work, however, is precisely the principle of
coherence, above all, when it is transferred from individual consciousness to the level of world history. Indeed, the question of the status of
objective mediations guaranteeing this coherence commands our attention, and we fall back again into the difficulties of the Baden School.
It is the kinship among these thinkers in the dilemma of asserting both
the primacy of historical comprehension and the transhistorical character of norms and values that the author succeeds in revealing, a
dilemma wherein the former assertion served to undermine the latter—
in which it was supposedly grounded.

He further clearly illustrates the mediating role exerted by theology
in the formation of Heidegger's thought. On one side were historicist
and culturalist theologians such as Ernst Troeltsch and Adolf von
Harnack, who encountered the dilemma of the critical philosophy of
history, that of the transhistorical, indeed ahistorical, character of cultural phenomena. The cultural approach to Christianity was condemned to engender the same dilemma, which Karl Barth denounced
with force in his famous *Römerbrief* (Epistle to the Romans) of 1919.
On the other were antihistoricist and anticulturalist theologians such as
Karl Barth, Rudolf Bultmann, and Friedrich Gogarten. And we discover the Heidegger of the period immediately following the First World
War, a Heidegger who is almost Protestant after having been almost
Catholic in his prewar neo-Thomist phase. We also note the appearance of the term "destruction"—cultural destruction, destruction in the
history of the spirit—in Heidegger's "Annotations" to the *Psychology
of Worldviews* of Karl Jaspers, a term inseparably linked to "life experience" and "interpretation of existence by the self [*Selbst*]."

What is most important, along with the author, we appreciate the
dimensions of the collapse of the pre–World War I thinkers' convictions—a spiritual collapse running parallel to that of political Germany—
which an entire generation of thinkers had to face in the postwar period.
Nothing remained stable: neither the methodological formalism of neo-
Kantianism nor the phenomenological immediacy of Husserl. In this
regard, the shock produced by publication of Spengler's *The Decline of the
West* becomes comprehensible, even if it astonishes us today.

Emerging from this background were Heidegger's attempts to resolve the problem of historical meaning in the courses he gave at Freiburg in 1920 and 1921—"Introduction to the Phenomenology of Religion" and "Augustine and Neoplatonism"—and then more boldly in his conference of 1927, "Phenomenology and Theology." Barash precisely analyzes, on the one hand, the consensus among the neo-orthodox Protestants on the negative potential of modern culture (already denounced by Nietzsche in the second meditation of his *Untimely Meditations*) and, on the other, the hidden discord that insinuates itself between this dialectical theology and Heidegger's purely philosophical attempt to respond to the challenge of historicism and nihilism. A philosophy of culture could no longer respond to the question of historical meaning: the methodological debate (*Methodenstreit*) that such a philosophy had brought about in preceding decades had lost all sense. A return to the eschatology of primitive Christianity was placed out of reach, however, as Franz Overbeck had perceived, even if it was in meditation on Augustine and Luther and in friendship with Bultmann that Heidegger learned to discern in "curiosity" and "lust of the eyes" the first manifestation of fallenness and of the forgetting of the sense of existence, and to locate in vigilant anticipation and in decision the deep-seated origin of historicity. What had to be radically changed were the categories of *philosophical* thought.

It is at this point that Barash raises several key questions. Did Heidegger not exacerbate the ordeal, the dilemma of historical thinking of his times? Did he respond better to the question of what it means to think historically than his predecessors, who had become the target of his critique? In subordinating this question to that of the meaning of Being, did he resolve it? Or did he rather neutralize it by showing its irrelevance? Armed with these questions, the author gives his own reading of *Being and Time,* a reading already so concise I will not attempt to summarize it. His altogether original approach never loses sight of the dilemma of historicism, even while recognizing the change in perspective introduced by Heidegger's analysis of *Dasein* and its reference to the question of Being. He offers a powerful interpretation of the paragraphs on the "they," which precisely occupied the terrain delimited not long before by a philosophy of culture—a term absent from *Being and Time*—and of the final paragraphs of the section

"Temporality and Historicity," dedicated to the critique of Dilthey by Count Yorck von Wartenburg. Here we assess to what extent Heidegger's extreme subordination of the epistemological problem amounts to a dismissal of the entire critical philosophy of history, henceforth eclipsed by the question of the forgetfulness of Being. But has the initial question concerning the coherence of history thus disappeared? No, Barash tells us, it has simply changed position and taken refuge in the question of the unity of the temporal *ekstases* and the choice between an authentic and an inauthentic mode of bringing about this unity. To the extent that anticipatory resoluteness and repetition, authentic modes of temporalization, now constitute historicity, the coherence of this historicity, which permits historical thought, cannot be separated from the decision in favor of authenticity and can no longer be an objective phenomenon, not even on the cultural level.

As the author makes clear, the shift in the question of coherence—a shift that, according to him, does not suppress the question—renders more opaque the transfer of the authentic choice of *Dasein* that we each are to a historical community and to the destiny of a people. We clearly see what the inauthentic community is: it is the "they." But what of an authentic community? It is here that Heidegger's well-known swerve in circumstances requiring reflective discernment encounters the least resistance, if not perhaps its explanation. Also more opaque are Heidegger's elaborations on the "world-historical" dimension accompanying the facticity of *Dasein,* a dimension Heidegger claimed could be apprehended without the aid of historiography.

I appreciate the tenacity with which the author returns to the question of coherence once it is shifted from the history of cultures to that of the historicity of *Dasein.* I do so because what is finally in question is the truth status of the historicity propositions themselves, a question homologous to the one not resolved by the critical philosophy of history. Yet must we not attribute a universal ambition to ontology for the historicity of an each-time singular *Dasein* to make sense? Does not the notion of finitude thus establish itself on an ahistorical basis? Does not the forgetfulness of Being designate—in the negative—a transhistorical unity of intellectual traditions of the West? This last question provides the starting point for the second part of the book.

The author might have justifiably concluded his work with the questions raised by *Being and Time.* Indeed, however close this masterwork

was to the same space of questioning as critical philosophy or phenomenology, Heidegger's work following the *Kehre* seems to have come
adrift, not only from his the previous way of situating the question of
meaning in history, but from the question itself. Does not Heidegger's
dialogue with the poets and with the pre-Socratics radically and definite-
ly remove thought from the previous field of battle? It is precisely in
opposition to this apparently reasonable conclusion that Barash has written the second part of his book. There he tests his bold hypothesis whereby the new notion of the "history of Being," despite its apparent lack of
a tie to the historian's history, bears witness to a resurgence of the original question of historical meaning, the very question that had given birth
to the famous *Methodenstreit* at the beginning of the century.

As the author sees it, after the enthusiastic reception of *Being and
Time,* fostered by the famous debate with Ernst Cassirer at Davos,
Heidegger passed through a profound crisis brought on by anthropological interpretations of *Being and Time.* Certainly such interpretations proceeded from a miscomprehension of the very term *"Dasein"*
and the entire ontology of finitude. This Heidegger never disavowed.
But how might it be proved that an anthropological reading was tantamount to miscomprehension? To reverse the accusation: in deploying
a world of representations structured in the human image, all of
Western metaphysics is secretly anthropological, even when it projects
into an ahistorical absolute a foundation of meaning that remains under
the control of the human subject who projects. It is this "reversal" itself
that places Being, set aside from human control, at the origin of its own
history. Yet, if it is true that the question of Being offers itself only in
an epochal way, another question unavoidably arises, that of the coherence of a history of Being, to which the history of mortals provides neither the measure nor the key. This coherence is evidently not that of a
cultural production; it is rather that of an errancy, although this errancy has a structure, a way of orientation, which is precisely what makes
it an epochal movement. Anthropocentric criteria may vanish; the history of Being nonetheless has articulations of its own, which permit the
designation of a certain unity of Western metaphysics. Certainly, the
"historical consideration" this history of Being authorizes does not
coincide with the "coherence of history" presented by a periodization
of great cultures. It remains that there is a tie of filiation and affinity
between Greek antiquity and the modern West, with its technology,
which is equivalent to a coherence underlying the history of mortals.

On the basis of the hypothesis that guides his reading, Barash asks two questions. How can one think of the history of Being as a nonhuman source of the historical movement of truth? And in what way does this historicity of truth, incorporated within the unity of Western history, place in question the criteria of truth of scientific rationality—permitting one to think of the meaning of history in terms that go beyond these criteria? It is in the formulation of these questions that the author sees the resurgence of the same problem of meaning and of coherence that led the critical philosophers of history, phenomenology, and perhaps also *Being and Time* itself into an impasse. Yet how can one not speak of coherence, be it even in errancy, if one wants to grant some meaning to the ever repeated affirmation that the basic retreat of Being is the thread that makes the epochs of the history of Being up to modern times "hold together"? The question of the coherence of the movement that constitutes the unity of Western intellectual traditions thus returns to the foreground by way of the forgetfulness of Being and errancy. The increasing errancy of metaphysics and the ever more opaque retreat of Being are, in relation to variations of truth, in the position of an inverted foundation. But it is ever and again for the historicity of truth that the philosopher seeks a nonhuman foundation in a history that mortals do not direct.

Considered in this way, Heidegger's thought appears less as an incessant moving away from itself than as a rethinking of the problem of historical meaning that had set in motion his research and that of his predecessors since before the First World War. It is for the boldness of this hypothesis and for the care taken in its support that I warmly recommend Jeffrey Andrew Barash's fine book.

—Paul Ricœur

---

*   The German word "Dasein" is untranslatable in English. Used to signify "existence," *Dasein* literally means "there-being." In Heidegger's terminology, *Dasein* refers to the finitude underlying human being: more primordial than humans, as he writes, is the "finitude of existence in them" (*Ursprünglicher als der Mensch ist die Endlichkeit des Daseins in ihm*). Heidegger, *Kant und das Problem der Metaphysik, GA*, vol. 3, p. 229. With the understanding that for Heidegger finitude provides the ground for human being, we have, for simplicity's sake, translated the term *Dasein* throughout this work as "finite human existence."

INTRODUCTION

I

One of the most profound intellectual developments of the modern period has been the genesis of a specifically historical worldview, attentive not only to changing events and circumstances, but also to the subtly changing ways by which human understanding structures its world as a coherent unity. Between the late eighteenth and early twentieth centuries, when principles of historical understanding received their deepest conceptual foundation, this worldview gave rise to the conviction, most profoundly expressed in Germany, of the essentially historical character of human existence.

Loosely designated under the heading "historicism," the conviction informed a number of diverse and at times conflicting intellectual currents of the time. It guided bold philosophical speculation about the overall significance of the course of history, more prudent and empirically oriented works of historical analysis, and—especially toward the end of the nineteenth century—critical attempts to evaluate the principles and scope of historical understanding. Diversity and conflict notwithstanding, there has been general agreement among sympathizers that the historical worldview engendered insights unprecedented in the Western intellectual heritage, opening a theoretical eye to the kinds of coherence specific to the variable, developmental, and uniquely individual aspects of the human world. During the nineteenth century the historical style of understanding came into its own, not only as a tool for the historian's fact gathering, but as a fundamental approach to human culture in a broad variety of social sciences.

Not all observers of the course of modern historical thinking have been unqualified admirers, however. The period following World War I, above all, constituted a watershed in German thought, when historical methods of understanding were subjected to searching interrogation in the German universities and when wide segments of the

German intelligentsia questioned the meaning of thinking historically with a new intensity.

In what proved to be a highly influential expression of this questioning, Martin Heidegger (1889–1976) took up the basic claim about the historical character of human existence and, integrating it after his own fashion into an overarching philosophy, assessed its theoretical foundations. While early admitting the distinctiveness of modern historical styles of thought, Heidegger called into question their ability to retrieve the authentic sense of the past.

In a philosophical position he began to articulate in the 1920s, Heidegger criticized philosophies of history—above all, that of Hegel—as well as those of major historians and pioneers of modern historiographical theory, such as Leopold von Ranke. The brunt of his attack was aimed, however, at critical theories of the late nineteenth and early twentieth centuries that tried to provide a scientific foundation for historical methods of understanding. As can be seen in his published works and (until recently) unpublished course lectures of the period, Heidegger's explicit attack was leveled at contemporary thinkers of the two preceding generations, in particular, at Wilhelm Windelband, Heinrich Rickert, Wilhelm Dilthey, Ernst Troeltsch, and Georg Simmel.

In divergent ways, each of these thinkers critically appraised the insights of earlier currents of historical thought. Each attempted to emancipate historical methods of understanding from the predominant metaphysical speculation concerning the meaning of the historical process as a totality. Despite discord concerning *how* such methods should proceed, there was consensus among these thinkers, as among a wide segment of the German intelligentsia in the years before World War I, that historical understanding, once made independent from theoretically unacceptable speculation, could fulfill a unique scientific role. In their respective ways, each of these theorists sought to develop logical rules governing historical methods that, taken collectively, spanned a wide variety of fields, from history and sociology to law, economics, theology, and philosophy.

After an initial period of qualified approval for this critical approach to history and an attempt to mediate between the diverse strands of its elaboration in his *Frühe Schriften* (Early writings), Heidegger took historical theory to task for skirting what he saw as the essential role of historical analysis. His writings of the period just following World War I demonstrate that, before concentrating on the historical ontology that was to be the hallmark of his thought of the late 1920s, he grappled intensely with the conceptions of history advanced by the above-mentioned theorists. In particular, and despite a certain admiration for Wilhelm Dilthey, he denigrated the aim of establishing a scientific (*wissenschaftliche*) historical method, viewed by Dilthey and other critical theorists as the culminating point of historical insights of the previous century. Heidegger understood that such a notion of historical method evolved within a set of assumptions based on the spontaneous meaning and objective coherence of the historical process. It presupposed that the deciding factors of history, though irreducible to the kind of lawful regularity manifested in nature, were nonetheless part of an empirically verifiable process obeying logical patterns often beyond the express will of individuals. Whether these patterns were placed on the plane of action or in the interchange of ideas, they imbued the genesis and historical development of the human world with an essential theoretical significance.

It was this synthetic concept of an objective sense of the human world as the wellspring of historical meaning that Heidegger began to question in his thinking of the 1920s. Rather than discern in the critical theories a novel approach to the human world that had cast off the trammels of metaphysical dogmatism enmeshing the larger Western intellectual tradition, Heidegger came to view their quest for objective coherence in human culture in a wholly different light. By the period of *Sein und Zeit* (Being and time; 1927), he considered the critical theories—and the earlier currents of thought whose metaphysical assumptions they had criticized—to be tacit extensions of that very dogmatism. Heidegger came to the opinion that a "deconstruction [*Abbau*]" of this tradition and of its inadequate estimation of the meaning of historical existence must constitute the aim of authentic historical thinking.

During the period of the thirties and forties that Heidegger characterized as a "reversal [*Kehre*]" in his thinking, he thoroughly reappraised the terms of this deconstruction as set forth in *Being and Time*; his understanding of the shortcomings of what he took to be the metaphysical roots of Western intellectual traditions underwent a crucial metamorphosis. All the more significant in view of this reversal,

Heidegger again called (though in different terms) for a radical redefinition of the meaning of historical reflection as it had emerged in the
philosophy of history and in the human sciences since the demise of
Hegelian speculative idealism.

The present work will reconsider Heidegger's critique of earlier
forms of historical thinking. It will explore the emergence of a coun-
terconception of historical understanding, both in his earlier and in his
later thought, as the central aspect of Heidegger's excoriation of
Western intellectual traditions.

At this preliminary point, I should note that the shift or reversal that
became manifest in his writings of the 1930s and 1940s has led me to
vary my approach to Heidegger's thought in the periods before and
after its occurrence. Because of the proximity of Heidegger's earlier
philosophy to a larger debate surrounding the problem of historical
meaning, one that reached its climax in the two decades before and
after World War I, the first and longer part of this study will closely
attend Heidegger's relation to this debate. If at a later time, however,
as his thought shifted focus, he departed from his own earlier conception of the meaning of historical reflection, I will argue that his later
position continually returned to the issues that this debate elicited,
although in a very different universe of thought and discourse. As I
will illustrate in part II of this study, Heidegger's later thought
assessed all previous historical reflection in the context of an unprecedented analysis of the destiny of Western intellectual traditions, focusing, above all, on what he took to be the historical meaning of the
philosophies of Hegel and of Nietzsche. With this in mind, let us turn
to the principal themes we will address in part I.

II

Our examination of the early Heidegger has a twofold purpose. First,
it attempts to locate and clarify the theme of historical thought as a predominant topic of Heidegger's philosophy in the period culminating
with the publication of *Being and Time*. As we have noted, Heidegger
incorporated an essentially historical view of humanity into his larger
philosophical orientation. Several related questions arise. What did
Heidegger mean by "history" and "historical," given his refusal to

equate historical understanding primarily with comprehension of objective, empirically verifiable coherences in an evolving world? Did his historical philosophy surmount limitations inherent in past historical ideas? Or, rather, did the breach with Western intellectual traditions Heidegger claimed as historical thought's authentic task presuppose, at its very core, the historicist insights of the previous century?

Second, the purpose of our analysis of the early Heidegger is not only to examine Heidegger's thought on historical matters and its relation to nineteenth-century historical theory, but also to use his ideas as a prism through which we may refract the theme of historical thinking in Germany. Of significance in this regard, Heidegger's negative stance toward historical theory, despite its originality, did not occur as a purely isolated decision, but arose during a period when the fundamental assumptions of a historically oriented generation of theorists came increasingly under attack.

Even before the First World War, insights of a historical worldview had already become the subject of deep ambivalence among scholars who, even as they affirmed its significance, could also appreciate its potential drawbacks. This ambivalence was conveyed through the pejorative sense that the word *historicism* acquired by the beginning of the twentieth century. It issued from the belief that historical analysis, applied with insouciance to all aspects of the human world, complemented a modern relativization of values and normative standards.[1] Already in the decade before the outbreak of the war, critical theorists such as Heinrich Rickert and Ernst Troeltsch, while confident that a rigorous theoretical foundation for historical methods could only confirm the coherence of norms in the historical process, also recognized the negative implications of an unfettered historicism for which all comprehension became relative to the historical culture in which it arose.[2]

I hope to show that Heidegger's historical ontology of the twenties and early thirties, which came to fruition after the war when the historicist dilemma grew to alarming proportions, had intimate ties to deeper concerns of his period that, I will argue, can be traced to his conception of the problem of historical meaning. I approach his philosophy with the idea that, however original, its reflections on historical understanding were founded on an altered perception of historical matters shared by important segments of the post–World War I intelligentsia. And, as I also hope to show, a view of the development of historical thinking of

the nineteenth and twentieth centuries sheds light not only on the emergence of Heidegger's historical ontology, but also on the dilemma of
historical understanding that first became evident at this time.

III

A number of important objections might be raised to this way of analyzing Heidegger's early philosophy and the historical thinking of his
period. Let us now consider two that seem crucial.

First, it might be objected that to investigate Heidegger's thought in
relation to historical themes is to isolate part of his thought from the
spirit of the whole. After all, what is the justification for concentrating
on the theme of historical understanding with regard to a thinker whose
central contribution lay in the field of philosophy?

While a full response to this objection can only be given in the
course of the following chapters, a preliminary justification of this
focus of analysis becomes apparent with a brief reconsideration of the
way in which Heidegger's works have been comprehended. In the
Anglo-American world, as in France, the subject of historical understanding has received sparse treatment in investigations of Heidegger's
philosophy.[3] Philosophers and intellectual historians in these parts of
the world have often classified Heidegger (against his own predilec-
tion) as an existentialist, and therefore as an unhistorical thinker.
Despite all talk of what Heidegger termed humanity's "fundamental
historicity," he is seen to take historical premises to altogether unhistorical conclusions.[4] Perhaps not without a certain justice, his very
approach to thinking has been attacked for giving rise to questions
about its underlying historical character.[5]

This viewpoint, involving the semantic and conceptual problem of
what exactly Heidegger's philosophy means, rarely takes into consideration the reception of Heidegger's works in the twenties and early
thirties. In this context, Heidegger was not alone in believing that his
thought offered an essential contribution to the question of historical
understanding and interpretation; the perception of his ideas by those
who were familiar with his works at the time also tended to corroborate this opinion. As Karl Heussi, the foremost scholar of the predicament of the historical understanding in this period, noted in 1932: "In

the second half of the 1920s the transformation of phenomenology accomplished by Martin Heidegger began to very strongly influence the historical problematic; decisive here was the connection of Husserlian phenomenology, which remained neutral in regard to the problems of the philosophy of history, with Dilthey's thought."[6]

Heidegger's influence in this area is directly noticeable, to take a prominent example, in the work of the theologian Rudolf Bultmann, whose 1930 article "Die Geschichtlichkeit des Daseins und der Glaube" (The historicity of existence and faith) employed Heidegger's notion of historicity to justify what Bultmann viewed as a radical hermeneutic principle in the historical interpretation of scripture.[7] From a very different standpoint, the young Herbert Marcuse, comparing Heidegger's thought very favorably with that of the noted critical theorists of the prewar period, in particular, Wilhelm Dilthey, Max Weber, and Heinrich Rickert, concluded that Heidegger's analyses in *Being and Time* "have discovered in the most primordial way the phenomenon of historicity."[8] In a later period, Heidegger's former students Hans-Georg Gadamer and Hannah Arendt would each emphasize the originality of Heidegger's contribution to historical aspects of understanding.[9]

The divergence in approach to Heidegger suggests the need for a reappraisal of the theme of historical understanding in his early philosophy, one taking into account how it was intended by him—and how it was received in the context of the times. Cutting across any problem of mere semantics, this divergence reveals a central difficulty concerning exactly how Heidegger comprehended historical thinking and the relation of this comprehension to previous historical reflection.

A second objection to the approach to Heidegger outlined above might be that it levels down the original aspects of his thought to a set of preconditions and influences all too often ill fitted to account for unique characteristics that do not conform to the preestablished model.[10] Such an objection, which might be voiced by disciples of Heidegger's philosophy, would be based on statements scattered throughout his works indicating his rejection of the standard practice of intellectual history, whereby a thinker is considered in relation to a larger milieu.

To this it might be added that Heidegger was highly secretive about his past. His collected works, which will eventually comprise as many as eighty volumes, are characterized by an unusual lack of autobiographical detail and by the omission of much of his correspondence.

For more than a decade following his death, many of his early course lectures and much of his correspondence were kept locked in the Deutsches Literaturarchiv at Marbach, to which only librarians and Heidegger disciples had access. Indeed, it might well be argued, it was precisely Heidegger's hostility to the methods of intellectual history that had inclined him to remain reticent about his relation to the events and major ideas shaking Germany since World War I, the period during which his thought came to fruition.

For many years, Heidegger's actions in this regard had a curious effect. They led to the circumstance that almost the only known records of his life remained official documents, for the most part reflecting the somber story of his eight months of political activity in favor of Hitler, as rector of the University of Freiburg in 1933–34. The result has been a polarization of opinion about his thought, either toward reductively understanding it as a prelude and afterlude to his political involvement or else toward omitting that involvement from consideration.[11] In the former case, Heidegger's philosophy is read as a document of totalitarian ideology; in the latter, his disciples, ignoring the importance of any contemporary intellectual context, exaggerate his own desire to stand out as far as possible within the topography of the times. This has led to the standpoint, often voiced by Heidegger's disciples, that the meaning of his early philosophy is much more clearly discernible in relation to Aristotle or Kant than to the vibrant years between the decline of the *Kaiserzeit* and that of the Weimar Republic.[12]

Without seeking to reduce Heidegger's originality to a product of his milieu, and without denying the influence of thinkers of distant ages on his philosophy, the following examination of his early development will proceed from the assumption that ignoring the concerns of his contemporary epoch can only lead to distortion. It is my hope that, by addressing the unique significance of historical thinking in the modern period, which informed Heidegger's philosophy and decisively distinguished it and his intellectual world from that of Aristotle or Kant, my inquiry will help restore the link between Heidegger and his times, and thus lead to a more equilibrated view of him as a thinker.

The concept of "generation [*Generation*]," one of the central historical concepts of *Being and Time* explicitly borrowed by Heidegger from Wilhelm Dilthey, and, as we will see, one strewn throughout this major work, clearly relates to this attempt to understand Heidegger's own thought. Heidegger stated that *Dasein*'s "own past . . . always bespeaks the past of its 'generation.'"[13] It is precisely in relation to *his* generation that we will try to place the early Heidegger's thought in perspective, in the working out of what he came to see as the philosophically vital dilemma of historical understanding in his times.

IV

In his essay "Die Wahrheit des Kunstwerkes" (The truth of the work of art), Hans-Georg Gadamer wrote that *Being and Time* "conveyed with one stroke to broad circles of the public the new spirit [*Geist*] that had taken hold of philosophy due to the tremor of World War I."[14]

If this affirmation of Heidegger's communication of a "spirit" of the post–World War I period suggests a cardinal theme to be investigated through our analysis of the historical dimension of his thinking, the pursuit of this theme after Heidegger's *Kehre* in the thirties and forties proves far more problematic. Revealing as it may be to analyze the implications of Heidegger's early philosophy in relation to parallel currents of thought in this period, the immediate intellectual context surrounding his work between 1933 and 1945, and even after 1945, tells us far less about the implicit contours of his thought. If, as we will see, a consideration of German and world history after 1933 figured among his analytical themes, in comparison to the contemporary background to his earlier work—and, especially for our purposes, the broad debate on the problem of historical meaning—the context of these later years provides us with only the most general information about the nature of his later orientation. In no small part, this was due to Heidegger's isolation in what he belatedly recognized to be the intellectual and spiritual bankruptcy of Nazi Germany, and to his seclusion in the years following the war. By the 1960s, moreover, as Gadamer's account confirms,[15] Heidegger's early thought no longer commanded its former influence and, except among specialists, his works after the *Kehre* never received the wide acclaim accorded his previous philosophy.

Accordingly, our analysis of later transformations in Heidegger's orientation will limit itself to changes in the way he investigated the theme of historical coherence, while continuing to draw on insights that he derived from his perception of the problem of historical meaning, and which presupposed a century of reflection in Germany on the essentially historical character of human understanding. Because, I will argue, the later Heidegger's historical reflection results less from his interaction with other thinkers in this period than from the internal movement of his thought on historical meaning itself, it is this topic, much more than the question of an immediate intellectual milieu, that animates my discussion of his later appraisal of the historical destiny of the Western intellectual heritage. That discussion is of course also limited by what is appropriate for a study concentrating on Heidegger's earlier philosophy.

Chapter 1 investigates the course of major currents of historical reflection from the late eighteenth to the early twentieth centuries to place in relief a set of motifs examined in Heidegger's philosophy. By calling attention to his broad conception of its intellectual framework, my aim is to gain an independent perspective on the immanent movement of historical reflection and the emergence at this time of the problem of historical meaning. As we will see, this problem began to reveal itself with the sober quest for stable systems of cultural norms and theoretical structures that could withstand the historical variation of human understanding.

Chapter 2 deals with the young Heidegger's ideas at the time of his *Early Writings* (1912–16), when the historical contemplation of philosophical problems would cause him "spiritual disquiet [*geistige Unruhe*]."[16] His reflections took into consideration a complex array of intellectual orientations. He was deeply concerned with the metaphysics of Catholic theology, but also influenced by that of German idealism; he was stimulated by the phenomenology of Edmund Husserl and the thinking of contemporary historical theorists such as his mentor of that time, Heinrich Rickert. To a lesser degree, Heidegger's interests were directed toward other critical theorists such as Georg Simmel, Wilhelm Dilthey, and Ernst Troeltsch. Given the context of his early intellectual endeavors, chapter 2 focuses on Heidegger's growing awareness of the difficulties that historical investigation posed for systematic coherence in the theoretical sciences; it unveils the presuppositions he adopted to resolve, albeit tentatively, those difficulties at this time.

Chapters 3 and 4 deal with the years following World War I. They analyze the context of the deepening crisis of historical understanding and the sweeping metamorphosis in Heidegger's early thought. We will see the central role that the gradual shift in historical outlook played in the broader changes in his early orientation as a whole. Chapter 5 concludes the first part of this study with a consideration of historical thinking and ontology in *Being and Time* in relation to the problem of historical meaning.

My discussion of the later Heidegger in chapter 6, which constitutes the second part of the present work, explores the shift in the basis of Heidegger's thinking from an ontology of history to the history of Being (*Seinsgeschichte*) and the implications of this shift for the problem of historical meaning.

NOTES

1. This is convincingly demonstrated in Heussi, *Die Krisis des Historismus*, 4–9.

2. Rickert, "Geschichtsphilosophie," 321–420; Troeltsch, *Gesammelte Schriften*, 4:628. Troeltsch's reference to historicism cited here first appeared in 1913.

3. When the first edition of the present work was published in 1988, no full-length studies of Heidegger's relation to the contemporary theories of historicity were available. The following articles were consulted: Wren, "Heidegger's Philosophy of History," 111–26; Rollin, "Heidegger's Philosophy of History in *Being and Time*," 97–113; Hoy, "History, Historicity, and Historiography in *Being and Time*," 329–33. The question of historical reflection in Heidegger has also been dealt with in the following studies: Gadamer, *Wahrheit und Methode: Grundzüge einer philosophischen Hermeneutik* (English translation: *Truth and Method*); Birault, *Heidegger et l'expérience de la pensée;* Murray, *Modern Philosophy of History: Its Origin and Destination;* Pöggeler, *Denkweg Martin Heideggers;* Ricœur, *Temps et récit* (English translation: *Time and Narrative*), vol. 3: *Le temps raconté;* Vattimo, *Avventure della Differenza;* Derrida, *De l'Esprit, Heidegger et la question* (English translation: *Of Spirit: Heidegger and the Question*). See also Brandner, *Heideggers Begriff der Geschichte und das neuzeitliche Geschichtsdenken;* Fynsk, *Heidegger: Thought and Historicity;* and the concluding chapter of Motzkin, *Time and Transcendence:Secular History, the Catholic Reaction and the Rediscovery of the Future.* Still more recently, Charles Bambach, in *Heidegger, Dilthey and the Crisis of Historicism,* draws on sources quite similar to those used in the present work, while also going

back over territory similar to that covered here. Bambach concludes, however, that the prewar crisis of historicism was "narrowly academic" in scope and that Heidegger helped "rehabilitate the positive sense of crisis that he believed defined the project of modernity" (p. 185). Heidegger's own reflection was at the same time "antimodern and postmodern" (p. 271). In my opinion, such arguments do not do justice to the deeper scientific and cultural implications of early-twentieth-century critical philosophy of history. Nor do the categories of "modernity" and of "postmodernity" in which these arguments are couched, by imposing on Heidegger an implicit philosophy of history latent in timely academic discourse, seem appropriate to uncover the untimely dimension of Heidegger's historical reflection.

4. In Germany, this opinion has been forcefully supported by Theodor W. Adorno, who, in *Negative Dialektik,* 135, has written that Heidegger's notion of historicity "places history to rest in the unhistorical." Unless otherwise indicated, all translations in this work are my own.

5. This has been the conception of noted intellectual historians such as Georg Iggers. See Iggers, *The German Conception of History,* 243–45.

6. Heussi, *Krisis,* 37.

7. Bultmann, "Die Geschichtlichkeit des Daseins und der Glaube," 72–95.

8. Marcuse, "Beiträge zu einer Phänomenologie des historischen Materialismus," 61 (*Schriften,* 1:373).

9. Gadamer, *Wahrheit und Methode,* 214–35. Referring to the later Heidegger, Hannah Arendt noted in *The Life of the Mind,* 2:179: "The difference between Heidegger's position and those of his predecessors lies in this: the mind of man, claimed by Being in order to transpose into language the truth of Being, is subject to a history of Being [*Seinsgeschichte*], and this history determines whether men respond to Being in terms of willing or in terms of thinking."

10. In later years, Heidegger did not fail to add grist to this mill: "Historical research does not deny greatness in history, but explains [*erklärt*] it as the exception. In this explanation greatness is measured by the ordinary and the mediocre." Heidegger, "Die Zeit des Weltbildes," in *Holzwege,* 76.

11. According to Peter Gay, *Weimar Culture: The Outsider as Insider,* 82: "Whatever the precise philosophical import of *Sein und Zeit* and of the writings that surrounded it, Heidegger's work amounted to a denigration of Weimar, that creature of reason, and an exaltation of movements like that of the Nazis, who thought with their blood, worshipped the charismatic leader, praised and practiced murder, and hoped to stamp out reason—forever—in the drunken embrace of that life which is death." In the opinion of W. R. Beyer, *Vier Kritiken: Heidegger, Sartre, Adorno, Lukács,* 20: "All typical formulations of Heideggerian thought can be evaluated in National Socialist

fashion. . . . All his 'decisions' he met with National Socialist verbosity." During the decades that followed the publication of these early critiques, the tendency to consider Heidegger's philosophy to be a mere expression of Nazi ideology has become ever more common.

12. Following early biographical analyses of Heidegger such as Hühnerfeld, *In Sachen Heidegger: Versuch über ein deutsches Genie;* and Palmier, *Les écrits politiques de Heidegger,* Heidegger's philosophical development has been further clarified by several intellectual biographies, most notably, Van Buren, *The Young Heidegger: Rumor of the Hidden King;* Kisiel, *The Genesis of Heidegger's* Being and Time; Ott, *Martin Heidegger: Unterwegs zu seiner Biographie* (English translation: *Martin Heidegger: A Political Life*); and Safranski, *Ein Meister aus Deutschland: Heidegger und seine Zeit* (English translation: *Martin Heidegger: Between Good and Evil*).

13. Heidegger, *Sein und Zeit,* 20. Since the pagination of the Niemeyer edition of *Sein und Zeit* is indicated in the margins of both the *Gesamtausgabe* edition and the English translation by John Macquarrie and Edward Robinson, I will use only the Niemeyer pagination here.

14. Gadamer, Introduction to Heidegger, *Der Ursprung des Kunstwerkes,* in *Heideggers Wege: Studien zum Spätwerk,* 82.

15. Gadamer, "Martin Heidegger—85 Jahre" (1974), in *Heideggers Wege,* 94–95.

16. Heidegger, *Frühe Schriften,* 342.

Part I

Toward an Ontology of History: 1912–1927

1

The Emergence of the Problem of Historical Meaning in Nineteenth-Century German Thought

IN THE YEARS just before and after the middle of the nineteenth century, there was a change in the orientation of the German universities that would significantly mark the intellectual context of the six decades leading up to the outbreak of the First World War. As we will see, reference to this change was widely made by late nineteenth-century contemporaries; Heidegger mentioned it in his *Frühe Schriften* (Early writings) and in his later course lectures and other works. In a course lecture of the 1920s, where he traced this theme in some detail, Heidegger spoke of a "shift in scientific consciousness, pertaining not only to philosophy but to all sciences."[1]

Voicing what has been a general assessment of nineteenth-century thought, Heidegger identified this shift with the decline in influence of the diverse currents of German idealism. This influence had been most powerfully exerted by the thought of Fichte, Schelling, and especially Hegel, whose philosophy had commanded a preeminent authority in the first decades of the nineteenth century. The German idealist philosophies had each proposed a unified, metaphysically grounded view of the world of human experience, but, as Heidegger noted, the approach to this world as a unity gave way after midcentury to a pronounced specialization and fragmentation of concerns in the empirically oriented university disciplines.

The demise of the German idealist systems, with their speculative methods of metaphysical reasoning, coincided not only with the rise of specialized disciplines of empirical research to predominance in the German universities, but also with the development of philosophical inquiry intimately related to these disciplines. Two styles were most influential in this regard. The first, comprising a succession of theoretical standpoints that proved especially persuasive after the mid-nineteenth century in Germany, may be generally characterized under the heading "naturalistic worldview," whose essential distinction lay in the assumption that, to explain the workings of reality as a whole, theorists might draw extraempirical inferences from the principles of the natural sciences. For reasons that will become clear, such inferences skirted, and would shed little light on, the radical implications of insight into the human historical world that had emerged in Germany since the late eighteenth century. A second influential style of philosophical inquiry arose with the resurgence of the prudent, critical orientation, mindful of the limiting dependence of human reason on the data of experience, originally propounded by Kant—an orientation the German idealist systems had earlier attempted to surpass. A group of critical thinkers strove to discern, each in his characteristic way, the historical limits of reason, much as Kant had in their view established boundaries of reason for the natural sciences. Among this group were thinkers briefly mentioned in my introduction, including neo-Kantians such as Wilhelm Windelband, Heinrich Rickert, and Georg Simmel, as well as thinkers who, like Wilhelm Dilthey and Ernst Troeltsch, diverged in a fundamental way from Kant's specific epistemology. Each may be called a "critical theorist of history" in that each evolved a theory that, on historical grounds, called into question any ambitious claim to grasp an all-encompassing meaning of reality.

Our immediate task will be to trace the emergence of a complex new awareness of the sense of historical thinking in the nineteenth century and, with it, a heightened appreciation of the diversity of different epochs, cultures, and the normative truths holding sway in each of them. This appreciation of diversity inspired the unprecedented conviction of the contingent, perspectival character of human consciousness in its grasp of the normative criteria of truth, traceable to the essentially historical mode—or historicity (*Geschichtlichkeit*)—of human experience. It was precisely this historicity, which each of the critical theorists invoked to preclude any claim to an ultimate truth beyond the particular, multifaceted perspectives on truth through which experience becomes meaningful.

In conjunction with this view of historical diversity and the historicity of human experience, the problem of historical meaning made its appearance, emerging within the gap between attempts to grasp history as a metaphysical whole and the critical response to such attempts. By examining the sources of this problem among generations of thinkers whose insights influenced the assumptions of the critical theories of history of the late nineteenth and early twentieth centuries, we will be able to see how the larger issues of critical theory affected both Heidegger's early and—from a different vantage point—his later thought. We will see that Heidegger's redefinition of the purpose of historical thought presupposed the complex new awareness of historical reflection that arose in Germany in the years between midcentury and the outbreak of World War I.

I

In an often-quoted statement from *Sein und Zeit* (Being and time), Heidegger proclaimed his intention to "foster the spirit of Count Yorck, in order to serve the work of Dilthey."[2] As we will see in chapter 5, however, *Being and Time* hardly represented a mere application of the insights of Wilhelm Dilthey or of Count Yorck von Wartenburg, Dilthey's friend and correspondent. Indeed, Heidegger aimed to reconsider their respective ideas on the historical character of human life from the standpoint of an ontology of *Dasein* (finite human existence) that moved far outside the range of these thinkers' original purpose. Nonetheless, his expressed desire to consider Dilthey and Yorck in elaborating the historical dimension of his thought indicates his debt to their "shared interest" (as Yorck wrote to Dilthey) "in understanding historicity."[3]

This shared interest unveiled an awareness of the critical implications of modern historical thought for what these authors each took to be unwarranted metaphysical presuppositions about the ahistorical foundation of truth that had long dominated Western intellectual traditions. In the words of Yorck, here in close agreement with Dilthey and anticipating an important theme of analysis later taken up by Heidegger, "the nonhistoricization of philosophizing seems to me, in relation to method, to be a metaphysical residue."[4]

The endeavors of Dilthey and of Yorck expressly retraced the ground surveyed by previous generations of thinkers whose unprecedented insight into historical meaning was closely tied to heightened attentiveness to the historical movement of normative standards of truth in relation to the development of specific nations or cultures. Indeed, Dilthey alluded to the roots of this notion of a relation between the historicity of truth and its specific cultural incarnation:

> Culture is above all the interweaving of coherent, purposeful relations [*Zweckzusammenhängen*]. Each of them, such as language, law, myth and religion, poetry, philosophy, possesses an inner lawfulness [*Gesetzlichkeit*], which conditions its structure, and this determines its development. . . . [In the mid-nineteenth century,] the historical constitution of this development had been comprehended. This is what Hegel and Schleiermacher accomplished: they penetrated its abstract systematics with the consciousness of the historicity of its essence.[5]

Dilthey's description sheds light on the origins of his idea of historicity and, as we will see, on a source of presuppositions about the character of truth that were shared by contemporary critical theorists of history.[6] In this regard, precisely because they only partially accommodated the variegated standpoints of later critical theories, the specific assumptions of late-eighteenth- and early-nineteenth-century thinkers set in clear relief the intellectual groundwork and incipient aporias of these theories.

Reflection on the essentially historical character of normative truths, closely tied to the deepening comprehension of the embodiment of truth in the historical movement of a specific nation or culture, first emerged in Germany in the late eighteenth century. This comprehension placed in a profoundly new light the radical divergence in normative standards between cultures and epochs, a divergence that—to thinkers such as Johann Gottfried Herder or Friedrich Schleiermacher—appeared more fundamental than any common denominator to which these norms might be reduced by the human intelligence. If Herder's manifesto *Auch eine Philosophie der Geschichte zur Bildung der Menschheit* (Yet another philosophy of history for the cultivation of humanity; 1774) heralded Germany's new comprehension of the implications of normative divergence, this was clearly due to his will to expose what he considered his century's tendency to universalize contemporary standards of rationality, to assume that the course of history could be understood as a unified whole, manifesting the gradual cultivation (*Bildung*) or education (*Erziehung*) of humanity in its progression to the contemporary epoch.[7] Directing his attack at diverse targets, including the historical and philosophical works of Hume and Voltaire, the histories of Robertson and Iselin, and the philosophical and literary writings of d'Alembert, Herder reproached all for their common assumption that truth could be judged according to a uniform standard, leading to the presumption that the present age represented the "highest peak of human cultivation [*Bildung*]."[8] As different as such thinkers might have been from each other, to cite only three notable examples, Voltaire's thought of progress in the rational enlightenment of humanity, Hume's postulate of the progress of human sentiments under the tutelage of universally valid rational appreciation of socially useful virtues, and Iselin's identification of a universal principle in the "fervor to do good and to become useful" all presupposed the evidence of universally valid rational standards that comes to expression in the movement of history.[9] In their very different intellectual contexts, these thinkers each assumed that the meaningfulness of history depends on the intelligibility of a progressive human domination of blind and uncontrolled forces and their subjection under universally recognizable rational ends. By contrast, Herder's manifesto has rightfully been regarded as the harbinger of the nineteenth-century historicist insight that the movement of history embodied divergent cultural standards, each valid and comprehensible in its own context, and that it is only obscured when subjected to an alien standard—such as the eighteenth century's presuppositions concerning the universality of its ideas of rationality.[10]

Two and a half decades later, Friedrich Schleiermacher's *Über die Religion: Reden an die Gebildeten unter ihren Verächtern* (On religion: Speeches to its cultured despisers; 1799) would also emphasize the diversity of truths expressed in historical epochs and in their particular cultural contexts—and the incomprehensibility of a culture or an epoch not approached in terms of specific norms dwelling within it. At the same time, it would deepen Herder's insight: supersession of truths predominant in an earlier epoch by those predominant in a later one in no way invalidates these earlier truths but, on the contrary, may indicate a deficiency in the approach to truth characteristic of this later epoch. Principally concerned with what he took to be his more radical contemporaries' misconception of sacred truths affirmed in past epochs, Schleiermacher employed the principle of the historicity of truth as a plea for comprehension of historical divergence to neutralize contemporary ideas of the merely vestigial status of religious practices in the progress of enlightenment over superstition. From this standpoint, religious truth, far from overtaken by the rationalization of social customs, had only been eclipsed, for it "had not let itself be glimpsed in its distinctive form [*in ihrer eigentümlichen Gestalt*] for quite some time."[11] This eclipse, for Schleiermacher, was closely tied to that of earlier truths in a more general sense, engendered by the standardization of particular cultural modes of thought and expression:

> The distinctive kind of sensibility [*Sinnesart*] of the different cultivated peoples no longer represents itself so clearly and determinately in particular actions since contacts of all sorts have given rise to many-sided relations among them and have increased their communal quality. Just as the imagination [*Einbildungskraft*] alone can grasp the total idea of these characteristics, which in their particulars cannot be encountered except mixed with many foreign elements, so it is also with spiritual things, and among them with religion.[12]

From Schleiermacher's viewpoint, the eighteenth century's subsumption of experience under the "uniformity of a universal concept"[13] coincided with a dulling of the sense of cultural uniqueness and a dampening of the ardor inspiring the religious insight through which this uniqueness had been expressed.

Herder and Schleiermacher are chiefly significant for our purposes, not because they were precursors of the later intellectual development of the nineteenth century, nor because Heidegger, in a still later period, occasionally quoted Herder and counted Schleiermacher among the influences on his thinking during his early years as a student of theology.[14] Rather, they are cited to illustrate the emergence of the late-eighteenth- and early-nineteenth-century conviction that, for consciousness to posit truth, the perspective of a particular historical culture is essential. Indeed, the perspectives of individual cultures and their interaction and movement over historical epochs serve as the medium of truth's metamorphoses in the unified course of history as a totality. Hence, even as they questioned Enlightenment faith in history as the arena of progressive application of universally valid rational norms, thinkers like Herder or Schleiermacher shared the conviction that history was a meaningful, coherent whole, which, if not necessarily intelligible to human understanding, could be ascribed to what each took to be its inscrutable sacred foundation.[15]

This emphasis on the diversity of truths articulated by particular cultures and epochs came to its most influential expression in the philosophy of Hegel, an expression Heidegger deemed the "most powerful system of a historical worldview, which no essential encounter with the history of philosophy could fail to engage in discussion."[16] Having freely assimilated insights that had been the special acquisition of the eighteenth and early nineteenth centuries, Hegel invoked the historicity of truth, at once to vindicate Enlightenment faith in the validity of universal standards of reason for rendering history coherent and to underline the limits of the Enlightenment conception of reason. His marriage of the universal validity of rational standards with historical diversity gave rise to a metaphysical tension that, as we will see, would have fateful consequences for the future of historical reflection in Germany.

At one crucial point in his critique of the Enlightenment, Hegel engaged in a rebuttal of Kant, who had turned against the empiricist outlook that dominated Enlightenment orientations in England and France through the emphasis placed by thinkers such as Locke, Hume, and Voltaire on sense experience as the ultimate foundation of human thought and of the normative truth it deploys. From Kant's perspective, the precarious and contingent character of experience could never provide the universality of rational criteria these thinkers had presupposed, and certainly not the apodictic character of universality that Kant comprehended as the highest expression of normative truth. If such universality could not be founded on experience, from Kant's well-known viewpoint, it could be traced to the activity of consciousness itself, conceived not as the product but as the precondition of experience, providing it with a universalizable structure in the pure forms of temporal and spatial intuition and in the pure logic of the understanding. Beyond these faculties, the constitutive activity of consciousness was confirmed at its highest level by the universally valid normative truths applied by the autonomous faculty of reason through its critical grasp of the range of consciousness in the meaningful constitution of a world—above all, in its establishment of moral laws to regulate action in that world.

Even though Kant's view of the constitutive activity of consciousness served as a precondition for later German idealism, notably that of Hegel himself, Hegel took aim at the limitations of that view. He challenged Kant's stipulation that consciousness, while providing a universal and necessary intuitive, conceptual, and rational structure to experience, nonetheless could not penetrate the appearances it gave to things in themselves and provide certain knowledge of the ultimate metaphysical foundations underlying those appearances. To be sure, Kant deemed such foundations essential to the postulation of human freedom in the moral realm. Yet this critical application of reason to exclude a metaphysical foundation for the universality of truth claimed by theoretical science only confirmed a noteworthy assumption of Enlightenment thought—most consistently argued by Hume—and led Hegel to characterize Kant's theoretical standpoint as the "Enlightenment made methodical."[17]

Denied both a metaphysical and an empirical foundation for the strict theoretical certitude of its constitutive activity, Kant had recourse to his transcendental model of consciousness—"consciousness in general [*Bewusstsein überhaupt*]"—isolated in its pure acts from anything outside itself and considered an ideal regularity in the ways its faculties render a world coherent. Beheld essentially from the standpoint of the universality and necessity of its acts, the normative capacity of such a consciousness achieves its purpose to the extent that it is generalizable apart from specific considerations of time and place. This model of a normative capacity of consciousness prior to the qualitative influences of individual historical context dominated the conceptual sphere of theoretical science and served to found the criteria of truth in the moral application of freedom and in aesthetic and teleological judgment. Indeed, when, at the end of his life, Kant dealt with the truth of religion, he subjected it to the same abstract criteria of universality that prevailed in the other domains of philosophy. He identified the essence of religious truth with a "pure religious faith [*reiner Religionsglaube*]," capable of fostering rationally deducible standards of moral action, and thus asserting a universally valid role superior to the particular historical claim of sacred revelation.[18]

In all spheres of human endeavor, the history of truth for Kant comes to light essentially as an accommodation of imperfect principles to pure norms, which themselves are as timeless as the underlying structures of consciousness through which they are posited.[19] Kant's model of uniform consciousness in general, however, admitted of no *historicity* in the sense it would acquire only in the nineteenth century: Kant allowed no essential determination of truth's character by the movement of a history rendered coherent through the mediation of individual cultural perspectives.

Already in his 1803 essay "Über die wissenschaftlichen Behandlungsarten des Naturrechts" (On the scientific ways of treating natural law), Hegel adumbrated his epoch-making approach to the thought of historicity in his critique of Kant on this point. Hegel rejected the formalism of Kant's notion of the universality of pure reason, applied in abstraction from the concrete contents of experience in the moral as in the theoretical sphere. He then stipulated, essentially in relation to the rational derivation of moral law, that reason must be incorporated in the "living individuality of a people—an individuality whose highest determinations are to be grasped again in terms of a universal necessity."[20]

In the full vision of his later years, Hegel's dissolution of the critical limitations on the metaphysical reach of theoretical consciousness coincided with his rejection both of Kant's model of a pure consciousness reduced to a consciousness in general and of the assumption of a static uniformity as the essential mark of the criteria of universality and necessity in all fields of human thought and action. Instead, these criteria were to be interpreted within the specific articulations of the experience of the Spirit, mediated by the concrete particularity of historical perspective. In his *Vorlesungen über die Geschichte der Philosophie* (Lectures on the history of philosophy), Hegel described the concrete embodiment of the interrelated spheres of philosophy, political history, national constitutions, art, and religion in the life of a people: "It is *one* determinate essence or character that penetrates all aspects and represents itself in the political and in the other, as in diverse elements; it is *one* condition that coheres [*sich zusammenhängt*] in all of its parts and whose different aspects, as manifold and contingent as they might look and as much as they might seem to contradict one another, contain nothing heterogeneous in their foundation."[21]

The far-reaching implications of this proposition became apparent at many points in Hegel's philosophy of history as it traversed the divergent ancient, medieval, and modern worlds. Yet these implications stand in their clearest light where Hegel responded to that continual spur to historical reflection posed by the problematic relation of moderns to antiquity, which he confronted in his portrayal of the unity of the ancient Greek experience of truth embodied in art and religion. This unity, for Hegel, served to highlight the opacity of antiquity to moderns, to whom it could only appear as a long-dead world, whose "[s]tatues are but corpses, whose animating soul is as the words of a hymn, the belief in which has taken flight."[22]

Hegel pursued this insight in his *Vorlesungen über die Ästhetik* (Lectures on aesthetics); writing in the late 1930s, Heidegger singled out its profound implications, not just for aesthetics or theology, but for later interpretations of the coherence of history per se.[23] Hegel went so far as to state that the truth of art in its highest Greek form, as the metaphysical embodiment of the Divinity, remains for us an irretrievable vestige.[24] Beholding the interrelation of art and religion in its past historical expression, Hegel's radical vision of the historicity of truth affirmed the absolute foundations of the ultimate harmony of religion and art for the ancient Greeks—thus redeeming the validity of past truth in its original historical context despite its opacity to contemporary minds.

Nonetheless, unlike earlier affirmations of historicity in terms of normative truths that resist systematization according to uniformly rational principles, Hegel's historical metaphysics restores the rational intelligibility of history. For, if the harmony of religion and art characteristic of Greek antiquity—and, with it, the ultimate spiritual expression of art—forfeits its ultimate meaning as it relinquishes its power to express the absolute, this loss is by no means to be lamented. Indeed, the higher determination of the experience of Spirit, which Hegel always thought of in terms of a given structural interrelation of the specific (religious, artistic, political, etc.) aspects of a people's existence, requires the divestiture of its absolute incarnation in the sensuous medium of art. Within the horizon of a different cultural context and a later epoch, the divestiture entails reconfiguration of this interrelation through Hegel's celebrated passage of the absolute into the supersensuous truth of revealed religion and the rational truth of philosophy, a passage corresponding to the advent of the modern political articulation of the consciousness of freedom. All the more significant in view of this movement was Hegel's assumption that the *universal* meaning of truth comes to expression in the individual context of the "spirit of the people itself."[25] Here the rational and universal basis of truth prevails, not through uniform principles in their autonomy from historical experience, but directly amid the diversity and particularity of the cultural and epochal context of this experience and of the heterogeneity of the media of its expression. The opacity of historical experience arising from cultural and epochal cleavages in the fiber of

history is vanquished at its very core through the absolute, metaphysically founded coherence of the historical movement of truth.

By midcentury, Hegel's metaphysical synthesis and the viability of
metaphysics per se came into question in the German universities,
although, at least in part due to Hegel's legacy, few thinkers would have
questioned the presupposition that truth and the historical process were
fundamentally coherent and meaningful amid diversity and change.
Nevertheless, for any thinker who viewed historical themes as more
than just shadow issues, the insight into concrete historical diversity and
the loss of faith in all-encompassing metaphysical syntheses left a central problem unresolved. Given the diversity of normative standards and
values and their perpetual modification through history, what assurance
might be adduced for coherent foundations of truth so necessary to
intellectual endeavors? How might a systematic theoretical framework
for philosophy and the other human sciences be achieved? The recognition of truth's historical diversity with no assurance that human
thought could penetrate the inner depths of reality presented a perplexing challenge—how to unify the concrete foundations of the truths of
different epochs into an interpenetrating totality, without which each
epoch would remain locked within its specific historical context.

The realization of the seriousness of such issues dawned only gradually among discerning members of the German intelligentsia between
midcentury and the cataclysm of 1914. These were years of rapid
change, both in the universities and in German society as a whole.
What had been the attitude of a small minority of thinkers who mistrusted the speculative methods and metaphysical claims of German
idealism and who sought a factual and empirical emphasis in intellectual endeavors quickly began to gain ground during the 1840s and
1850s. Heidegger employed the label "positivism"—in an especially
broad sense—to characterize the growth of a more empirical outlook
in Germany after the fall of German idealism at midcentury:

> This is knowledge whose claim to truth is from beginning to end based
> on what one calls "facts [*Tatsachen*]." One holds that there can be no
> argument about facts; they are the highest tribunal for the decisions con-
> cerning truth and untruth. What is proved by experiments in the natural
> sciences and what is verified by manuscripts and documents in the his-
> torical-cultural sciences [*Geisteswissenschaften*] is true, and is the only
> comprehensibly verifiable truth.[26]

As Heidegger also noted, this turn toward facts involved a breaking free from the confines of metaphysics to seek another principle of systematization, either because metaphysics seemed irrelevant to the operational needs of science or, in a more critical vein, because the complexity and diversity of real particulars did not seem to lend itself to the kind of all-encompassing synthesis that German idealism had proposed.

The turn toward inductive, empirical guidance and away from speculative metaphysics to achieve standards of truth did not obviate the need to make nonempirical decisions, however. The entire question of *method,* by which facts were to be analyzed, ordered, and integrated into a conceptual system, entailed, not factual or empirical, but epistemological decisions about the criteria of theory and their coherence in history. In the empirical climate of the period following Hegel's death, different conceptions of method arose in the natural and humanistic disciplines; in response to this, the problem of historical meaning moved into the forefront of intellectual investigation in the late nineteenth and early twentieth centuries. Our consideration of the development of method in the human sciences will lead us directly to the promise and the predicament of historical reflection in this period, when Heidegger's thought first began to take shape.

II

In historiography, a new, more empirical attitude had already begun to make its appearance in the first decades of the nineteenth century, as German idealism was exerting its most vigorous influence. This attitude, with its immediate theoretical roots in the ideas of Hegel's contemporary Wilhelm von Humboldt, anticipated the direction of critical historical thinking of the late nineteenth century by making two significant distinctions: first, between individual diversity, which the historian attempts to render coherent in its concrete national or cultural embodiment, and the philosopher's abstract metaphysical speculation; second, between empirical reality interpreted by the human sciences and the mechanically conceived processes of physical nature.[27]

Humboldt's conception of historical method based on empirical representations independent of the philosopher's speculative deductions became a working precept for an important group of historians and philologists. Most notable among these was Barthold Georg Niebuhr. In sharp contrast to Hegel, who deduced historical meaning from the canons of a priori reason, Niebuhr emphasized philological criticism of texts and careful factual analysis—above all, in his *Römische Geschichte* (History of Rome)—as the principal source of historical understanding.

Humboldt's theoretical principles and Niebuhr's conception of historiography heralded a shift in emphasis in historical scholarship: by midcentury, the preference for a more factual and inductive style of analysis began to establish itself in the humanistic disciplines. This preference was adopted by a number of influential thinkers in the generation that followed, above all, by Leopold von Ranke, who directly attacked Hegel's metaphysical understanding of history as a progressively advancing totality in his lecture series "Über die Epochen der neueren Geschichte" (On the epochs of modern history). For Ranke, history could not be constructed out of a priori ideas, such as progress or reason, presumed to be its universal ground. Rather, insofar as they were comprehensible in history, ideas had to be gleaned inductively as a posteriori manifestations of Spirit in reality (*realgeistig*).

Ranke proceeded from a conviction of the diversity of historical epochs and of the nations composing them, each epoch manifesting its own dominant tendencies (*leitende Tendenzen*) in accord with an immanent structure of singular, interacting principles of national development. Rather than attempting to derive real historical existence from the all-encompassing axioms of a presupposed totality, he placed special stress on reconstructing national histories and historical epochs through careful archival research and documentary verification. In reestablishing the actual course of events, this reconstruction aimed to revive normative standards specific to a given epoch, which, in Ranke's estimation, general, all-encompassing criteria could not intuit: "[E]ach epoch must be viewed as valid for itself and appearing most worthy to consideration."[28]

Ranke articulated his sharp distinction between a priori first principles and the study of a concrete empirical reality in terms of the respective tasks of philosopher and historian. Although not hostile to philosophy per se, Ranke consistently rejected the metaphysical claims of German idealist thinkers, who sought to derive a world of concrete facts from a limited system of ideas. The philosopher's ideas were to be complemented by, not imposed upon, historical facts. Only in this sense could Ranke accept philosophy, and only from this perspective was he ready to acknowledge that history "is not a denial but a fulfillment of philosophy."[29]

Given Ranke's view, a salient question arises. How are the coherence of ideas and the absolute character of religious, moral, aesthetic, intellectual, and other normative principles to be conceived? If every epoch is understood according to leading tendencies immanent within it, how might we arrive at systematic foundations that transcend the temporal horizons of any one given age?

Such questions did not present the same problem for Ranke that they would for critical historical theorists at the dawn of the twentieth century. His presupposition of absolute underpinnings of the manifestations of world history reposed on a conviction of their origin in the Divine will. This conviction, untroubled in its serenity by self-conscious doubt, insulated his thinking from the troublesome issues that would devolve upon later generations.

No less than Hegel, Ranke thus affirmed the objective coherence of world history (*Weltgeschichte*) sustained by Providential will, although he stressed the limits of human understanding in the face of real diversity. His notion of reality sought to restore the complexity and mystery of the historical, which could only be glimpsed discursively within an infinite metaphysical ocean of totality. Ranke taught a style of realism for which the sense of empirical fact could never be exhausted. For him, the metaphysical constancy of eternal norms was transposed into the finite realm, not as pure, invariable ideas or a fixed human character, but amid a flux of historical tendencies, subject to painstaking empirical research, yet offering no response to purely rational dialectic or deduction. Such research made the study of history more than a simple recapitulation of accidental facts, elevating it to a quest for traces of the Divine will hidden in the ephemeral realm.

With Humboldt, Ranke distinguished between the methods of natural science and those of history. For Ranke as for Humboldt, natural scientific thinking issued from the analysis of mechanical generalities; historical individualities, by contrast, could not be expected to conform to the kind of lawful regularity that natural processes manifest.

During the productive decades of Ranke's career, the attempt to articulate such distinctions between natural science and history was overshadowed by a desire to safeguard historiography from the encroachments of an enormously influential speculative philosophy. With the decline of German idealist influence after midcentury, an increasingly favorable climate for empirical research nurtured the development of the natural sciences, which at times challenged the historian's autonomy from another direction. This was especially the case where the growth of natural scientific preponderance in the German universities between 1850 and 1890 spawned the highly popular (if pseudoempirical) naturalistic worldview, claiming to explain cultural as well as natural affairs on the basis of natural scientific methods. By the 1880s, the assertion of the independence of the methods of the humanistic disciplines from those of the natural sciences became a central focus of debate. The battle against the naturalistic worldview, or naturalism, increasingly preoccupied both philosophers and thinkers in other humanistic disciplines, shaping the direction their theoretical pursuits took in the period leading up to the First World War.

Diverse groups of thinkers from many disciplines joined the battle over method; philosophy became the special province of methodological controversy (*Methodenstreit*), touching on the inner articulation of each of the university disciplines. As we will presently see, in a number of its most significant forms, German philosophical orientations favored the separation of humanistic from natural disciplines; here the theme of historical understanding—beyond the narrow domain of research by the specialized historian, but shorn of any pretension to account for metaphysical totality—would play a paradigmatic role as a method of analysis for the human sciences.

To get a better idea of what the historical styles of understanding had to arm themselves against, let us briefly consider the naturalistic worldview. Because the rebuttal of naturalism remained in the forefront of Heidegger's first published articles, we will also consider certain key descriptions he offered and the specific thinkers he analyzed.

III

An important stimulus to factual-empirical research in Germany proceeded from the successive waves of theoretical discoveries and technological innovations that grew in significance toward midcentury. Previously, experimental advancement in physics, chemistry, biology, and the other natural sciences had for the most part been achieved else-where, especially in England or in France. In Germany, where thinkers such as Schelling or Hegel claimed to legislate on matters concerning biology and physics as well as history and logic, the experimental method had advanced more slowly.[30]

The shift in scientific consciousness during the 1840s and 1850s brought with it a complete reversal in this situation: logical standards of empirical method transformed Germany's academies of higher learning and brought astounding success to the natural sciences, whose development was reinforced by the rapid ascent of an urban middle class, which readily appreciated the important connection between empirical research and industrial progress. This shift manifestly justi-fied the independence of the natural sciences from the speculative con-cerns of metaphysics, unfettering natural scientific research for the pursuit of more utilitarian goals that favored its development in harmo-ny with the demands of industry.

The "predominance" of the natural sciences in the 1860s and 1870s, as Heidegger—echoing a general opinion—would later characterize it,[31] encouraged a growing number of enthusiasts who trumpeted the arrival of a new all-encompassing vision of reality, a vision not sur-prisingly most prevalent among natural scientists. The ascendance of the naturalistic worldview in Germany paralleled the revitalization of empiricism in England and the rise in influence of August Comte's positivism in France, although it never made the headway in Germany that it did in these two other countries.[32] Occupying the traditional province of philosophy, naturalism claimed to supplant the intellectu-al grasp of the world totality with methods of law construction. Wilhelm Dilthey described the change in intellectual perspective that the advent of naturalism brought about: "As I began in philosophy, the idealistic monism of Hegel had been replaced by the domination of the natural sciences. When the scientific spirit became philosophy, as among the Encyclopedists, Comte, and philosophizing natural researchers in Germany, it attempted to conceive the spirit as a prod-uct of nature."[33]

Quite often, especially in its early forms, German naturalism assumed the philosophical standpoint of materialism, which, in the words of Wilhelm Windelband, "overflowed the fields of German spiritual life in the middle of the nineteenth century." Indeed, Windelband went on to say, "[i]n the great breadth of the literature, materialism occupied the predominant place for decades."[34] Those who realized that materialism lapsed into metaphysical presuppositions at least as hypothetical as those of idealism often preferred a more sophisticated form of naturalism, one in which the metaphysical contents of natural being—whether ultimately matter or idea—were simply left unspecified.

From the middle of the nineteenth century until 1914, naturalism was elaborated and refined by successive generations of thinkers. Its most significant stages of development were represented, first, by a wave of materialistic thought in the 1850s, typified in the systems of Jacob Moleschott and Ludwig Büchner; second, by an influx of Darwinist notions of evolution, expounded in a popular style by Ernst Haeckel; and third, by the more epistemologically refined works of the empiriocriticists Ernst Mach and Richard Avenarius. It is worth briefly considering the latest and most sophisticated of these thinkers, Mach and Avenarius, both for the counterargument their epistemologies would elicit in the first writings of the young Heidegger and for the naturalistic style of systematizing history their works exemplify.

These two like-minded philosophers expressed a common aim of adapting the theory of human consciousness to the model of the natural sciences, avoiding all the while the assumptions of metaphysics. Developed independently by Richard Avenarius, most notably in his *Kritik der reinen Erfahrung* (Critique of pure experience; 1888–90), and by Ernst Mach, most clearly in his *Beiträge zur Analyse der Empfindungen* (Contributions to the analysis of sensations; 1886), their empiriocritical theories were to find a wide resonance among the German intelligentsia in the years before 1914 and well beyond.

The epistemological astuteness of thinkers like Avenarius and Mach derived in large part from their respective reinterpretations of earlier British currents of empiricism, especially the thought of David Hume. In a 1912 article, "Das Realitätsproblem in der modernen Philosophie" (The problem of reality in modern philosophy), Heidegger evidenced a clear appreciation of Hume's thought as the source of these philosophies and as an intellectual and spiritual wellspring for "the philosophy of the times."[35]

Mach and Avenarius shared with Hume the conviction that all human understanding arises in experience, not in ideas independent of experience, and that a faithful account of experience gives us, not objects in any definitive sense, but only sense impressions or sensations characteristically associated with objects. Or, as Heidegger put it: "The thing, the body, the matter is nothing beside the cohesion of its elements [i.e., sensations], of colors, sounds, and so on, beside the so-called qualities."[36]

By considering experience solely in terms of sense impressions, an end could be put to metaphysically freighted concepts such as "substance" or "thing in itself," which, in the opinion of the empiriocriticists, had haunted earlier attempts to formulate a scientific philosophy. These concepts had no place in a truly empirical account of the world, and the speculative tendencies they occasioned could only be banned from philosophy by focusing on the sense data of what Avenarius termed "pure experience."

Sowing the field originally cultivated by Hume, Avenarius and Mach independently theorized that even fundamental concepts such as causality could not be attributed to an ultimate substance of which we have no immediate experience. The very concept of causality, like that of substance itself, is rooted in a conviction or feeling of necessity, arising from continuous psychological associations of given kinds of action with related kinds of circumstance, rather than from an ontological structure in the world itself. Commenting on Hume's philosophy, Heidegger might just as well have been describing empiriocriticism: "The fundamental concepts of substance and of causality are stripped of their objective, real character, in which the former is dissolved into a 'bundle of sensations,' the latter referred back to a subjective feeling of necessity."[37] In the empiriocritical style of reasoning, such an outlook had interesting ramifications, some of which shed light on the attempt to systematize the historical dimensions of thought on naturalistic foundations.

With the idea that causality arises, not in an intrinsic relation between ontological substances, but through the association of sense data, both Mach and Avenarius arrived at a crucial conclusion: that the genesis of human reflection and of the higher spheres of normative thinking and valuing could be traced to laws of association on which all experience is based. According to this viewpoint, the plenitude of the human historical world and the coherent manifestations of meaning within it originate—just as surely as does the experience of natural phenomena—in the association of given kinds of circumstances with their outcomes. Mechanical laws of causality, from this standpoint, could be uniformly applied as a sufficient explanatory principle both to the natural world and to the historical sphere of human national or cultural development.[38]

Just how far conformity between the realms of human history and nature could be extended is nowhere better demonstrated than in the biological and physiological arguments developed by both Avenarius and Mach from the so-called psychological laws of association. In Avenarius's "principle of least action" and in Mach's notion of the "economy of thought," which closely resembled one another, some of the most important results achieved by the methods of natural science were directly applied to a theory of consciousness. Here nineteenth-century physical conceptions of the conservation of energy and biological conceptions of natural selection found direct psychological application. Consciousness, it was held, proceeds according to a law of economy, at bottom the expression of a will to conserve a maximum amount of effort and energy. Or, as Avenarius put it: "The change imparted by the mind to its representations when new impressions enter is always the least possible."[39]

Whether called the "principle of least action" or the "economy of thought," this principle had at its source a quasi-Darwinian explanation: conservation of energy permitted an optimal adaptation of the human organism to its environment. All experience, historical as well as natural, was founded in the associative activity of human thought conceived as a strict function of vital processes.

This form of thinking, in which psychological, biological, and physical laws were intermingled, reduced human normative standards to a subordinate moment in an entirely operational system. It deprived the human world of autonomy, subjugating the criteria of meaningful action and truth to the rigid laws of a mechanical teleology. Nowhere was this more evident than in Mach's understanding of the theoretical work of the researcher, which was not to discover empirical reality with the aid of autonomous normative standards of truth, but to refine vital instincts: "[T]he conscious psychic activity of the [natural] researcher [is] a methodologically clarified, sharpened, and refined variety [*Abart*] of the instinctive activity of animals and humans, which is practiced daily in natural and in cultural life."[40] For all who opposed the enormous simplifications of this outlook, the assertion of meaning transcending this merely operational sphere and valid in its own right became a primary quest.

IV

One of the earliest and most influential attempts to elaborate a counterargument to the naturalistic worldview revived Kant's transcendental thinking as a buttress against subsuming normative standards under the functions of a mechanistically interpreted world. Indeed, the revival of Kant would play a pivotal role in the debate over the orientation of all the humanistic disciplines.

In dealing with the epistemological innovations of neo-Kantianism, this section will consider Wilhelm Windelband's and Heinrich Rickert's reflections on historical method and systematic philosophy, while section V will treat Edmund Husserl's and Wilhelm Dilthey's epistemological divergence from neo-Kantianism, in particular, Dilthey's critical theory of history. This will lead to some general observations about the horizon of historical thought and the quest for a systematic ground for the human sciences in the period leading up to the First World War, during which Heidegger found his early orientation.

After midcentury and concurrently with thinkers such as Hermann Lotze, who tried to reconcile the new scientific outlook with a more empirically oriented metaphysics, the German neo-Kantians sought to establish the autonomy of human thought in harmony with the factual bent and enormous strides of the sciences. Unlike Lotze, however, they were unanimous in emphasizing an epistemological approach that eschewed any suggestion of metaphysical reasoning. In the 1860s, a number of parallel works began to lay the groundwork for a counterattack against the panoply of naturalistic assumptions that would only grow in popularity as the century advanced. Kuno Fischer's *Geschichte der neueren Philosophie* (A history of modern philosophy; 1852–77), Otto Liebmann's *Kant und die Epigonen* (Kant and the epigones; 1865), and Friedrich Lange's *Geschichte des Materialismus und Kritik seiner Bedeutung für die Gegenwart* (The history of materialism and a critique of its significance for the present day; 1866) signaled the relevance of critical philosophy for the intellectual concerns of the generation of the 1860s and 1870s.

Over the next four decades, the intellectual setting in Germany was to be profoundly affected by the emergence of a variety of expressions of neo-Kantian thought. Among the most important were those of Hermann Cohen and Paul Natorp, whose Marburg School distinguished itself, above all, in its analyses of the logic of the natural sciences and of mathematics, and those of Windelband and Rickert, whose Baden School concentrated on the logic of the historical-cultural disciplines.

Cohen's philosophy, like that of Kant, stood on a conviction of epistemological idealism, by which consciousness, instead of conforming to objects, constitutes them in accord with its logical, rule-giving faculties. For Cohen, who was especially concerned with the logical foundations of the natural sciences, this outlook gave rise to what he saw as the only effective counterposition to the naturalistic worldview: instead of being real entities to which the mind must conform in a naturalistic sense, natural laws are ideal emanations of the logical and productive capacities of consciousness. The laws of nature pertain to the world only because consciousness tacitly introduces them as a precondition of possible experience. The theoretical basis of science becomes conceivable, not from the hypostatization of natural laws as part of the fabric of reality in itself, but solely from their character as constructs of consciousness corresponding to logical rules.

In his masterwork, *Kants Theorie der Erfahrung* (Kant's theory of experience; 1871), Cohen interpreted Kant in a way that retreated farther into the ideal structures of consciousness as the source of meaning than even Kant had intended. For Kant, the ultimate source of the sensory content of experience, to which pure intuition and pure logic give form, remained a mystery, calling for the postulation of a thing in itself. Distrusting any kind of metaphysical principle, however, Cohen did away with this last holdout of metaphysics. He separated the consideration of nature from any ontological problem of the world in itself. Making sense impressions entirely subservient to the logic of the natural sciences, he detached them from the question of an origin outside consciousness. In a confident statement of principle, Cohen explained: "What nature might be is revealed to the philosopher not by common sense perceptions—neither healthy nor hallucinatory ones—but only by natural science. Only this must be conceivable to us; thus no forces or principles can seek validity, except those required by our scientific conceptualization. As for nature itself—who would hope to grasp it [*sie zu begreifen*]!"[41]

For Cohen, the problem of what nature might be, independent of the mind, was not necessary to any consideration of the systematic, theoretical certitude of the sciences. Only this certitude, he expressly averred, concerned him in his theoretical investigation; it reposed neither on nature in any ontological sense nor on a thing in itself presumably operating behind nature, but strictly on the ideal premises from which scientific concepts were constructed.

Cohen's exclusion of any metaphysical considerations from his analyses and his correlated foundation of natural science in consciousness guaranteed the logical autonomy of mind and the systematic character of natural scientific theory by totally absorbing nature within a fixed logic of mental capacities. This was related to the conclusion that all possible experience of nature was a function of logical operations underlying the actual natural scientific disciplines. Natural science was interpreted as an ongoing clarification and codification of the universal and necessary forms of all kinds of natural apprehension. Here the criteria of the natural sciences became the fundamental criteria of natural experience per se.

After expressing qualified admiration for Cohen in his *Early Writings,*[42] Heidegger took him to task in the 1920s for overemphasizing the centrality of the criteria of scientific theory to the evaluation of experience:

> The very precisely oriented theoretical-scientific rediscovery of Kant concentrated itself directly on a positivist interpretation of Kantian philosophy. This work was accomplished by H. Cohen, the founder of the so-called Marburg School, in his work *Kant's Theory of Experience.* From the title, one sees the way in which Kant is basically seen: "theory of experience," where experience is understood as scientific experience in the way it has become concrete in mathematical physics, that is, a Kant-oriented theory of positivism of the sciences.[43]

Windelband's and Rickert's extension of neo-Kantian principles to the cultural-historical disciplines and their contributions to the development of a critical philosophy of history lend their writings a special importance, one bearing both on the role of historical understanding in the humanistic disciplines and on the problem of the coherence of normative truth in view of its historical diversity. From a critical standpoint, both thinkers were sensitive to what they considered the irreconcilability of historical understanding with any form of metaphysical speculation, based either on naturalistic or on idealist precepts. Moreover, in extending critical analysis to the logic of the cultural-historical disciplines, both thinkers raised a novel set of themes. Each sought to demonstrate the unique character of historical thought, which he attempted to define in relation to the logic of the natural sciences in their strictly empirical application. Far from being confined to the humanistic sphere, however, the problem of historical coherence that developed from this kind of theoretical approach extended to the systematic articulation of the sciences as a whole.

Between 1912 and 1916, Rickert served as mentor of the young Heidegger and as director of his *Habilitationsschrift* (postdoctoral dissertation), completed in 1916. Heidegger's writings of this period, above all, his *Habilitationsschrift* and the accompanying *Habilitationsvortrag* (postdoctoral presentation), manifested the unmistakable imprint of Rickert's Baden School. As we will see in later chapters, these neo-Kantians, whose epistemological idealism received only qualified support in Heidegger's *Early Writings,* became a principal target of his work in the 1920s. Even at this later time, however, Heidegger would affirm in a letter to Rickert that his former mentor's teachings in the area of historical reflection had led him to grasp the "fundamental importance of the historical for phenomenology," thus enabling him to distinguish his thought from contemporary interpretations of phenomenological philosophy.[44] Moreover, even as he subjected Windelband's and Rickert's philosophy of values to caustic verbal attack in his lectures, Heidegger did not fail to credit them with having had a "special function between 1880 and 1900" in "the struggle against rationalism and the predominance of the natural sciences in philosophical thought."[45]

Windelband harmonized a number of diverse intellectual strands in his rendition of neo-Kantian logic. He began from Kant's primacy of logic over an empirical world of natural processes. With Hermann Cohen, he diminished the margin of difference between the possible sense of experience and its actual articulation in the logic of the theoretical sciences. For Windelband as for Cohen, the logic of human understanding, arising in the ideal faculties of consciousness, expressed itself both as possibilities of experience in general and as rules in the sciences, although understanding in the sciences was elevated to a different order of clarity and condensed into more rigorously structured propositions.

Windelband was keenly aware that Kant's logical categories had originally attempted to comprehend the natural scientific thinking of his day. Influenced by the historical insights achieved since Kant's time, he sought to extend the Kantian logic to encompass an independent sphere of research investigated by the cultural-historical disciplines.[46] Drawing on the thought of Hermann Lotze, who had established a significant conception of values alongside logic as autonomous criteria of truth, Windelband formulated his philosophy of value (*Wertphilosophie*). Taken in Lotze's sense, values were seen, not simply as empirical facts reducible to immanent biological, psychological, or other natural motivation, but as transcendental, autonomous norms, like the logical principles governing the natural sciences, lending coherence at once to experience in general and to the theoretical disciplines that bring experience to clarity.

Proceeding from the notion of values capable of regulating empirical life, Windelband founded his method of the historical-cultural sciences in the a priori structures of consciousness, as Kant had his logic. In Windelband's view, natural scientists seek lawful, generalizable constructions, and the logic they employ is tailored to this end. From these lawful generalizations, the scientists are able to proceed from experimentation to prediction of the structure of factual interaction.

Values, on the other hand, are of a different character. In his "Strassburger Rektoratsrede" (Strassburg rector's address; 1894), Windelband succinctly justified in neo-Kantian terms the current of German historiography given theoretical expression by Humboldt and Ranke. Instead of being subject to uniform, repetitive, and generalizable methods of analysis, values provide the key to an autonomous kind of meaning characterized by its nonrepetitive and uniquely individual quality. The concepts of the natural sciences—which Windelband termed "nomothetic"—were thus not the only kind of logical expressions available to the sciences, but had to be supplemented by an "idiographic" method of the human sciences, whose subject matter could not be brought into focus by mechanical methods.[47]

Windelband's central premise concerning the ground of normative certitude in the cultural-historical disciplines paralleled the idealist assumptions through which Cohen claimed to establish the validity of the natural sciences. Far from assuming a metaphysical or ontological source beyond the material under investigation, historical and natural disciplines alike were pure constructs of consciousness. Such objectivity as might be ascribed to their material referred only to the immanent capacity of consciousness to formulate universally valid, necessary judgments, and could have no recourse to objects independent of the mind.

By founding the certitude of the sciences on their character as pure constructs of consciousness, Rickert developed a systematic philosophy, giving the Baden School's critical-historical method its fullest expression. In Rickert's detailed analysis, neo-Kantian epistemological idealism posited both historical understanding as a method for the human sciences and universal criteria of coherence, which transcended historical individuality and diversity of perspective.

A major theme underlying Rickert's theoretical work centered on the nominalistic concept of the "irrationality" of empirical being, that is, the absolute heterogeneity of its real particularity. For Rickert, empirical being encompassed the innumerable psychic and physical sense data enmeshed in myriad levels of quantitative components and qualitative differences. In the face of the elusiveness of the empirical, truth could not be conceived as an understanding of order and meaning in reality, but only in terms of an a priori system of forms of understanding that consciousness (taken in the general sense of *Bewusstsein überhaupt*) imposed on the real world. Truth did not arise from the correspondence between a knower and the anarchic diversity of individuals, but from the logical coherence of the understanding itself.

From the irrationality of empirical being, Rickert concluded that any ontological inquiry attempting to locate configurative order or meaning in reality itself must prove meaningless. For both varieties of understanding that he, following Windelband, admitted in the construction of concepts—the natural scientist's general laws and the historian's representations of unique individuality—the forms through which understanding arose could not be considered as ontologically present in the material but only in the thought through which understanding was constituted.

In neo-Kantian style, Rickert subsumed empirical matter under categories of understanding that engendered the laws of nature. These laws comprised a system of principles according to which every possible fact might be identified. Through the evolution of research this system became ever more comprehensive as empirical reality was increasingly rationalized. Nonetheless, despite all potential progress the logical coherence of natural laws always remained separate from reality in itself. It was precisely because of their generality that laws could never be ontologically situated in a reality that, beyond all general forms, presented itself only in the guise of absolute particularity.

In the case of historical science, the irrationality of empirical facts and the mind's inability to give ontological status to patterns it discerned among them signified that historical concepts would never be able to penetrate, or even approximately comprehend, the actual complexity of events themselves. The historian's reconstruction of unique individuality in the flux of the empirical could never duplicate the infinite particularity of possible circumstances involving any individual agent, each circumstance exhibiting a different kind and degree of significance. For this reason, Rickert faced the problem of how, in the face of this multiplicity, the historian could systematize empirical particularity in the form of valid representations.

To solve this problem Rickert, following the lead of Windelband, brought to bear his notion of values. Historical understanding constructed its concepts amid an infinity of possible facts, not by employing laws, but by focusing on individual unities—both persons and objects—in view of what it judged to be their unique historical *value*. This value was the principle that guided the selection of particular facts in the formation of historical concepts.

According to Rickert, the construction of concepts in relation to values permitted the historical sciences to approach the domain of culture (*Kultur*), involving the politics, religion, art, and so on of a given collectivity. Inaccessible to the generalizations of the natural sciences, culture constituted the field of historical systematization through which individual unities constructed by value concepts were made coherent. To understand how Rickert envisioned individualization in the historical sciences, we need to examine his notion of values in the field of culture.

"Valuing" and the "Theoretical Relation to Values"

Through values, Rickert believed that historically relevant individuality could be revealed and made coherent in the field of culture. On the one hand, objectified in the events of the past, values form the contents that the historian seeks to bring to coherence; on the other, they reside in the historian's own capacity to make value judgments. In all cases, however, values remain separate from psychophysical reality and are what Rickert termed "nonreal [*irreale*]" forms of consciousness, irreducible to psychophysical facts.

Let us take the example of a historical personality such as Napoleon. We could understand Napoleon, Rickert argued, not because of general characteristics attributable to every human being, but because we could penetrate generality to grasp his unique personality. In Rickert's view, this personality, unfathomable in the infinity of his real characteristics, became understandable in relation to a given set of values involving certain people, objects, and events; it was the actualization of these values that we had to study to comprehend the historical sense of Napoleon.

For Rickert, the attempt to comprehend historical personalities did not mean the application of the same sort of evaluative judgments that the personalities themselves employed. This would involve the approval or condemnation of the personalities and their heritage. Historians attempted to understand the past, not by taking sides for or against historical personages and the events they produced, but only by attempting to understand their theoretical sense for history, in a way that might be recognized objectively by each historian. Thus they asked, not whether Napoleon's actions exercised a beneficent or deleterious effect for Europe, but how his actions shaped the direction of European history. In regard to this stipulation, an important question remained. How could historians guarantee that the sense of a historical personage was scientifically understood, ensuring the objective validity of judgments that were made?

Rickert responded by explaining that the historical meaning of people, objects, and events depended on the application of values from a different perspective, which he termed the "theoretical relation to values [*theoretische Wertbeziehung*]."[48] In this relation to values, historians proceeded by seeking out the normative role of values in the community under study. In conjunction with these values, they attempted to reconstruct the logical end that specifically brought about the action of a personage (or of different personages), and the motivation governing the effect this action had in a unique historical situation. This procedure permitted historians to place in relief the essential characteristics relevant to a historical representation, separating them from the infinity of past persons and events.

The significance of this theoretical relation to values could be clearly seen in the construction of historical concepts of individuality by historians treating a community in a context of cultural coherence other than their own. If they judged the community according to criteria they took to be valid—"valuing [*praktische Wertung*]"—their choice of all that was essential might no longer correspond to that community's criteria. With the application of the theoretical relation and the suspension of all inclination toward evaluation that it involved, Rickert believed this difficulty could be surmounted. Through the theoretical relation, historians could attempt to relive (*hineinleben*) the normative values of the community they were investigating. Once this was accomplished, they would be able to reconstruct objectively essential historical individuality.

That empirical being comprised an infinitude of heterogeneous particulars meant, for Rickert, that the historical sciences, whose method aimed toward representation of individuality, came closer to reality than the natural sciences, which built their general concepts only by ignoring the particular. Nevertheless, the concepts of history never attained the capacity to comprehend reality in its infinity. As for natural concepts, the multiplicity of irrational Being always remained beyond historical concepts, whose logical validity, Rickert reiterated time and again, could never achieve an ontological status.

The Structures of Signification

As Rickert understood them, the structures of signification (*Sinngebilde*) represented a historical actualization of values in the form of larger cultural unities—persons and objects comprising an institution, a state, or the spirit of an age.[49] The structures of signification were neither physically nor psychologically real, but were the expression of groups of "nonreal" values that imbued (*sich haften*) particular empirical elements and made possible their coherence as a related set of individual unities in a given culture.

To illustrate this idea, let us take a typical object, whose meaning resides in a structure of signification: a copy of the Napoleonic code, objectifying the values of the First Empire. The copy exists materially as a book, bringing together the manifold particularity of ink patterns, pages, and binding. However necessary to the existence of the copy, this material particularity is not what distinguishes its specific sense from that of any other book. This sense depends on an entire structure of signification that arose during the First Empire, giving empirical objects their historically unique quality. In this perspective, the Napoleonic Code evinces values predominant during the Napoleonic epoch, forming a coherent whole with the values of Napoleon, as well as those exemplified in the legal thinking of J. E. M. Portalis and in the ideas and actions of other relevant personages of the First Empire.

In stating that a structure of signification lends historical coherence to empirical objects, Rickert did not mean to suggest that such a structure might have an intelligible existence independent of the individual personages and objects constituting it, which would imply a coherence of value structures in reality, beyond the objects and individuals in which they are empirically manifest, a conclusion that, for Rickert, was not supported by the facts.

On the other hand, Rickert claimed that the structures of signification characterizing the uniqueness of a community or group of communities considered as the spirit of an epoch are knowable only in the ensemble of singular qualities of a determinate number of significant people and objects. The spirit of the Italian Renaissance, for example, did not spontaneously inhere in each person who lived in Florence, Verona, or Venice during the fifteenth and sixteenth centuries; rather, it was expressed in values that certain great painters, sculptors, statesmen, and so on objectified in an original fashion.

As is clear from this example, Rickert conceived his structures of signification as groups of atomized individuals. Wishing to deny structures of signification autonomous real coherence, and thus ontological status, Rickert rejected the idea that there might be a real, factually verifiable unity that exerted an extraindividual influence behind the manifestations of empirical individuality. By confining all extraindividual influence to the realm of nonreal values, he precluded the reduction of structures of signification and the values empirically objectified in them to general forces operating in reality itself, whether in the guise of ideal spiritual agents or material laws. Far from being accounted for in their real embodiment through such general forces, cultural values themselves provided an autonomous basis of coherence through which alone the structures of signification might be understood.

For Rickert, nothing better demonstrated this premise than the fact that the theoretical forms of human understanding are themselves subsumed under the evolution of culture and of the values constituting it. This dependence of understanding and any structure of signification it might discern in reality on autonomous, nonreal values comes to light with fundamental historical changes in the theoretical orientation of the natural and human sciences. Such changes occur in relation to broad cultural values prefiguring the direction and meaningfulness of areas of research. Cultural values, sustaining and propelling the theoretical work of the sciences, do not arise in accord with a discernible plan or law inscribed in reality's texture. Rather, they originate in an indefinable sphere governing the infinite process of representation and rationalization of the irrational substratum of the empirical. The historicity of theory is the best evidence of the inability of mental constructs to move beyond the significance of beings to encompass the meaning of Being in its infinite particularity.

Given this image of the finitude of human understanding in the face of the infinity of Being, what is the possible source of our confidence in the historical evolution of theoretical standards? More to the point, given the individuality and diversity of empirical contexts in which all values come to expression, how could Rickert presume the systematic stability and coherence of normative values?

The Transcendent Values

To assure the stable foundation and coherence of value manifestations, Rickert posited a transcendent form of values.[50] Such values served to found every form of meaning that evolved historically within culture—including all scientific activity—whose perpetual, sometimes anarchic evolution seemed to contradict the possibility of stable and objective criteria of truth. By contrast, transcendent values, whose validity might be considered extratemporal, remained entirely untouched by empirical being and, ultimately, beyond the reach of human understanding. Although here it might seem that Rickert has gone beyond what he himself designated as the legitimate concern of science and into the domain of metaphysics, he reserved the term "metaphysics"—joining it to ontology—for real existence as such, and did not apply it to what was unknowable. Scientific concepts and faith, he stressed, should not be confused.

The separation of ideal meaning conferred by values from the empirical process of reality served an important critical function in Rickert's philosophy. Working backward from this insight, he brought to light what he viewed as the illegitimate metaphysical presuppositions in nineteenth- and early-twentieth-century thought. In a Germany influenced first by post-Kantian idealism and then by naturalism, he took special pains to criticize the respective presuppositions inherent in these two styles of thinking, especially as exemplified by Hegel and by proponents of the naturalistic worldview. In his classic work on historical understanding, *Die Grenzen der naturwissenschaftlichen Begriffsbildung* (The limits of concept formation in the natural sciences), Rickert juxtaposed the two as typical representatives of extremes in historical understanding, reaching beyond the bounds of legitimate theoretical inquiry.

On the one side, Hegel had postulated the progressive apprehension of the real by ideas, assuming that ideas achieve a rational capacity to apprehend irrational individuality; on the other side, Comte—much like the German proponents of naturalism—had dissolved ideality within a closed system of laws in which the scientist's generalities were taken as adequate, undistorted copies of reality, replacing the heterogeneous irrationality of particulars.[51] In both cases, the plenitude of real being had been forgotten and the distinction between the configurations of mind and empirical givenness blurred. As a result, historical theorists had "discovered" meaning in reality in the form of intelligible teleological relations, manifested either as Hegel's notion of rational purpose in history, operative even beyond the express will of individuals, or as Comte's idea of general laws according to which all historical cultures necessarily evolve.

In its critical aspect, Rickert's work provided a clear analytical standard according to which empirically founded historical research could be sharply distinguished from wishful thinking about historical development. Like his colleagues influenced by the neo-Kantian spirit—such as Max Weber, Ernst Troeltsch, and Georg Simmel—Rickert attempted to demystify a historical field heavily freighted with varieties of historical speculation, all claiming the status of established truth. In so doing, he assured the autonomy of the historian's endeavor.

Rickert's adaptation of the concept of history as a study of individual uniqueness and his reliance on empirical research to arrive at a nonevaluative conception of the past sustained the insights of earlier German historical theorists such as Humboldt and Ranke. Despite trenchant criticism of what he saw as metaphysical illusions, Rickert shared their confidence in the strength of the European scientific heritage. In Rickert's case, this confidence rested less on theological conviction than on his theoretical faith in the existence of transcendent meaning. In this faith alone, and in the philosophical quest that strove to give it justification, Rickert found the key to the problem of historical relativism, which he was among the first to label "historicism [*Historismus*]."[52] Faith in transcendent values seemed to justify the conviction of eternal continuity amid the uncontrollable flux of the empirical.

V

The neo-Kantian style of thinking, which vigorously animated the German intellectual climate in the late nineteenth and early twentieth centuries, did not lack its farsighted opponents. To better understand two themes central to our investigation—the predicament of historical understanding and the intellectual development of Martin Heidegger in this period (pursued more closely in chapter 2)—we need to consider two of these opponents, Wilhelm Dilthey and Edmund Husserl.

At first sight, it might seem inapt to juxtapose two such different thinkers: Dilthey was a generation older than Husserl, and their conflicting temperaments and intellectual persuasions expressed themselves in conflicting evaluations of historical and psychological aspects of thinking. Their mutual opposition to neo-Kantianism constituted an important affinity, however, one revealed in Dilthey's anticipation of certain insights of Husserl's epistemology and, as an old man, in his fruitful interpretation of Husserl's *Logische Untersuchungen* (Logical investigations; 1900–01), and one described by Heidegger himself:

> The first to recognize the central significance of these investigations was Dilthey. He designated these investigations as the first great scientific progress in philosophy since Kant's *Critique of Pure Reason*. Dilthey was seventy years old when he first became familiar with Husserl's *Logical Investigations,* an age when others have long felt secure and at home with their system. Dilthey immediately began to

study this book in the circle of his closest students, which he continued for semester after semester. Indeed, insight into the meaning of this work was facilitated for him by an inner affinity with its basic tendency. In a letter to Husserl, he likened their work to boring into a mountain from opposite sides, by which they came to break through and meet one another. Here Dilthey found a first fulfillment of what he had sought for decades, and had critically and programmatically formulated in an academic treatise of 1894: a fundamental science of life itself.[53]

Heidegger traced this affinity to the fact that Dilthey and Husserl's mentor, Franz Brentano, were both students of the great Aristotle scholar of the early nineteenth century, Adolph Trendelenburg. The realist style of thinking that developed from Trendelenburg's renewal of Aristotle's philosophy influenced the respective epistemologies of Dilthey and Brentano, and is also present in Husserl's *Logical Investigations*. Even after Husserl abandoned the starting point of the *Logical Investigations* for a novel phenomenological idealism in the years that followed, and subsequently rebuffed Dilthey's style of thinking, the young Heidegger continued to focus on these investigations in close relation to the philosophy of Aristotle.[54]

In dealing with Dilthey and Husserl we will first explore the aspects of Husserl's epistemology that helped to shape the counterthrust against neo-Kantianism. Although the order of treatment of the two thinkers violates the chronology of events (Husserl was considerably younger than Dilthey) we need to consider Husserl's epistemological breakthrough and the grounds for his critique of Dilthey at the same time to place the elder thinker in the light necessary for our analysis. This order of treatment will help clarify both the important character and the problematic side of what Heidegger would later describe as "the positive aspect of Dilthey's work: the tendency toward the actuality [*Wirklichkeit*] itself that is the theme of the historical sciences."[55]

Beside elucidating Heidegger's conception of Dilthey and distinctions between Dilthey and Husserl and, more markedly, between Dilthey and neo-Kantian idealism, we will consider how Husserl and Dilthey understood the possibility of systematic coherence of normative criteria of truth in view of its historicity. This will give us our first serious look at the emergence of the problem of historical meaning, reflected in the conflict between these two thinkers in the aftermath of Husserl's turn to phenomenological idealism and his 1910 criticism of Dilthey.

This section will also prepare the ground for reflection, in section VI, on the wider assumptions that—despite their disparate points of epistemological departure—informed the critical theories of history of Windelband, Rickert, and Dilthey. Such assumptions, I will argue, were shared with a number of the ablest theorists of the day, those responsible for the modern articulation of the methods of the human sciences. Our interest will be focused on how these assumptions fitted within the larger context of systematic concerns of nineteenth- and early-twentieth-century historical thinking, concerns Heidegger's ontology of the 1920s sought to satisfy. To lay the epistemological groundwork for an investigation of this theme, let us briefly turn to the thought of Husserl.

In his *Logical Investigations,* Husserl proposed an alternative both to the naturalists' view of all possible experience as an epiphenomenon of laws of nature, and to the neo-Kantian idealists' view of experience as a pure expression of the conceptual acts of universal, meaning-giving structures of consciousness. To this end, he reinterpreted and refined a realist tenet borrowed from the Scholastics by his mentor, Franz Brentano: the notion of intentionality, that is, the orientation of consciousness beyond itself toward a real world of objects.

Where the naturalistic orientation in Germany, including the ideas espoused by Husserl's opponents, Mach and Avenarius, attempted to account for consciousness on the basis of elements of an explanatory psychology, placing the psychological association of sensations at the root of all forms of meaningful experience, Husserl's effort stressed what he viewed as a more faithful description of the actual experience of consciousness itself. In interpreting experience, his guiding notion of intentionality highlighted the meaningful contents of phenomena. Consciousness chiefly experiences not sensations but meanings, which, he argued, the association of sensations could never fully bring to account. Comprising a universe of variegated meanings, the unity of experience cannot be pieced together by the uniform method of mechanical association. Rather, it has to be grasped as a structural interrelation of diverse modes of apprehension synthetically correlated with the meaningful content of phenomena brought to clarity. In the elucidation of meaning, only the logical analysis of consciousness, not its piecemeal psychological aggregation, would serve as an adequate starting point.

The idea of a primacy of meaningful or logical contents of phenomena over psychological processes struck a chord that harmonized with the aims of the neo-Kantians. Like them, Husserl was alarmed by the skeptical implications of the naturalists' reduction of human meaning to a system of operations. In the first part of the *Logical Investigations*— "Prolegomena to Pure Logic"—he presented detailed arguments to advance the idea that any theoretical reduction of logical meaning to laws of psychology could only prove self-defeating. The subsumption of logical meaning under psychological processes, according to Husserl, could only compromise the autonomous truth value of logical standards, a claim nowhere better substantiated than in the naturalists' theoretical propositions, which, according to their interpretation, were mere results of psychological functions, having no truth value in their own right.

Husserl's "Sixth Investigation," in the second volume of the *Logical Investigations,* cut forcefully against the grain of neo-Kantian idealism. Heidegger later singled out this investigation for its importance in guiding him toward the idea of phenomenology expressed in the fundamental ontology of *Being and Time.*[56]

Husserl rejected the neo-Kantian presupposition that consciousness served as a total, self-enclosed source of meaning. He explicitly criticized Rickert's position that reality was composed of irrational and utterly amorphous empirical being, a position that assumed experience was given sense only in the form of concepts; he proposed another interpretation.[57] Presenting a subtle realist argument, Husserl's intentionality stressed that concepts were founded in a priori fulfillment of meaning in what he termed a "straightforward [*schlichte*]" perception of objects themselves.[58] For Husserl, meaning had its source in the intention of a structure implicit in "things themselves," rather than in the projection of meaning onto incoherent sense data. Categorical concepts were founded in straightforward perceptions of objects, having neither the amorphousness of mere sense data, at one extreme, nor yet the conceptual determinateness that reflection first gave them, at the other. Husserl stressed the primordial presence of objects, appearing perspectivally as an only partially apprehendable plentitude, within which the complement of an intentionally projected sense was already tacitly situated. Reposing below the higher conceptual clarity dictated by rules of thought, the conferring of sense never exhausted the possible perspectives of real givenness, but drew out of it essential unified structures.

With one bold stroke, Husserl broke through the intellectualism of the neo-Kantian position, which had identified all meaningful experience with the constituted product of categorical logic or of transcendental values. In so doing, he indicated the way toward a new style of epistemology in which meaning reposed on the straightforward, preconceptual intentions of consciousness, interwoven with a correlated world. Here variegated nuances of meaning in the limitless territory of experience could be made to appear in layers beneath the fully explicit level of concepts and the rules of the theoretical sciences. Husserl's insight restored an intricacy to a world of tacit sense.

As Heidegger saw it, this insight undercut traditional Western notions of Being as either the ideal reflection of concepts or else wholly undiscoverable. This left room for the elaboration of an unprecedented ontology that would gradually emerge in Heidegger's thinking, giving the question of Being a fresh point from which to advance.

For his part, however, Husserl would place strong limitations on this insight. Despite his distance from the neo-Kantian epistemology in the *Logical Investigations,* he never wavered in the conviction, shared by them, that philosophy had to provide an absolute foundation for scientific endeavors. With regard to this aim, Husserl's stipulation that meaning depended on fulfillment through straightforward intentions exposed his theory to important difficulties, withdrawing the fundament of thinking from the apparent stability of an unequivocal sphere of concepts. What assurance could he give that the determination of sense by consciousness actually corresponded to an essential dimension revealed by things themselves—that the most basic norms of consciousness were not subject to important metamorphosis, however minutely discernible and tacit? Was it not also possible that the specific givenness of an objective world in relation to consciousness might be subject to systematic historical modification, as Hegel's phenomenology had announced a century before?

Husserl attempted to clarify his position in his *Logos* article "Philosophie als strenge Wissenschaft" (Philosophy as a rigorous science; 1910)—which Heidegger, as we will see, later criticized in his early Marburg course lectures.[59] Husserl lashed out against naturalism and especially against historicism (*Historizismus*), which he identified closely with the "weakening of philosophy's scientific impulse."[60] Husserl's use of the term "historicism," employed throughout the article as a synonym for "historical relativism," is itself highly significant. Husserl traced the problem of historicism back to the philosophy of Hegel, in particular, to the intellectual results of the breakdown of his all-encompassing metaphysical system: "Hegelian philosophy pro- duced aftereffects by its doctrine of the relative justification of every philosophy for its own time—a doctrine, it is true, that in Hegel's sys- tem, with its claim to absolute validity, had an entirely different sense than the historicist [*historizistischen*] one attributed to it by genera- tions that had lost along with their belief in Hegelian philosophy any belief whatever in absolute philosophy."[61]

Among his contemporaries, Husserl targeted Wilhelm Dilthey, whom he saw as responsible for transforming Hegel's metaphysical system into a philosophy of worldviews, with no absolute foundation against the tides of change. The growing fear of historicism that gripped Husserl and a number of his perspicacious colleagues only helped sharpen his conviction that "science is a title, standing for absolute, timeless values,"[62] and led him to advocate all the more earnestly a philosophical orientation corresponding to such a theoretical ideal. The foundation of normative certitude he proposed was situated in an ideal sphere of consciousness isolated from the world it was meant to com- prehend. Where the neo-Kantians had postulated fixed methods of con- cept formation and an ultimately stable source of conceptual meaning, Husserl sought a similar ground of stability in primary structures of what he saw as the universal "region" of consciousness, preceding and prefiguring the reflective level of conceptualization. Husserl's phenom- enological idealism claimed to distinguish a realm of consciousness from a world of facts by a turn toward immanent modes of the consti- tution of meaning. In the immanent encounter between universal struc- tures of consciousness and the essential phenomena of experience, Husserl claimed to have delineated an ideal universe of possible sense resisting the forces of historical variation. He insisted that his normative certitude could fix in its immediacy the essence of an infinitude of par- ticulars and determine the individuality of things in a way that "a mere subsumption under concepts cannot accomplish."[63]

Where, in the Baden neo-Kantians' view, meaning was formed according to two separate conceptual methods—natural and historical reflection—in Husserl's view, the presupposition of a preconceptual ground of meaning signaled the priority of its phenomenological immediacy to any consideration of its relation to history or to nature. Only in this prenatural and prehistorical sense could a truly absolute foundation be established.

As earnestly as Husserl sought to provide a foundation for the sciences, his claims ultimately created an enormous chasm between phenomenology and the empirical domain. Dilthey did not hesitate to criticize the course that Husserl's thought took, and castigated his endeavors after the *Logos* article as a new form of Platonic quest for the invariable.[64] In the 1920s, as we will see, Heidegger parted company with Husserl on the grounds of some of the very objections Dilthey had raised. In his mature years Heidegger charged that Husserl never understood the significance of the historical, trying only to dispel what he saw as its specter.[65]

Like Husserl and the neo-Kantians, Dilthey was inspired by a quest for scientific foundations of the academic disciplines. He shared with Windelband and Rickert a special concern for the human sciences, but in closer epistemological accord with the realist implications of Husserl's *Logical Investigations*.[66] Dilthey affirmed that an ideal, form-giving activity of consciousness, conceived as separate from the material it organizes, can never sufficiently account for the presence of meaning, which has its origin in the interplay between a full range of faculties of consciousness—firmly rooted in willing as well as in thinking—and a real world of objects.[67] The objects of consciousness are not irrational individuals, nor can they be comprehended either by the activity of pure concepts on merely subjective sensations or by the piecemeal collection of atomized sense data. For Dilthey, the objects themselves are involved in the activity of consciousness, notwithstanding all complexity and heterogeneity. Like Husserl before his turn to phenomenological immanence, Dilthey went beyond idealism, which would situate meaning uniquely in the operations of consciousness. Like Husserl, he also affirmed that the fulfillment of sense does not exhaust all of the object's possibilities, thus avoiding the naive realist presupposition of a simple correspondence between consciousness and object. Dilthey's epistemology steered between strictly conceptual reflection brought to clarity in the theoretical sciences and the anarchy of mere sensations or atomistically conceived sense data. This middle course allowed him to explore the tacit realm of experience, from which his world of meaning took its starting point.

Such epistemological considerations had a clear-cut influence on Dilthey's conception of method. His realist orientation led him to conclude that the idealist detachment of methodological concerns from any possible objective matter of experience was too formalistic and limited in scope to do justice to the plethora of meaning in experience. Whereas Windelband and Rickert had attributed the distinction between the natural and the human sciences entirely to the kind of method directed toward empirical contents, Dilthey stressed the dependence of method on the generic quality of the material contents themselves. For this, pure conceptions of individuality and generality, applicable to any kind of material, could never be sufficient. The distinction between human and natural sciences, grounded in the character of the material itself, could only be adequately approached by taking into account the difference between discretely given external phenomena of nature and interrelated coherent structures within human life, examined in the humanistic disciplines. As Dilthey concisely put it in "Ideen über eine beschreibende und zergliedernde Psychologie" (Ideas on a descriptive and analytic psychology)—the treatise (*Akademieabhandlung*) he presented to the Prussian Academy of Sciences in 1890: "The human sciences most readily distinguish themselves from the natural sciences in that the latter have as their objects facts appearing before consciousness from outside, as phenomena, and separately; whereas [the objects] of the former arise from inside, as reality, and as a living coherence [*als ein lebendiger Zusammenhang*] in the original sphere."[68]

Here an important qualification must be introduced: the coherence of human life studied by the human sciences was not to be based on immediate, ideal modes of apprehension in the Husserlian sense, detached from a factual world of psychological patterns manifested in history. Such coherence was to be uncovered by observing structural relations, whose meaning could not be neatly disassociated from the real depths of a world of psychological and of historical facts.

Dilthey's treatment of the factual world in the years before 1900 emphasized the central place of psychology, which he called the "fundamental science [*Grundwissenschaft*]" of the humanistic disciplines. His was not the constructive psychology of the naturalist, who insisted on reducing consciousness to discrete and fragmentary moments patched together out of an experience analogous to the distinct processes of external nature. Dilthey's descriptive and analytic psychology was meant to encompass what the naturalists could not help but overlook: the diversity of historical variation and the psychological subtlety of human creativity manifested in history. Dilthey hoped to discover life coherences capable of penetrating and systematizing the complex human world.[69] For insight into human life, he drew on great literature, rather than on the experimental psychology of his day:

> In the works of the poets, in the reflections about life as they have been expressed by great writers such as Seneca, Marcus Aurelius, Augustine, Machiavelli, Montaigne, Pascal, an understanding of man in his full actuality is embodied, in relation to which all explanatory psychology must lag very far behind. . . . One would wish for a psychology capable of catching in the net of its descriptions what, beyond all previous doctrines of the psyche [*Seelenlehre*], these poets and writers have embodied.[70]

Here the important question arises concerning exactly what Dilthey meant by "life coherence." Although Rickert—and later Heidegger—would criticize what they saw as the vagueness of the term "life," which applied to plants and animals as well as to humans,[71] Dilthey's concept was more precise than these criticisms implied. Shifting the accent on psychological method, his later writings expanded the psychological focus and clarified the concept of life. Psychology, especially where founded on an analysis of personal lived experience (*Erlebnis*), gave way to a more specifically social and cultural investigation of structures of life experience (*Lebenserfahrung*), mediated by the objective coherences of a historical world. [72] In his late essay "Der Aufbau der geschichtlichen Welt in den Geisteswissenschaften" (Construction of the historical world in the human sciences), Dilthey made clear that human life was distinguished by the character of its relation (*Lebensbezug*), which, though far from restricted to individual experience, was mediated as life experience (*Lebenserfahrung*) by objective structures in a collective, historically evolving cultural experience.[73] In chapter 3, we will see that Heidegger borrowed Dilthey's notion of life experience (*Lebenserfahrung*), which—for telling reasons—he understood in a different sense than Dilthey intended.

For Dilthey, life and life experience served as an immanent incarnation of meaning that Rickert had situated, in the form of transcendent values, above and beyond the historical process. In dynamic rapport with the world, meaning emerged in factual relation to historically evolving objective structures of reality, influencing individuals and modified in turn by them.

This notion of the real foundations of historical meaning set Dilthey's idea of history sharply apart from that of Rickert, who understood the objective coherence of history as an actualization of ideal values in the activity of individual agents living in, but discretely separated from, the empirical substratum of a factual world. Such a conception excluded any possible constitutive force of a real, extraindividual context, such as a national character or the spirit of an age.

Dilthey's incarnation of values in an objectively real medium precluded both their discrete restriction to an ideal seat in consciousness and their reduction to historical or natural processes. This preclusion lent objective and empirically real status to an overarching context as the bearer of meaningful structures, while leaving individuality a primary constitutive role in their reception and potential modification. To use Dilthey's term, one could speak of a common "worldview" as more than an outlook shared by several great representatives of a society, having its foundation in the objectivity of language, institutions, and general cultural patterns of relation, and exercising a determinate force that Rickert's theories would not allow.

Such a style of thinking might seem to represent a shift in emphasis from an epistemological examination of the range of consciousness to a positing of fundamental structures of Being in the sense of Hegel's ontology. Dilthey himself often acknowledged the importance of Hegel's thought for his own historical view of the human sciences. Yet he remained committed to a critical standpoint.

Drawing on his conviction of the inexhaustibility of the real by the meanings of consciousness, Dilthey refused to endorse the metaphysical conclusion that had characterized Hegel's phenomenology. While affirming the basis of historical meaning in reality—rather than simply in the "nonreal" constructs of consciousness—Dilthey denied that reason could ever claim to comprehend the essence of reality in its total form. His aim remained the foundation of historical *science*. Influenced by the empirical turn after midcentury and the consonant concept of history voiced in the tradition of historical scholarship of Humboldt and Ranke, Dilthey refused to admit philosophical speculation into the range of historical theorizing. As most strongly articulated in his early work *Einleitung in die Geisteswissenschaften* (Introduction to the human sciences), the task of historical understanding had to be separated from ontology or metaphysics as much in the Hegelian sense as in the implicit, all-encompassing sense of the naturalists.[74]

Dilthey's standpoint, both Rickert and Husserl were quick to point out, had difficulties of its own. The implicit connection between ideal and real, between epistemology and factual circumstance, left the problem of a scientific foundation without the kind of absolute solution that these fastidious theorists sought. Although Dilthey claimed to provide universally valid criteria (*Allgemeingültigkeit*) that no science could forgo, at the same time, he considered theorists to be too closely linked to the factual presuppositions of their own historical worldviews to be able to posit the kind of presuppositionless absolute standpoint they confidently believed themselves to have found. In his own, rather blunt terms: "Presuppositionless epistemology is an illusion."[75]

The dilemma immediately arising from this orientation—as Husserl did not hesitate to point out in his *Logos* article—was as follows: If it is impossible to speak of an absolute, presuppositionless foundation for the sciences; if even the intellectual bases of science are intermingled with psychological assumptions and historically conditioned assertions, how can we arrive at clear normative principles in logical, aesthetic, religious, ethical, and other domains?

While he no longer relied on the metaphysical underpinnings of Hegel's thought, nor on the transcendent theological foundations of Ranke's, nor even on the ethereal values of Windelband and Rickert, Dilthey assumed that a universal scientific validity was possible, one founded on a thread of stable coherence running through world history as a totality.[76] To the extent that this coherence could be neither empirically ascertained nor absolutely verified, it remained always intermixed with an opacity that was, at bottom, what Dilthey discerned as the opacity of the human condition itself.

VI

Despite significant differences in their approaches to the historical world, a common critical aim underlay the thought of the Baden neo-Kantians and Dilthey.[77] Rooted in a long-standing pursuit and originally nurtured in the theoretical works of the nineteenth-century tradition of German historiography, it sought to establish historical methods of understanding on an autonomous basis, free from the encroachments of idealist speculative metaphysics or naturalistic tendencies, which had presumed to grasp the essential possibilities of human reality in a closed system of theoretical postulates.

By identifying this aim and examining its implications, we will be able to extend our observations to critical-historical thinking of the period as a whole. Three related themes are of special importance in this regard: first, a qualitatively new awareness of the limits of human understanding engendered by historical forms of thinking; second, similar ways of depicting the development of the history of ideas in the light of this new awareness; and third, congruent ideas concerning the relation between historical understanding and coherent normative standards and values.

Thus the common aim of the critical theorists under consideration involved, first, a deepening appreciation of the historical dimension of thought, not only as an advance in the capacities of human understanding, but also as a heightened comprehension of its boundaries. Armed with the resources of historical thinking, critical reasoning was tasked with apprehending the limits of human ideas which, tied to the variations of consciousness and the contingencies of its perspective, could never reach an ultimate conclusion about the character of reality itself. In the sense of a historical critique of reason, this style of thinking paralleled Kant's critical intent (if not always his epistemology), which had attempted to demonstrate that the quest for an ultimate comprehension of nature was fraught with inherent contradictions and had to be kept within distinct limits.

For his part, Rickert summed up this standpoint, which was in full agreement with the conclusions of his mentor's own philosophy, in his 1915 tribute to Windelband: "Philosophy is a science [*Wissenschaft*], and no science can hope one day to come to the end of its work. In spite of this, the systematic philosopher will ever strive for an end and for a conclusion. For him, then, nothing else remains but to ignore the fact that he is a historically contingent [*historisch bedingtes*] individual. He must be able to forget history if he himself wants to make history. For the historian such forgetfulness is forever precluded."[78]

Historical theorists, Rickert concluded, had an essential lesson to teach to overambitious systematic philosophers, or to other theorists who would seek to replace the philosophers' systematic quests. For them, the historicity of philosophy corresponded to an unavoidable historicity in the theoretical structure of all science, and this represented a critical conclusion that no aspect of thought could hope to surmount. As we noted earlier, the ongoing objectivity and coherence of theoretical systems could never be grounded in the empirical world but only in faith in absolute transcendent values.

Dilthey placed the source of objectivity in an immanent, meaningful coherence of the life world; his conclusion about the finitude of human understanding was equally firm, and was advanced for parallel reasons. As stated in *Einleitung in die Geisteswissenschaften,* both a naturalistic sociology and an ontology of history were false because they

> discern in the representation of the singular [*des Singularen*] a mere raw material for their abstractions. This superstition subordinates the work of the historian to a mysterious process in order alchemistically to change the singular material found in this work into the unalloyed gold of abstractions and to force history to divulge its final mystery. This is just as adventurous as ever the dream of the alchemist was, who thought he had discovered nature's last word. There is as little such a last word of history, which would express its true sense, as there is of nature.[79]

Beyond this conclusion about the limits of human understanding and the role of historical reflection in bringing it into clear focus, a second underlying theme that united the critical aim of the Baden neo-Kantians with that of Dilthey is to be found in their respective interpretations of the advent of critical-historical thought in Western culture. Designating an explicit direction in the history of Western ideas, *Einleitung in die Geisteswissenschaften* dealt with what Dilthey saw as a gradual "dissolution of the metaphysical standpoint of man" in contradistinction to the "emergence and the legitimacy of modern scientific consciousness."[80] He neither dismissed speculative metaphysical reasoning nor acknowledged it as a necessary, if often illusory, characteristic of human thought, as Kant had proclaimed a century before.[81] Rather, he dealt with the logical fallacies of speculative metaphysics by relativizing it as a "historically limited appearance,"[82] whose illusory character had to be exposed before one could undertake truly scientific reflection. In Dilthey's teleology, Western thought had as an important cultural goal its gradual (if perhaps never total) liberation from metaphysical presuppositions in the natural sciences of the seventeenth and eighteenth centuries and in the historical science of the nineteenth.

From a very different methodological perspective, Windelband expressed an almost identical interpretation of the movement of Western thought. His essay "Was ist Philosophie?" (What is philosophy?) traced the development of philosophy from the metaphysics of the Greeks and the medieval Scholastics to the critical approach introduced by Kant and further extended through the critical-historical insights of nineteenth-century theorists.[83]

This progressive movement of Western thought, finally, received strong support from Rickert, whose essay "Geschichtsphilosophie" (The philosophy of history; 1905) dealt with the emergence of critical awareness as part of a long historical process, in which thought passed through the three phases of dogmatism, skepticism, and criticism.[84] Western science progressed to the dawn of the critical style of thought—beginning with Kant—which understood the impossibility of ascribing metaphysical reality to any sense or value that might be perceived in the course of historical development.[85]

The third theme running through the critical theories of history of the Baden neo-Kantians and Dilthey concerned the relation between historical understanding and coherent norms and values. Leaving aside the formal sphere of logic, how might the diversity and individuality of cultures or worldviews revealed by historical understanding be reconciled with the universal normative criteria required by the theoretical sciences?

For Dilthey as for Windelband and Rickert, world history (*Weltgeschichte*) was not a simple record of accidents and contingencies, but conveyed an overarching objective sense. Once the quest for metaphysical finality was renounced, researchers were free to pursue limited systematic insights. To that end, historical induction was the more appropriate mode of analysis for the human sciences. In the wide range of particularly embodied normative meanings actualized in the course of history, this more modest mode of analysis presupposed a universally comprehensible sense, a sense that, from a purely theoretical standpoint, could guide researchers in their studies. Thus historical understanding presupposed a higher universality, above and beyond the diversity and individuality of historical contexts, which it helped bring to ever greater clarity.

Nowhere did the role of historical understanding in the clarification of the universal meaning of normative principles become clearer than in the three theorists' respective conceptions of philosophy itself. Dilthey expressed his most developed elaboration of the concept of philosophy in his late essay "Das Wesen der Philosophie" (The essence of philosophy). To the question, "Is it possible to speak of an essence of philosophy?" Dilthey argued, the proper response is to be found in the inductive study of history, and not in the deductive operations of reason.[86] Philosophy is not to be constructed from pure concepts. It must be grasped by study of what philosophy has meant in the cultural contexts where it has arisen; it cannot be characterized within the confines of a single determining factor. To understand philosophy, researchers must follow the tissue of meaning that its development has woven, in a plurality of ways, across the history of ideas:

> [A] great number of attempts to determine the concept [of philosophy] are the expression of what particular philosophers, determined by a given cultural situation and oriented by their own system, have considered philosophy to be. Thus these definitions are abbreviations for what characterizes one historical form of philosophy. They provide insight into the inner dialectic by which philosophy has run through [*durchlaufen*] the possibilities of its position in the coherence [*Zusammenhang*] of culture. Each of these possibilities must be able to be made fruitful for the determination of the concept of philosophy.[87]

Only in such inductive comprehension of the historical forms that philosophy has assumed can the emergent profile of philosophy as a search for universal validity (*Allgemeingültigkeit*) be clarified and placed in the context of a larger cultural role.

Windelband, who had written a number of famous histories of philosophy, expressed a parallel conception. The study of the history of philosophy, in his estimation, was closely bound up with the formulation of normative standards that guide the theoretical sciences and the life of culture:

> The historical process of the human spirit . . . can be considered from the [following] standpoint. [G]radually, in the midst of work on particular problems, in the modification of its interests, in the shifting of its single threads, the [historical] consciousness of norms [*Normen*] has broken through to the effect that, in its progressive movement, it represents an ever deeper and more comprehensive grasping of normative

consciousness [*Normalbewusstsein*]. Nothing stands in the way when, from the standpoint of this determination of the concept of philosophy, the gradual coming to awareness of norms is conceived as the genuine sense of the history of philosophy.[88]

For his part, writing in "Geschichtsphilosophie," Rickert affirmed the importance of inductive historical research for the task of rising beyond the historical contingency of a particular period toward clarification of the universally valid norms sought by the philosopher. The systematization of values objectified in the past, if never capable of yielding the sense of ultimate, transcendent values, nonetheless provides ever more comprehensive material traces of this sense as the objective coherence linking together the course of world history.

The fin de siècle critical aim of the Baden neo-Kantians and of Dilthey endowed historical understanding with methodological significance for the systematic concerns of the sciences as a whole. In harmony with it, a wide variety of theorists in the humanistic disciplines broke free from idealist metaphysical speculation and from naturalism by elaborating critical-historical approaches to social science in accord with the specific needs of their disciplines. To better appreciate the scope of historical understanding in this period, let us turn now to several of the most significant of these theorists, whose writings are also analyzed in Heidegger's works.

To take a noted example, Georg Simmel contributed in significant ways to extending the critical style of historical theorizing into the different realm of sociology and the philosophy of economics. Simmel's early thinking provided what Heidegger would later describe as an "epistemological elucidation of historical comprehension."[89]

Like Windelband and Rickert, Simmel was deeply influenced by the revival of Kant's philosophy in the second half of the nineteenth century. Concurrently with them, he sought to expand the Kantian conception of understanding to encompass the historical world. Like Rickert, who openly admired his work, Simmel postulated that all thought, natural as well as historical, is confronted with an infinity of possible choices in the selection of its material. For Simmel as for Rickert, this infinitude precluded the speculative metaphysical deduction of real historical particularity—thus also the naturalist's naive realist presupposition (as in the sociology of Comte) that laws discerned by consciousness are simple copies of the real world.[90]

Although sensitive to the distinction between logic and psychology that the Baden and other neo-Kantians had drawn, unlike them, Simmel focused his analysis on the psychological factors that influenced historical understanding, fixing his attention, especially in *Die Probleme der Geschichtsphilosophie* (The problems of the philosophy of history), on the interest guiding the historian's choice, nuanced by psychological motives. His focus on psychology, however, did not imply that the historian's methods, once liberated from the naturalist's naive realist claim, were to imitate the laws constructed by the natural scientist. Psychological factors propelled interest in given historical contents, and the meaning of these contents was intertwined with psychological propensities of the historical agents under study; ultimately, however, these contents had to refer to an essential core of individuality beyond the generalizing methods of natural science and irreducible to psychological law. We could understand this individuality precisely because the psychological aspects it embodied referred back to a logical structure, one that called for an autonomous method of historical understanding.

In the notion of interest guiding the historical sciences, complementing that of law construction in the natural sciences, Simmel's critical-historical aim was clearly revealed: history and the natural sciences constituted different ways of selecting material in an infinitely heterogeneous world. This selection bespoke the distance between mind and reality and, given the limits of finite mind, the never-ending attempt to bridge this distance engendered the historicity of all human concepts.

Simmel's historical-critical conception of the limits of human understanding and his quest for autonomous methods of historical investigation joined his ideas to the other critical theories of history of this period. In *Die Probleme der Geschichtsphilosophie,* a further thread linked his thought with the aims of the other theorists in question. Like the Baden neo-Kantians and Dilthey, Simmel relativized metaphysical speculation as a historical stage that, to his mind, critical thinking had overcome. He spoke freely of a "destiny of development of our knowledge," in which speculative philosophy and the ontological hypostatization of natural laws served as important "anticipations" of more exact, critical forms of scientific knowledge.[91]

About the relation between historical understanding and the quest for universal norms, Simmel was less explicit than the other theorists under consideration. On the one hand, he agreed that the task of historical understanding was to probe the historical world as a source of material to be systematized by sociohistorical research.[92] He conceived such systematization along the lines of a comparative study of social patterns. On the other, he held that the coherence of normative standards through which a system became possible had to be conceived (in Kantian fashion) in terms of stable categories of concept formation.[93] Simmel acknowledged that, though there might very well be an absolute basis to this understanding, nowhere was this basis in evidence.[94] Nonetheless, despite all historical variation in natural and in historical concepts, he was confident that the failure to locate such an absolute basis did not condemn human thought to skepticism. Simmel's own efforts in *Die Probleme der Geschichtsphilosophie,* as first stated in the 1907 edition, were meant to help overcome such skepticism by freeing human consciousness from the dangerous tendencies of historicism (*Historismus*).[95]

Another major figure allied with the critical style of historical theorizing in this period was Max Weber. In an early article, Heidegger described Weber's method as an adaptation of Rickert's neo-Kantian principles of historical understanding to the socioeconomic world.[96] Indeed, notwithstanding the originality of Weber's ideas, there is much in his writings, especially in his application of value theory to the social sciences, that testifies to a strong neo-Kantian influence.[97]

Like the other theorists under consideration, Weber agreed that the historical-cultural disciplines needed a rigorous foundation to keep them independent of both the law-constructing methods of the natural sciences and the speculative tendencies of all forms of metaphysics. With them, Weber emphasized the unbridgeable gap between our ideas or laws and the plenitude of empirical reality itself.

Weber's social scientific method emphasized the empirical study of the manifestation of ideas in world history; it grouped together heterogeneous empirical contents by relating them to an "ideal limiting case [*idealer Grenzfall*]."[98] For this purpose, Weber suggested ideal type constructions—conceived as coherent models of reality, not as its copies—which were to remain of cardinal importance in the methodology of the social sciences. Using ideal type constructions, historical study was directed to inductively gather empirical material from an infinite arena and to classify that material typologically.

To be sure, Weber's emphasis on the ideal type (*Idealtypus*), which constructed a general pattern from heterogeneous samples of material, departed from the traditional view of history as a recapitulation of individuality. In explaining the use of types, however, Weber was careful to distinguish between the sociologist and the historian. Rickert responded with a parallel distinction of his own, between the "historical-individual concepts" of the historian and the more general "relative historical concepts" of the sociologist.[99] For both thinkers, relative historical concepts were in no way to be confused with the pure generalities of natural scientific law. The autonomy of historical thinking was thus safeguarded.[100]

Looking over the course of history, Weber also recognized an unmistakable progression of rational values. Yet confidence in an absolute source of rational principles, guiding the course of world history in indecipherable fashion, gave way in his thought to a less optimistic outlook. Weber was deeply sensitive to the loss of spontaneous metaphysical harmony with the world that the rationalization of life, and the growth of critical awareness, had engendered. He remained deeply ambivalent toward the disenchantment (*Entzauberung*) of the world and the sense of ultimate purposelessness that the rational challenge to religious values had set in motion. Nevertheless, Weber maintained his faith in the soundness of Western intellectual traditions. He continued to argue for the stability of theoretical norms and for the reconcilability of the systematic needs of human understanding with the unwavering historicity of theoretical configurations.[101]

Yet another significant critical-historical thinker in the decades preceding the outbreak of World War I was theologian Ernst Troeltsch, whom Heidegger would target in the years just following the war, as we will see in chapter 4. Like Weber, Troeltsch was deeply influenced in the prewar decades by the neo-Kantian orientation of Windelband and Rickert. In his comprehensive review of Rickert's *Grenzen der naturwissenschaftlichen Begriffsbildung,* Troeltsch would note: "Thus I can only express spirited agreement with the basic thought of Rickert's work."[102] Along with other critical-minded theorists, Troeltsch wrote of the need for an autonomous, rigorously founded science of history, free from the naturalistic and speculative-idealist orientations to which it had been subordinated at different periods over the course of the nineteenth century. To his mind, at least in the prewar period, Rickert's philosophy fulfilled this task most efficaciously.

Troeltsch's interest in historical themes and the inspiration he drew from Rickert's *Wertphilosophie* (Philosophy of value) were intimately connected with the deeper theological motives of his thought. Rickert's clear logical separation of naturalistic methods and idealist metaphysical constructions from historical science bolstered his defense of an autonomous value for religious manifestations in the historical world, irreducible to functional processes of nature and undeducible from concepts of reason.

Troeltsch's theological concerns enriched his idea of the historical world and lent his thinking on historical matters an uncommon profundity. With the march of secularization and of modernization that accompanied and complemented the general shift in German scientific consciousness after midcentury, theology fell into a period of widely acknowledged crisis. Far more directly than that of secular values, the systematic coherence of religious values came increasingly into question in a period when—as Troeltsch was all too aware—the traditional teachings of the Protestant churches grew increasingly out of touch with empirical-minded sectors of the intelligentsia.

Nowhere, perhaps, was the crisis of theology more evident than in the epoch-making work *Das Wesen des Christentums* (The essence of Christianity; 1900) by Troeltsch's colleague, Adolf von Harnack, whose attempt to reconstruct the essence of the Christian faith on strictly historical grounds touched off a controversy that would last for decades. Indeed, as chapters 2 and 4 explore in greater detail, the rebuttal of Catholic modernism by orthodox Catholics and (somewhat later) that of Protestant liberalism by neo-orthodox Protestants revolved around the issue of historical treatment of religious phenomena, of which Harnack's work was the most straightforward expression. In Protestant and Catholic Church alike, the problem of positing coherent standards of truth in the face of truth's historical diversity erupted with extraordinary force.

At the apex of an age of liberal-historical Protestant theology, Troeltsch's teaching steadily refused to retreat before the problem of historical meaning. His openness to the historical world was drawn from faith that, despite the whirlwind of cultural change that characterized the late nineteenth and early twentieth centuries, Christian values would prevail and prove themselves anew. In his remarkable treatise *Die Absolutheit des Christentums und die Religionsgeschichte* (The absoluteness of Christianity and the history of religion; 1902), Troeltsch argued that theologians had no need to fear historical relativism—or "historicism [*Historismus*]"[103]—but could instead place their confidence in the coherence of history as an arena of actualization of normative standards. "History," he wrote, "does not exclude norms [*Normen*]; indeed, its most essential work is the bringing forth of norms and the struggle for the comprehension of these norms."[104] If cultural norms were never simply products of historical development and had to be considered as arising from an a priori source, the only possible arena open for their disclosure was that presented by the historical world itself.

In Troeltsch's estimation—as was also most clearly pronounced in the thought of the Baden neo-Kantians and Dilthey—historical thinking, far from being a threat to normative values, was crucial to the development of the human spirit. By engendering awareness of the limits of human understanding, it brought an end to "the dogmatic formation of concepts that naive claims to validity hypostatized with whatever comparatively simple concepts [came to hand],"[105] and it made room for a new phase of inductive-historical understanding.

Despite his distaste for the speculative metaphysics of German idealism, Troeltsch was not entirely in accord with the neo-Kantian tendency to exclude all forms of metaphysics from consideration in the foundation of social science. In his view, the ultimate separation of metaphysics from empirical reality was achieved only at the cost of an extreme fragmentation of the social world, on the one hand, and of tension in the underlying premises of thought and belief, on the other.[106] Although Troeltsch would attempt to resolve this problem by moving farther away from Rickert's formalism, especially in the postwar period, that his own conception of metaphysics never broke with the inductive approach of social science only demonstrated the inner congruence of his thought with the empirical style of scientific consciousness of his age.

Having considered the major critical theorists of history in Germany of the late nineteenth and early twentieth centuries, we can see how, following the shift in scientific consciousness toward a more empirical style of research, inductive and historical methods of understanding became synonymous with rigorous, scientific thought in the humanistic disciplines. They served as the means by which a wide variety of disciplines could assert their autonomy as styles of cognition specially suited to the human world.

In each case, the adoption of historical methods of understanding was based on a central presupposition. Underlying the historicity of human understanding, a stable set of normative criteria enabled objective systematization of human phenomena across the boundaries imposed by vast changes in cultural values and in the very preconditions of human existence itself. This presupposition was transmitted between the generations of historical thinkers of the nineteenth and early twentieth centuries, withstanding all criticism of metaphysics and the decline of faith in Divine guidance as the immediate support of events in the world.[107]

The presupposition of stable normative standards by critical theorists of history, as has been stressed, precluded consideration of such standards as products either of factual circumstance or of an all-powerful absolute spirit. After the critique of Hegelian ontology, naturalism, and historicism, such stability was commonly sought in one of two directions—either (with the neo-Kantians) in the constitution of world history by ideal, meaning-giving values of consciousness or (with Dilthey) in the interrelation of ideal capacities of consciousness with objective structures of the life world. In both cases, it was presumed that the meaningfulness of world history could be characterized according to schema having universal validity, making the norms of the past objectively comprehensible to theorists of the present.

Conceived according to this outline, the assumption of world historical coherence remained vulnerable to the extent that it could not be empirically verified. Because the assertion of universal principles according to which such coherence was elaborated could not convincingly result from the conglomeration of standards manifested by historically variable individuality, it had to be adopted on faith—as a methodological postulate.

With the presupposition of the objective meaningfulness of world history came a second, closely interrelated presupposition: that historical meaning was indeed accessible from the course of historical development—that the norms and values manifested in the past and objectively verifiable by the historians' methods were in fact the repositories of an original meaning the past had to offer. In chapters 3, 4, and 5, we will consider the emergence, in important sectors of the post–World War I German intelligentsia, of various lines of attack against this second presupposition.

Although the critical theorists admitted that the universal validity assumed by historians operated within the range of a historically limited perspective and never exhausted the past's original meaning, there was one possibility arising from the critical standpoint that they never seriously considered—the possibility of radical disharmony between the alleged coherence of world history and the inner meaning specific to the heterogeneous moments of that history. Indeed, the presupposition of world historical coherence in the manifestation of normative principles—especially for Windelband, Rickert, Dilthey, and Troeltsch, who assumed a clearly formulated idea of the progress of human understanding—implied a higher order of reconciliation and harmony of the individual moments of history within the overarching framework of the whole.

In this ongoing coherence, any negation, falsification, and forgetfulness that adaptation to cultural standards might engender eluded the systematic eye on the lookout for universally valid standards. From the doubting perspective of postwar thought, the prewar style of historical theorizing seemed not to have considered the possible radical incompatibility of certain norms with the process of cultural development and with the theoretical forms of interpretation that looked to history as a fundamental source of normative meaning. The presupposition of critical-historical thought in this regard, with roots deep in the intellectual soil of nineteenth-century forms of historical understanding, withstood the critique of speculative metaphysics and the naturalistic worldview, two intellectual tendencies in which this presupposition had gained a most pervasive force.

In the prewar period, condemnations of what was viewed as an overextension of the historical understanding centered for the most part on the fear (shared by Husserl, as we have seen) that the objective needs of science could only be undermined by a too exclusive concentration on historical forms of analysis. Even Windelband, who had done so much to promote historical methods of thought, would near the end of his life describe what he saw as the propagation of an exaggerated style of historical analysis in late nineteenth-century philosophy. In 1909, a year before the publication of Husserl's critique of historicism in "Philosophy as a Rigorous Science," Windelband described the identical phenomenon that Husserl was to pinpoint, yet with greater sensitivity to the predicament of historical understanding that this phenomenon symptomized. In Windelband's estimation (as in that of Husserl and Troeltsch), this exaggerated style of historical analysis had roots in Hegel's principle of historical comprehension, adopted without consideration for his (or any other) standard of objective truth. Here the dissolution of philosophy into its history "organized itself in a different way than was the case for Hegel. The single systems were no longer valid as moments of truth, but of untruth. Their opposing and contradictory variety was taken to be the refutation of their strivings. For general opinion the result of the entire laborious work of historical reflection resulted only in the relativity of all world apprehensions."[108] Writing in response to the development of historical relativism, Windelband described a great danger posed by an important faction of the younger generation at the end of the century. According to him, these younger thinkers "began to feel tradition, the great historical schoolbag of modern man, to be a burden; and boasting about the originality of their own deeds, they believed themselves capable of easily throwing it off."[109]

The philosopher who most clearly anticipated the critique of the exaggerated style of historical analysis among members of the post–World War I generation was Friedrich Nietzsche. Well before the affirmations of historical understanding by the critical theorists, the second essay of his *Untimely Meditations* had forcefully stigmatized the unchecked application of historical understanding and what Nietzsche viewed as its particular incompatibility with philosophy and theology.[110] In remarks that proved prophetic, Nietzsche warned that, although "[f]or a good while, one can indeed occupy oneself with history in a fully harmless and thoughtless way, as if this were an occupation like any other," eventually historical science becomes a burden, not only because it relativizes the customs of life and brings into question the normative standards of truth by which life is maintained, but also because it reduces to factual reality even those highest and most sacred values whose transcendence of the historical process—even where wholly illusory—is necessary as a vital principle of robust health.[111]

On this ground, Nietzsche took what he viewed as the rise of an overconcern with historical matters as a bad omen for modern culture. Absorption in the past, for him, only augmented a real danger modern humans had to face: that of becoming mere epigones, numbed by a throng of details about creations of the past, but for whom the source of creativity had run dry.

The shortcomings that Nietzsche attributed to historical thought and the doubt he felt toward a modern culture he believed had become preoccupied with historical matters touch on a theme to which we will return in our examination of the post–World War I period, where his thought played its most decisive role. In chapter 2, however, we will turn from the macrocosm of German historical theory and philosophy of the prewar period to the intellectual microcosm of the young Heidegger, whose thought, among all the representatives of the post–World War I generation, is most centrally at issue.

NOTES

1. Heidegger's reference to this change appeared first in his 1912 article "Das Realitätsproblem in der modernen Philosophie," 354, and then in a later lecture, "Prolegomena zur Geschichte des Zeitbegriffs," printed in *Gesamtausgabe,* 20:13.

2. Heidegger, *Sein und Zeit,* 404.

3. Ibid., 398.

4. Yorck, "Die Nicht-Vergeschichtlichung des Philosophierens erscheint mir in methodischer Beziehung als ein metaphysischer Rest," as quoted in ibid., 402.

5. Dilthey, "Rede zum 70. Geburtstag (1903)," in *Die geistige Welt: Einleitung in die Philosophie des Lebens,* 7.

6. Leonhard von Renthe-Fink has demonstrated that the very word *historicity (Geschichtlichkeit)*, with which Dilthey and Yorck characterized their task—and which, from a different perspective, Heidegger took up in his *Daseinsanalyse*—first emerged in the writings of Schleiermacher and of Hegel. Renthe-Fink points out that, even if these thinkers were the first to employ the word, *historicity* did not carry then the same semantic connotations that it would in the late nineteenth century, when it acquired its problematic nuances, which Heidegger sought to rid it of throughout his working life. See Renthe-Fink, *Geschichtlichkeit: Ihr terminologischer und begrifflicher Ursprung bei Hegel, Haym, Dilthey und Yorck,* and also "Geschichtlichkeit," 404–5.

7. See, for example, Cassirer, *Das Erkenntnisproblem in der Philosophie und Wissenschaft der neueren Zeit,* 230; Gadamer, Afterword to Herder, *Auch eine Philosophie der Geschichte zur Bildung der Menschheit,* 146–77.

8. Herder, *Auch eine Philosophie,* 16, 69, 96–97.

9. Hume, *Enquiry Concerning the Principles of Morals;* Iselin, *Über die Geschichte der Menschheit,* 433.

10. Or, as Heidegger himself expressed this idea in his Freiburg course lecture series, "Phänomenologie und Transzendentale Wertphilosophie," *Gesamtausgabe,* 56/57:133:

> Indeed, with Herder, historical consciousness [*historisches Bewusstsein*] attained a decisive elucidation. He brought a transformation in that he viewed historical reality [*geschichtliche Wirklichkeit*] . . . in the diversity of its irrational plenitude [*in ihrer mannigfaltigen irrationalen Fülle*] and above all recognized the autonomous value of every nation, of every epoch, of every historical phenomenon as such. Historical reality is no longer exclusively viewed according to the schematic regularity of a rational-linear orientation toward progress in which each level meets its limit in that it overcomes barbarity and achieves rationality. The goal of progress is as such no longer one of abstract, rational happiness and virtue, rather "every Nation bears the center of its happiness within itself, as every ball its center of gravity."

11. Schleiermacher, *Über die Religion: Reden an die Gebildeten unter ihren Verächtern,* 23.

12. Ibid., 23.

13. Ibid., 30.

14. Heidegger, *Unterwegs zur Sprache,* 96–97. In his early Freiburg course lectures, Heidegger noted the importance of Schleiermacher's historical method of interpretation for Christian theology. See Heidegger, *Gesamtausgabe,* 59:21–22.

15. Hence, as Herder, *Auch eine Philosophie,* 40, said: "Only the Creator is able to think of the complete unity of one and all nations in their diversity, without thereby losing sight of this unity"; or as Schleiermacher, *Über die Religion,* 47, could affirm: "If you seek to gain an inkling of a sublime unity, an immense coherence [*Zusammenhang*], it must be found, not only in a general tendency toward order and harmony, but in a singular relation that cannot be fully intelligible by itself."

16. Heidegger, *Frühe Schriften,* 353.

17. Hegel, *Vorlesungen über die Geschichte der Philosophie III, Werke,* 20:333.

18. Kant, *Die Religion innerhalb der Grenzen der blossen Vernunft, Werke,* 8(2):777–815.

19. See, in this regard, the last section of Kant's *Kritik der reinen Vernunft,* "Die Geschichte der reinen Vernunft," *Werke,* 4:709–12, and especially his

1784 essay "Idee zu einer allgemeinen Geschichte in weltbürgerlicher Absicht," *Werke,* 11:33–50. See also Herder's critique of Kant's "Idee zu einer allgemeinen Geschichte" and of Kant's epistemology in its application to history in Herder's 1785 letter to C. M. Wieland in Herder, *Briefe,* 102–3. In his 1799 work *Vernunft und Sprache,* Herder applied judgments to the Kantian epistemology that had become familiar in his earlier, general critique of the Enlightenment: he criticized the Kantian epistemology for deducing the possibility of experience on the basis of an abstract notion of the faculties of consciousness and of "universally valid [*allgemeingültige*]" criteria of truth. This doctrine, according to Herder, only projected empty propositions "because, referred back to the particular, they are nowhere valid." Herder, *Vernunft und Sprache: Eine Metakritik zur* Kritik der reinen Vernunft: *Mit einer Zugabe, betreffend ein kritisches Tribunal aller Facultäten, Regierungen und Geschäfte,* 313.

20. Hegel, "Über die wissenschaftlichen Behandlungsarten des Naturrechts, seine Stelle in der praktischen Philosophie und sein Verhältnis zu den positiven Rechtswissenschaften," *Werke,* 2:525; see also Görland, *Die Kantkritik des jungen Hegel.*

21. Hegel, *Vorlesungen über die Geschichte der Philosophie I, Werke,* 18:74.

22. Hegel, *Phänomenologie des Geistes, Werke,* 3:547. For a discussion of Hegel's relation to Greek antiquity in regard to this point, see Taminiaux, *La nostalgie de la Grèce à l'aube de l'idéalisme allemand: Kant et les Grecs dans l'itinéraire de Schiller, de Hölderlin et de Hegel,* 239–48.

23. Heidegger, *Nietzsche,* 1:91–108.

24. Ibid., 100–101.

25. Hegel, *Vorlesungen über die Philosophie der Geschichte, Werke,* 12:69.

26. Heidegger, *What is a Thing?,* 59.

27. Humboldt, "Über die Aufgabe des Geschichtsschreibers" and "Betrachtungen über die bewegenden Ursachen," in *Schriften zur Anthropologie und Geschichte,* 583–89.

28. Ranke, "Über die Epochen der neueren Geschichte," 141.

29. Kessel, "Idee der Universalhistorie," 293–94. According to Heidegger in his Freiburg course lecture series "Phänomenologie und Transzendentale Wertphilosophie," in *Gesamtausgabe,* 56/57: 135, Ranke "avoided any kind of speculative dialectics and aimed toward the contents and the real center point of world historical narrative [*Mär der Weltgeschichte*] in its genuine universal-historical coherence [*Zusammenhang*]. His work therefore provided a point of orientation for the future. With the ever new onrush

of empirical material of historical life, its mastery within the domain of experience was attributed priority and privilege. The capacity to comprehend the philosophical interrelation of ideas and the formation of principles disappeared, for which philosophy itself was in part responsible."

On this point, Leonard Krieger wrote in *Ranke: The Meaning of History,* 132: "Ranke was open to philosophy when it was the way to unitary principles within the framework of history, as he was opposed to it when it was a rival structure of a priori knowledge outside the framework of history."

30. See, for example, Schnabel, *Deutsche Geschichte im 19. Jahrhundert,* 3:198.

31. Heidegger, *Gesamtausgabe,* 21:63.

32. Heidegger's use of the term "positivism," which he applied to neo-Kantians as well as to thinkers who are more generally considered to be positivists, should not be confused with the original positivism of thinkers like Comte. His broad usage tended to encompass not only thinkers who attempted to apply mechanistic laws to human consciousness, but to what he saw as those who concentrated too exclusively on facts and factual analysis. M. W. Simon has convincingly argued the latter point in *European Positivism in the Nineteenth Century,* 238–64.

33. Dilthey, *Geistige Welt,* 3.

34. Windelband, *Die Philosophie im deutschen Geistesleben des 19. Jahrhunderts,* 64–65.

35. Heidegger, "Realitätsproblem," 354.

36. Ibid., 356–57.

37. Ibid., 354. Heidegger interpreted the empiriocriticists in explicit relation to this kind of associationist psychology above all by specifying that, according to them, "the real lawfulness in the connection of acts of thought is indeed also psychic facts [*Tatbestände*]," ibid., 358. Although the empiriocriticists sought to do away with the distinction between psychic and physical to the extent that it carried quasi-ontological implications, all experience was referred back to a psychological relation of sense data, in which the ontological status of the psyche remained neutral.

38. Such a viewpoint had also been anticipated by Hume in *Enquiry Concerning Human Understanding,* 74: "And indeed, when we consider how aptly *natural* and *moral* evidence link together, and form only one chain of argument, we shall make no scruple to allow, that they are of the same nature, and derived from the same principles."

39. Avenarius, *Philosophy as Thought about the World According to the Principle of Least Action: Prolegomena to a Critique of Pure Experience,* as quoted in Husserl, *Logical Investigations,* 1:198. On the empiriocritical theory of consciousness, see Kolakowski, *Philosophie des Positivismus.*

40. Mach, *Erkenntnis und Irrtum: Skizzen zur Psychologie der Forschung*, v.

41. Cohen, Introduction to Lange, *Geschichte des Materialismus und Kritik seiner Bedutung für die Gegenwart*, 1:x–xi.

42. Heidegger, *Frühe Schriften*, 5.

43. Heidegger, *Gesamtausgabe*, 20:18.

44. Heidegger, letter to Heinrich Rickert, March 15, 1921, in Heidegger and Rickert, *Briefe*, 54. In the same letter, Heidegger informed Rickert he was planning to teach a seminar on Rickert's *Die Grenzen der naturwissenschaftlichen Begriffsbildung*. Ibid., 55. That this was more than just flattery of an elder former mentor on the part of a young *Privatdozent* seems plain from Heidegger's letter of February 15, 1928, to Rickert, where he again mentions the importance of Rickert's *Grenzen* for the development of his thinking. Ibid., 58.

45. Heidegger, *Gesamtausgabe*, 21:85.

46. Windelband, *Präludien*, 1:154–55.

47. Ibid., 2:136–61.

48. Rickert, *Grenzen*, 244–56. Although Rickert reworked some of his concepts in the third and fourth editions, these essentially recapitulated ideas already expressed in the first and second editions (1902 and 1913).

49. Ibid., 404–65.

50. Rickert, "Geschichtsphilosophie," 321–420.

51. Rickert, *Grenzen*, 1–26. In general, Rickert's references to Comte are not directed toward specific aspects of Comtean positivism, but criticize elements of Comte's thought shared in common with other forms of elaboration of the naturalistic worldview.

52. Rickert, "Geschichtsphilosophie," 321–420.

53. Heidegger, *Gesamtausgabe*, 20:30.

54. Heidegger, "Mein Weg in die Phänomenologie," in *Zur Sache des Denkens*, 81–90.

55. Heidegger, *Gesamtausgabe*, 20:20.

56. Heidegger, "Mein Weg," in *Zur Sache des Denkens*, 86–87.

57. Husserl, *Logical Investigations*, 1:387.

58. Ibid., 2:791.

59. Heidegger, *Gesamtausgabe*, 17:88–100.

60. Husserl, "Philosophy as a Rigorous Science," 78.

61. Ibid., 77.

62. Ibid., 136.

63. Ibid., 116.

64. Dilthey, *Geistige Welt*, cxii.

65. Heidegger's sharpest criticism of Husserl on this matter appeared in his "Brief über den Humanismus," in *Wegmarken*, 170.

66. For Dilthey's comments on Husserl's *Logical Investigations*, see Dilthey, *Der Aufbau der geschlichtlichen Welt in den Geisteswissenschaften*, 14.

67. By 1890, before the appearance of Husserl's *Logical Investigations*, much of Dilthey's epistemology had already been elaborated in essays such as "Beiträge zur Lösung der Frage vom Ursprung unseres Glaubens an die Realität der Aussenwelt und seinem Recht," in *Geistige Welt*, 90–139.

68. Dilthey, "Ideen über eine beschreibende und zergliedernde Psychologie," *Geistige Welt*, 143.

69. Ibid., 152–53.

70. Ibid.

71. Heidegger stated his concurrence with Rickert on this point in *Gesamtausgabe*, 21:216.

72. The concept of mediation in Dilthey's philosophy has received clear exposition in Michael Ermarth's work, *Wilhelm Dilthey: The Critique of Historical Reason*. Ermarth points out the distinction, especially in Dilthey's later thought, between the immediate *Erlebnis* and the mediated *Lebenserfahrung*, the most genuine material of the human sciences. Ermarth convincingly demonstrates that between the treatise (*Akademieabhandlung*) Dilthey presented to the Prussian Academy of Sciences in 1890 and his later analyses of the organization of the historical world, Dilthey shifted his emphasis away from descriptive psychology of lived experience (*Erlebnis*) toward the study of life experience (*Lebenserfahrung*) crystallized in structures (such as linguistic expression) more evidently mediated by history. As seems apparent both in Dilthey's thought and in Ermarth's treatment of it, the key concept of *Lebenserfahrung* should be seen, not as a total change, but rather as a shift in accent.

73. Dilthey, *Aufbau*, 130–52.

74. Dilthey, *Einleitung in die Geisteswissenschaften*, 76–120. Dilthey dedicated the *Einleitung* to the memory of his friend and correspondent Count Yorck von Wartenburg, mentioned in connection with Dilthey at the outset of this chapter. Because Yorck remained practically unknown to the German intelligentsia until the publication of his correspondence with Dilthey in 1923, we will consider Yorck's relation to Dilthey in the context of Heidegger's commentary in *Being and Time*. On Dilthey's complex relation to Hegelian metaphysics, see esp. Cacciatore, *Scienza e filosofia in Dilthey*, 1:167–68, and Makkreel, *Dilthey: Philosopher of the Human Sciences*, 306–10.

75. Dilthey, *Geistige Welt*, 150.

76. Dilthey, *Aufbau*, 120–88.

77. My understanding of this theme has benefited from the classic work of Raymond Aron on this subject, *La philosophie critique de l'histoire*. Aron's

insights have been elaborated on in Henri-Irénée Marrou's informative treatise on historical understanding, *De la connaissance historique.* See also Mandelbaum, *History, Man and Reason: A Study in Nineteenth-Century Thought.*

78. Rickert, *Wilhelm Windelband*, 23.

79. Dilthey, *Einleitung*, 91–92.

80. Ibid., 352.

81. In the *Critique of Pure Reason*, 56, Kant had written: "In all men, as soon as their reason has become ripe for speculation, there has always existed and will always continue to exist some kind of metaphysics." While it would perhaps be an exaggeration to attribute to Dilthey the conviction that metaphysical speculation would forever be banished from philosophical thinking, there is a historical emphasis in his thinking that is not evident in the eighteenth-century philosophy of Kant. Dilthey's attitude toward speculative metaphysics, as reflected in his late essay "Das Wesen der Philosophie," in *Geistige Welt*, 371–417, remained constant throughout his work.

82. Dilthey, *Einleitung*, 133.

83. Windelband, "Was ist Philosophie?" in *Präludien*, 1:17–19. The role of critical-historical thinking in the development of Western intellectual history is most clearly examined in the essay "Nach Hundert Jahren," in *Präludien*, 1:154.

84. Rickert, "Geschichtsphilosophie," 404.

85. Ibid., 418.

86. Dilthey, "Wesen der Philosophie," in *Geistige Welt*, 339.

87. Ibid., 344.

88. Windelband, "Was ist Philosophie?," in *Präludien*, 1:47–48.

89. Heidegger, *Sein und Zeit*, 375.

90. During the final period of his life, and toward the end of the First World War, Simmel began to elaborate a new style of metaphysics, which he set out in *Lebensanschauung: Vier metaphysische Kapitel.*

91. Simmel, *Probleme der Geschichtsphilosophie,*120, 20.

92. Simmel, "Problem of Sociology," 25.

93. For this reason, Maurice Mandelbaum placed Simmel among the "counterrelativists," although, for Mandelbaum, Simmel's ideas are not brought to sufficient clarity on this point. See Mandelbaum, *Problem of Historical Knowledge*, 101–19.

94. Simmel, *The Philosophy of Money*, 164.

95. Simmel, *Probleme der Geschichtsphilosophie*, vii.

96. Heidegger, "Anmerkungen zu Karl Jaspers *Psychologie der Weltanschauungen*," 97. Heidegger's original review was written between 1919 and 1921. See also Heidegger, *Wegmarken* (vol .9 of *Gesamtausgabe*), where this review has been reprinted.

EMERGENCE OF THE PROBLEM OF HISTORICAL MEANING   63

97. Weber specially acknowledged his indebtedness to Simmel, Windelband, and Rickert, emphasizing how important Rickert's value philosophy was for his understanding of the logical problems of the science of culture. See Weber's essay "Die 'Objektivität' sozialwissenschaftlicher und sozialpolitischer Erkenntnis," in *Wissenschaftslehre*, 146–214, esp. 146.

98. Ibid., 195. The English translation of Weber's term "*idealer Grenzfall*" has been taken from Weber, *The Methodology of the Social Sciences*, 94, a work that translates three of Weber's early essays (1904–17), most notably, "Die 'Objektivität' sozialwissenschaftlicher und sozialpolitischer Erkenntnis" (see note 97). All three derive from Weber, *Wissenschaftslehre*.

99. Rickert, *Grenzen*, 248.

100. Rickert stressed that the historian's portrayal of reality can never attain absolute individuality: the words that are used to describe historical action, to take one example, are themselves typical constructions. Nonetheless, the objects under historical consideration may be depicted in a more individual light through the general medium of words than would be the case in the construction of sociological concepts. The third edition of Rickert's *Grenzen* was dedicated to the memory of Max Weber, whom Rickert had known since his boyhood in Berlin.

101. Weber, *Wissenschaftslehre*, 213.

102. Troeltsch, "Moderne Geschichtsphilosophie," *Gesammelte Schriften*, 2:79.

103. The use of the word *Historismus* in this sense is already to be found in Troeltsch's 1898 article "Geschichte und Metaphysik." As would Husserl, Troeltsch traced the origin of the problem of historical meaning to the decline of German idealism. See Troeltsch, *Absolutheit*, 83.

104. Troeltsch, *Absolutheit*, 69.

105. Ibid., 30.

106. Troeltsch, "Moderne Geschichtsphilosophie," 719–27, and "Geschichte und Metaphysik," 68–70.

107. Although, from his theological perspective, Troeltsch maintained faith in Divine guidance, it is interesting to note his critique of Albrecht Ritschl's notions of supernaturalism in Troeltsch, "Geschichte und Metaphysik," 68–70. On the presupposition of stable normative criteria in history assumed by the critical theorists, see also Iggers, *German Conception*, 269–86.

108. Windelband, *Philosophie*, 87.

109. Ibid., 104.

110. Nietzsche, "Vom Nutzen und Nachteil der Historie für das Leben," in *Friedrich Nietzsche: Erkenntnistheoretische Schriften*, 45, 59.

111. Ibid., 59, 21.

2

Metaphysics and Historical Meaning in Heidegger's *Early Writings*

HEIDEGGER was born in 1889 in the small southern German town of Messkirch, near Konstanz. His early life gave little indication of the role he would play in twentieth-century German thought. His father, Friedrich Heidegger, served as a sacristan at the local Saint Martin's Church, across from the Heidegger family's small house. Young Martin served as an altar boy.

Of the circumstances that influenced the young Heidegger, his Catholic upbringing was later the most vividly recalled, and proved highly significant for his early life, as one of his rare published recollections, written at the age of 65, makes plain:

> The secret juncture in which the church festivals, the devotional days, and the course of the seasons fused together; the joining of morning, afternoon, and evening hours of each day, so that one peal of the bell continually sounded through young hearts, dreams, prayers, and games—this is indeed what, with one of the most magical, blessed, and lasting secrets, was sheltered in the bell tower; it was offered, ever transformed and unrepeatable, until the last peal into the mount of Being [*Gebirg des Seyns*].[1]

Heidegger's Catholic family orientation was complemented by his education. At fourteen, he was enrolled at the Jesuit secondary school in Konstanz, where he spent four years, followed by two at the Jesuit Bertholdsgymnasium in Freiburg im Breisgau, with a strong emphasis on theological and classical studies. At nineteen, Heidegger entered the novitiate in the Jesuit institution at Feldkirch, Austria, but discontinued his studies after several weeks due to ill health. He then enrolled at the archdiocesan Jesuit seminary in Freiburg and also at the University of Freiburg, where he pursued his theology studies for three semesters before devoting himself entirely to philosophy.[2]

The significance of these early years should not be underestimated. It was during his six years of secondary education, as Heidegger noted late in life, that he "acquired everything that was of lasting value."[3] "Without this theological origin," he went on to say, "I would never have reached the path of thought."[4] Indeed, it was also during his secondary school and university years, Heidegger recalled, that he awakened to a theme of lifelong interest and one central to his later philosophical inquiries: the question of the sense of Being—the fundamental topic of metaphysics.[5]

In the rapidly industrializing Germany of the late nineteenth and early twentieth centuries, there was unprecedented interest in empirical methods among the humanistic and natural disciplines; the traditional subject of metaphysics no longer attracted the wide attention it had in the past. Since Hegel's death in 1831 and the demise of German idealist metaphysics by midcentury, the question of the ultimate sense of Being, to which empirical methods could give no response, had lost its once powerful hold on German intellectual life.

Despite the general decline of metaphysical speculation, however, an older and altogether different metaphysical tradition subsisted within the Catholic Church, a tradition reaching back to Aquinas and the Scholastics and still farther, to Aristotle. Although they remained in the minority, Catholic intellectuals in Germany took metaphysical themes quite seriously.

Indeed, Heidegger's gymnasium and university years were a time of Thomist revival in Catholic ecclesiastical and intellectual circles throughout Europe. Pope Leo XIII's 1879 encyclical *Aeterni Patris* gave the works of Saint Thomas Aquinas a special priority in expressing the Church's philosophy. And at Freiburg when Heidegger began his studies in Catholic theology in 1909, neo-Thomism was the predominant Catholic intellectual orientation.

Numerous studies consider the neo-Thomist orientation to have exerted a paramount influence on Heidegger's early thought and on the direction it would take in later years.[6] Nonetheless, though central to fathoming Heidegger's first ideas both on metaphysics and on history, this thesis needs to be carefully qualified in light of other early influences and of the exact line of development his *Frühe Schriften* (Early writings) follow. To facilitate this task, we will examine the young Heidegger's ideas in relation to two questions:

1. What did neo-Thomist philosophy and metaphysics imply for an understanding of the historical world?
2. To what extent did Heidegger's comprehension of philosophy and history in his *Early Writings* conform to neo-Thomist teachings?

In responding to these questions, we will pay particular attention to Heidegger's growing awareness of the problem of historical meaning in the period spanned by his *Early Writings* (1912–16), and we will more closely situate that problem in Heidegger's immediate intellectual environment.

II

Juxtaposing neo-Thomism, which reached back to the Middle Ages and beyond, to antiquity, with the modern philosophical orientations that dominated the late nineteenth and early twentieth centuries in Germany unveils wholly disparate postulates on the source of meaning in human experience. The most influential philosophies of this period drew inspiration from the revival of the thought of Hume and of Kant. Although Humeans emphasized the empirical and psychological framework of experience, whereas Kantians separated empirical and psychological aspects from what they viewed as experience's a priori preconditions, both schools of thought agreed that the content of experience is sense data and not Being in any metaphysical sense. Neo-Thomism, by contrast, with roots in a medieval worldview in which the possibility of metaphysical knowledge had not yet been placed in question, considered this theme in a wholly different light.

Neo-Thomism found inspiration in Aristotelian realism, according to which the conceptual categories of thought and meaningful relation to the world, predicated in language, are not merely arbitrary formulations or styles of classification grounded solely in human experience or in the pure faculties of consciousness. Rather, they refer to the essential character of objects independent of the mind, in which attributed meanings structurally inhere.

For Aristotle, the inherence of meaning in objects referred to fixed, formal characteristics that human concepts discerned and that really determined objects according to kind. Despite all variation among individuals of a kind—which Aristotle accounted for by differences in their material composition—they were imbued with form, an immaterial and universally homogeneous rational principle that shaped the amorphous particularity of material contents and responded to the specific ways in which it could be.

Taken together, the formal characteristics of all objects participate in a hierarchy of Being, in which all beings, from inanimate things to humans, find their place. Our special privilege in this hierarchy is that of discerning, through the capacities of the rational soul informing us, the universe of meaningful forms that this ontological hierarchy presents. Within this hierarchy, our own fixed role in society and cosmos is established.

The Thomist interpretation of Aristotle in the light of Christianity taught that the real inherence of meaning in the forms of objects resulted from the natural harmony of Divine creation: the created order of natural law comprised the correspondence between categories of understanding and real principles governing objects—between thought and Being. Within this order, Aquinas situated all created beings, inanimate as well as animate, nonhuman as well as human, each with its essential place in an overarching natural hierarchy. In line with his extrapolation from Aristotelian realism, he postulated a law of human nature, formally inhering in the soul of each human individual, and analogous to the uniformity and continuity observed in nonhuman aspects of nature, as the basis of unchanging fundamental norms of society. Over 600 years after his death, Aquinas's understanding of human society arising out of the continuous and stable harmony of the created natural order was reaffirmed to support the Catholic Church's metaphysical claim that no historical modification could touch the core of human reality and its fundamental truths.

In the light of this doctrine as it was embodied in the late nineteenth and early twentieth centuries, let us turn to the early influences on Heidegger and to the early development of his thought. Heidegger recorded that his first contact with the question of Being occurred while he was at the Bertholdsgymnasium, when Father Konrad Gröber, a "fatherly friend" who later became Freiburg's archbishop, presented him with a copy of *Von der mannigfachen Bedeutung des Seienden nach Aristoteles* (On the several senses of being in Aristotle; 1862) by Franz Brentano, who had himself been a Catholic priest.[7] Heidegger later described this work as the "rod and staff of my first awkward attempts to penetrate into philosophy" and also as the "first philosophical text through which I worked my way, again and again, from 1907 onward."[8]

As Heidegger would note in a course lecture of the 1920s, Brentano's general interpretation of Aristotle in this work had been strongly marked by the Scholastic synthesis of Aristotle's ideas with the Christian thought of Saint Thomas Aquinas.[9] The 1862 publication of *On the Several Senses of Being in Aristotle,* Brentano's doctoral dissertation and first book, antedated by seventeen years Pope Leo XIII's encyclical in favor of Saint Thomas's philosophy.

Although anticipating perhaps the orthodox self-interpretation of the Catholic Church and later refining the Thomist idea of *lex naturalis,*[10] Brentano's thinking was never restricted to the confines of Catholic dogma. His approach to philosophy remained open to the modern tendencies of the natural scientific and psychological methods of his age, which he brought into the analytical field of his neo-Scholastic and Aristotelian style of inquiry. One of his major contributions in this domain, as we have seen in chapter 1, was his revival of the Scholastic notion of intentionality—later reinterpreted by his pupil, Edmund Husserl, and stripped both of its traditional basis in categorical concepts and of its metaphysical reference—to represent the way thought illuminates beings.

Brentano's independent thinking would lead him to leave the priesthood. The period of neo-Thomism in the decades prior to World War I was also a time of growing rigidity among Catholic conservatives in response to an age of scientific and industrial progress, of nationalism and modernization, and of the increasing secularization of social institutions, all of which proved inhospitable to the Catholic faith. The time-tried traditions of the Catholic Church were, as a result, being buffeted by the forces of unprecedented historical change. *Aeterni Patris* was one of a series of attempts by the Catholic Church to assert its temporal authority in the decades prior to World War I. The reassertion of Aquinas's doctrines by Leo XIII, turning Aquinas's powerful justification of the ahistorical character of fundamental truth to conservative ends, followed by ten years the highly controversial attempt to shore up ecclesiastical authority by Pius IX in the 1869 declaration of papal infallibility. This declaration, as Heidegger would also note in a lecture of the 1920s, was entirely foreign to Brentano's style of thinking and led to his break with the Church hierarchy.[11]

The work that so vividly stimulated the young Heidegger's philosophical imagination, *On the Several Senses of Being in Aristotle,* presented a lively defense of metaphysical reasoning that accorded with the neo-Scholastic movement. Nonetheless, its interest went far beyond mere apologetics. Brentano offered a defense of the Aristotelian conception of the categories of thought, building on the prior work of his teacher, the great Aristotle scholar Adolf Trendelenburg, to whom the work was dedicated. As Brentano noted, Trendelenburg charted out a precise relationship between the Aristotelian categories and the grammatical structures of language. In an erudite and lucid set of arguments, Brentano attempted to go beyond the theme of language, which remained within the sphere of human modes of cognizance, by underlining the metaphysical doctrine of Aristotle. He emphasized, above all, that the manifold distinctions among beings (*Seienden*) conveyed by the categories articulate in analogous ways primary Being (*Sein*)—universal to all. In so arguing, Brentano revived for contemporary intellectual debate a keen explication of the metaphysical differentiation between beings (*Seienden*), which manifest themselves in their diverse modes of coordination, and primary Being (*Sein*), which underlies them and makes them possible.

In Brentano's way of phrasing this distinction, Heidegger found the terms for posing the question that would impel his thought in the years ahead: "How is Being as such [*das Sein als solches*]—not only beings as beings [*das Seiende als Seiendes*]—determined?"[12] He admitted that this question was not asked at this time in the same way it would be in the 1920s, when it would provide a guiding motif for *Sein und Zeit* (Being and time). A brief analysis of Heidegger's first article, "Das Realitätsproblem in der modernen Philosophie" (The problem of reality in modern philosophy; 1912), provides a preliminary clue toward understanding how he comprehended the question of Being at this time and its relation to the theme of history.

Published in the *Philosophisches Jahrbuch* of the influential Catholic Görres Gesellschaft, Heidegger's "Das Realitätsproblem" presented a brief review of some of the contemporary proponents of philosophical realism, with which he also identified himself. He defended the ideas of three realist thinkers, August Messer, Joseph Geyser—a proponent of neo-Thomism—and Oswald Külpe, against the epistemological orientations of empiriocriticism and Kantianism. His review briefly analyzed the contention advanced, on the one hand, by empiriocriticists inspired by Hume, and, on the other, by thinkers influenced by Kant, that understanding has no reference to objects independent of the mind but operates essentially on immanently presented phenomena.

One central idea presented by Heidegger in this short article—which was heavily dependent on Külpe's work *Einleitung in die Philosophie* (Introduction to philosophy; 1895)—provided the basis for his argument: the progress of the natural sciences, instead of corroborating the phenomenalist or immanentist presupposition accepted by Hume and Kant, has helped uncover its profound limitations. Heidegger pointed out that, far from a scientific conclusion, this premise remains foreign to the practice of scientific researchers, who investigate objects and not merely immanent phenomena or sense data:

> When the morphologist determines the form of plant and animal matter, when the anatomist analyzes the inner structure of living beings and their organs, when the cell biologist studies cells, . . . when the chemist investigates matter and its elements and bonds, . . . all of the researchers in these different branches of science are convinced that they are not analyzing mere sensations or working with pure concepts; rather, they are in agreement that they locate and determine real objects that are independent of them and of their scientific research.[13]

The scientist's conviction, Heidegger argued, is grounded on sound reasoning. He took the Humean and empiriocritical notion of experience as composed by a psychological association of sense data and turned it around to assert that we primarily experience meaningful objects. The whole notion of experience as a psychological association of sense data, according to Heidegger, can only arise through a failure to distinguish between the logical sense of an object and the psychological act by which it is presented to consciousness.[14]

Heidegger's thinking here may seem to tread on ground prepared by the Kantian critique of Hume's failure to distinguish between logical and empirical aspects of experience. The realist stance Heidegger favored, however, underlined what he viewed as the inadequacy of Kant's stipulation—denying independent objects of experience—that the phenomena of the senses and the logical understanding that comprehends them must be entirely confined within the sphere of consciousness. This results in what Heidegger, following Külpe, saw as an overemphasis on the constitutive role of consciousness.

With Külpe, Heidegger offered an alternative interpretation, one that refused the notion of a pure logic of thought working on sense data detached from any independently conceived reality. He favored a dualistic epistemology that placed the concepts of consciousness and a coherent world of empirical objects in mutual interplay. A scientist, for example, can make all manner of potential discoveries through the independent understanding, which may or may not eventually be verified in relation to objects under investigation. The exclusively constitutive character of Kant's logic, however, did not seem to Heidegger to fully account either for the potentially independent and interdependent character of consciousness or for empirical reality in the genesis of conceptual meaning.

"Only then," Heidegger concluded, "when empirical and rational aspects work together, is the proper harmony established."[15] Such a notion of mutual interplay—which Heidegger referred to as "critical realism"[16]—can only be supported by the presupposition that consciousness apprehends meaning inhering in a world of independent objects.

In offering an insufficient account of the relationship between consciousness and the world, epistemologies inspired by Hume or Kant are unable to bring into the range of vision the very theme of reality that concerns the natural scientist, and which Heidegger, in company with Külpe, placed "on the threshold of the philosophy of the future."[17] He freely conceded that certain perspectives of the world may forever remain barred to human vision, but insisted that, in the history of science, "[b]eside material progress . . . forward movement is demonstrated in the standard determination of objects."[18] Bringing a distinctly metaphysical argument into his line of reasoning, Heidegger noted that the goal of uncovering reality, of its "realization [*Realisierung*]," is "to determine the given in itself [*in seinem Ansich*] by eliminating modes of apprehension that modify it and attributes superimposed by the subject's own conceptions."[19]

At the beginning of "Das Realitätsproblem," paraphrasing ideas he found in Külpe's *Einleitung in die Philosophie,* the young Heidegger pointed out that realism had been the predominant mode of thinking of the Western intellectual tradition up until modern empiricism and Kantianism. In a somewhat facile interpretation, which adopted Külpe's argument nearly verbatim, Heidegger wrote: "To obtain the historical basis for a discussion of the problem, it is briefly to be noted that the manner of thought of Greek philosophy is oriented through critical realism. The Neoplatonists think in realist fashion, as do the philosophers of the Middle Ages and the modern period. If one encounters many variants in the way of determining the real, unanimity predominates over the positing of a transsubjective object [*eines Transsubjektiven*]."[20]

Heidegger succinctly traced the deviation from this long historical line of realist thinking, which, he argued, began with empiricism and was reinforced by Kant. He saw this deviation from realism as a kind of aberration from philosophy's true path: "It will remain [Külpe's] achievement that he set philosophy, which strayed far from its path, back on its authentic course. Aristotelian-Scholastic philosophy, which always professed realism, will not lose sight of this new epistemological movement; it must be supplemented by further work in this direction."[21]

Corresponding to his conviction of the correctness of a neo-Thomist, realist epistemology in this article is the essentially unitary and static view of truth in which the history of thought was to be founded. The neo-Thomist worldview, as described above, is clearly consonant with the metaphysical basis of the standpoint Heidegger was defending.

Here it is important to note that one aspect of neo-Thomist thinking, central to the theme of historical meaning we are pursuing, nowhere appeared in Heidegger's brief analysis. For the neo-Thomists, static foundations of human understanding followed as a logical consequence from what they considered to be the fixed character of human nature. This aspect is all the more important for our investigation because, in denying the possibility of understanding the metaphysical foundations of the world, Hume and Kant had provoked a series of momentous breaches in the Western intellectual tradition, in large part because they placed in question our ability to gain metaphysical comprehension of our own nature. In their respective writings on epistemology, both Hume and Kant cast doubt on the postulate that a graspable metaphysical form or essence could be made the basis for theories of knowledge or human society.

From a different realist standpoint than that of the Thomist tradition, Wilhelm Dilthey had seen Hume and Kant as decisive steps on the way to a dissolution of the dogma of a fixed human nature, opening the door to a more fluid idea of the human character.[22] Such a progression,

Dilthey stressed, was a precondition for the development of a fundamental insight instilling a historical worldview. The structures of
human understanding, rather than being governed by a fixed form or
nature capable of definitively establishing the fundamental norms of a
human and a natural world, evolve dynamically in an ongoing movement of discovery and reassessment of all such normative principles
within the opaque and inexhaustible context of reality.

Perhaps because the philosophy supported in his first article
assumed static metaphysical foundations, Heidegger's writings
between 1912 and 1914—including a 1912 article on contemporary
logical theory and his 1912 *Dissertation* (doctoral dissertation)—
remained insulated from any concern with the topic of human historicity. In the years before 1916, however, various influences would draw
his interest in this direction.

III

A further source of inspiration to Heidegger during his early years was
Professor Carl Braig, who taught him systematic theology at Freiburg.
Heidegger continued to frequent Braig's lectures after changing over
to philosophy in 1911; from Heidegger's comments, it is evident that
his personal contact with Braig continued well beyond this date.

Braig's works—notably, *Vom Sein: Abriss der Ontologie* (On
Being: An outline of ontology), which Heidegger found most significant[23]—questioned the foundations of the modern sciences in a style
Braig found entirely compatible with the kind of metaphysical inquiry
he proposed. Indeed, he faulted modern researchers for being too concerned with superficial detail and neglectful of the metaphysical underpinnings that, in his opinion, no truly scientific outlook could avoid.
He noted that even the most exact scientific disciplines absorb themselves in their own fragmented fields of research, neglecting a systematic overview of the reality that each observes. It was here, in his
estimation, that the most basic questions of metaphysics and the concerns of the sciences had to find a point of profound accord.[24]

Braig's work on Being, Heidegger would later write, was of special
interest in presenting "extensive quotations from texts of Aristotle,
Thomas Aquinas, and Suarez, as well as the etymology of words for

the basic concepts of ontology."[25] His outlook was not restricted to a study of the problem of Being in an Aristotelian-Thomist sense, however. It was through Braig that Heidegger became aware of the importance of modern conceptions of metaphysics outside the framework of the Catholic Church, especially those of Hegel and of Schelling:

> In the years after 1911, I attended still another course in theology, the one on dogmatics given by Carl Braig. There I became interested in speculative theology, above all in the impressive style of thought that this teacher vividly displayed in every lecture. During a few walks on which I was permitted to accompany him, I heard for the first time of the importance of Schelling and Hegel for speculative theology, in contrast to the systematic teachings of Scholasticism. In this way, the tension between ontology and speculative theology in the constitution of metaphysics came into the purview of my inquiries.[26]

Heidegger added that Braig was "the last [thinker] in the line of the Tübingen Speculative School. He gave Catholic theology quality and breadth by his manner of coming to terms with Hegel and Schelling."[27] Inspired in the early nineteenth century by thinkers such as Johann Adam Möhler in Tübingen and F. A. Staudenmaier in Tübingen and Freiburg, the Catholic Tübingen Speculative School, also known as the "school of historical theology," early acknowledged the significance of a historical understanding of the Church's development, in unique relationship with the cultural circumstances surrounding it.[28] From a Scholastic viewpoint, with its focus on a statically conceived human nature and fixed categories of human understanding, human history could only be of incidental significance in the expression of Divine meaning. Without vitiating dogma, the Tübingen theologians elevated its historical interpretation to a heretofore unprecedented place in Catholic thought. At the same time, with their clear emphasis on a distinction between Divine transcendence and human historical immanence, they distinguished themselves from the predominant philosophies of German idealism, especially that of Hegel, whose pantheistic notions comprehended God and the doctrines of Christianity entirely within the framework of human historical development.

Although Heidegger mentioned none of the other Tübingen thinkers nor the significance of their deliberations on historical matters in his published writings, as we will later have occasion to note, Otto Pöggeler has discerned traces of Tübingen speculative philosophy in

Heidegger's ideas in his 1916 *Habilitationsschrift* (postdoctoral dissertation) on John Duns Scotus.[29] Of primary importance for our purposes is not the question of direct influence—which remains conjectural—but a change in the intellectual context of Braig's theology and, subsequently, of Heidegger's thinking. We can see this in the acute difference in tenor regarding historical matters manifested by the early Tübingen thinkers such as Staudenmaier, on the one hand, and by their later counterparts such as Carl Braig, on the other. A brief comparison of the writings of Staudenmaier and Braig will help demarcate two distinct periods in German Catholic thought, the later period coinciding, not fortuitously, with the wide emergence of a problem of historical meaning in Germany in the years before the First World War.

F. A. Staudenmaier's writings stemmed from the early nineteenth century, when captivation with historical understanding focused on its value as a source of speculative truth. His ideas abounded with confidence in the worthiness of historical contemplation of religious phenomena, which, in his estimation, provided primordial insight into the positive, progressive course of world history as a whole. In accord with what he termed the "speculative method," Staudenmaier could affirm: "Humanity evolves according to the principle of its development, which is the religious principle. This development proceeds according to a steady progression, as an organic unity [*organische Einheit*]."[30]

Like the Scholastics, whose systematic efforts he viewed as a vital historical moment in theology, not as its apotheosis, Staudenmaier admitted a divinely created human nature as the bearer of truths discerned by human understanding.[31] Nevertheless, he placed emphasis on a gradual spiritual ascent in harmony with these truths in the progressive stages of human history. In this ascent, a historically self-conscious philosophy had a special role to play: "Philosophy is the free and conscious Spirit of humanity, and it is disseminated in the world by God. The Spirit's eternal movement is its eternal development. From the power of the Spirit's free personality [*Persönlichkeit*], it produces a world history [*Weltgeschichte*], whose true and luminous content it is itself at the different levels of its development."[32]

Against this background, Braig's writings bore the traces of a period of dogmatic retrenchment in Catholic thought, when speculative historical themes no longer had any ready rapport with the Catholic worldview. To be sure, the growth of modernism in the Catholic

Church throughout Europe in the first years of the twentieth century signified an important application of scientific historical criticism to the doctrines of the Church, although with a different emphasis from that of the Protestants for the previous half century.[33] This current of thought—of which Braig was one of the foremost German opponents—was roundly condemned by Pope Pius IX both in the famous *Pascendi* encyclical of 1907 and in a supplementary papal bull of 1910. The antimodernist declarations of the pope provoked heated debate in all parts of Germany, renewing controversies that dated back to the declaration of papal infallibility.[34]

The enthusiasm of Staudenmaier and his early-nineteenth-century Tübingen colleagues for historical understanding of religious doctrines was overshadowed in Braig's disquisitions by an authoritarian approach to truth more characteristic of neo-Thomism than of the original Tübingen School. Although, by and large, he defended Staudenmaier's historical ideas, Braig criticized what he viewed as the Staudenmaier's exaggerated concern for "exact science, poetry, rhetoric, and philosophy."[35] He also criticized Scholasticism for what he considered to be its too ready assumption of a spontaneous correspondence between the categories of thought and empirical reality.[36] Nonetheless, even as liberal Protestants opened their religious convictions ever wider to accommodate a more pluralistic conception of truth taught by critical and inductive styles of historical science, and seemed to be drawing Catholic modernists toward their way of thinking, Braig and other intellectuals close to orthodox Catholicism clung all the more firmly to an idea of the singularity of truth in history, withstanding all variation. As Braig noted: "Christian truth is presented to the subject through a visible institution, the Church. The teachings it presents are in essence and in substance the underpinnings of truth, which are immutable throughout the centuries. These teachings are the *norma normans,* not the *norma normanda,* of Christian thought, feeling, and will."[37]

Where Staudenmaier's writings waxed optimistic about the course of history and the value of human speculative reason that reaches out to grasp it, Braig's were full of reservations on these matters. Braig evinced a deep fear of the consequences of too thoroughgoing an application of historical scholarship, forcefully criticizing the attempt to reconstruct the absolute in history on the basis of history itself, without the necessary metaphysical presuppositions provided by systematic theology. In this regard, he attacked what he considered to be the aim of liberal Protestant thought—above all, the historical ruminations of Adolf von Harnack—and its attempt to define the essence of Christianity on historical grounds alone, without relying on the systematic metaphysical basis provided by Catholic dogma and theology. In his opinion, this erroneous line of thinking was rooted in neo-Kantianism.[38] Pushed to its logical extreme, it would lead, in Braig's estimation, to a troublesome and exaggerated preoccupation with historical variation and to the skeptical void of "historicism [*Historizismus*]."[39] Even though Heidegger made no mention of them in his works, Braig's comments on the potential dangers of historical understanding clearly reflect the broadening of awareness of a potential problem of historical meaning in the Catholic circles with which Heidegger was closely affiliated in this period. In the years to come, his orientation began to take a different turn.

By 1912, Heidegger had already begun to study with one of the foremost theorists of historical method, the neo-Kantian Heinrich Rickert. Whereas Braig's religious persuasion emphasized the irrelevance of an autonomous, impartial historical science and the pluralistic conception of the values it discovers in the face of the unitary truth of Catholic dogma, Rickert affirmed their value, although, like Braig, he appreciated the potential dangers of a reckless historicism (*Historismus*). Ironically, this insight, shared with his opponent and contemporary, Rickert, separated Braig irrevocably from his greatly esteemed predecessor, F. A. Staudenmaier. In view of Heidegger's work with these two thinkers, it is perhaps not surprising that between 1912 and 1916 his thought widened in scope, especially in relation to historical themes.

IV

From Heidegger's *Early Writings,* we know that his studies with Heinrich Rickert in 1912 were chiefly on the subject of logic. Completed in that same year, both a second review article, "Neuere Forschungen über Logik" (Recent investigations into logic), and his *Dissertation* (doctoral dissertation), "Die Lehre vom Urteil im Psychologismus" (The doctrine of judgment in psychologism), dealt essentially with the logical refutation of psychologism.[40] Indeed, in his *Dissertation,* Heidegger expressed his gratitude for Rickert's counsel on logical questions.[41]

Neither of these two works evinces the hostility toward the Kantian epistemology evident in Heidegger's first article, "Das Realitätsproblem," also published in 1912. Heidegger did not fail to reiterate his special praise in both works for what he viewed as the unequaled clarity of the distinction that Edmund Husserl (at the time in Göttingen) made in his *Logische Untersuchungen* (Logical investigations) between psychological acts and the logical content of experience.

In the preface to his *Dissertation,* the body of which criticized the logical theories of five contemporary thinkers (including Franz Brentano), Heidegger referred to himself as an "unhistorical mathematician,"[42] a curious self-assessment, but one borne out by his *Dissertation* and the second review article, which nowhere evoke the relevance of historical themes to the problem of logic, and by "Das Realitätsproblem," which illustrates his static view of the foundations of human understanding. He nevertheless thanked Professor Heinrich Finke, who held the chair in history associated with the Freiburg faculty of Catholic theology, for having "awakened" in him "love and understanding for history."[43] This was the same "Dr. Finke" whom the staunchly Protestant Friedrich Meinecke, also a professor in Freiburg in these years before 1914, described as one "who possessed an uncommonly vivacious intuition of the medieval world," and one from whom Meinecke "learned the meaning of Catholic culture."[44]

Beside his early contact with philosophy, history, the natural sciences, and mathematics, Heidegger much later recalled other sources of inspiration in the "exciting years between 1910 and 1914." He experienced "a growing interest for Hegel and Schelling"; he read Dilthey's works for the first time and also began to reflect on the radical forms of questioning that had begun to stir the German intellectual landscape, and which would play so important a role in Heidegger's later thought. Such questioning included the impassioned works of Nietzsche, Kierkegaard, Dostoyevsky, Rilke, and Trakl.[45] Aside from a few favorable, if innocuous, references to Nietzsche in his 1916 *Habilitationsschrift,* the influence of these thinkers is nowhere in evidence in his first published writings.

By 1914, Heidegger had become a prominent participant in Rickert's celebrated philosophical seminar at Freiburg. Julius Ebbinghaus, another participant, has left a revealing impression of Heidegger:

I had become acquainted with Heidegger in Rickert's seminar, in which I participated during the summer of 1914. Heidegger was still in the attire of an alumnus of the Freiburg seminary (the so-called Sapienz). As far as I remember, I supposed at that time that he intended to submit his candidacy for the chair in philosophy, linked to religious persuasion, that had been accorded to the Catholic Church through an agreement with the State.[46]

Following the outbreak of World War I, Ebbinghaus, Heidegger, and a large number of other Freiburg students went to enlist for active duty. After a medical examination, Heidegger was rejected on account of poor health.[47] At this time, he began work in earnest on his *Habilitationsschrift,* for which Rickert served as director. The first product of his work was the customary *Habilitationsvortrag* (postdoctoral presentation), made in 1915. In this speech, "Der Zeitbegriff in den Geschichtswissenschaften" (The concept of time in the historical sciences), Heidegger sought to vindicate a central premise of historical method, explicitly related to Rickert's neo-Kantian idea of historiography and adapted from the earlier tradition of German historical thinking: while natural concepts are essentially distinguished by the general patterns or laws they formulate, the basis of historical understanding lies in its thematization of individuality. To demonstrate this principle, Heidegger investigated the concepts of time employed in the natural disciplines (for example, in physics) and in the historical-cultural sciences.

In physics, Heidegger explained, references to objects are always general in the sense that they do not deal with unique entities, neither with "this or with that determinate body," nor with "this or that period of time, or this or that space."[48] They are valid insofar as they judge bodies, time, and space as general concepts. For the sense of time as such, this generality translates itself in terms of uniformly measurable temporal units. "Only when measurable," Heidegger noted, does time have a "meaningful function in physics."[49] By contrast, in the historical sciences, a similar methodological straightforwardness would be difficult to attain in delineating the concept of time. Indeed, he noted, the major theorists of historiography themselves have been unable to resolve the basic contention over the purpose and the object of historical science.[50]

Nevertheless, Heidegger ventured a judgment concerning the concept of time in the historical sciences, based on what he saw as the two fundamental tasks of historical method. The first task, which he justified with a quotation from Johann Gustav Droysen's *Grundriss der Historik* (Sketch of the methodology of historical science), lay in a verification of the factuality of historical data—what Droysen referred to as an "investigation of sources."[51] In this case, temporal sequence plays a clear role, which Heidegger illustrated with the famous proof of the falseness of the pseudo-Isidorian decrees of the Middle Ages. One could demonstrate their falseness by showing, for example, that the notion of canon law the decrees employed did not arise until an epoch later than the epoch to which they were wrongly attributed.

By referring them to a chronological order of epochs, the critical appraisal of documents thus constitutes a special domain of historical analysis in which the concept of time plays a key role. But how specifically can we distinguish this role from that of time concepts in the natural sciences? To do so, Heidegger pointed out the necessity of touching on a second, more comprehensive methodological task, in which the function of temporal concepts in historiography is exhibited: the designation of an inner coherence (*Zusammenhang*) of the epochs making up the chronological order that temporal concepts investigate.

To facilitate this analysis, Heidegger took as an example Ernst Troeltsch's recently published work, *Augustin: Die christliche Antike und das Mittelalter* (Augustine: Christian antiquity and the middle ages). In Heidegger's words, Troeltsch demonstrated that Augustine "is truly the end and completion of Christian antiquity, its last and greatest thinker, its spiritual representative and popular leader. He must be understood above all from this perspective."[52]

Troeltsch characterized the function of the concept of time in the historical sciences by situating Augustine in relation to distinct periods of history, periods distinguishable from one another as cultural individualities. Augustine was understood in relation to the period in which he lived, and the delimitation of periods in the history of Christianity was, in turn, made possible in relation to thinkers such as Augustine.

In his extrapolation from this example, Heidegger demarcated the separate principles of time differentiation operative in the natural and the historical sciences. Temporal concepts of history, far from dealing with quantitative measure, focus on the individual, qualitatively distinct style of an epoch. To be able to conceive of a historical time period (*Zeitalter*), it is necessary to reconfigure its individual structure—its "leading tendencies [*leitenden Tendenzen*]," to use Ranke's term.[53] In contrast to the natural sciences, there is no homogeneous sequence of time periods or epochs in the historical sciences, and no general law of progression to predict how the epochs will follow one another. History is essentially the orderly consolidation (*Verdichtung*) of structures of objectified life, which are qualitatively different in each epoch.[54]

The qualitative principle of time distinction in history, Heidegger concluded, is characterized by a relation to values (*Wertbeziehung*), which constitute the criteria of selection in the construction of historical concepts, as Rickert averred in *Die Grenzen der naturwissenschaftlichen Begriffsbildung* (The limits to concept formation in the natural sciences). Values, as a theoretical construct of historical understanding, allow us to recognize individuality and the manifestations of its coherence that characterize the specific domain of historical science and of historical time concepts.[55]

A close reading of Heidegger's 1915 *Habilitationsvortrag* demonstrates that, despite these favorable comments vis-à-vis the theories of his mentor, Rickert, Heidegger nevertheless maintained a certain distance. This became especially evident when the young Catholic scholar evoked the issue of epistemology, and vaguely affirmed, notwithstanding his mentor's teachings, the necessity of basing the theory of knowledge in metaphysics. Here he challenged Rickert's extreme epistemological idealism, which presumed the futility of all forms of metaphysical questioning.

Adumbrating a point more fully explored in his *Habilitationsschrift* on Duns Scotus, where he attempted to mediate between epistemological idealism and metaphysical realism, Heidegger expressed the conviction that epistemology taken in isolation could only prove insufficient. A self-conscious theory of knowledge, in his opinion, needed to be moored to metaphysics:

> For several years a certain "metaphysical impulse" has been stirring in scientific philosophy [*in der wissenschaftlichen Philosophie*]. The continuous preoccupation with mere epistemology no longer suffices. The insistence on epistemological problems, arising from a justified, energetic awareness of the necessity and value of criticism, does not let the purpose and the final questions of philosophy attain their immanent meaning. Hence the sometimes hidden, sometimes open tendency toward metaphysics.[56]

To comprehend the full sense of Heidegger's comments on this matter, we will analyze the most significant of his first works, his 1916 *Habilitationsschrift* on Duns Scotus. Here, in relation to the systematic concerns of metaphysics, a deepening awareness of the historicity of human understanding emerged; in harmony with the deeper intellectual contours of his times, Heidegger began to consider the problematic character of historical reflection.

V

On the first page of his *Habilitationsschrift*, "Die Kategorien- und Bedeutungslehre des Duns Scotus" (The theory of categories and meaning in Duns Scotus), Heidegger presented a quotation from the writings of Hegel's youth: "With regard to the inner essence of philosophy, there are neither forerunners nor successors."[57]

Heidegger's express motive for writing about the celebrated medieval "Subtle Doctor," Duns Scotus, was to make a statement about the inner essence of philosophy and its historical development. He aimed to demonstrate the possibility of a systematic approach to the problems of philosophy, notwithstanding all of the historical modifications to which they had been subject.

At the very beginning of the *Habilitationsschrift*, Heidegger evoked the complexity of the philosophical problem of achieving a system of the sciences. By this he meant a coordination of the verities attained by the university disciplines, as they changed historically and evolved in unforeseeable ways:

> The concept of a "system of the sciences" is not a directly unequivocal concept. One may readily understand by it an arrangement of factually available sciences, oriented toward specific standpoints at a determinate period of time. Such a classification of a historically given system, encompassing the accomplishments up to a determinate period in the history of thought, can only have limited validity. Like everything that is subject to historical development, it must change. Such a system of sciences can be most significant for practical purposes in its times. It may be a fruitful means of characterizing a cultural epoch in the history of ideas. On the basis of its merit from a purely theoretical standpoint, however, it can only be of little worth. Hence, a system of sciences can only be valuable when it is not limited to a compilation of

immediately present sciences, but comprises all sciences per se. How is such a "system" possible? . . . How can one know in a given period which new sciences will arise in the future, when their number will be exhausted, or if it will be exhausted?[58]

According to Heidegger, philosophy, whose task it is to attain such a system, has no facile answer, for "*directly it* is subject to very strong modifications."[59]

Thus, in the first pages of his work, Heidegger stated the problem of historical relativism. As we have briefly noted, this problem preoccupied Carl Braig, Heidegger's early professor of dogmatic theology, and emerged in the works of thinkers such Windelband, Rickert, Husserl, and Troeltsch, to whose ideas Heidegger was attentive at this time. At stake in his attempt to grapple with the problem, was what Heidegger realized to be the validity of any fundamental idea he might propose concerning the systematic character of philosophical thinking. Nor could the problem be addressed by way of history itself. Expressing an assumption that may at first sight seem ingenuous, but, as we will see, corresponds to the overall conception of metaphysics informing his ideas in this period, he explained that strictly historical considerations must be set aside. "If the religious, political, and, in the narrow sense, cultural aspects of a period are unavoidable for an understanding of the *origin* and the historical determination of a philosophy, these aspects can nonetheless be ignored by a purely philosophical interest that concerns itself only with [a] problem *in itself:* Time, understood as a historical category, is, so to say, excluded."[60]

How did Heidegger justify this standpoint? In a brief comment in the introduction to the text, he adumbrated what he considered to be the metaphysical foundations for systematic continuity in philosophy: "Due to the constancy of human nature [*Konstanz der Menschennatur*]. the repetition of philosophical problems in history becomes understandable. . . . This continuous renewal of effort in regard to a more or less similar group of problems, this perseverance of the identity of the philosophical spirit, not only enables but *requires* a corresponding conception of the 'history' of philosophy."[61]

With this reasoning, Heidegger might seem to furnish a more intricate substructure to the epistemology developed in "Das Realitätsproblem," albeit with a greater awareness of the difficulties his reasoning might encounter. The idea of human nature as a stable basis of human thought, evidently arising from the kind of neo-Thomist outlook he defended there, would seem to confirm his kinship with this movement's approach to the theme of meaning in history. But, as his analysis of Duns Scotus and the "inner essence of philosophy" reveal, Heidegger's ideas of history and of metaphysics were more complex than his introductory comments might suggest.

The body of Heidegger's *Habilitationsschrift* is divided into two parts. The first deals with Scotus's doctrine of the categories, an elaboration of the "element and means of conferring meaning on possible experience,"[62] whereas the second part treats the relation of the categories to meanings evoked in parts of speech. In analyzing this work, we will emphasize themes Heidegger set in relief for their relevance to the overarching question of metaphysics and history constituting the most original characteristic of the work as a whole.[63]

At the outset of his depiction of Scotus's doctrine of the categories, Heidegger maintained a certain distance from Aristotelian philosophy,[64] distinguishing Aristotle's conception of the categories as possible predicates of thought and of Being, from Scotus's high Scholastic conception of them. Although not questioning the validity of Aristotle's categories, Heidegger stated clearly that he did not take them to be "*the* categories per se."[65] He also affirmed his preference for the wider categorical distinctions of the Subtle Doctor over those of Aristotle and those of the medieval school philosophy he so strongly influenced.[66] He made the grounds for this preference quite plain. Scotus, though sensitive to the abstract world of mathematics, also "discovered a greater and more subtle proximity [*haecceitas*] to real life, to its variety and possible distinctions, than any of the Scholastics before him."[67] For Scotus, Heidegger noted with approval, the structures of thought could neither entirely encompass nor entirely exhaust the phenomenon of individuality in its manifold real forms (*haecceitas*). Reality retained a character of irreducible particularity that always transcended the meanings of consciousness and resisted any reduction to them.

This observation led Heidegger to reject any theory that the categories of thinking were mere copies (*blosse Abbilder*) of real objects (*dem realen Objektbereich entnommen*).[68] Thus he rejected any unproblematic form of realism postulating a discrete correspondence between thought and Being.[69]

Heidegger emphasized the proximity of Scotus's concept of individuality to that of the director of his work, Heinrich Rickert. Like Scotus, Rickert conceived of the world of Being as ultimately composed of real particulars, an uncircumscribable multiplicity (*unübersehbare Mannigfaltigkeit*) of heterogeneous components separate from the homogeneous world of conceptual thought.[70] Beyond this common starting point, however, Heidegger was also aware of the considerable philosophical differences between the fourteenth-century Scholastic thinker and the twentieth-century neo-Kantian. Perhaps so as not to risk antagonizing his domineering *Doktorvater,* [71] Heidegger did not analyze those differences. He contented himself with noting that, though he admired Rickert's views, his *Habilitationsschrift* on Duns Scotus would search for an "independent standpoint."[72]

If he admired Rickert's critique of a correspondence theory of truth on the ground of the fundamental distinction between thought and the real particularity of Being, Heidegger was by no means ready to admit the radical conclusions that Rickert proposed as a result of this presupposition. To Rickert's way of thinking, the very heterogeneity and particularity of real Being precluded the possibility that consciousness might find in reality, in however vague or implicit a form, any ground for the meanings with which it dealt. Given in its immediacy, reality was nothing but a blur of sense data, without structure, to which consciousness alone added meaningful form.

Heidegger's reasoning was guided by the Subtle Doctor's conviction that understanding deals with real Being independent of the mind, even if Being must be taken as far more opaque and particular than the earlier medieval realist tradition acknowledged. Although Heidegger rejected an unproblematic correspondence theory of truth in his work, he stopped short of the kind of pure coherence theory that constructs the object of perception out of immanent sense data and locates understanding entirely within consciousness. The judgments by which understanding is achieved, according to Heidegger, arise from what the Scholastics termed "intentionality," the primary directedness of consciousness toward an object. To the notion of intentionality, Scotus's epistemology brought its own carefully nuanced approach: the soul intends an object, it directs meaning toward it, and if the manifold Being of objects is never exhausted by these meanings, they nevertheless achieve their character of validity only in relation to an object itself.[73] If the real is to be characterized by its particularity, ever transcending the generality of meaning, this does not, at the other extreme, relegate meaning to a purely immanent sphere, precluding the possibility that it may be illuminated, "encountered [*betroffen*]"—however implicitly—in reality.[74]

The subtle variety of realism that Heidegger extrapolated from Scotus's thought actually bore a close resemblance to that of Edmund Husserl's *Logical Investigations,* whose seminal importance Heidegger did not fail to acknowledge. Although well aware that Scotus's conceptions, in their medieval formulation and metaphysical application, remained distant from the theoretical aims of Husserl,[75] Heidegger was nonetheless willing to venture that in the "Scholastic type of thought, indeed, perhaps most strongly in this type of thought, aspects of phenomenological observation lay hidden."[76] This judgment seemed warranted by his retrieval of the Scholastic concept of intentionality—renovated, as we have seen, by Brentano and refined by Husserl—to explore its connotations in Scotus's thought. Looked at in a certain light, the analysis of intentionality by the Subtle Doctor might have anticipated Husserl's ideas in an essential sense. Husserl described intentionality as the primary character of consciousness moving beyond itself into the midst of heterogeneous, infinitely faceted phenomena, which its meanings illuminate without ever exhausting.

In bringing this resemblance between Husserl and Scotus to light, Heidegger carefully avoided treating the complex idealist nuances that the concept of intentionality had received in Husserl's thinking since its first exposition in the *Logical Investigations,* and especially in the years just preceding Heidegger's own work. Ironically, whereas Husserl stressed the need for a radical new beginning for philosophy and emphasized the originality of his concept of intentionality in contradistinction to Scholasticism, Heidegger emphasized the opposite. Indeed, his juxtaposition of the two thinkers, lending metaphysical overtones to Husserl's ideas that Husserl himself had never intended, and his suggestion of a possible systematic unity (but not identity) of philosophies of different ages served to exaggerate the elasticity of Husserl's theoretical framework. It is no wonder that Husserl later referred to Heidegger's *Habilitationsschrift* in private correspondence as a "beginner's work."[77]

In the second part of the *Habilitationsschrift,* Heidegger charted out the conclusions for a theory of language to be drawn both from Scotus's separation of the realms of ideal thinking and real Being and from his idea of the different kinds of possible unity of these two realms. Heidegger's construction of intentionality and the conclusions he drew from it are highly relevant to our present theme. Heidegger worked forward from Scotus's premise that the distinction between ideal meaning and real Being indicated an a priori origin of the meanings consciousness intends. Meaningful intentions can only be independent of experience, hence a priori, because experience presents solely particulars and cannot by itself account for the meaningful universals with which consciousness deals. Although Heidegger developed his argument by way of Scotus, he also invoked contemporary theorists such as Hermann Lotze, who also contributed toward an a priori grasp of language on the basis of the split between empirical reality and ideal meaning.[78] If language itself can be neither simply reduced to categorical forms of logic nor deduced from them, it nonetheless finds its grammatical foundation in the a priori logical structures of the soul, distinguishable from a world of heterogeneous, particular being.

Referring to the *Grammatica Speculativa,* Heidegger stated that, despite all the accidental features of language, grammatical forms could be led back to an initial a priori logical sense. In writing this, Heidegger explicitly sought to detach the meaning expressed in grammatical forms of language from the empirical world of psychological acts and of historical development. As he explained at the very beginning of his remarks on the doctrine of language:

> In the broad, sometimes deeply rooted sphere of influence that the concept of development has universally attained in the scientific ideas of the present, a dangerous tendency has arisen: the interpretation of the way in which an object has developed serves to explain it and, along with this, the ultimate possibilities of knowledge about it. This way of positing historical and psychological thought as absolute nonetheless disregards the possibility of another, it might be said contradictory, mode of questioning in regard to given objects. Next to the question, How has language arisen? another kind of question is possible: What should language accomplish?[79]

In a complex and highly detailed analysis of the different parts of speech, Heidegger explicated what he perceived to be Scotus's (actually Erfurt's) severing of the a priori content of linguistic meaning from all empirical considerations. In thus projecting the foundations of grammar into a sphere structured by logical forms, Heidegger arrived at a major conclusion of the second part of his work, namely, that "psychological and historical investigations of language do not belong in a philosophy of language."[80]

Though he denied neither the historical evolution nor the psychological character of language, Heidegger relegated such empirical considerations to second place. In this instance, as in his earlier considerations on the theory of the categories, Heidegger attempted to work beyond the ideas of Scotus (Erfurt) to find their modern complement in the philosophy of Edmund Husserl. A similar view of the a priori foundations of grammar appeared in the fourth essay of Husserl's *Logical Investigations.* In the years after the publication of this work, Husserl had been energetically attempting to work out the logical basis for language in relation to the phenomenon of meaning in general, independent of historical or psychological factors.[81]

The contiguity Heidegger perceived between Scotus's concerns and those of contemporary philosophers, above all, those of Husserl, provided him with an argument for the relevance of medieval thinking to the most modern of logical questions. More important, Heidegger's view of the a priori character of logical meaning and of the foundations of grammar provided him an argument for the relevance of such thinking to his presupposition that historical time can be set aside in dealing with philosophical questions, and that a systematic ground for philosophy exists in the midst of all historical flux. Anchored, as Heidegger intimated, in the metaphysical identity of human nature, it is by no means surprising that recurring themes in the history of philosophy would suggest themselves.

What is of interest in this regard is not the extent to which Heidegger is faithful to the thought of Scotus (Erfurt), Rickert, or Husserl.[82] Most important is the idea of a metaphysical ground for the history of thought that Heidegger developed from his observations. Compared with the static underpinnings of thought in "Das Realitätsproblem," Heidegger's analysis in the *Habilitationsschrift* demonstrates a more nuanced approach to the problem of historical meaning. Evidence of his reconsideration of the theme of history and metaphysics becomes especially noticeable in the conclusion of this work, where Heidegger extends his examination of the dualism Scotus established between the individuality of real Being and the general a priori structures of meaning in a further direction. In the body of his work, Heidegger emphasizes this dualism to suggest the possibility of an autonomous universal realm of meaning, given the individuality of objects toward which meaning is addressed. Moving explicitly beyond the medieval worldview, while also extrapolating from its principles, the conclusion announces that meaning must be considered in fundamental unity with the individual acts that express it. Heidegger perceives this unity of a priori meaning and the concrete, individual act in which this meaning is expressed as joined in the "metaphysical Spirit" (or "living Spirit"): "In the concept of the living Spirit and its relation to the metaphysical 'origin' insight is given into the Spirit's metaphysical foundation, in which the singularity and individuality of *acts* are interrelated with the universal validity of autonomous *meaning*."[83]

If the dictum that the real is individual—and inexhaustible by the forms of thinking—applies not only to external objects but to the real soul itself,[84] the notion of such a living unity is entirely consistent: the acts of the individual soul are always the medium through which, in an infinitude of unforeseeable ways, the universally valid a priori meaning structures are expressed. These acts of the individual soul, in which the a priori is embodied, Heidegger places on the plane of history: "Taken objectively, the problem presents itself concerning a relation between time and eternity, change and absolute validity, world and God, and from the standpoint of theoretical science it is reflected in *history* (constitution of values) and *philosophy* (validity of values)."[85] Still more explicitly, he notes:

> The living Spirit is *essentially a historical* spirit in the widest sense of the word. The true worldview [*Weltanschauung*] is far removed from the mere . . . existence of a theory abstracted from life. The Spirit is only conceivable when the complete plenitude of its accomplishments, that is, *its history,* is incorporated within it. With this continually growing plenitude in its philosophical articulation, an ever increasing means is given toward the living apprehension of the absolute Spirit of God.[86]

The history that Heidegger refers to as a "history of the Spirit" concerns, not the historian's inductive science of facts, but the history of truth with which the philosopher alone is competent to deal.[87] Nonetheless, toward the historical formulation of philosophical problems, Heidegger also admits that the philosopher must always feel a spiritual disquiet (*Unruhe*).[88] History, Heidegger argues, must steadily be viewed from the perspective of a timeless, systematic moment actualized in time.

Clearly, Heidegger's metaphysical interpretation is laden with manifest theological presuppositions supporting his larger theoretical framework. The possible continuity of a priori structures of meaning is related, for Heidegger as for Scotus, to the human vocation in quest of God, anchored in fundamental capacities of human metaphysical nature. Heidegger's view of this continuity is nuanced by a greater appreciation for Scotus's medieval conception of individuality (haecceitas), which opens for Heidegger's modern conception the possibility of an ongoing systematization of the history of truth.

But it is precisely here, in the historical expression of individuality and its coherence, that Heidegger's overall endeavor to assert a systematic unity of philosophy runs adrift. The young Catholic thinker conveniently fits themes that seem to repeat themselves into a systematic framework, while failing to consider other themes that might place his theory in question. Thus, as long as one maintains, with Heidegger, a strictly abstract analysis of individuality, relating it to the heterogeneous particularity of all possible Being whatsoever, the parallel between medieval and modern seems to hold. But, as soon as one refers the concept of history to a concrete human context, the unbridgeable gap between medieval and modern becomes glaringly evident.

At various points in the body of the work, Heidegger succinctly, though somewhat ambiguously, admits this difficulty. On the one hand, he intimates that Scotus can be credited with anticipating both the abstract and—albeit unwittingly—the concrete historical view of individuality as it has arisen in modern times.[89] On the other hand, he suggests elsewhere that the moderns were indeed the first to conceive of an autonomous historical individuality and of the methods for bringing it into focus; a footnote then refers readers to the works of Rickert, Simmel, and Dilthey.[90] In still another isolated passage, Heidegger comes closest to acknowledging that an irreconcilable difference exists:

> The concepts of the "personality [Persönlichkeit]," of the spiritual individual, are not, it is true, entirely foreign to Scholasticism (one thinks of the teaching of the trinity and of angels, of the anthropology). Yet the complexity of the historical personality, its specific character, its contingency and manifold effects, its interconnection with its surroundings, the idea of historical development and of problems tied to this are present to medieval spiritual life only in inadequate conceptual form.[91]

Heidegger's recognition of this fundamental difference in the notion of individuality between the period of high Scholasticism and the contemporary epoch introduces an inconsistency into his interpretation of the systematic character of philosophy. In this early work, Heidegger never seriously considers the implications of a qualitatively new orientation, represented by the emergence of the historical conception of the individual and of humanity in Germany during the eighteenth and nineteenth centuries. Nor does he attempt to square the appearance of this unprecedented way of thinking with the assumption of an overarching systematic continuity of philosophy. Above all, he fails to take into account in any consequent way the challenge of historical thinking to facile assumptions concerning the continuity of human logical conceptions and other normative standards.

Instead, Heidegger fell back on the metaphysics of Catholic theology, for which the response to such pressing issues of the times had already been decided. Although the problem of historical meaning had become a major concern for the authors he cited during these years, and although Heidegger himself had begun to take definite cognizance of its scope, his own metaphysical presuppositions cushioned his thinking from the shock of its radical challenge.

Given the metaphysical basis of Heidegger's early thinking, the widely shared viewpoint that Heidegger's use of words such as *life* or *spirit* in his *Habilitationsschrift* reflected Dilthey's essential influence should perhaps be qualified.[92] However aware Heidegger may have been of Dilthey's ideas (and those of others who employed the terminology of a life philosophy, such as Simmel and Nietzsche), his metaphysical conception of history as the individualized expression of the "life" of the Spirit grounded in an evolving human nature called to mind ideas springing from another source. The Tübingen Speculative School, which had inspired Heidegger's mentor, Carl Braig, applied the word *life* (commonly employed in modern Catholic theology as a whole) in a way that very much resembled Heidegger's style of thought.

As Otto Pöggeler has perceptively written, the Tübingen School should be mentioned in another regard—Heidegger's terse polemic against Hegel (a major opponent of the Catholic Tübingen thinkers) in the concluding sentence of the *Habilitationsschrift:* "A theory of the categories directed especially from the basic tendencies of a philosophy of the living Spirit, of devout fervor for God—a philosophy whose most general basis could only be hinted at here—stands before the great task of coming to terms with . . . the most powerful system of a historical worldview [*Weltanschauung*], with Hegel."[93]

By the time Heidegger's *Habilitationsschrift* was accepted (1916), an important change had taken place in his immediate intellectual environment. Heinrich Rickert had moved to Heidelberg to occupy the chair of Windelband, who had died in 1915. Husserl, who had come to Freiburg from Göttingen to occupy Rickert's position, was thus brought into personal contact with the young Heidegger. This circumstance proved fruitful for the young scholar's academic career.

A year after Husserl's arrival in 1916, Heidegger was called up to serve with the Ersatz-Bataillon Infanterie-Regiment 113. In 1918, he was transferred to Verdun to work with the meteorological service.[94] Upon his discharge from the army, he began teaching in Freiburg. The extraordinary change in his intellectual orientation at this time will be the subject of analysis of chapter 3.

NOTES

1. Martin Heidegger, "Vom Geheimnis des Glockenturms," 10.

2. On Heidegger's early schooling, see Franzen, *Martin Heidegger,* and Sheehan, "Heidegger's Early Years: Fragments for a Philosophical Biography," 3–21. For further information, see also Ott, *Martin Heidegger: A Political Life.*

3. Heidegger, *Frühe Schriften,* ix–x, as translated by H. Siegfried in Heidegger, "M. Heidegger."

4. Heidegger, "Aus einem Gespräch von der Sprache," in *Unterwegs zur Sprache,* 96.

5. Heidegger, "Mein Weg in die Phänomenologie," in *Zur Sache des Denkens,* 81–90. On this theme, see also Pereira, *Tradição e crise no pensamento do jovem Heidegger*; Kisiel, *The Genesis of Heidegger's* Being and Time; Van Buren, *The Young Heidegger: Rumor of the Hidden King*; and Giugliano, "Intorno al concetto di *Weltanschauung* nel primo Heidegger."

6. Note, for example, Beyer, *Vier Kritiken,* 55–58; Hühnerfeld, *In Sachen Heidegger,* 24; Palmier, *Les écrits politiques de Heidegger,* 35. See also Farías, *Heidegger and Nazism;* Ott, *Martin Heidegger: A Political Life;* Safranski, *Martin Heidegger: Between Good and Evil.*

7. Heidegger, "Aus einem Gespräch von der Sprache," in *Unterwegs zur Sprache,* 92.

8. Heidegger, "Mein Weg," in *Zur Sache des Denkens,* 81, and Introduction to Richardson, *Heidegger,* x. English translations of Heidegger's account are from Sheehan, "Heidegger's Early Years."

9. Heidegger, *Gesamtausgabe,* 20:23. Brentano highly approved of Saint Thomas Aquinas's interpretation of Aristotle. After citing two extensive passages from Aristotle's conception of Being near the end of his work, he observed: "Truly, this commentary does not itself require a commentary, for the definitions are given with admirable clarity and precision. It should also be compared with Saint Thomas's remarks in his commentary to the *Auscultationes Physicae.* . . . Both passages essentially agree with our entire previous discussion." Brentano, *On the Several Senses of Being in Aristotle,* 122.

10. Note, in this regard, Brentano's later work, *Vom Ursprung sittlicher Ertenntnis,* 6–7.

11. Heidegger, *Gesamtausgabe,* 20:23.

12. Heidegger, Introduction to Richardson, *Heidegger,* xi.

13. Heidegger, "Realitätsproblem," 355–56.

14. Heidegger cited Husserl's *Logical Investigations* in support of his argument; evidently, the phenomenological realism implied in this work would not have supported the kind of ready correspondence between concepts and objects as the source of knowledge that, as we will see more clearly, Heidegger's position would suggest.

15. Heidegger, "Realitätsproblem," 362.

16. Such realism is critical because empirical and logical moments complement each other and correct for each other's shortcomings. On the one hand, rational thought depends on a correspondence between the senses and objects themselves, which can help compensate for mistakes of the rational faculty; on the other hand, the shortsightedness of empirical perception is revealed by rational insight. Heidegger touched on this point in ibid., 361–62.

17. Ibid., 355.

18. Ibid., 362.

19. Ibid., 361.

20. Ibid., 353. Compare Heidegger's words with those of Külpe in *Einleitung in die Philosophie,* 152–53.

21. Heidegger, "Realitätsproblem," 363.

22. Dilthey, *Weltanschauungslehre: Abhandlungen zur Philosophie der Philosophie,* 76–77. This theme has also been treated in Meinecke's *Die Entstehung des Historismus.*

23. Heidegger, "Mein Weg," in *Zur Sache des Denkens,* 81.

24. Braig, *Vom Sein: Abriss der Ontologie,* 4–13.

25. Heidegger, "Mein Weg," in *Zur Sache des Denkens,* 81–82.

26. Ibid., 82. For a discussion of the importance of Braig in the development of Heidegger's thought and also for an examination of Heidegger's later critique of Scholasticism, see Caputo, *Heidegger and Aquinas: An Essay on Overcoming Metaphysics.*

27. Heidegger, *Frühe Schriften,* xi.

28. According to historian Franz Schnabel, Möhler's "special accomplishment lay in his juxtaposition of historical and systematic theology. Thus, in the history of ideas he belongs alongside Savigny, J. Grimm, Niebuhr, Ranke, and Schleiermacher." Schnabel, *Deutsche Geschichte,* 3:121.

29. Pöggeler, *Denkweg,* 23.

30. Staudenmaier, *Johannes Scotus Erigena und die Wissenschaft seiner Zeit,* 3.

31. Ibid., 307.

32. Ibid., 11.

33. Benedetto Croce, in *Histoire de l'Europe au 19e siècle,* 360, has concisely characterized modernism in the Catholic Church:

> Between the last years of the nineteenth century and the first years of the twentieth, the movement called "modernism" arose impetuously among the most cultivated Catholics, under the influence of secular philosophy and historiography. Modernism embodied the contradictory idea of opening Catholicism to historical criticism, while conserving the unity of Church tradition and maintaining the authority of the sovereign pontiff and dogmatic form, while fleeing from Protestantism and declaring abhorrence of it.

On the theme of tradition and continuity in late nineteenth-century Catholic thought, see also Motzkin, *Time and Transcendence.*

34. See Braig's own comments in *Der Modernismus und die Freiheit der Wissenschaft,* 1–4, on the impact of the pope's declarations in Germany.

35. Braig, *Über Geist und Wesen des Christentums,* 46.

36. Ibid.

37. Ibid., 20.

38. Ibid., 19.

39. Ibid., 19–29.

40. Heidegger, "Neuere Forchungen über Logik" and "Die Lehre vom Urteil im Psychologismus," in *Frühe Schriften,* 465–72, 517–24, 565–70 and 3–129, respectively.

41. "Lehre vom Urteil," in *Frühe Schriften,* 3.

42. Ibid.

43. Ibid.

44. Meinecke, *Autobiographische Schriften,* 184–86.

45. Heidegger, *Frühe Schriften*, x.

46. Ebbinghaus et al., *Philosophie in Selbstdarstellungen*, 3:30–31. On Heidegger's role in the Rickert seminar, see Heidegger and Rickert, *Briefe: 1912–1933,* and also Glockner, *Heidelberger Bilderbuch,* 169, where Glockner deals briefly with Rickert's prewar years in Freiburg.

47. See Heidegger's letter to Heinrich Rickert, November 3, 1914, in Heidegger and Rickert, *Briefe,* 20. For an understanding of details surrounding Heidegger's personal experiences in regard to military service, see also Ott, *Martin Heidegger: A Political Life,* and Sheehan, "Heidegger's Early Years," 7.

48. Heidegger, "Der Zeitbegriff in den Geschichtswissenschaften," in *Frühe Schriften,* 361–62.

49. Ibid., 366.

50. Ibid., 368.

51. Ibid., 370.

52. Ibid., 372.

53. Ibid., 373.

54. Ibid.

55. Ibid., 374.

56. Ibid., 357.

57. Heidegger, "Die Kategorien- und Bedeutungslehre des Duns Scotus" (1916), in *Frühe Schriften,* 135.

58. Ibid., 150.

59. Ibid.

60. Ibid., 138.

61. Ibid.

62. Ibid., 342.

63. Heidegger's treatment of Scotus in his *Habilitationsschrift* is somewhat complicated by the fact that the *Grammatica Speculativa,* on which much of Heidegger's argument is based, was not actually written by the Subtle Doctor himself, as Heidegger presumed, but by one of his disciples, Thomas of Erfurt, as Martin Grabmann subsequently proved. Nevertheless, this fact changes little in the overall character of Heidegger's argument. See Grabmann, *Mittelalterliches Geistesleben,* vol. 1.

64. Heidegger, "Duns Scotus," in *Frühe Schriften,* 205, 229.

65. Ibid., 153.

66. Ibid.

67. Ibid., 145.

68. Ibid., 223.

69. Ibid. Even Külpe's critical realism, which Heidegger had endorsed in 1912, was criticized now for taking too little notice of the moment of judgment in understanding, which had been underlined in Rickert's philosophy

and highlighted the form-giving, constructive act of consciousness in understanding. See ibid., 346.

70. Ibid., 194–95.

71. Rickert's domineering character is well documented in a number of personal recollections of his students and colleagues. See, for example, Marcuse, *Mein zwanzigstes Jahrhandert: Auf dem Weg zu einer Autobiographie*; Jaspers, *Philosophische Autobiographie*. Rickert's overbearing disposition may help explain Heidegger's change in attitude toward him from one of strong praise (as in the *Habilitationsschrift*, which was dedicated to Rickert) to disdain (as evidenced in Heidegger's lectures of the 1920s).

72. Heidegger, "Duns Scotus," in *Frühe Schriften*, 133.

73. Heidegger used the term *"Hingeltungscharakter"* to describe this relation. Ibid., 223.

74. Ibid. Heidegger's description of the intentional relation between consciousness and object was throughout colored by the language of Emil Lask. Lask, a young professor in Heidelberg, had been Rickert's preferred pupil, and attempted in two of his works to mediate between Rickert's neo-Kantian idealism and the subtle realism of Husserl's *Logical Investigations*. The terms *"Hingeltungscharakter"* and *"Betroffenheit"* were taken from Lask's thought. See Lask, *Die Logik der Philosophie und die Kategorienlehre* and *Die Lehre vom Urteil, Gesammelte Schriften*, 2:83 and 2:173–78, respectively. In his report on Heidegger's *Habilitationsschrift*, Rickert characterized the importance of Lask's influence on Heidegger's work as "perhaps greater than [Heidegger] himself is aware." See Rickert's report in the appendix to Heidegger and Rickert, *Briefe*, 96. In 1915, while Heidegger was composing his *Habilitationsschrift*, Lask was killed in an early battle of the First World War.

75. Heidegger, "Duns Scotus," in *Frühe Schriften*, 143–44.

76. Ibid.

77. Husserl, letter to Paul Natorp, October 10, 1917, as cited in Sheehan, "Heidegger's Early Years," 8.

78. Heidegger, "Duns Scotus," in *Frühe Schriften*, 265–68.

79. Ibid., 247.

80. Ibid., 282. Heidegger's philosophy of language was explicitly directed against the linguistic theories of Karl Vossler, philologist of the romance languages and close friend of Benedetto Croce. Like Wilhelm von Humboldt, Vossler advocated a more alogical, historical approach to linguistic phenomena. Note Heidegger's comments in this regard in ibid., 280.

81. In his treatment of the philosophy of language, Heidegger relied both on Husserl's *Logische Untersuchungen* (1900–1901) and on his *Ideen zu einer reinen Phänomenologie* (1913). Heidegger, "Duns Scotus," in *Frühe Schriften*, 245–340.

82. Heidegger's *Habilitationsschrift* did not go without criticism on this point. In his *Historische Zeitschrift* review (pp. 497–98), Adolf Dyroff gave the following commentary:

In part, Duns Scotus comes off too well, as the author himself actually admits on page 27. In part, something is interpreted in Scotus's statements that is not there. What is clear and understandable in Latin becomes opaque and difficult to understand, at the very least stilted, under Heidegger's influence. Heidegger works with the expressions of Rickert and Husserl. In view of the display of ingenuity, and after the proud words of the "introduction," the result of the [*Habilitationsschrift*] left me somewhat disappointed.

83. Heidegger, "Duns Scotus," in *Frühe Schriften*, 352.

84. Heidegger evokes Scotus's idea of the real individuality of the soul at various points in his *Habilitationsschrift* (cf. ibid., 219), distinguishing it from the universal validity of the soul's acts.

85. Ibid., 352.

86. Ibid., 349–50.

87. Ibid., 138–39.

88. Ibid., 341–42.

89. Ibid., 307.

90. Ibid., 295.

91. Ibid., 206.

92. In his article on Heidegger's *Habilitationsschrift,* J. D. Caputo has rightly pointed out the influence of Dilthey and Nietzsche on Heidegger's use of the word *life*. Heidegger's "life philosophy" at the same time could draw on earlier ideas alive in the German Catholic tradition. See Caputo, "Phenomenology, Mysticism, and the 'Grammatica Speculativa': A Study of Heidegger's 'Habilitationsschrift,'" 112.

93. Pöggeler, *Denkweg,* 23; Heidegger, "Duns Scotus," in *Frühe Schriften,* 352–53.

94. Sheehan, "Heidegger's Early Years," 7.

3

Existence and History: Heidegger's Radical Turning Point between 1918 and 1923

A LETTER written by the thirty-one-year-old Heidegger in 1920 to his young student Karl Löwith, and published in part in a *Temps Modernes* article by Löwith twenty-five years later, has for good reason often been cited in works on Heidegger. It is one of the few published traces of Heidegger's correspondence during his period as a Freiburg *Privatdozent* (university lecturer; 1919–23), and deals with his personal reaction to the general social and cultural instability in Germany between 1918 and 1920:

> Instead of abandoning oneself to the general need to become cultivated, as if one had received the order to "save culture" it would be necessary through a radical reduction and disintegration, through a *destruction* [*Destruktion*], to firmly convince oneself of the "only thing" necessary without paying attention to the idle task and agitation of enterprising and intelligent men. . . . My will at least is directed toward something else, and it is not much: living in the situation of de facto upheaval [*Umsturz*], I am pursuing what I feel to be "necessary" without worrying whether the result will be a "culture" or if my quest will precipitate ruin.[1]

Among the interesting notions expressed in this letter, one seems to be of special importance and was, indeed, underlined in the text: the suggestion of a need for cultural "destruction." Further clarification of this notion is offered by another document of this period, discovered among Karl Jaspers's papers and published for the first time in 1973. In this text from the years 1919–21—Heidegger's "Anmerkungen zu Karl Jaspers *Psychologie der Weltanschauungen*" (Annotations to Jaspers's *Psychology of Worldviews*)—the notion of destruction also played a central role.[2]

With regard to this document and the letter to Löwith, it is of interest to note that previous writings, as late as Heidegger's 1916 *Habilitationsschrift* (postdoctoral dissertation) on Duns Scotus, which attempted to mediate between the conflicting orientations of Catholic theology, Husserl's phenomenology, and Rickert's neo-Kantianism, contained little that foreshadowed the motif of destruction.

For this reason, the use of "destruction" in these two texts signaled an important turning point in Heidegger's early thought. It reflected his serious doubts about Western intellectual traditions and his profound questioning of the leading contemporary theoretical concerns of the German academic milieu. This theme of destruction would become a keynote of the "fundamental ontology" of Heidegger's *Sein und Zeit* (Being and time; 1927).

Contrary to what it might seem to imply, and as was already clear in the "Annotations," "destruction," which Heidegger also termed "destruction in the history of thought [*geistesgeschichtliche Destruktion*]," did not signify a mere rejection of intellectual traditions or disavowal of contemporary theoretical pursuits.[3] Rather, in its affirmative sense, it aimed to reassert the truly essential themes of philosophy.[4] In Heidegger's estimation, such themes had been obscured by intellectual orientations contemporary philosophy had chosen from the legacy of the past. Far from inaugurating a new philosophy, then, "destruction" was to separate the wheat from the chaff in the philosophical heritage, to bring to light what Heidegger considered to be the authentic philosophical endeavor, within an intellectual landscape where fundamental meaning had become obscure.

In philosophical matters, as elsewhere, the separation of wheat from chaff assumes the ability to distinguish which is which. Against a hardened intellectual tradition, how might the fundamentally meaningful be brought into view and set aside from the accidental and inauthentic? If, as Heidegger suggested to his contemporaries, "we are perhaps occupying ourselves with merely subordinate affairs, instead of receiving rigorously conceived major philosophical questions,"[5] how might such major questions be made indisputably clear? Having asserted that the essential had been obscured and could be brought to light only with destruction, Heidegger could not simply claim to have sighted what had been missed—he had to provide a principle of interpretation to demonstrate *what* was essential and *how* it had been brought into view.

In the "Annotations," this principle of interpretation rested on the historical understanding of what Heidegger termed "life experience [*Lebenserfahrung*]," considered as existence. A far cry from his 1916 *Habilitationsschrift* on Duns Scotus, where Heidegger had postulated a fixed human nature as the metaphysical basis of truth, the "Annotations" claimed that human existence is radically historical; from this new vantage point, only a more fundamental understanding of historical existence than that attained heretofore might stir up the stock categories of his intellectual world and, at the same time, provide a criterion for separating genuine philosophical issues from superficial ones.

Our purpose in this chapter is twofold: first, to grasp the historical sense of "life experience" that we ourselves are and that destruction was meant to bring into focus and, second, to discern its place in a wider horizon of concerns of an important segment of Heidegger's generation. For this second purpose, we will make use (in section II) of Heidegger's course lecture series of the academic year 1920–21, entitled "Einleitung in die Phänomenologie der Religion" (Introduction to the phenomenology of religion), first published in 1995.

I

Heidegger divulged little about his life in the years between 1917, when he was called up for military service, and 1923 when he was appointed *Professor extraordinarius* at the University of Marburg, after having taught for five years as a Freiburg *Privatdozent*. Because his works contain almost no reference to World War I or to the 1920s, one might conclude that the momentous events of his age were of little importance for Heidegger's development as a thinker. And yet, as difficult as it is to place the turning point in Heidegger's early thought in direct relation to the events of the period, it hardly seems accidental that his turn toward destruction in the history of thought took place against the background of an important metamorphosis in German social and cultural life.

In this metamorphosis, the focus of intellectual concern among broad segments of the younger generation began to change. Important groups of students and younger intellectuals, many of them returning from the front, became dissatisfied with the traditional academic pursuits of the German universities. In the words of Hannah Arendt, who studied with Heidegger in the 1920s, a "widespread discontent" spread after the war "in all the faculties that were more than just professional schools, and among all the students for whom scholarship meant more than preparation for a profession."[6]

From articles by Arendt and other students of Heidegger in the 1920s, including Karl Löwith and Hans-Georg Gadamer, we can see that Heidegger attracted his first important audience among this younger generation of students. As Gadamer wrote, Heidegger's "questions were also the urgent questions of an agitated, crippled generation, shaken in its cultural pride by the devastating battles of World War I."[7] To describe the link between Heidegger's questions and those of his generation on the plane of thought, however, is no easy matter. Such a description must proceed with caution if we are not to fall into facile generalizations.

To be sure, one plausible link suggests itself in the terminology of life philosophy (*Lebensphilosophie*)—especially, the term "life experience," which Dilthey had brought into current usage—that Heidegger began to employ. Indeed, this style of philosophy had immediate roots in the thought of Dilthey, which Heidegger characterized as the "highpoint" of *Lebensphilosophie*.[8] At times blended with ideas of Nietzsche or of the late Simmel, *Lebensphilosophie* enjoyed a far greater popularity than it had before the war.

For this reason, it was fitting that the "Annotations" concerned Jaspers's recent work, *Psychology of Worldviews,* which Heidegger took to be an example of *Lebensphilosophie*'s contemporary expression. Born in the difficult years of the war, Jaspers's work sought to describe the extreme limiting situations (*Grenzsituationen*) of life—including war, accident, and death. In sharp contrast to the strongly affirmative view of culture that characterized the prewar thought of philosophers like Dilthey, it emphasized the contradictions (*Widersprüche*) in individual existence that no culture could alleviate, and even the potential death of a culture itself. In these limiting situations and the contradictions of life, Jaspers set out to demarcate "life as a whole."

As Heidegger pointed out in the "Annotations," Jaspers's thought was only one of the highly heterogeneous tendencies of *Lebensphilosophie,* which extended to fields as diverse as history, psychology, biology, and philosophy. Heidegger refused to be identified with any tendency of *Lebensphilosophie*; he sought to distinguish his thought from it, as well as from thinkers such as Rickert or Husserl who had already declared their hostility to Dilthey's *Lebensphilosophie* in the prewar period. In the postwar period, they continued to view this philosophical impulse as ambiguous at best and lacking in theoretical rigor.

On the one hand, Heidegger was careful to insist that none of the contemporary orientations, whether those of young or those of older thinkers, could serve as a point of departure for his thought. On the other, he expressed esteem for Dilthey and admitted to being inspired by his mode of phenomenological observation. He also described Jaspers's work as a "positive step,"[9] writing in a letter to Rickert that it "meets a trend of the times [*einem Zug der Zeit entgegenkommt*]." Nevertheless, in this same letter, he affirmed the necessity of combatting Jaspers's book "in the strongest way [*auf das schärfste bekämpft werden muss*]"—the acknowledged purpose of the "Annotations," which he sent Rickert in unpublished form.[10] At this early time, Heidegger claimed to proceed independently, a claim that resounded in the German universities of the early 1920s, where, on the basis of his celebrated course lectures, the rumor circulated that Heidegger "is a man who has really attained to the things [*Sachen*] proclaimed by Husserl; one who knows that they are not an academic affair, but the interest of thinking people and, it is true, not since yesterday and today, but from time immemorial [*seit eh und je*]. This man is able to discover the past anew precisely because for him the thread of tradition has been rent."[11]

In the "Annotations," Heidegger attempted to disengage his thought from a number of the leading contemporary intellectual orientations, above all, those of Husserl, Rickert, Dilthey, and Jaspers. To better understand the turning point in Heidegger's early thought and to prepare the way for reflection on its place within the intellectual milieu of his times, let us examine Heidegger's critique of these thinkers, beginning with Heidegger's former mentors, Husserl and Rickert, then proceeding to Jaspers and Dilthey. Although the earliest of these thinkers, Dilthey (d. 1911) will be treated last so that examination of his original notion of "life experience" in relation to Heidegger's might be more fruitful.

In the "Annotations," Heidegger rejected both the theoretical character of Husserlian phenomenology and the theoretical standpoint of the historical sciences, for which Rickert's neo-Kantian philosophy was cited as the foundation.[12] He found their respective emphases on theoretical concerns too remote from factical-historical "life experience," considered as existence.[13] The sense of existence, as he put it bluntly, "cannot be genuinely had in theoretical reckoning [*Meinen*]."[14]

Heidegger's assertions undercut the fundamental basis of Husserl's and Rickert's thought. Whatever differences existed between Rickert's neo-Kantianism and phenomenology, their systematic concepts were grounded in a priori theoretical norms secure against historical change. Their followers saw any attempt to unmoor these concepts from the absolute anchorage of thought—whether situated in Husserl's immanent sphere of consciousness or guaranteed by Rickert's transcendent values—as casting them adrift on the currents of relativism and skepticism.

Heidegger, for his part, rejected such concepts as "absolute validity of truth," "skepticism," and "relativism" in the "Annotations," although he did not allude to their central importance for his former mentors.[15] The train of his thought was nevertheless clear: far from being accepted or tacitly presupposed, such concepts were themselves to be made the objects of a radical critique, as products of a sclerotic and inauthentic (*unechte*) tradition.

"Life experience," for Heidegger, was not to be judged according to nonexperiential concepts. Rather, the spell of such concepts, which were no more than the expression of a primary experience and its underlying motives, was to be broken by a destructive reversal. Destruction was therefore tantamount (*gleichbedeutend*) to the "explanation of the motivating, original situations bringing forth fundamental philosophical experiences, of which such ideal premises (skepticism, relativism, absolute validity of truth) are to be understood to be the expression."[16]

Heidegger emphasized that, rather than to reach outside the evidence of factical experience to grasp absolute standards of judgment, one had to remain faithful to the factical character of experience recalcitrant to such standards. To grasp this primordial sense of experience, critical analysis had to begin from presuppositions or "preconceptions" flowing from that experience.

Such preconceptions orient theoretical methods in their assumptions about phenomena to be sought and concerning the boundaries within which they are to be found. The conception of history, for example, presupposes in its method historical phenomena to be sought in the field of the historical; biology presupposes biological objects, which may overlap with the historical field yet, at a given point, shade off into their own specific realm. Such preconceptions and the methods rooted in them were not, for Heidegger, directed by ideal standards independent of experience. The preconceptions providing access to a field of experience incarnated in theory themselves arose with the experience of the theorist. The problem Heidegger posed was that of uncovering experience *by* experience, moving beyond theoretical determinations of different fields and methods of analysis to reach back to what he saw as a variety of possible *motives* expressed in the experiential preconceptions governing theoretical analysis.

Heidegger attributed a fundamental importance to such motives and to the preconceptions they express because they involve a "self" that interprets its existence. "Having the self" is not a set relation (*Bezug*) established by uniform logical rules, but arises in continuous fulfillment (*Vollzug*); this fulfillment of the self's sense of existence—which Heidegger referred to as the self's "factical-historical [*faktisch-historischer*]" character—orients the preconceptions of experience and all theory. The self is "historical" in the sense that it is not a fixed relation, but can determine the ways of its fulfillment; it is factical, not due to an interest in "facts [*Tatsachen*]," but for the impossibility Heidegger saw of abstracting it from the fact—or, in more precise terms, the "facticity"—of its fulfillment to posit its existence as something preconceived in the theoretical realm, and thus as already acquired or definitively established. In his Freiburg course lectures, he described "facticity" as "life's sense of being [*Seinssinn des Lebens*]," characterized by its essential mobility (*Bewegtheit*), which fades (*verblasst*) and goes to waste (*abfällt*) when it is reified through inappropriate theoretical standards.[17]

Beyond a disavowal of an absolute starting point for thought, the broad implications of Heidegger's position were clear, vis-à-vis both phenomenology and Baden neo-Kantianism. The generally accepted method of phenomenology, rather than beginning from preconceptions of experience, laid claim to a presuppositionless constitution of phenomena in their immediacy, which it sought to reduce to an essential core of meaning. For Heidegger, the central presupposition of this allegedly presuppositionless viewpoint was that meaning is rooted in what Husserl termed the universal "region" of consciousness, whose foundations were insulated from any contingent experiential context of historical modification. Against such a viewpoint, Heidegger exclaimed: "A view that, to avoid an inappropriate, constructive standpoint is concerned merely with its immediacy, only too easily falls into blindness in regard to its own, in the end nonprimary, motives. The meaning of primacy is not an extra- or ahistorical idea, but shows itself in the sense that presuppositionlessness can only be won in factical-historical self-criticism."[18]

Rickert, it is true, had distinguished himself from Husserl by doubting that method could be applied from the standpoint of mere immediacy. Because he viewed immediately given phenomena as nothing more than an infinite multiplicity of fleeting, unintelligible sense impressions, the level at which such phenomena became coherent could not, therefore, be prior to their historical emplacement. Coherence, Rickert thought, became manifest in the alternative perspectives through which objects could be rendered meaningful: either as historical individualities or as natural, law-obeying generalities. Not immediate apprehension but mediation by natural or historical concepts was the meaning-conferring act.

Nevertheless, as the juxtaposition of natural and historical methods of concept formation indicates, the notion of the historical was not guided by concern for the sense of life experience, but was formally deduced as one of two possible theoretical methods of constituting objects. Where the natural and historical worlds underwent constant flux, both of these methods and the meaning-conferring structures of the consciousness in general (*Bewusstsein überhaupt*) through which they were expressed were insulated from factical-historical considerations.

If Heidegger had distinguished between historical and natural methods in his *Habilitationsvortrag,* which owed much to Rickert, the new starting point in "factical-historical" life experience signaled a decisive departure from this earlier idea. Now he openly referred to what he viewed as Rickert's "disputable ideal of philosophical knowledge."[19]

The radicalism of Heidegger's standpoint, at the core of his rejection of both neo-Kantian methodological formalism and phenomenological immediacy, came home in the central thrust of his broader attack. As different from each other as they were, both styles of analysis could claim absolute foundations in focusing on consciousness in its fixed generality. Their respective theoretical pursuits were sustained, not by open fulfillment of a factical-historical self in restless search of a sense of existence, but by universal structures of consciousness. This was the way in which, at different levels of analysis, Husserl understood his "regional consciousness" and Rickert his "consciousness in general [*Bewusstsein überhaupt*]." Heidegger sought to place such structures in factical-historical flux by denying their role as the decisive factor in the meaning-conferring activity of the self: "Factical life experience itself, in which I can have myself in various ways, is not, however, something like a 'region' in which I stand, not the universal whose isolation would then be the self; this experience is an essentially 'historical' phenomenon, according to the how of its self-fulfillment."[20]

Heidegger proposed to dislodge principles of truth from a priori universal standards in his search for a method originating in factical-historical experience, and adequate for an analysis of the phenomenon of existence. This meant elaborating a different aim for phenomenology. Heidegger sought to demonstrate that abandoning the presupposition of a universal, a priori basis for meaning-conferring acts of consciousness was a necessary step toward clarifying the fundament of existence. His phenomenology sought to distill, not universal structures of consciousness, but a basic preconception equal to the task of investigating that fundament. Even when a thinker claimed only to deal descriptively with the phenomenon of existence, it could not be brought into focus without a suitable preconception. This observation was the key point in Heidegger's critique of Jaspers's *Psychology of Worldviews*.

According to Heidegger, the abstract preconception Jaspers brought to bear in his analysis manifested itself in the following way. Jaspers characterized "life as a whole," the potential situations of existence, as infinite, yet this infinitude was analogously applied to life in its psychological, biological, and historical dimensions. Jaspers's concept of infinitude was not guided by the kind of material it intended to comprehend. He did not differentiate among the varieties of infinity, positing both historical existence and biological organisms as infinite. Nowhere did he attempt to disentangle the historical aspects of existence as separate, because self-directed and fulfilled, from the spontaneous occurrences of natural organisms. Jaspers's preconception, subservient to theoretical assumptions at hand in the scientific environment, leveled all phenomena down to similarly comprehended objects involved in infinite processes. This abstract preconception brought existence into view as a vaguely formulated theoretical product, which Heidegger criticized in the following terms:

> The "concept" of infinitude explicitly appears to have been taken from a biological entity. It is also applied to the life of the spirit [*des Geistes*], in such a way that, in a closer delineation of the latter, an ulterior concept is interposed. . . . [When Jaspers speaks] of an "infinite whole" and of "infinite process," the two unclear concepts of infinity shine through one another. According to its intentional relation [*Bezug*], Jaspers already has life as a totality in a preconception intending a thing-object: "It is there," a process of movement (movement: intentionally directed; process: "occurring" as an event).[21]

For Heidegger, the understanding of "life" and of "life reality" could not be gained through the application of a preconception considering all objects in terms of an identical scale of uniformity. Jaspers's approach rested on an imprecise theoretical basis and, in its abstraction, missed the central principle for clarifying the phenomena it examined. Although he claimed to merely contemplate phenomena that presented themselves, his preconceptual approach presupposed a comparison nowhere given in contemplation, nor in experience per se. This comparison obscured the basic quality of life experience as existence; it is not an object among other objects, which can be conceived according to the same groups of concepts, like infinity abstractly applied. "Life" as existence is, in Heidegger's words: "*the* area, *the* fundamental reality, unified and encompassing, into which all phenomena are built [*eingebaut werden*]."[22]

But did not Heidegger's insistence on the unique, irreducible character of human life experience, and his pursuit of this uniqueness in factical-historical existence, bring him into the theoretical camp of Dilthey? Did not Heidegger's distinction between human historical and nonhuman biological realities extend and radicalize the historicist view of late-nineteenth-century German historical thinking, at least insofar as Dilthey had embodied it?

Our adumbration of Heidegger's notion of factical-historical life experience in the "Annotations" permits us to draw a preliminary distinction between Dilthey's and Heidegger's respective interpretations of "life experience." As we have seen in chapter 2, life experience was preeminently historical for Dilthey: he represented it as the mediation of personal lived-experience (*Erlebnis*) by the cultural domain of institutions, language, and expression. Historical understanding, for Dilthey, was the study of objectified life experience crystallized in the past and made accessible by threads of coherence universally spanning the generations of human life in the historical world.

By contrast, Heidegger's notion of life experience in the "Annotations" was considerably different. Articulated through the variable sense that the self could give to existence, Heidegger's comprehension of life experience denied Dilthey's foundation of historical meaning on a core of coherence running through world history and making the objectified products of human thought and activity universally accessible. For Heidegger, the authentic sense of the historical had to be sought primarily in the way in which the past was made meaningful to the self. The past had meaning only according to the mode in which it was appropriated by the self in its concern (*Bekümmerung*) for fulfillment of a sense of existence.

Dilthey's way of disclosing the past, according to Heidegger, focused on personalities (*Persönlichkeiten*) of the past, from which the question of fulfillment of the sense of existence was left out. Heidegger traced Dilthey's tendency to omit the self from investigation to what he termed "aesthetic" motives of contemplation,[23] by which he meant, not the artistic motives behind investigation, but rather motives that fail to consider the sense of self of the researcher.

The distance Heidegger perceived between his own thought and that of Dilthey becomes evident in Heidegger's tendency to liken Dilthey and Jaspers. Even though Dilthey had never endorsed Jaspers's style of abstract application of uniform categories to conscious life and to nature, Heidegger nevertheless attributed "aesthetic motives" of thought to both thinkers. For Heidegger, Dilthey's concentration on objective expressions of personality in the past arose from the same motives as Jaspers's classification of worldviews according to *type* in *Psychology of Worldviews*. He viewed both Dilthey's approach to the past and Jaspers's typology of worldviews as shortsighted, holding that all classifications of the past on the basis of types systematizes objects in a manner indifferent to the sense of existence of the one undertaking systematization.[24]

As Heidegger saw it, in the concept of historical meaning of both Dilthey and Jaspers the forgetfulness of the self was not, however, tantamount to its obliteration. In both approaches, the self tacitly came to expression in the preconception guided by an aesthetic motive, clouding given potentialities for revealing meaning, and robbing the possibilities for fulfillment of the sense of existence of primordial prefiguration in the past. Thus, for Heidegger, the attempt to arrive at meaning by an inductive assortment of past appearances remained unenlightening so long as the theme of the existing self was not considered beforehand to guide the way meaning was sought: only on the basis of concern for the sense of existence of the self could the potentialities of this sense implicit in the past emerge from out of its depths.

In a brief but important observation, Heidegger went beyond his objections to type schemata, inveighing against a traditional principle adopted of German historical thinking, rooted in the thought of Wilhelm von Humboldt and Leopold von Ranke, that he himself had favored in his earlier *Habilitationsvortrag*. Even if historical thought were to de-emphasize type schemata and focus on unique individuality, he noted, this in itself would not be sufficient.[25] For him, the existential sense of the self had to take precedence over any consideration of past objectifications of unique individuality, just as it did over typical articulations of historical personality.

Moreover (to anticipate section II), historical meaning for Heidegger was not even primarily founded in the basic distinction of the historical from the natural agreed upon by all of the critical theorists and by the earlier theorists of history Humboldt and Ranke. His attributing the same aesthetic motives to Dilthey, who distinguished sharply between the historical and the natural, as to Jaspers, who blurred this distinction with his abstract categories, prefigured Heidegger's later tendency to view any such considerations as of minimal importance without prior clarification of the principle of existence as he saw it.

Beyond this point, Heidegger's ruminations in the "Annotations" were vague as to the precise activity of historical thought. He contented himself with observing that authentic roots of the historical had to be sought in arousing concern of the self through the reawakening of conscience (*Gewissen*). Conscience was to constitute the mode of self-awareness of life experience in which historical meaning was primordially revealed.

Heidegger traced the darkening of the phenomenon of conscience, which signified the exclusion of a sense of responsibility elicited by the past, to various forms of the historical thinking of his times:

The historical is today almost exclusively an objective interest, something to know and to be curious about, an occasion and place to gain practical instruction for future behavior, . . . a conglomeration of "cases" for universal systematic contemplation. We no longer experience the sense of conscience and of responsibility that lies in the historical itself, because we do not genuinely see the phenomenon of existence today. The historical is not only something from which one gets information, and about which there are books; it is, much more, what we ourselves are, what we bear. Thus the motives for a return to the historical are also, throughout our own history, lifeless and obscure.[26]

In what Heidegger viewed to be traditional ideas of the self, in the scientific path to knowledge of it, historical thinking had tended to hide the phenomenon of existence. The neglect of a genuine historical self-concern thus resulted in the borrowing of a sense of existence from an already objectified, traditional interpretation at hand in the environment. Whether such objectifications were conceived, for example, in terms of an "ideal of humanity [Humanitätsideal]" or of a "personal character [Persönlichkeit]," they relied on traditional interpretations of the past, precluding an authentic responsibility for fulfillment of existence's sense.[27] In Heidegger's view, the phenomenon of existence had to be fulfilled continually, not understood once and for all. This quest for a definitive, systematic philosophy was, in his estimation, basically misguided: rooted in life experience, thought was always historical in character.

Moreover, to avoid entanglement in the objectified meanings of the traditional intellectual environment, Heidegger warned, one had to destroy tradition: "As soon as the characteristic burdening [Belastung] of factical life through tradition is seen . . . the insight grows that the concrete possibility of bringing the phenomenon of existence into view and of explicating it according to genuine concepts is *only* revealed when the concrete, in any way still effectively experienced, tradition [is] destroyed."[28] This point, introduced near the end of the "Annotations," gave little direction to the problem of destruction with which the text was introduced. Clearly, the thrust of Heidegger's reflections on historical meaning was more powerfully directed toward peeling away traditional accretions than toward establishing the historical foundation Heidegger sought. If it involved historicizing reified modes of interpretation of the self, destruction provided little to retrieve the sense of the self beyond its open and wholly indeterminate character.

Finally, with the rejection of purely logical consciousness or of universally comprehensible objectifications as a possible unifying tissue of the historical world of life experience, the necessary locus of history, as a mediated relation between self and community, remained fragmentary. Although, at certain points in the "Annotations," Heidegger suggested that experience had to be taken as a revelation of environment, community, and the self, he did not explore the dimensions of this larger sense of experience. This gap in Heidegger's analysis was also to be of crucial importance, as we will see, in Heidegger's later attempt to root historical meaning in the fundamental ontology of *Being and Time*.

II

In his *Philosophische Autobiographie* (Philosophical autobiography), Jaspers reported that he only "glanced over" the "Annotations" that Heidegger sent him shortly after the publication of the *Psychology of Worldviews*.[29] At the end of the "Annotations," Heidegger suggested a thoroughgoing revision of the work. Jaspers commented in a handwritten note to the second edition that little could be changed without writing an entirely new book.[30] The *Psychology of Worldviews* was composed in a period when Jaspers was changing over from clinical psychology to philosophy. His later work, in the 1920s and 1930s, attested to Jaspers's independent development, during which his own experience drew him away from the kind of thinking Heidegger had found objectionable.

In the years between 1919 and 1923, the two thinkers became friends, with Heidegger traveling to Heidelberg on occasion as Jaspers's guest. In his *Philosophical Autobiography*, Jaspers recounted the importance for him of contact with Heidegger, and his satisfaction at being "able to speak seriously at least with one member of the philosopher's guild."[31]

Jaspers went on to explain that the two young thinkers were most firmly bound together by their common conviction that philosophy in the German universities needed to be thoroughly reoriented, by their "common opposition to the traditional professors' philosophy."[32] In his letters to Jaspers at this time, Heidegger also wrote of the need to overthrow the whole interpretation of philosophy in its general relation to the other disciplines in the German universities.[33] For both thinkers, academic philosophy had become estranged from its life source and needed to be directed toward a more fundamental path.

During one of Jaspers's rare trips to Freiburg at the beginning of their intellectual relationship, he and Heidegger paid a visit to the home of the elder Husserl. Jaspers and Heidegger got into a mild argument with Husserl over a trivial administrative question concerning the university, a dispute Jaspers interpreted as a symbol of "a kind of solidarity of both the younger ones against the authority of abstract regulations [Ordnungen]."[34] Whereas Jaspers remained distant from Husserl, Heidegger continued a close relationship with his former mentor until the open conflict that followed publication of Being and Time. Referring to his preoccupation with Husserlian phenomenology, he recalled that he had been "learning and teaching in the proximity of Husserl since 1919."[35] And, as the "Annotations" and the Freiburg course lectures of this period indeed show, after 1919, Heidegger considered his approach to philosophy to be phenomenological, although his interpretation of phenomenology as a factical explication of historical life experience clearly diverged from Husserl's "theoretical" phenomenology, anchored as it was in a basis of truth resistant to historical contingency. At this early point, the grounds for their later break were already laid, if not yet apparent.[36]

The separation of both Heidegger and Jaspers from the neo-Kantian "school philosophy" was more direct; their personal relations with Heinrich Rickert quickly cooled. On a visit to Heidelberg, Hans-Georg Gadamer recorded Rickert's deep disappointment in changes he perceived in Heidegger's orientation, with Rickert mournfully asking Gadamer "why his student [had] kept so little to his teachings."[37] Between 1921 and 1928, only one letter exists between Heidegger and Rickert (about Rickert's article on Emil Lask); their correspondence after 1928 testifies to a marked cooling of their philosophical and personal relations.[38] In his autobiographical statements, Jaspers recounted that he quickly drew away from Rickert after the death of their mutual friend and colleague, Max Weber.[39]

During the academic year 1920–21, Heidegger presented his series of course lectures at the University of Freiburg entitled "Introduction to the Phenomenology of Religion." The two-semester series comprised two parts, the first (touched on here) dealing with methodological problems, and most specifically with the problem of historical understanding; the second (touched on in chapter 4) dealing with phenomenology and applying the historical understanding achieved in the first part to the theme of religion.

In this lecture series, Heidegger rarely mentioned the thought of Husserl. Instead, he focused on the thinking of those whom he considered to be the major historical theorists among his contemporaries. He dealt with the important prewar theorists Wilhelm Windelband, Heinrich Rickert, Wilhelm Dilthey, Georg Simmel, and Ernst Troeltsch, and spoke of Oswald Spengler's more recent book, *Der Untergang des Abendlandes* (The decline of the West; 1918–22). Although Heidegger did not use the provocative term "destruction," which played such a central role in the "Annotations," he spoke of the need "to burst [*sprengen*]" the categories of Western thought, expressing the hope that his work would contribute toward this task.

The "Introduction to the Phenomenology of Religion" complemented ideas expressed in the "Annotations," making these ideas more concrete and relating them more closely to the intellectual milieu in which Heidegger was thinking and writing. To clarify the still vague perspectives in Heidegger's understanding of the problem of historical meaning at this decisive time in his intellectual development, we need to examine his critique of the older generation of historical theorists and particularly of Oswald Spengler. Of central importance in his approach is not only what Heidegger said, but also the crucial way in which he related the prewar varieties of historical thinking to the more controversial theories of the young Spengler.

An understanding of Heidegger's highly critical appraisal of Spengler, and of how it relates to the analysis of the other thinkers in question, is complicated by one important circumstance that must be clarified at the start: thinkers close to Heidegger in the early twenties have tended to pass over his criticism of Spengler, focusing instead on points of *affinity* between his and Spengler's styles of thinking.

In the *Temps Modernes* article cited at the beginning of the chapter, Karl Löwith compared the thought of Heidegger and of Spengler at this time—to which he also joined the early theological writings of Karl Barth.[40] In characterizing the intellectual climate that fostered the "death of the liberal epoch" at the end of the war, Gadamer alluded to the significance of Spengler's *Decline of the West* and to the simultaneous emergence of the Heideggerian standpoint; he mentioned Barth's neo-Reformed theology as moving in a complementary direction.[41] Furthermore, Heidegger himself, in his 1928 course lectures on Leibniz, felt it necessary to dispel speculation that his thought might be a reformulation of the Spenglerian worldview.[42] However far away from a Spenglerian outlook Heidegger might have been, his need to disavow Spengler's influence suggests that still other intellectuals of this period had perceived an affinity between the two thinkers.

To a present-day mind, such comparisons may seem curious. On the face of it, Spengler's philosophy of history, with all its abstruse facts and its broad judgments about the stages of Western history, would seem to have little in common with the philosophy of existence Heidegger was beginning to articulate. On the other hand, a superficial look at Spengler's philosophy is likely to miss its broad implications— why, in the early 1920s, an affinity was perceived between Spengler's and Heidegger's thinking. As Spengler liked to observe, all philosophy symbolizes the spirit of its times, an observation perhaps nowhere truer than for Spengler's philosophy itself. Indeed, it is in understanding how Spengler's writings were appreciated as a symbol of their times that the broader meaning of his work and its possible relation to Heidegger's must be sought.

The thrust of Spengler's notion of a decline of the West, as Gadamer made clear, directly contradicted liberal attitudes strongly entrenched in the prewar academic milieu. Most generally associated with the widespread neo-Kantian worldview,[43] but also with thinkers like Dilthey, Simmel, and Troeltsch, such attitudes attributed a spontaneously meaningful character to the broad process of history and evinced strong faith in the soundness of the German cultural heritage. Spengler's work formed a symbolic rallying point for a break with prewar liberal confidence in German and Western culture, and brought into sharp question the forms of liberal historical scholarship through which cultural development had been laboriously recapitulated and interpreted.

In this sense, Spengler's significance was affirmed in quite diverse circles, and at times even where some of his more central conclusions could not be accepted. This was the case, to take an important example, in theology, where a group of university theologians including Friedrich Gogarten, Eduard Turneysen, Rudolf Bultmann (Heidegger's future Marburg collaborator), and Karl Barth were struggling against what they saw as a "liberal-historical" emphasis in prewar religious studies.[44] In 1919, Gogarten, of whom Heidegger would express high esteem to Bultmann in 1923,[45] wrote a highly acclaimed manifesto, "Zwischen den Zeiten" (Between times; which later gave its name to the group's theological review). In it, he declared: "We are jubilant over the Spengler book. It proves, whether one agrees with its details or not, that the hour has struck when this fine, clever culture [*Kultur*] discovers, out of its own cleverness, the worm that is eating it; when trust in the development of culture receives the deathblow. And the Spengler book is not the only sign."[46]

Given the historical and largely nontheological references that Spengler marshaled to support his theories (Troeltsch referred to them as "atheistic"),[47] the affinity between theologian Gogarten and philosopher Spengler found its firmest roots in their shared radical perspective, involving widespread disenchantment with presuppositions of self-sustaining transcendent values, objective spirit, and other forms of spontaneous historical meaning. Such a perspective had been far less evident in the period before the war and the collapse of Germany.

Thus, as illustrated by Gogarten's use of Spengler, one can acknowledge a general affinity between Spengler and Heidegger in the *impact* of their thinking, while recognizing significant differences in the substance of that thinking, as Heidegger's relentless criticism of Spengler in the 1920–21 lectures "Introduction to the Phenomenology of Religion" makes plain. Undoubtedly, the most varied criticisms of the spontaneous coherence of the historical process—from Spengler's idea of decline, to Gogarten's scorn for cultural development, to Heidegger's "destruction" in the history of thought—owed their ready acceptability and popularity to a radicalism favored by the circumstances of the period.

Given the general radicalization of historical perspectives in the German universities, it is not surprising to find Ernst Troeltsch's 1923 reference to a "crisis of the historical understanding" in contemporary culture. In an interpretation since reaffirmed by successive generations of scholars of historical reflection, Troeltsch located the crisis in the "general philosophical basis and elements of historical thinking, in the conception of historical values from which we think and construct the coherence of history."[48]

Troeltsch's assessment of the contemporary situation provides a backdrop against which the varieties of doubt in the prewar vision of the historical world may be set in relief. Nonetheless, there is a complication we must address. In his lecture series "Introduction to the Phenomenology of Religion," Heidegger advanced an unusual interpretation, one that only serves to make matters more problematic for our analysis. Far from regarding Spengler as a comrade-in-arms in "destruction," or even as a significant symbol of the rupture in intellectual traditions, Heidegger paradoxically counted Spengler's thought as a radicalized *continuation* of the prewar theorists' fundamental approach to history.[49] Thus, ironically, even as the two surviving elder theorists with whom he dealt in his lectures—Troeltsch and Rickert—were earnestly attempting to discredit Spengler,[50] Heidegger was arguing that all three thinkers had taken a similar underlying approach in their respective interpretations of the historical world!

At the very least, this disharmony in interpretation testifies to the complex character of the problem of historical thought in the postwar period. The task at hand requires that we untangle the tangled contours of the problem, as they touch on the principle of historical understanding Heidegger attempted to demarcate. To this end, let us proceed with a closer investigation of Spengler, whose controversial writings are at the heart of the paradox under consideration.

Spengler's enormous impact and unprecedented literary success in Germany, both among the intelligentsia and the larger reading public, has often been described as indicating a wide consensus among Germans in this troubled time.[51] It reflected a deeply held German opinion that, whatever victories the Western democracies might have wrung from Germany, in the decline of the West, they themselves participated in the German loss. Indeed, victory in battle was only incidental; beneath it, the underlying current of history was inexorably flowing. The World War was a final episode, according to this interpretation, ushering in the fall.

Breaking out of the mold of epistemologically cautious, critically inspired historical theory of the prewar period, Spengler's ideas served as a focal point for intellectual discontent. His vision fueled dissatisfaction with the historians' idea of their craft as a faithful interpretation of events, and with the philosophers' contention that historical reasoning must be limited to an analysis of the development of ideas, the objectification of values, or the exchange of dynamic worldviews. By themselves, these were treated as surface occurrences, permitting only a fragmentary view of the past without providing a basis for understanding the contemporary situation in relation to the historical "life principle" at its source. Only when this historical "life principle" was properly grasped could one understand the metaphysical destiny of Western culture and the hidden reason for its impending decline.

For Spengler, such understanding only became available when Western culture was viewed against the total backdrop of world history (*Weltgeschichte*). Here informed observers could discern not only Western culture, but all culture, as subject a priori to rise and decline. From Spengler's perspective, cultures "live" like other organic realities and, like all life units, are individually distinct. Each can be characterized as an individual type—for example, the self-sufficient, harmonious "Apollonian" culture of ancient Greece, or the infinitely striving "Faustian" civilization of the modern Occident. For Spengler, such types were not to be taken nominalistically, in the neo-Kantian fashion, as convenient logical ways of grasping entities that in themselves remained irreducible to any common schema; nor were they to be understood in the sense of Dilthey or Jaspers, as having a solid basis in reality, without ever being able to comprehend and exhaust the essential possibilities of objects they meant to unify. Spengler proposed his vital cultural types as hypostatizations of a metaphysical life principle making possible the primary forms (*Urgestalten*) through which cultural reality was constituted.

Beside the individual-typical aspects of distinct cultures, Spengler saw another, more general character in the phenomenon of culture itself. This general character related both to culture as a whole organism and to the place of individual people in the vital process of this organism. On the one hand, culture, like all living organisms, was subject to a uniform style of existence, with its life rhythm and its end in death. Just as the individual person underwent the stages of youth, maturity, and senescence, so did culture. On the other hand, Spengler proposed that the life of individuals was determined by this vital cultural rhythm: as their individual selves were limited by personal finitude, so were they limited, and their consciousness profoundly shaped, by the historical position—or "destiny"—of the cultural whole. This cultural destiny took precedence, for Spengler, over all personal choices and circumstances: philosophical, scientific, artistic, and other expressions could not escape the essential impression of culture at a given stage of its life cycle. Thought was spiritually informed, or decadent and bereft of spirit, due not to personal intentions but because of an objective position in the cultural life cycle.

Subjugating personal consciousness to the determinacy of a historical culture and erasing any possible transcendence of historical reality by thought became especially controversial in the postwar intellectual environment. Defying more than two generations of inoculation against relativism and skepticism by critical theorists and philosophers in the German universities, Spengler dared to introduce his highly popular "morphology," in which the validity of all thought, from philosophy to mathematics, was seen as strictly relative to the cultural life reality in which it was expressed.[52] The challenge of Spengler—as Heidegger noted in the "Introduction to the Phenomenology of Religion"—lay in his disbelief in the conception of science founded in ideal continuity, transcending the purely relative elements of culture. Heidegger aptly characterized this as "Spengler's radical self-deliverance unto the historical process."[53]

Nevertheless, Spengler had strong faith in the rigorous nature of his own philosophy of history. The depths of his faith were extensively demonstrated in *The Decline of the West*. For him, because the expressions of thought and of action were relative to culture, on the basis of a close examination, one could rigorously deduce the stages of the cultural cycle in which such expressions occurred. Furthermore, because all cultures had identical general phases of growth and decline, all cultural type particularities appeared at analogous stages of cultural development. For example, despite all differences between "Apollonian" Greece and the "Faustian" West, Spengler postulated that in both cultures the appearance of similar kinds of thought, such as metaphysical or nonmetaphysical philosophies, analogously indicated the onset of cultural growth or decline.[54]

From this kind of argument by analogy, Spengler developed his larger vision of the goal of historical reasoning: on the basis of analogy, one could not only study past culture, but also come to precise conclusions concerning the future development of present culture. History was not only capable of an inductive survey of the past, but of deductive predictions concerning what was to come. As Spengler averred in the very first sentence of *Decline:* "In this book the attempt to predetermine [*vorauszubestimmen*] history will be made for the first time."[55]

Thus the method of history, conceived as a predictive discipline, was "raised" to the level of exactitude of a law-constructing natural science. Where elder theorists such as Windelband and Rickert, Dilthey, Simmel, and Troeltsch—following in the footsteps of an older German historiographical tradition—had hoped to establish history as an autonomous discipline with an epistemological goal independent of prediction, Spengler's formulations blurred the difference in *purpose* between the two varieties of thought.[56]

On the basis of this epistemological transformation, finally, Spengler sought to justify his doubt about the course of Western culture. The decline of belief in metaphysics, the growth of skepticism, the imperialistic motives of the Great War—all were amalgamated within the framework of Spengler's work: "Ever and again [the] type of strong-spirited, thoroughly nonmetaphysical man emerges. In his hands lies the spiritual and material fate of every late epoch. He carries out the Babylonian, Egyptian, Indian, Chinese and Roman imperialism. In such periods, Buddhism, Stoicism, and socialism ripen into final world temperaments, which allow a fading humanity to conceive and transform its substance one more time."[57]

Setting aside the elaborate historical constructions on which Spengler's doubt was based, his larger message of decline would hardly seem to have been new. As Heidegger pointed out in a later lecture, Spengler's doubts about modern Western civilization had been anticipated several decades before in far subtler form by Nietzsche.[58] A crucial difference was that Nietzsche, despite his deep sensibility and seductive prose, remained an outsider—even an object of reproof—to the academic world until 1914.[59] Only in the postwar climate of radical questioning did such expressions of loss of faith penetrate the academic world on a large scale. The German collapse and the broad revelation of the negative potential of modern culture brought a new and more general urgency to the problem of historical meaning—and new doubts about its traditional solutions.

While Spengler's philosophy of history gained an enormous audience, more demanding thinkers who questioned the soundness of Western cultural traditions often drew from the philosophy of Nietzsche. Reminiscing in 1937 on what he saw as the more profound relevance of Nietzsche, Heidegger wrote:

What a revelation it was two decades ago [1917] for the multitude unfamiliar with genuine thought and its rich history, as Spengler himself believed to have found out for the first time that every age and every culture has its own worldview. However, this was all just a very skillful and spirited popularization of thoughts and questions that had long ago—and most recently by Nietzsche—been more deeply thought. These [matters], nevertheless, were by no means mastered, and to this hour have still not been mastered.[60]

In treating Spengler and the critical theories of history in the "Introduction to the Phenomenology of Religion," Heidegger did not speak of Nietzsche's philosophy. Nevertheless, Nietzsche's argument in the "Use and Abuse of History," which Heidegger drew on in *Being and Time,* anticipated the central theme of Heidegger's methodological introduction to these course lectures on religion in 1920–21. In the opening pages of these lectures, Heidegger identified what he considered to be the predominant quality of historical reflection in contemporary culture: its burdensome, disturbing character for factical life experience.[61]

The suggestion that historical understanding presented difficulties for life was a new note in Heidegger's thought. Only a few years before, he could approach history as the natural arena of human realization; the problematic character of historical thought had not yet become the commanding theme of analysis. In an intellectual setting where the utter complexity of the problem of historical meaning had begun to reveal itself, Heidegger's attention, too, was focused on this more disturbing theme. In the series of lectures "Introduction to the Phenomenology of Religion," Heidegger emphasized, above all, what he characterized as the multiple expressions of historical consciousness lending significance to the "problem of the historical [*Problem des Historischen*]."[62]

But why, Heidegger asked, should historical understanding prove disturbing? What relation did this bothersome character of historical thought have to the theories of Windelband, Rickert, Simmel, Troeltsch, Dilthey, and Spengler? The response to these questions requires a closer examination of the sense of the historical as Heidegger presented it in the text of his lectures.

Heidegger first pointed out what he saw as the dual character of historical understanding, which is not purely problematic, but can exercise an affirmative role in directing attention away from all that is merely present, opening awareness to other periods and the possibility of other life aspects. Nonetheless, especially in contemporary culture, the quest for historical understanding exercises a detrimental influence by intruding on the impulse toward creative production (*Schaffen*). In a passage reminiscent of Nietzsche's earlier ideas, Heidegger explained that this intrusion is experienced as a dampening of enthusiasm to create; history testified to the ephemerality of all creation and proclaimed that all creation itself had to give way and become historical.[63]

Against this disturbing aspect of the historical, Heidegger asserted that factical life experience continually sought a means of self-assertion, which became the central motive for historical reflection. He sought to relate this motive to the predominant forms of historical thinking of his times, which he divided into various ways of establishing security against the burden of the historical. In this lecture series, Heidegger separated the forms of contemporary historical theorizing into groups, according to their response to the most extreme attempt to resolve the problem of the historical. This extreme attempt, exemplified by the Platonic heritage, was situated at the center of contemporary historical thinking, and sought to escape from the burden of the historical through a denial of its fundamental meaning. For the Platonic style of reasoning the historical, as ephemeral, was only secondary: truth lay in the discernment of ideal, eternal meaning which the historical only faintly reflected. The historical had no claim over eternal elements it could never vanquish.

Heidegger situated Windelband and Rickert closest to the Platonic style of questioning, albeit modified by their Kantian viewpoint. Both of these thinkers ascribed a fundamental meaning to the historical, which did not, however, contradict Platonism, because this meaning did not originate in historical reality itself, but in the value-conferring acts of consciousness. Where on the level of human comprehension, meanings or values were subject to variation, they nonetheless manifested a basic coherence. This coherence, withstanding the erosive forces of historical reality, was ultimately ascribable to an eternal, transcendent source. The aim of historical thinking was to provide an empirical manifestation of ideal traces of coherence in which this transcendent source revealed its work.

Even if Windelband and Rickert did not represent a *Lebensphilosophie,* in Heidegger's view, their ideas nonetheless clearly manifested the self-assertion of life against the historical. For them, historical meaning was purely an affair of consciousness, which determined the historical character of the objects it investigated. History was not a process capable of menacing values or meaning in any ultimate sense because the transcendent source of the consciousness that formed them remained at a distance from the caprices of historical variation.

Heidegger considered Simmel and Dilthey to be more distant from the Platonic influence. Described as the contemporary advocates of *Lebensphilosophie,* these thinkers made the transcendent values of Windelband and Rickert immanent expressions of life. In their respective ways of theorizing, life became a repository of ideas that served to orient it in a continuous process. A kernel of Platonism manifested itself in their philosophies in the presupposition that each adopted of an ongoing coherence in the ideas that life objectified in its historical development. For Simmel and Dilthey, this coherence offered a measure of security against the burden of historical transience.

In a preamble on the theme of the phenomenology of religion, Heidegger divided Troeltsch's theory of history into two periods: in the first, Troeltsch was most strongly influenced by Windelband and Rickert; in the second, he moved close to the ideas of Dilthey.

Heidegger described Spengler's thought as an inverted form of the Platonic outlook, where meaning arose in the generative matrix of the historical process, and any possibility of transcendence of the historical was negated. Consciousness did not retain an autonomous base of coherence in the midst of the historical material it analyzed: consciousness, meaning, and value were all determined by a historically evolving cultural soul.

Despite Spengler's bold anti-Platonic stance, Heidegger discerned in his work yet another set of ideas entangled in the Platonic web. In Heidegger's estimation, Spengler fell prey to the very style of Platonic reasoning he sought to negate. To comprehend this, Heidegger asserted that one needed only to examine what Spengler described as the source of decline of Western culture. Spengler discovered this source in an estrangement of the self from its meaning-giving acts, yet the self was not ultimately responsible for its acts. Rather, Spengler presupposed this estrangement as an unavoidable condition arising in a blindly objective historical process. The possibility of coherence was simply displaced onto a larger, anonymous milieu. Spengler thus transferred the production of objective meaning from an ideal seat in conscious-ness to an ironclad flow of the historical process. Platonism, the theo-ry of a preeminence of objective meaning beyond merely factual appearances, was maintained in an inverted form.

For Heidegger, Spengler's approach radicalized the tacit motives impelling each of the other theories in pushing historical objectification to its limit.[64] In each case, however, objective coherence remained the source of historical meaning, and responsibility for the factical sense of human existence (*des menschlichen Daseins*) as the root of the disturbing aspect of historical transience was conveniently set aside (*eingestellt*).

To clarify his viewpoint, Heidegger introduced the theme of type construction, which we have already encountered in the "Annotations." Noting that Spengler and each of the other thinkers in question employed a kind of type construction in their theories of history, he described it as the most characteristic form of historical thinking in con-temporary culture, and the most effective means of displacing the bur-den of the historical onto an objective coherence of history.[65]

In Heidegger's view, Spengler's use of type demonstrated, in all cases, an identical motive, one that tacitly unified his thought with that of the elder theorists—despite the extremes to which his morphology of culture pushed the concept of type construction. In each case, type construction neglected the source of the burden of the historical in the self and in its care (*Bekümmerung*), as elicited by factical life experi-ence. Because the past was arranged and objectified, the threat of the historical was disguised by means of theoretical abstractions.

From the notion of a tacit unity of motives underlying all the impor-tant examples of contemporary historical thinking he investigated, Heidegger drew a conclusion with important consequences: the central dichotomy in the historical theories of his times was not between Platonism and anti-Platonism; rather, it was between the historical considered as science and the historical comprehended as the focus of philosophy standing outside the domain of the contemporary sciences. Only the latter, according to Heidegger, could break through the rei-fied systems of thought in the contemporary intellectual environment to reinterpret the sense of the self in factical life experience. If the objectifications of contemporary science precluded the genuine con-sideration of this theme from the outset, only a philosophy capable of seeing through the motives of science could bring it back into view.

Heidegger's manner of opposing science (*Wissenschaft*) to philosophy throughout his lectures bears more widely on the problem of historical meaning. Most significant in this respect, though he recognized important variants in the notion of historical "science" along the path from neo-Kantian values to Spengler's theories, Heidegger refused to ascribe a fundamental character to *any* of them. At the level of tacit motives, he viewed each variant as far less than a genuine confrontation with the problem of the historical.

Heidegger's thinking proved significant as much for the distinctions it omitted as for the ones it expressly made. He passed over the central features that united all of the critical theorists and set their style of theorizing apart from that of Spengler: unlike Spengler, all had distinguished between historical and natural methods of understanding and between *all* science and the claim of naturalistic metaphysics.

Considering Spengler's goal to "predetermine history"—to make history a predictive discipline, achieving on a metaphysical foundation the exactitude of a law-constructing natural science—Heidegger's omission is highly significant. By referring the historical to nonobjectifying philosophy, as opposed to objectifying science, Heidegger called into question the distinction between two contradictory conceptions of history, carefully separated by a long tradition of German historiography rooted in the thought of Humboldt and Ranke: history as a law-constituting discipline on the naturalistic model and history as an autonomous science, operating according to its own unique methods. Heidegger simply bypassed the *Methodenstreit* of prewar Germany: all authentic historical understanding was merged with philosophy as he conceived it.

The refusal to admit such fundamental distinctions in historical thinking harmonized well with Heidegger's quest to explode the contemporary categories of thought. Most directly, it served to undermine not only what Heidegger viewed as pretensions to a "systematic" philosophy abstracted from historical concerns, but also any conception of the historical that claimed independence from philosophy. Here, too, Heidegger contradicted the tradition of German historical scholarship that sought to establish history as an autonomous science. As we saw in chapter 2, this tradition aimed to liberate historical scholarship as much from the tutelage of a fixed philosophical orientation as from the mechanistic methods of natural science. Whatever disagreements Windelband, Rickert, Troeltsch, Simmel, and Dilthey might have had among themselves over historical method, all viewed the establishment of an autonomous historical science as a primary goal.

From Spengler, who sought to solve the riddle of history through a naturalistic form of comprehension, on the one side, and from Heidegger, who placed historical thinking under the wing of a philosophy of existence, on the other, the German historical tradition faced formidable opposition. Whereas Spengler's variety of argumentation proved less convincing in the long run, Heidegger's approach, which came to full expression in *Being and Time* and his works of the 1930s, introduced a highly influential countercurrent to respond to the "question of the sense of historical being [*Frage nach dem Sinn des geschichtlichen Seins*]."[66]

NOTES

1. Löwith, "Les implications politiques de la philosophie de l'existence chez Heidegger," 343–60. See also Löwith, *Mein Leben in Deutschland vor und nach 1933: Ein Bericht*, 28 (English translation: *My Life in Germany before and after 1933: A Report*), and "Der europäische Nihilismus: Betrachtungen zur Vorgeschichte des europäischen Krieges," in *Weltgeschichte und Heilsgeschehen: Zur Kritik der Geschichtsphilosophie*, 515–16 (English translation: *European Nihilism*).

2. Heidegger, "Anmerkungen," 70–100 (reprinted in *Wegmarken*; vol. 9 of *Gesamtausgabe*).

3. Reflecting back on this period, Karl Löwith observed, in Löwith et al., *Martin Heidegger im Gespräch*, 38–39:

These years after World War I were the most beautiful, the richest, and the most fruitful of my generation. They brought forth almost everything from which, even today, we spiritually live. At the same time these years were designated by a critique of all that had been handed down [*an allem Überlieferten*] and that still remained. The younger generation cannot rightly imagine the radicalism of this critique because, after surviving a similar catastrophe, its members rebel, not out of genuine hunger and inner urging [*Drang*], but out of boredom and satiety [*Überdruss*]. The slogan of *Being and Time,* the "destruction" of all traditional metaphysics and ontology, had its driving motive in this situation after World War I. It spoke to us in an immediately positive [*positiv*] way because the conviction lived in one's consciousness that nothing remaining could remain, if it had not been fundamentally questioned and renewed.

4. In the lectures "Phänomenologische Interpretationen zu Aristoteles: Anzeige der hermeneutischen Situation" (written in 1922 and first published in 1989), 267, Heidegger characterized the task of "destruction" as "the authentic path on which the present in its own fundamental movements [*Grundbewegtheiten*] must be encountered, and, indeed, encountered in such a way that the perpetual question of how far [the present] itself appropriates and interprets the radical possibilities of fundamental experience surges out of history."

5. Heidegger, "Anmerkungen," 73.

6. Arendt, "Martin Heidegger ist achtzig Jahre alt," 893–94.

7. Gadamer, *Kleine Schriften*, 3:205.

8. Heidegger, "Anmerkungen," 79. Heidegger expressed a similar admiration for Dilthey in his course lectures of this period, which remained unpublished until recent years. See, for example, Heidegger's 1919 Freiburg lecture series "Phänomenologie und transzendentale Wertphilosophie," in *Gesamtausgabe*, 56/57:164–65, and also his 1920 lecture series "Phänomenologie der Anschauung und des Ausdrucks," in *Gesamtausgabe*, 59:155–58.

9. Heidegger, "Anmerkungen," 99.

10. See Heidegger, letters to Heinrich Rickert, January 27, 1920, and June 25, 1921, in Heidegger and Rickert, *Briefe*, 49, 56.

11. Arendt, "Martin Heidegger," 894.

12. Heidegger, "Anmerkungen," 93, 97.

13. Following the example of John Macquarrie and Edward Robinson, translators of *Being and Time*, to preserve a key distinction, I have throughout translated Heidegger's "*faktisch*" (referring only to *Dasein*) as "factical" and his "*tatsächlich*" (taken in the more general sense) as "factual."

14. Heidegger, "Anmerkungen," 89.

15. Ibid., 71. In a contemporary course lecture, "Phänomenologie der Anschauung und des Ausdrucks" (written in 1920 and first published in 1993), in *Gesamtausgabe*, 59:154, Heidegger went even further in this direction: "*Lebensphilosophie* is for us a necessary step on the path of philosophy, in contradistinction to empty formal transcendental philosophy. One sets Dilthey under the concept of historicism and fears in him the specter of relativism; but we must lose the fear of this specter." In the appendix to this lecture (p. 190), he went on to say: "Standard [is] never an absolute, [it is] above all relative, when one considers, that in this we [not only] strive toward the origin [itself] as idea, but toward the concrete and unique. Relativism [is] unavoidable!"

Windelband's and Rickert's attempts to overcome historicism by positing absolute values met with Heidegger's sharp criticism in the Freiburg course lectures of 1919, "Die Idee der Philosophie und das Weltanschauungsproblem," in *Gesamtausgabe*, 56/57:27–39. Husserl's call, in his 1910 *Logos* essay

"Philosophie als strenge Wissenschaft," for an absolute foundation for philosophy, capable of withstanding the threats of relativism and historicism, was criticized by Heidegger in the 1923–24 course lectures "Einführung in die phänomenologische Forschung," in *Gesamtausgabe*, 17:88–100. On this theme, see also Heidegger's remarks in app. 1 to the lectures "Phänomenologische Interpretationen zu Aristoteles: Einführung in die phänomenologische Forschung," in *Gesamtausgabe*, 61:162–67. Four years later, Heidegger returned to this theme and questioned the presuppositions of both Rickert and Husserl in his lecture course series "Logik: Die Frage nach der Wahrheit." See *Gesamtausgabe*, 21:31–127.

16. Heidegger, "Anmerkungen," 72.

17. See, in this regard, Heidegger's early Freiburg course lecture series "Phänomenologie der Anschauung und des Ausdrucks: Theorie der philosophischen Begriffsbildung" (1920), in *Gesamtausgabe*, 59:36–41; "Phänomenologische Interpretationen zu Aristoteles: Einführung in die phänomenologische Forschung" (1921–22), in *Gesamtausgabe*, 61:110–17. In light of Heidegger's critique of the theoretical criteria of contemporary historical reflection in *Being and Time* (discussed in chapter 5), it is also important to note his attack in the early Freiburg lectures on the criteria of "general validity [*Allgemeingültigkeit*]," which each of the critical theorists had taken to be fundamental standards of historical understanding and central to the task of overcoming "relativism" and "skepticism"—and which Heidegger berated as a "miscomprehension of the fundamental sense of facticity [*Verkennen des Grundsinns der Faktizität*]" in "Phänomenologische Interpretationen zu Aristoteles," in *Gesamtausgabe*, 61:87.

18. Heidegger, "Anmerkungen," 72. It remains unclear how Heidegger could have hoped to achieve presuppositionlessness in any generally accepted sense, given the interrelation of all thought with the preconceptions of factical-historical experience.

19. Ibid., 78. This critique did not prevent Heidegger from acknowledging his debt to Rickert for his comprehension of historical reflection. Heidegger, letter to Heinrich Rickert, March 15, 1921, in Heidegger and Rickert, *Briefe*, 34–35. In this same letter, Heidegger announced he was planning to hold a seminar in the coming winter semester on Rickert's *Grenzen*, which was in fact never held. Ibid.,126.

20. Heidegger, "Anmerkungen," 91. That such statements were indeed directed against Husserl and Rickert (among other possible targets) became clear in course lectures of the 1920s. Rickert's notion of a consciousness in general (*Bewusstsein überhaupt*) was the object of reproof in Heidegger's 1919 course lectures "Die Idee der Philosophie und das Weltanschauungsproblem," in *Gesamtausgabe*, 56/57:29–58, as it was in the 1920–21 lectures "Einleitung

in die Phänomenologie der Religion," in *Gesamtausgabe,* 60:3–66—where he also took Husserl's description of "regional consciousness" to task (pp. 55–62)—and in his 1928 lecture series "Die Grundprobleme der Phänomenologie," in *Gesamtausgabe,* 24:183.

21. Heidegger, " Anmerkungen," 81.

22. Ibid., 82.

23. Ibid., 96.

24. For an account of Dilthey's conception of the typology of worldviews, see Dilthey, "Beiträge zum Studium der Individualität," in *Geistige Welt,* 241–317. In the "Annotations," Heidegger underlines the "aesthetic" motive that to his mind impels Jaspers's typology and Dilthey's concept of life. That this aesthetic motive directly concerns Dilthey's typology of worldviews comes to the fore, above all, in Heidegger's 1920 Freiburg course lecture series "Phänomenologie der Anschauung und des Ausdrucks," in *Gesamtausgabe,* 59:155–68, where he took Dilthey's typology of worldviews to task, along with what Heidegger qualified as the aesthetic motive governing Dilthey's concentration on form (*das Gestalthafte*). This would become a central topic of Heidegger's critique of Dilthey in *Being and Time,* as we will see in chapter 5.

25. Heidegger, "Anmerkungen," 92.

26. Ibid.

27. Ibid. On this theme, see also Heidegger, *Gesamtausgabe,* 63:14–33.

28. Heidegger, "Anmerkungen," 93.

29. Jaspers, *Philosophische Autobiographie,* 94–95.

30. Hans Saner, the editor of the work in which the "Annotations" were first published, commented on Jaspers's note at the end of the article. Heidegger, "Anmerkungen," 100.

31. Jaspers, *Philosophische Autobiographie,* 94.

32. Ibid.

33. Heidegger, letters to Karl Jaspers, June 27, 1922, and July 14, 1923. Heidegger and Jaspers, *Briefwechsel, 1920–1963,* 26–43.

34. Jaspers, *Philosophische Autobiographie,* 92–93.

35. Heidegger, "Mein Weg," in *Zur Sache des Denkens,* 86.

36. Heidegger's critical attitude toward Husserlian phenomenology, which was already apparent in the "Annotations," came to light in other of his utterances of the period. For example, in his letter to Heinrich Rickert, January 27, 1920, Heidegger explained that Husserlian phenomenology was essentially inspired by the "mathematical natural sciences," while he sought to ground his own approach in "living historical life itself [*im lebendigen geschichtlichen Leben selbst*]." Heidegger and Rickert, *Briefe,* 48. Later, in his letter to Jaspers, December 26, 1926, on the eve of *Being and Time*'s publication (1927), Heidegger expressed bitterness over Rickert's having recently blocked

his appointment to a chair in Heidelberg; he then made the surprising assertion that *Being and Time* was written against Husserl, above all (it was in fact dedicated to Husserl "in friendship and veneration"; see *Sein und Zeit,* iii). Heidegger and Jaspers, *Briefwechsel,* 71–72.

37. Gadamer, *Philosophische Lehrjahre,* 34.

38. Heidegger and Rickert, *Briefe,* 56–58; see esp. Rickert's letter to Heidegger, July 17, 1929, on Heidegger's sharp criticism of neo-Kantianism and of Rickert's philosophy during Heidegger's 1929 debate with Ernst Cassirer at Davos.

39. Jaspers, *Philosophische Autobiographie,* 35–40.

40. Löwith, "Implications politiques," 347. Löwith made this comparison on the basis of what he viewed as the strong impact of these three thinkers on the younger generation in Germany: "It is from a single source that it is necessary to understand the extraordinary fascination that Spengler, Barth, and Heidegger, despite the diversity of their spiritual tendencies, exerted over the young generation of Germans after World War I."

41. Gadamer, Introduction to Heidegger, *Ursprung,* 102–4.

42. Heidegger, *Gesamtausgabe,* 26:177. After mentioning the problem of temporality, Heidegger asked if the importance of the problem arose from its having been dealt with by thinkers such as "Bergson and his follower Spengler," by Husserl, Dilthey, or Kierkegaard:

> Thus the analysis of finite human existence [*Dasein*] would have been devised in relation to time because it was thought that it arranged things very well to fuse together the above-named thinkers? . . . It is all too often little Moritz's representation of philosophy, who reckons that out of five authors a sixth will be made; (I already came to terms with Kierkegaard before there were any dialectical writings, and with Dilthey when it was still unbecoming to mention him in a philosophical seminar).

43. Gadamer, Introduction to Heidegger, *Ursprung,* 102–4.

44. Note, for example, Bultmann's instructive words in 1924: "Liberal theology receives its character essentially through the predominance of *historical interest.*" According to Bultmann, the major representatives of liberal theology included Wilhelm Herrmann and the great "Aporetician" of liberal theology, Ernst Troeltsch. Bultmann, "Die liberale Theologie und die jüngste theologische Bewegung," in *Glauben und Verstehen,* 1:1–2.

45. Bultmann, letter to Hans von Soden, December 23, 1923, as cited in Jaspert, *Rudolf Bultmanns Werk und Wirkung,* 202. Heidegger again praised Gogarten and also Karl Barth in an unpublished letter addressed to his student at that time Karl Löwith and dated August 24, 1925: "What still shows signs of 'life' is the Barth-Gogarten movement, which is carefully and independently

represented by Bultmann in Marburg, and since, indeed, theology is continually . . . being imputed to me, I may travel along with this movement, although I
have expressed my skepticism clearly enough." I am grateful to the late Ada
Löwith and to Klaus Stichweh for permission to read and cite this letter, mentioned by Löwith in *Mein Leben,* 29.

46. Gogarten, "Zwischen den Zeiten," in Barth et al., *Anfänge der dialektischen Theologie,* 2:98.

47. Troeltsch, *Der Historismus und seine Probleme,* ix.

48. See, for example, Heussi, *Krisis*; Iggers, *German Conception of
History*; Troeltsch quotation is from *Historismus,* 4.

49. See, in this context, Heidegger's 1920 course lectures
"Phänomenologie der Anschauung," in *Gesamtausgabe,* 59:16–17.

50. Troeltsch, *Gesammelte Schriften,* 4:684; Rickert, *Grenzen,* 478.

51. In Max Scheler's opinion, for example, "The immense effect of [*The
Decline of the West*] and the exciting impression of novelty it created [are]
psychologically understandable only in relation to Germany's defeat in the
war." Scheler, *Deutsche Philosophie der Gegenwart,* 323.

52. Spengler, *Der Untergang des Abendlandes,* 1:514. In Spengler's
words: "There are no eternal questions; there are only questions that are felt
and asked in the existence [*Dasein*] of a historical-individual humanity, within the context of a single culture." Apparently, Spengler's philosophy was the
only one capable of transcending the historical horizon of its culture.

53. Heidegger, "Einleitung," in *Gesamtausgabe,* 60:38. In later works,
Heidegger was especially critical of this aspect of Spengler's thought, and
especially of the suggestion that philosophy might be reducible to an expression of culture. In a 1930 essay, Heidegger wrote of an enslavement of philosophical thought, "whose destitute sort hides itself in the subterfuge of
making philosophy valid as an 'expression' of 'culture' (Spengler), and as an
ornament of a productive humanity." Heidegger, "Vom Wesen der Wahrheit,"
in *Wegmarken,* 95.

54. Spengler, *Untergang,* 1:62.

55. Ibid., 3.

56. This is true despite Spengler's superficial distinction between history
and nature.

57. Spengler, *Untergang,* 1:44.

58. Heidegger, "Der Spruch des Anaximander," in *Holzwege,* 301.

59. Ernst Cassirer pointed out, with considerable justice, that Spengler's
methodology was anticipated by Karl Lamprecht's prewar historical psychology. Cassirer, *The Problem of Knowledge,* 282. Spengler's extension of ideas
that Karl Lamprecht and Kurt Breysig had developed in the pre–World War I
period was also mentioned in passing by Heidegger in his 1920 course lecture

series "Phänomenologie der Anschauung," in *Gesamtausgabe,* 59:16. An important difference was that Lamprecht, a university professor in the prewar intellectual context, came to the liberal conclusion that German culture was experiencing *progress* and not decline.

60. Heidegger, *Nietzsche,* 1:360.

61. Heidegger, "Einleitung," in *Gesamtausgabe,* 60:33–38.

62. Ibid., 37–38.

63. Ibid., 38.

64. Ibid., 40–52.

65. One might object that Windelband's and Rickert's theories seem to contradict Heidegger's statement because, for them, the historical searched out the unique quality of the past. Heidegger anticipated such an objection by arguing that Windelband's and Rickert's assumption of transcendent values presupposed typification of relative human values in relation to an alleged absolute source. See ibid., 44.

66. In 1925, Heidegger wrote that the question of the sense of historical being had arisen ever more forcefully since the end of the nineteenth century. Heidegger, "Wilhelm Diltheys Forschungsarbeit und der gegenwärtige Kampf um eine historische Weltanschauung" (Kasseler Vorträge), 146–47; see also Rodi, "Die Bedeutung Diltheys für die Konzeption von 'Sein und Zeit': Zum Umfeld von Heideggers Kasseler Vorträgen (1925)," 161–77.

4

The Theological Roots of Heidegger's Interpretation of Historical Meaning

As THE TITLES of his 1920–21 Freiburg lectures ("Introduction to the Phenomenology of Religion" and "Augustine and Neoplatonism") indicate, Heidegger was at this time concerned with religious thinkers and religious themes. For one who had written from a Catholic neo-Scholastic perspective only a few years before, this preoccupation with religious subjects might not seem surprising. Yet his more recent focus on historical existence betrayed an important shift in emphasis: the open, historically accomplished and variable sense of the self introduced in Heidegger's post–World War I lectures and writings could not have stood on the static ground of "human nature" borrowed from Catholic theology, as proposed in his 1916 *Habilitationsschrift* (postdoctoral dissertation) on Duns Scotus. The historicized approach to the self that Heidegger developed, invoking "destruction in the history of thought," was at least as foreign to the Catholic theological tradition as it was to the main currents of historical and philosophical thinking in the pre-1914 era.

Heidegger's departure from a neo-Thomist stance to a more fluid vision of historical meaning was accompanied by an important shift in his religious orientation, a shift witnessed by his mentor, Edmund Husserl. In a 1919 letter to the theologian Rudolf Otto, Husserl denied any responsibility for Heidegger's "passage over to the ground of Protestantism" (while admitting that his own "philosophical effect has something remarkably revolutionary about it: Protestants become Catholic, Catholics become Protestant").[1] Whether such a "passage" actually took place has been questioned.[2] Beyond question, however, were Heidegger's profound interest and personal involvement in Protestant theology, even though he never formally abandoned the Catholic Church.

At the time of Husserl's letter, Heidegger had been married for two years to a Protestant woman, Elfriede Petri. He had begun an intensive study of Luther's writings,[3] which he would favorably assess in his course lectures of the early 1920s, especially in the second part of the "Einleitung in die Phänomenologie der Religion" (Introduction to the phenomenology of religion). Contemporary reports show that he was deeply impressed by the modern Protestant thinkers Sören Kierkegaard and Franz Overbeck, and by the more recent neo-orthodox theologians Karl Barth, Rudolf Bultmann, and Friedrich Gogarten.[4] In a 1923 letter to Hans von Soden (referred to briefly in the previous chapter), Bultmann wrote of Heidegger's religious outlook, in much the same terms as Husserl had four years before. Here he describes Heidegger's participation in a theology seminar Bultmann attended shortly after Heidegger's appointment to Marburg:

> This time the Seminar is especially instructive for me, due to the participation of our new philosopher, Heidegger, a student of Husserl. He comes from Catholicism, but is entirely Protestant. This he demonstrated recently during a debate after one of [Heinrich] Hermelink's lectures on Luther and the Middle Ages. He not only has an extraordinary knowledge of Scholasticism, but also of Luther, and he somewhat embarrassed Hermelink by conceiving the question more profoundly than this latter thinker. It is of interest that Heidegger—also familiar with modern theology and having special respect for [Wilhelm] Herrmann—knows Gogarten and Barth as well. The former, above all, he values [einschätzt] exactly as I do. You can imagine how important it is for me that you come here to join in on the discussion. The older generation is unable to participate because its members no longer even understand the problem to which we are lending our efforts.[5]

It is clear that Heidegger's religious outlook, like his notion of the historical, underwent important changes at this time. Might the simultaneity of these changes be more than accidental? Might there be a relation between his new historical viewpoint and significant theological motives shared with the younger generation of theologians, setting them apart from the "older generation" to which Bultmann referred?

I

Before World War I, liberal Protestant theology constituted only one facet of a multifaceted Protestant following in Germany. Since Luther's time, Protestantism had split into a multitude of sects along social and economic lines: for this reason, it is impossible to speak of one unified Protestant Church. In an article published in 1920, Ernst Troeltsch described the "difficult situation of German Protestantism, . . . which is in part an annex to the conservative form of the State and its ruling strata, in part the corporate religion, in old Lutheran fashion, of peasant and petit bourgeois circles, in part a half-scientific religion concerned with culture, and in part an experimental field for religious subjectivity."[6]

In the period before the war, liberal Protestant theologians tended to share one conviction that generally cut across social differences: the German nation was participating in an extraordinary process of historical development. In its intellectual focus, however, liberal theology remained separate—even isolated—from other Protestant currents. Over the course of the nineteenth century, university theologians, who constituted the overwhelming majority of liberal theologians, embraced an inquisitive, scientific approach to religion as a cultural phenomenon. Like important currents of late-nineteenth-century philosophy and historical theory, liberal Protestant theology had been influenced by the scientific aims of the neo-Kantian movement. And like their philosopher and historian counterparts, these theologians sought a rigorous method of analysis that respected the autonomy of human ideas and values, which they saw as more than mere products of psychological, biological, or other purely causal processes. In arguing that the phenomena of human culture were not subject to analysis after the fashion of the law-constructing natural sciences, the neo-Kantian worldview fulfilled a crucial role. The question now arose, could analysis of religious phenomena using the methods of the human sciences indeed serve the genuine interests of religion?

As in philosophy and historical theory, scientific rigor in theology meant emphasizing inductive methods in the empirical study of, in this case, cultural manifestations of religion—and de-emphasizing the claims of a closed metaphysical system, in favor of a study of historical appearances. It meant, in short, tailoring theology to the concerns of the immanent cultural world.

An early proponent of this outlook was the influential theologian and Bible scholar Albrecht Ritschl. An important source of inspiration for liberal theology, Ritschl ascribed two fundamental tasks to a theology that had set aside the speculative concerns of metaphysics: first, to define the historical meaning of Christianity in the cultural world; second, to determine its relation to practical-ethical imperatives.[7] Theology was fitted to the task of critical research, and the quest for God was directed toward what were taken to be His workings in an immanent historical and moral universe.

Ritschl's theology reinterpreted the ideas of an earlier spiritual mentor of liberal theology, Friedrich Schleiermacher, with whom Ritschl affirmed the need to grasp religious belief as it is manifested historically.[8] For both thinkers, historical understanding presupposed an overarching meaning that tacitly informed empirical material. While this meaning never became explicit to the point where the empirical content of religion might be deduced in some grand metaphysical style, it provided an ongoing principle of coherence, which permitted inductive-historical demarcation.

With their respect for the empirical content of religion, Ritschl and Schleiermacher alike viewed religion as more than a mere vehicle for ethical maxims. Although neither thinker could accept Kant's derivation of the necessity of religion from the dictates of practical reason, Ritschl was unwilling to establish the autonomy of religion on a universal "religious feeling," as Schleiermacher had done.[9] Drawing upon Lotze, Ritschl used a value philosophy (*Wertphilosophie*) to mediate between the Kantian derivation of religion from ethics and Schleiermacher's intuition of it in feeling. He saw religion as autonomous with regard to ethics, although comprehensible in terms of value judgments that were more readily recognizable than Schleiermacher's *Gefühl*.[10]

The Ritschl school provided a starting point for two liberal theologians—who would become major targets of neo-orthodox theology— Ernst Troeltsch and Adolf von Harnack. In his course lecture series "Introduction to the Phenomenology of Religion" and "Augustine and Neoplatonism," Heidegger took these two thinkers (and Dilthey) to task for treating Christianity as a historical objectification.

Although Troeltsch moved well beyond the confines of neo-Kantian formalism, his emphasis on scientific, historical research, as opposed to final metaphysical conclusions, brought his thought within the intellectual orbit of Harnack and other liberal theologians closer to the neo-Kantian worldview. In harmony with critical historical scholarship, both Troeltsch and Harnack concentrated on historical evidence in biblical study. In his influential *Das Wesen des Christentums* (The essence of Christianity), Harnack affirmed the possibility of inductively discovering the essence of Christianity from its historical manifestations: "What is Christianity?—Here we want to attempt to answer this question only in its historical sense: that is, by means of historical science [*Wissenschaft*], and with the life experience [*Lebenserfahrung*] that has been acquired from lived history."[11]

Troeltsch, too, and thinkers who stood close to him, such as Wilhelm Bousset, Johannes Weiss, and Wilhelm Wrede, sought to study Christianity as a historical movement, focusing on its interrelation with a given cultural context, as opposed to approaching it as a purely transcendent phenomenon.Yet, as in philosophy, the application of historical methods in theology, while fruitful, was also fraught with difficulties, of which perspicacious thinkers such as Ernst Troeltsch were especially aware. Liberal historical study sought a sense of coherence in historical Christianity, but, as Troeltsch pointed out in his critique of Harnack's *Wesen des Christentums,* a systematic comparison of the various stages of Christianity could not be made on the basis of historical induction alone.[12] A synthesis of the reported teachings of Jesus in the early Gospels with Catholic ideas from various periods of the Middle Ages and with modern Protestant ideas would not, of its own accord, form a unified Christian essence. Such an essence could only be discerned by virtue of presuppositions.

Neither Harnack nor the more radical Troeltsch had ever gone so far as to declare that the absoluteness of the Christian essence could be historically verified.[13] Herein lay the heart of a paradox that the neo-orthodox thinkers and Heidegger did not fail to notice: while avowing the necessity of absolutes for religious belief, both Harnack and Troeltsch asserted the inability of historical scholarship to provide them. What, then, could be the purpose of historical understanding in theology?

The response to this question rested on an assumption having theological roots in the thought of Schleiermacher and Ritschl. Like these earlier thinkers, Harnack and Troeltsch shared a belief that historical study uncovers empirical manifestations of faith, which in turn confirm the assumption about coherence in the historical process. Empirical manifestations of faith are meaningful in pointing toward a higher source of coherence than history itself.

Such a conviction was clearly at work in Harnack's quest for an inductively ascertainable historical essence of Christianity. If Troeltsch considered the meaning of Christianity to be less readily comprehensible than did Harnack, he nonetheless did not deny its objective coherence in history.[14] With the passing years, he came to have greater doubts, without entirely surrendering his earlier faith.

Troeltsch's unwillingness to retreat before his doubts could be seen in his openness to the sociological conclusions of his colleague Max Weber, who had traced the effects of the spirit of Protestantism in the development of the modern social, political, and economic world. In pursuing some of Weber's central themes, Troeltsch could not help but draw similar conclusions about the secularization of older forms of belief in modern social institutions. As Troeltsch explained in *Die Bedeutung des Protestantismus für die Entstehung der modernen Welt* (The significance of Protestantism for the rise of the modern world), the changes that the Reformation had brought to all forms of cultural life gave the initial impulse to secular institutions, which soon moved beyond the framework of the original Protestant design.[15]

Such conclusions were not altogether optimistic for the future of belief. Writing about the distressing side of Troeltsch's prewar thought, Karl Barth observed: "If I am not mistaken, Troeltsch's exclamations about the preliminary sociological meaning of the Church and his gloomy outlook concerning ice ages to come, in which it all could come to an end, was the last prewar stage worth noting that this discussion was to reach. We listened to him then [Aarau, 1910] with the dark feeling that it had all reached a deadend."[16]

Because Troeltsch explicitly linked the certitude of theology to that of other normative concerns, including logic, the connection between theological conclusions and the problem of relativism, which was to become his chief concern, followed quite readily. At this sensitive point, the younger generation of theologians and, in his own fashion, Heidegger himself attempted to discredit Troeltsch's theological method.[17] The problem of relativism, seen as the inevitable outcome of liberal theology, was not pursued in Troeltschean fashion; the younger generation simply sought a different point of departure for theology.

Not all of the outstanding university theologians associated with the liberal movement, however, were prepared to follow Troeltsch or Harnack in their emphasis on scientific, historical research. Another distinguished theologian, Wilhelm Herrmann, who, though he did not rank himself among the liberals, shared their distrust of the older orthodoxy, argued against any possible consideration of theology as a science among other sciences. In pointed opposition to Harnack and Troeltsch, Herrmann asserted that historical scholarship can only analyze psychological manifestations of religion; it cannot account for the essential, otherworldly character of religious phenomena, which always remain beyond empirical-historical verification. Among the members of the older generation of theologians, Herrmann stood closest to the position Barth, Gogarten, and Bultmann would adopt, and to the persuasion of Heidegger.

A common presupposition united Herrmann with Troeltsch and Harnack and lent clear support to the title of "liberal theologian" often given Herrmann: like his two distinguished contemporaries, Herrmann was convinced of the inner harmony between faith and its historical manifestation in cultural institutions. Indeed, despite his opposition to the critical historical method, the presupposition of a coherent structure of the historical world, into which Christianity as a cultural phenomenon fitted closely, clearly figured in Herrmann's thought.[18]

The first significant assault on this worldview in the post-World War I period was launched by Karl Barth in his 1919 commentary on Saint Paul, *Römerbrief* (Epistle to the Romans). Like Bultmann, Barth had been a student of Wilhelm Herrmann at the University of Marburg and a convinced liberal in the prewar period. According to Barth's own testimony, the First World War had provoked a change in sentiment.[19] The nationalism of the German theologians, who did not hesitate to see a Divine purpose behind German involvement in the conflict, deeply repelled the young Swiss pastor and helped convince him of God's utter transcendence vis-à-vis the things of this world. While by no means accepted uncritically, Barth's radical commentary was warmly received by Heidegger at the time of its publication.[20] For this reason, let us briefly turn to Barth's central viewpoint, in loose relation to those of Gogarten and Bultmann, before considering Heidegger's own thought.

At every turn in his interpretation, Barth emphasized the dissonance between belief and knowledge. In themes highly reminiscent of Kierkegaard, Barth spoke of the contradiction (*Widerspruch*) that belief involved: "He who acknowledges a limitation of the world through a contradictory truth [*widersprechende Wahrheit*] and a self-limitation through a contradictory will; he, therefore, *who finally avows this contradiction* and bases his life upon it—he believes."[21] He explicitly thought of this contradiction in terms of God, on the one hand, and the cultural manifestations of religion, on the other. God was radically dissociated from the human world, so the traditional support for harmony between God and culture was withdrawn. Any possible relation between natural reason and the theological realm was disputed, along with the Protestant emphasis on history as the arena in which religious values emerge, as posited by a line of modern thinkers from Schleiermacher to Ritschl and Troeltsch. We are set apart in our world from the otherness of the transcendent God. Only in the realization of this otherness do we begin to find the road toward truth. All attempts to concentrate religious understanding on the immanent world, in the manner of liberal theology, were seen as forms of idolatry. Friedrich Gogarten, whom Barth described as having had "the exact same concerns as I did" at this time,[22] summed up this position succinctly in his "Zwischen den Zeiten" (Between times) article: "We have sunk so deeply into human affairs that we have lost God . . . not one of our thoughts reaches out toward him any longer. They don't get beyond the sphere of humanity. . . . Is it any wonder that we have become suspicious of anything human all the way to our fingertips [*bis in die Fingerspitzen*]?"[23]

The liberal theologians had attempted to understand the phenomenon of religion in terms of a historically evolving cultural world. Barth's epoch-making work pointed out that precisely this style of understanding obscured the otherworldly orientation of genuine Christian belief, evoked, above all, in the eschatological inspiration of Paul's writings. With his choice of Paul as a religious authority, Barth in another way traversed an important current of historical study of the prewar period: Harnack's historical orientation—in company with that of Wilhelm Wrede, Adolf Jülicher, and Paul de Lagarde—had led him to separate Paul's writings from the first three Gospels. He considered Paul a speculative misreading of the "historical Jesus'" true message.[24]

The reevaluation of Paul after the First World War, by contrast, constituted an attempt to revive the eschatological force of a pristine Christian message. In one of Bultmann's early essays, which came closest to the ideas of Barth he was hotly defending, Bultmann made this point especially clear:

"Liberal theology" would make the "historical Jesus" and His Religion the basis of piety, and thus would establish a limited historical Person in the place of Myth and Cult, which yet can be the only expression for the living, eternal, ahistorical aspect of a religion. In fact, liberal theology had for its part protested against the consideration of a limited historical form of Christianity, namely the Pauline dogmatic-ecclesiastical version, as normative.[25]

It is significant in this regard that, like Barth and Bultmann, Heidegger also turned attention to the eschatological spirit of Saint Paul's Epistles (in the second half of the "Introduction to the Phenomenology of Religion"), although irreconcilable conceptual differences in their respective interpretations of Paul suggest that he was not directly influenced by Barth's approach. Less marked differences in perspective between Heidegger, on the one hand, and Bultmann and Gogarten, on the other, can in general be traced back to Heidegger's philosophical starting point, as opposed to the more directly theological concerns of the three thinkers.

Before dealing with these differences in interpretation, however, let us examine more closely the affinities between these younger thinkers. A clue to help elucidate this theme is offered by what has been seen to be a key term in Heidegger's understanding of the problem of historical meaning—"objectification [*Objektivierung*]." Interestingly, this term was also present in the vocabularies of Bultmann, Gogarten, and Barth.[26] It provides an important guidepost to assumptions shared by Heidegger and his neo-orthodox contemporaries, and it indicates the theological roots of Heidegger's concern for historical meaning.

II

In the second half of the "Introduction to the Phenomenology of Religion," Heidegger joined his critique of the historical theories of the older generation to the theme of Saint Paul and original Christian devotion. For Heidegger, that Saint Paul's address to an original Christian community could be considered side by side with other historical expressions of Christianity already predisposed analysis to contemplation of objective manifestations of religious phenomena of the past. In his treatment of Paul's Epistle to the Thessalonians, however,

Heidegger sought to illustrate the radically unique character of original Christian belief.[27] He viewed the uniqueness of this belief as incompatible with any form of inductive comparison with other religious manifestations in the historical process.

To illustrate the grounds for this conviction, Heidegger turned to what he saw as a central aspect of original Christian experience: the expectation of Christ's second coming, or the Parousia. The original Christian attitude toward the Parousia, he told his listeners, could be interpreted as a kind of waiting, with Christian hope as its special form of articulation. This interpretation would restrict Paul's message to a purely relational sense (*Bezugssinn*) in the anticipation of a future event; it would deform the content of what Paul said by giving an objective structure to *time*, which would become a chronological order (*kronos*) implied in the waiting out of events.

Original Christian experience did not lend itself to this manner of conceptualization, however. It had to be characterized as a unique way of experiencing temporal events. In the Epistle to the Thessalonians, Paul did not say *when* the Parousia might be expected. He declared to the Thessalonians: "*You* know quite exactly!" To Heidegger's mind, this could only refer to a special kind of knowledge, lying beyond all objective events—that is, in the *self*. "You know quite exactly" signifies that the decision (*Entscheidung*) of the question depended on the Thessalonians themselves, in a unique temporal experience, the *kairos*.[28] To clarify this point, Heidegger recalled two approaches to life invoked by Saint Paul in his Epistles. Heidegger reminded his listeners that these approaches refer to ways of fulfilling experience, not to *types* of lifestyle.

One approach sought security: it banked on peace in life, fleeing all that might arise as a source of disquiet (*Beunruhigung*). This approach to life remained helpless against the onrush of decline. It remained estranged from the sense of its own self, which it could never have authentically (*eigentlich*). Waiting out events, and for the things of life in which it was absorbed, its insurmountable fate came as a surprise. In its unexpected suddenness, time was experienced as the Parousia, which, in the words of Saint Paul, arrived like a "thief in the night."[29]

In contrast, the genuine approach to life referred steadily back to a sense of self-accomplishment (*Vollzugssinn*). It expected the Parousia, not as an event among other objectively awaited events, but in sober, attentive preparedness for a wholly unobjectifiable grasping of the self and for decision (*Entscheidung*). Here Heidegger referred to the *kairos* as "temporal urgency [*zeitliche Bedrängnis*]," as "compressed temporality [*zusammengedrängte Zeitlichkeit*]," constitutive of Christian devotion.[30]

As Heidegger saw it, this eschatological sense of original Christian experience was falsified by later Christian tradition. Most fateful in this process, with the interjection of Neoplatonic ideas into the interpretation of original Christian experience, the primordial character of early Christian faith was abandoned: God became the object of speculation with the aid of Platonic-Aristotelian ideas. In contrast, Luther's distrust of Aristotle and Aristotelian Scholasticism testified to the Reformation attempt to return to an authentic Christian experience. Nonetheless, Heidegger explained, the sense of this attempt had been lost in the morass of more modern ideas, seeking to integrate the phenomenon of religion within the objectifiable sphere of human meaning.[31]

As an example of this kind of thinking, Heidegger pointed to the contemporary approach to religion through the concept of validity (*Geltung*), alluding to neo-Kantian value theory, in which the notion of validity was applied to value statements concerning religious phenomena.[32] Later comments by Heidegger confirmed that the neo-Kantian idea of religion formed one of his most explicit targets. In a rather sarcastic critique of neo-Kantian value theory during his 1924 lectures on logic, he made perfectly clear what he meant by objectifying religious experience in culturally acceptable values (as opposed to approaching them in their radical otherness):

> Now Kant also occupied himself with religion, but not in such a way that it might be possible to place his treatment of it on the same level as the *Critiques*. Religion must, however, also be brought into the system—and for this reason the value of the Holy was invented [*erfunden*]. According to Windelband, it is true, the Holy is no autonomous value. To say something like this around 1900, and before the war, might have been acceptable. Because the world, however, has become very religious since the war, and even world congresses are being announced, corresponding to the international association of chemists or meteorologists, one can risk saying that religion is also a value, and even the highest value.[33]

Struggling against what he viewed as the false premises of contemporary thought, Heidegger pointedly attacked the older generation of theologians in the first part of the 1921–22 lecture series "Augustinus und der Neuplatonismus" (Augustine and Neoplatonism), where again he centered his analysis on the problem of objectification.

From the outset, Heidegger focused on the conception of Augustine advanced by three of the great scholars of the prewar period: Adolf von Harnack, Ernst Troeltsch, and Wilhelm Dilthey.[34] For Heidegger, each of these thinkers placed greater emphasis on Augustine's accommodation of Christianity to objective historical circumstances than on the content of his thought and its implications for belief.

Thus, in his *Dogmengeschichte* (The history of dogma), Harnack concerned himself primarily with Augustine's role in adapting original Christian teachings to the needs of the Church for a dogmatic system. For Harnack, Augustine's major insight was the interpretation of early Christian ideas with the help of Greek concepts. For Troeltsch, as well, the synthesis of early Christian faith with the Hellenic worldview lent strength to Christian ethical teachings, which could then form the basis for a culture. Finally, for Dilthey, who focused on what he saw as Augustine's important role in the advance of epistemology, Augustine introduced the unique Christian concept of historicity into the static worldview of Hellenism, giving an essential impulse to the development of historical consciousness.

In this lecture series, Heidegger sought to penetrate Augustine's objective achievements to the inner content of his teachings and their meaning for belief. He set as his central task the discriminating assessment of those teachings, and not what could be seen or inductively traced in historical development. Nor did he shrink from "destruction" when Augustine became dependent on Neoplatonic concepts to express his belief.[35] Thus Heidegger's criticism was most trenchant where Augustine employed Neoplatonic theories to defend a concept of God as repose, which Heidegger saw as going against the original Christian sense of wakefulness and the need for resolute choice.

To Heidegger's mind, Scholasticism and modern theology only reiterated the speculative attempt to conceptualize God, which they took far beyond Augustine. Basing himself on Luther's interpretation of Saint Paul in the *Heidelberger Disputation* of 1518, Heidegger followed Luther's image of the genuine theme of theological comprehension. Theologians were not justified in trying to speculatively grasp the invisible Being of God through His works; on the contrary, Divine truth was only to be discerned in the aspect of God's Being that had been turned toward the world in the Cross and the Passion (*im Kreuz und Leiden*).

Moving beyond theologians' speculative understanding of God and Revelation on the basis of His worldly works, and their more modern preoccupation with a historical world of culture, Heidegger considered theological interpretation strictly in terms of the self and its way of fulfillment (*Vollzug*). Here the problem of *belief,* which served to relate the more specific question of theology to the broad historical issue of objectification, became paramount. Thus, for Heidegger, the significance of original Christian belief was of interest not only for its contribution to theological comprehension, but, even more immediately, for its role as a prototype of authentic factical-historical life experience per se.[36]

In theological matters, historical scholarship tended to impose the same kinds of secular criteria on theological phenomena as on other aspects of the cultural world. It subjected the personification of God in Christ to the same historical rules as other historical events. It applied the same categories of historical understanding to the primitive Church as to secular institutions. Theologians like Harnack and Troeltsch simply failed to consider the possibility that religious belief might be irreducible to the same forms of analysis as other phenomena, that belief might potentially infuse existence with a meaning that could not readily be analyzed by the methods of investigation of secular disciplines.[37]

Heidegger's application of specific theological conceptions to general philosophical notions of historical meaning was not only to be found in these early lectures. In the 1927 lecture series "Phänomenologie und Theologie" (Phenomenology and theology)—dedicated in published form (1970) to Rudolf Bultmann—Heidegger again related the problem of belief to that of historical understanding. Although he never went so far here as to model authenticity on a specifically religious dimension of experience, and continually insisted on the distinction between philosophy and theology, the clear reference of philosophical to concrete theological instances (such as "guilt" or "sin") manifested the translatability of terms between intimately parallel fields. In this lecture, he wrote: "All theological concepts necessarily conceal *the* understanding of Being within themselves that finite human existence [*Dasein*] as such reveals, insofar as it exists at all."[38] For this reason, philosophy could act as a possible corrective (*Korrektive*) for fundamental theological concepts.

In terms nearly identical to those employed in the 1922 lecture series "Augustine and Neoplatonism," Heidegger noted in this 1927 work that "belief" is, in Luther's terms, "the rendering of ourselves to aspects that we don't see." For Heidegger, the task of theology lay in an investigation of belief that "does not only belong to Christianity insofar as it is historical, in connection with the general appearances of culture; theology is knowledge of that which first and foremost makes Christianity as a world-historical event possible."[39] This "knowledge," he went on to explain, is related to the unique historicity of the phenomenon on which belief is centered: the primordial historical sense of Revelation and the Crucifixion.

The significant point in the two lecture series of the early twenties, as in "Phenomenology and Theology," was the dualism in Heidegger's thinking between the realm of belief and that of historically evolving culture. For Heidegger, belief remained "unseen" and could not be registered as an objectified, empirical-historical phenomenon. It revealed its meaning, not primarily through an inductive grasp of cultural development, but in fulfillment of the self having an eye for historical significance invisible to objective vision.

The dualism between historical significance revealed in belief and objectively verifiable manifestations of culture was clearly rooted in a style of thinking that first became evident during Heidegger's intense involvement with Protestant theology from 1919 to 1922. The theological motives of Heidegger's way of thinking about history, as well as some of the wider implications of this thinking, become all the more clear when considered in relation to the neo-orthodox theologians Karl Barth, Rudolf Bultmann, and Friedrich Gogarten.

During the early twenties, both Bultmann and Gogarten actively defended the new direction inaugurated by Barth's *Römerbrief;* both stressed the radical distinction between religious objectification in the cultural world and the phenomenon of belief. Hence Gogarten, responding to Adolf Jülicher's criticism that he and Barth mistrusted all that was great in the past, wrote: "It might indeed be that I would have wished to liberate the 'greatness of the past' from every humanizing diminution [*vermenschlichenden Verkleinerung*], which every panhistorical engagement [*Einstellung*] in general development, and in all-sided dependence on development, at once signifies."[40]

Taking up a similar idea two years later, Gogarten noted in a forceful critique that

> Troeltsch's knowledge threatens to completely deprive theology of its topic [*Gegenstand*]. Because its topic, the Divine advent, no longer is a topic when it becomes one among others in all-lawful historical understanding [*Historie*], thus having ceased being Divine advent. . . . But this knowledge can place theology before the problem that rightfully should be its only one, namely that of Revelation. It can no longer be taken by us, however, as a topic, as an object [*Objekt*], which indeed it is not.[41]

In an essay defending Barth and Gogarten, Bultmann provided his own attack on Troeltsch, and on the inductive approach that considered Christianity as an "innerworldly appearance, subsumed under a sociopsychological law."

> One can speak of a *historical* pantheism of liberal theology, which is closely related to naturalistic pantheism, and which is ultimately founded on the consideration of history in the same way as nature; that is, with concepts that are valid for nature [*mit den für die Natur geltenden Begriffen*]. Man, insofar as he participates in this history, is seen in the same way, as object [*Objekt*], seen, so to speak, from outside and not according to categories that he himself has attained.[42]

Bultmann thus concluded that "the world that belief seeks to grasp is not at all graspable with the help of scientific knowledge [*wissenschaftlichen Erkenntnis*]."[43]

The understanding of authentic religious devotion in terms of belief and the refusal to consider belief as discernible in the objective course of the development of Christianity were convictions shared by Heidegger and the neo-orthodox theologians, as expressed quite clearly in their common rejection of a tendency of Protestant theology most powerfully represented by Ernst Troeltsch. To their minds, Troeltsch placed too exclusive an emphasis on objective facts while ignoring the tacit dimension that belief alone could discern. For Heidegger (and also for Gogarten and Bultmann in their respective ways), this called for the elaboration of a different notion of historical meaning, detached from manifestations of faith within a world of cultural development, and reflected back into the primordial faith of the individual self.[44]

The emphasis on the nonconceptual aspects of belief marked a rupture in the liberal synthesis between belief and historical knowledge of a cultural world. In sounding the depths of faith in this intangible sense, scientific understanding could provide no reliable guidance.

In the thought of Heidegger, who readily translated theological issues into philosophical ones, this point was decisive. In *Sein und Zeit* (Being and time), God's "invisible Being" as conceived by Luther was made the basis of ontological insight. Heidegger invoked the source Luther himself had: Saint Augustine's investigation of "sight" as lust of the eyes.[45] In the *Confessions,* Augustine related lust of the eyes to the curiosity of the sciences that delved into all possible intricate detail in the world, yet missed the essential when not informed by belief. In explicit reference to Augustine (and to Luther), curiosity as sight (*Sicht*) became, for Heidegger, one of the modes of *Dasein's* fallenness (*Verfallenheit*), while also occupying a place in the ontological genesis of the objective sciences.[46] In this style of analysis, Heidegger's tendency to exclude the objective, theoretical character of both historical and natural sciences from the sphere of authentic thinking found its most concrete expression.

Despite this retreat from the cultural world toward a more individual and intangible source of faith, it would be a grave mistake to conclude that Heidegger and the neo-orthodox theologians adopted a kind of quietism. One of Heidegger's major motives for rejecting contemporary theory, as has been noted, stemmed from what he saw as a tendency to leave the self of the theorist—in the fulfillment of its possibilities—out of consideration. In the terminology of the "Introduction to the Phenomenology of Religion," speculation about God offers security and quiet, skipping over the disquieting need for preparedness and decision (*Entscheidung*).[47] In the language of *Being and Time,* the curiosity of sight involves forgetfulness of the sense of existence, which is brought to awareness only in the resoluteness of choice in light of existence's possibilities.

For Gogarten and Bultmann as for Heidegger, the engagement of religious phenomena in a universal historical framework neglected the genuine theological theme of belief and, in its passivity before objective phenomena, forgot the need for choice that belief demanded. Gogarten's "religious decision [*religiöse Entscheidung*]" and Bultmann's "religious rebirth [*religiöse Neugeburt*]" emphasized precisely this. And Heidegger, in "Augustine and Neoplatonism," which represented his most trenchant attack against the predominant contemporary theories of religion in the human sciences, explained that his lectures were meant to help his listeners reach a "decision

[*Entscheidung*]" and thus contribute to the overcoming of traditional criteria of knowledge.[48] For each of these thinkers, "decision" involved a return to the individual self, which chose its existence in resolute opposition to the inhibiting factors of the natural or historical objectivity surrounding it.[49]

III

> Rather than support the worldly success and the "historical power" of Christianity, its purest and most truthful adherents have always placed this success and power in question. In this way they took care to set themselves outside of the "world" and they did not bother themselves about the 'process' of the Christian idea. . . . Thus, expressed in Christian terms, the ruler of the world, and master of success and progress, is the devil.
>
> —Nietzsche, *Untimely Meditations*

Although, at times in his Freiburg lectures of the early 1920s, Heidegger might seem to have spoken like a Protestant pastor, his standpoint remained predominantly philosophical. Nonetheless, after his 1923 appointment to the University of Marburg, his contacts with Protestant theologians became more frequent and intense. At this time, Heidegger established a personal friendship with Rudolf Bultmann. The two met regularly to read the Gospel According to Saint John together, and Heidegger participated in Bultmann's 1923 seminar "Paul's Ethics."[50] Marburg, which had been a center of neo-Kantian influence in philosophy and theology, now became a stronghold of attack on the neo-Kantian worldview. In the conflict between neo-orthodox theologians and neo-Kantians, Heidegger and Bultmann (and other neo-orthodox theologians outside of Marburg) formed a common front.

Yet the philosophical starting point of Heidegger's thought made him immediately suspect to the more orthodox thinkers, most especially to Karl Barth, who refused Bultmann's repeated invitations in 1924 to come to Marburg to meet Heidegger.[51] Barth's refusal highlighted undeniable differences between his interpretation of theology and Heidegger's—indeed, between Barth's interpretation and that of Bultmann and of Gogarten as well.

First, the sharpness of Barth's isolation of theology from worldly concerns left it indifferent to the historical per se, and not just to the cultural world analyzed by the historical sciences. This position was too extreme for Bultmann, and distinguished Barth from Gogarten as well. In his review of the second edition of Barth's *Römerbrief,* Bultmann noted Barth's intransigent effort to separate the character of true belief from any kind of psychological or historical context. Although, like Barth, Bultmann heartily opposed reducing Christianity to a history or psychology of religious appearances, Barth had gone too far in negating what Bultmann considered to be the unavoidable historicity of interpretation.[52]

Second, a close examination of the writings of Bultmann, Gogarten, and Heidegger clearly reveals their common interest in the wider problem of historical decline. By contrast, Barth's radical retreat into transcendence made him insensitive to the special difficulty that belief faced in contemporary society; in his leap toward otherworldliness, he failed to discern nuances in historical thinking.

This difference in emphasis between Bultmann and Gogarten, on the one hand, and Barth, on the other, soon came to constitute a significant issue between them, leading Barth to break with Bultmann in 1927, when the latter attempted to introduce the Heideggerian notion of the "historicity of *Dasein*" into theology.[53] Gogarten, also manifesting the influence of Heidegger's historical thinking in his writings, was, for Barth, far too preoccupied with the issues presented by history and philosophy.[54]

While the concerns of Gogarten and Bultmann were thus closer to those of Heidegger than to those of Barth, their proximity—from Heidegger's perspective—should not be exaggerated. However fruitful his thinking might later have proved for theology, it remained tied to philosophy, which, by its very nature, questioned theological presuppositions. Indeed, Heidegger's own tendency to do so becomes all the more apparent when viewed alongside his attitude toward Nietzsche's friend and contemporary, Franz Overbeck, acknowledged in post–World War I Germany both as a forerunner of the neo-orthodox movement and as one of its subtler opponents.[55]

Written in the same period as the second meditation of Nietzsche's *Untimely Meditations,* Franz Overbeck's *Über die Christlichkeit unserer heutigen Theologie* (On the Christianness of our current theology) manifested a clear affinity with Nietzsche's work. Like Nietzsche, Overbeck was suspicious of movements claiming to represent the original Christian ideal, reasoning that a history of Christianity could never be anything more than a history of ongoing falsification. He inveighed against the view, most notably expressed by Adolf von Harnack,[56] that faith and historical understanding were part of a single, coherent system, and that faith could conceivably be served by theological science. As he pointed out in *Über die Christlichkeit,* faith was not grounded in knowledge, but was more likely to be threatened by it, especially in the guise of the critical apparatus of historical scholarship.[57]

Unlike Nietzsche, Overbeck never denounced belief per se, and steadily refused to embrace the reduction of all religious activity to an underlying will to power, which Nietzsche proclaimed in his later writings. Anticipating the orientation reinvigorated after World War I, Overbeck never ceased to admire original Christianity, with its intensely eschatological focus. For Overbeck, historical meaning was not to be sought in the progressive actualization of faith, but in the "primordial history [*Urgeschichte*]" of the original sect, before loss of belief in the Parousia prepared the way for rigid dogmatization and the decline of the spirit.

For thinkers like Ernst Troeltsch, Overbeck represented no more than a reprehensible negation of theology.[58] Barth, on the other hand, was naturally sensitive to Overbeck's reasoning, rightly seeing him as a precursor of many of the ideas that had become contemporary.[59] Like that other great source of inspiration for the neo-orthodox movement, Kierkegaard, Overbeck favored belief over logical forms of comprehension and over cultural institutionalization, although, unlike Kierkegaard (as Barth pointed out), he never claimed to represent a "true" Christian faith and could not envision a personal purification campaign against religious falsification.

Overbeck may thus be distinguished both from Kierkegaard and from Barth. Although all three thinkers represented a "theology of crisis" in which the ongoing relation of God to humanity had become thoroughly problematic, Overbeck's view of the dilemma prevented any ready leap toward transcendence and left him trapped in the immanence of a historical world. Focusing on the articulations of history led him to what he saw as the low point of Christianity in the modern period. Indeed, with primitive eschatology as his standard, Overbeck saw the attempt to infuse Christianity with liberal notions of development or progress as the ultimate contradiction of primordial Christian faith.[60] Most important, according to Overbeck, the plight of modernity could not be overcome by personal piety and vision. We could not extricate ourselves in any simple way from the world that engendered liberal thought. The historical consequences of religious decline motivated his writings throughout. Notwithstanding his own objections, however, he could see no clear-cut alternative to that decline.

Like Overbeck, Heidegger was sensitive to the dilemma of theological truth in the contemporary world. His manner of approaching this dilemma, especially after his appointment to the University of Marburg, set him distinctly apart from Karl Barth, and distinguished him even from theologians more favorably inclined to his philosophy, such as Bultmann and Gogarten. In his letters, Heidegger referred to the failure of contemporary theology to live up to Overbeck's challenge, and, in the words of Gadamer, he "assumed Overbeck's theological skepticism" in the Marburg debates of the mid-1920s.[61]

In ways reminiscent of Overbeck, Heidegger focused in the early Freiburg lectures on the decline of religious experience since the original Christian community. Granted the possibility of partial retrieval of authenticity—as in the case of Augustine or Luther—tradition's historical betrayal of that authenticity made it necessary to continually "deconstruct" tradition and renew original experience.

In *Being and Time,* the decline from original Christianity would find its complement in a history of the forgetfulness of Being (*Seinsvergessenheit*), propagated and deepened since the period of the ancient Greek thinkers, and recapitulating the theme of early Christianity. Yet, even though *Being and Time* would place *Seinsvergessenheit* at the origin of distortion in the Christian tradition, Heidegger here envisioned authenticity primarily in a philosophical, rather than theological, context. Moving beyond Overbeck, he imagined a possibility of resolute decision in the philosophical sphere. What remained continuous in his interpretation was a metahistorical notion, anticipated by Overbeck and raised to an ontological principle in *Being and Time:* accommodation to historical tradition has only distorted what was originally genuine in the ancient conceptual and spiritual sources of our modern world.

NOTES

1. Schütte, *Religion und Christentum in der Theologie Rudolf Ottos*, 139–42. Husserl's letter appears in the appendix to this work. See Thomas Sheehan, "Heidegger's 'Introduction to the Phenomenology of Religion,' 1920–21," 312–24.

2. Although, in his 1928 Freiburg diary, Husserl's translator W. R. Boyce-Gibson noted that "Heidegger became a Protestant and was baptized a Protestant," the diary's editor, Herbert Spiegelberg described this statement and the comments in Husserl's letter as "clearly a mistake." See Boyce-Gibson, "Excerpts from a 1928 Freiburg Diary," 58–81. For more on Heidegger's drift away from Catholicism and his relation to Protestantism, see Ott, *Martin Heidegger,* 106–19.

3. See, for example, Jaspers, *Philosophische Autobiographie,* 93–94.

4. See Löwith et al., *Heidegger im Gespräch,* 39; Fuchs, "Aus der Marburger Zeit"; Löwith, *Mein Leben,* 29–30; Pöggeler, *Neue Wege mit Heidegger,* 466–71.

5. Bultmann, letter to Hans von Soden, December 23, 1923, 202. As noted in chapter 3, Heidegger expressed his esteem (*Wertschätzung*) for the "Barth-Gogarten movement" in his unpublished letter to Karl Löwith dated August 24,1925.

6. Troeltsch, "Ein Apfel vom Baume Kierkegaards" (1920), in Barth et al., *Anfänge,* 2:134.

7. Tillich, *Vorlesungen über die Geschichte des christlichen Denkens,* 178. Ritschl's attitude toward metaphysics is most explicitly stated in his work *Theologie und Metaphysik.*

8. In his early Freiburg lectures, Heidegger described the influence of Schleiermacher, Ritschl, and, later, the neo-Kantians on Troeltsch's liberal theology. See "Einleitung in die Phänomenologie der Religion" and "Zu Schleiermachers zweiter Rede, 'Über das Wesen der Religion,'" in *Gesamtausgabe,* 60:19–20 and 319–22, respectively.

9. Ritschl, *Die christliche Lehre von der Rechtfertigung und Versöhnung,*1:469–70.

10. An example of Ritschl's use of value theory (*Werttheorie*) is provided in his work *Theologie und Metaphysik,* 7, where, like the neo-Kantians, he contrasts value theory with metaphysics: "For the metaphysical doctrine of the world value distinctions also prove indifferent. In this conception the metaphysician places himself, as spirit, on a level separate from all nature, to which he feels himself to be superior. Here, however, is the source of the distance of metaphysical cosmology from any religious worldview [*Weltanschauung*]."

11. Harnack, *Das Wesen des Christentums,* 16.

12. Troeltsch, *Absolutheit,* 47–51.

13. Harnack, *Wesen,* 22.

14. Iggers has convincingly demonstrated this point in *The German Conception of History.*

15. Troeltsch, *Die Bedeutung des Protestantismus für die Entstehung der modernen Welt,* 66–80.

16. Barth, "Unerledigte Anfragen an die heutige Theologie," *Die Theologie und die Kirche,* 2:8.

17. Note especially Gogarten's trenchant comments in this regard from his 1925 article "Historismus," in Barth et al., *Anfänge,* 2:178.

18. This aspect of Herrmann's thought was illustrated in passages like the following: "In history, which we really can separate from nature, something continually takes place which never and nowhere has occurred before. Creative forces reveal themselves in history. But people can only become the means of such a Revelation when they will to become true or truly alive in themselves." Herrmann, *Die Wirklichkeit Gottes,* 17.

19. Barth and Bultmann, *Briefwechsel,* 306.

20. Karl Löwith, for example, wrote of Heidegger's qualified admiration for Barth in the following terms: "Karl Barth's *Römerbrief* (which appeared in 1918) seemed to Heidegger to be one of the few signs of a genuine spiritual life; yet a capacity for compromise dominated in theology, which did not dare to take seriously Franz Overbeck's critique of all theology." Löwith et al., *Heidegger im Gespräch,* 39. The grounds for Heidegger's critique of Barth will become clearer in the last section of this chapter.

21. Karl Barth, *Der Römerbrief,* 16. See also Bultmann's favorable comments on this passage in his review of the second edition of the *Römerbrief,* in Barth et al., *Anfänge,* 1:125–26.

22. Barth and Bultmann, *Briefwechsel,* 308.

23. Gogarten, "Zwischen den Zeiten," in Barth et al., *Anfänge,* 2:98.

24. Tillich, *Vorlesungen,* 184. Troeltsch does not seem to have shared von Harnack's ideas on Paul, and tended to consider him in a more positive light. Yet he concentrated more on the importance of Paul in the foundation of a Christian culture than on the explicitly eschatological dimension of Paul's writings. Troeltsch, *The Social Teaching of the Christian Churches,* 85–89.

25. Bultmann, "Ethische und mythische Religion im Urchristentum," in Barth et al., *Anfänge,* 2:42.

26. Other terms such as "ahistorical" and "absolute" commonly encountered in the language of these theologians necessarily remained alien to Heidegger's vocabulary for reasons we noted in chapter 3.

27. Heidegger, "Einleitung," in *Gesamtausgabe,* 60:98–105.

28. For Heidegger's early thoughts on the kairological relation to time, considered outside the context of Christian theology, see *Gesamtausgabe*, 61:137–40. See also the analyses of Otto Pöggeler in his masterful work on Heidegger, *Denkweg*, 36–45.

29. Heidegger, "Einleitung," in *Gesamtausgabe*, 60:104, 150–51.

30. Ibid., 98–105, 113–20, 150.

31. Ibid., 31–54, 97, 104, 132–35. On this critique of the Hellenistic falsification of original Christian devotion, see also Heidegger, *Gesamtausgabe*, 59:91.

32. Heidegger, "Einleitung," in *Gesamtausgabe*, 60:39–40, 104.

33. Heidegger, *Gesamtausgabe*, 21:83.

34. Heidegger, "Augustinus," in *Gesamtausgabe*, 60:160–73.

35. Cf. Heidegger, "Zur Destruktion von *Confessiones* X," app. 1 to "Augustinus," in *Gesamtausgabe*, 60:247.

36. Heidegger, "Einleitung," in *Gesamtausgabe*, 60:129–46, 149–53; see also Heidegger, *Grundprobleme der Phänomenologie (1919–20)*, in *Gesamtausgabe*, 58:61–64.

37. With this kind of problem in mind, Heidegger explicitly separated philosophy from all of the sciences, and theology from the profane historical sciences in *Phänomenologie und Theologie* (originally a 1927 lecture), 24.

38. Ibid., 29.

39. Ibid., 18.

40. Gogarten, "Vom heiligen Egoismus des Christen," in Barth et al., *Anfänge*, 1:103.

41. Gogarten, "Wider die romantische Theologie," in Barth et al., *Anfänge*, 2:142.

42. Bultmann, "Die liberale Theologie und die jüngste theologische Bewegung" (1924), in *Glauben und Verstehen*, 1:5.

43. Ibid., 4.

44. In a letter to Heinrich Rickert written directly following this lecture series, Heidegger criticized Troeltsch sharply for his "Hegelianism," adopted for lack of any better persuasion ("Man ist Hegelianer, weil manches so besser geht"). He took Troeltsch's timid attempts to reconstruct metaphysics to task. From Heidegger's standpoint, such a reconstruction clearly could not be accomplished after the fashion of Hegel through an interpretation of the meaning of religion in relation to its historical development. "I consider a debate with Troeltsch," he nevertheless wrote Rickert, "to be urgently necessary." Heidegger, letter to Heinrich Rickert, March 15, 1921, Heidegger and Rickert, *Briefe*, 53–54.

45. Heidegger, "Augustinus," in *Gesamtausgabe*, 60:222–27; Heidegger, *Sein und Zeit*, 170–73.

46. Heidegger, *Sein und Zeit,* 358.

47. As we will have occasion to note in chapter 5, this decision motif emerged in relation to ontology in *Sein und Zeit.* A number of interesting attempts have been made to link Heidegger to different authors of this period who centered their writings on a call for individual decision. For analyses of Heidegger's philosophy in light of the current of "decisionism," see Löwith, "Der okkasionelle Dezisionismus Carl Schmitts" (including a section on Gogarten and on Heidegger), in *Heidegger: Denker in dürftiger Zeit,* 30–71; Krokow, *Die Entscheidung Eine Untersuchung über E. Jünger, C. Schmitt, M. Heidegger;* Strohm, *Theologie im Schatten politischer Romantik: Eine wissenschafts-soziologische Anfrage an die Theologie F. Gogartens;* Martin, "Dezisionismus in der Theologie Rudolf Bultmanns?"

48. Heidegger, "Augustinus," in *Gesamtausgabe,* 60:165–66.

49. Heidegger had already written in this regard in "Einleitung," in *Gesamtausgabe,* 60:124–25:

> Genuine philosophy of religion does not arise from preconceived concepts concerning philosophy and religion. It is rather from a determinate religious devotion—for us Christian devotion—that the possibility of its philosophical comprehension emerges. Why precisely Christian devotion lies at the center of our consideration is a difficult question; it is only answerable through the resolution of the problem of historical coherences [*Problem der geschichtlichen Zusammenhänge*]. The task is to achieve a genuine [*echtes*] and original relation to history, which is to be explicated through our own historical situation and facticity. It is a question of understanding what the sense of history can mean for us [*was der Sinn der Geschichte für uns bedeuten kann*], so that the "objectivity" of the historical "in itself [*an sich*]" disappears. History emerges only out of the present. Only as such is it possible to comprehend the possibility of a philosophy of religion.

50. Information about Heidegger's participation in Bultmann's seminar is provided in Bultmann's December 22, 1923, letter to Friedrich Gogarten. In a second letter to Gogarten, dated October 19, 1924, Bultmann recalled: "Moreover, during an afternoon each week I am now reading with Heidegger the Gospel According to Saint John. I hope to learn all sorts of things from these meetings." I am grateful to Frau Marianne Bultmann, Friedrich Gogarten's daughter, for her kind permission to cite directly from the text of these two unpublished letters.

51. Barth and Bultmann, *Briefwechsel,* 33, 42, 68, 117, 152. In a reminiscence published in the afterword to *La théologie protestante au 19ᵉ siècle* (p. 453), Barth wrote that, around 1922, Bultmann had come "to see me one day

at Göttingen to read to me for hours on end . . . from some notes he had taken at Marburg in the courses of M. Heidegger. [I]t was in [Heidegger's existential] sense . . . that we should try to understand the Gospels of the New Testament, just like any other spiritual manifestation." According to Bultmann, Heidegger was eager to make Barth's acquaintance, despite Barth's reluctance to meet him. Barth and Bultmann, *Briefwechsel*, 33.

52. Bultmann, "Karl Barth's 'Römerbrief' in zweiter Auflage," in Barth et al., *Anfänge*, 1:119–42.

53. Barth and Bultmann, *Briefwechsel*, 117 (letter dated June 20, 1931). Bultmann had compared and contrasted Heidegger's and Gogarten's notions of history in his article "Die Geschichtlichkeit des Daseins und der Glaube," 339–64.

54. For evidence of Heidegger's influence on Gogarten, see Gogarten, "Karl Barths Dogmatik," 60–61.

55. In the introduction to *Phänomenologie und Theologie* (the 1970 published edition of his 1927 lecture), after praising the first meditation of Nietzsche's *Untimely Meditations,* Heidegger added (p. 8) a laudatory comment about Overbeck's *Über die Christlichkeit unserer heutigen Theologie,* "which confirms the world-negating expectation of the End as the basis of primordial Christianity."

56. Overbeck, *Über die Christlichkeit,* 200–217.

57. Ibid., 35–42.

58. Troeltsch, "*Christentum und Kultur* von F. Overbeck," 279–81.

59. Barth, "Unerledigte Anfragen," in *Theologie und die Kirche,* 1–25.

60. Karl Löwith has provided a important analysis of this topic in his *Von Hegel zu Nietzsche,* 471–85.

61. Heidegger, unpublished letter to Karl Löwith, June 30, 1925. Gadamer paraphrased Heidegger's comments in his article "Heidegger und die Marburger Theologie," in *Kleine Schriften,* 1:82.

5

Historical Meaning in the Fundamental Ontology of *Being and Time*

FAR FROM AN ISOLATED OCCURRENCE, the turning point in Martin Heidegger's thought during the years just after World War I, when he attempted to grasp the historical meaning of human existence, emerged against the backdrop of a wider intellectual predicament in Germany, in which the problem of historical meaning played a cardinal role. The 1927 publication of Heidegger's major work, *Sein und Zeit* (Being and time), bore witness to another shift in the emphasis of his thinking, transferring many of the historical themes highlighted by his earlier philosophy onto different ground. Its principal topic, ontology, was introduced with what Heidegger described as the most universal of all questions: What is the meaning of Being (*Sinn des Seins*)? Although ontology might seem to lie close to a theme introduced in his 1916 *Habilitationsschrift* (postdoctoral dissertation), the transcendence of purely logical themes toward a metaphysical realist concern with Being in its categorical and linguistic articulations, *Being and Time* pursued a thoroughly different aim.[1]

On the basis of ideas adumbrated in previous chapters, this different aim has already been anticipated in two ways. First, in significance as well as chronology, we have seen how Heidegger's notion of the historical, interwoven with insights gained from Protestant theology, tore him away from the natural metaphysics of neo-Scholasticism to which his *Frühe Schriften* (Early writings) were bound. Second, as suggested at the end of the previous chapter, we have seen how his more recent preoccupation with Being coincided with his growing reluctance to consider philosophical topics from *any* theological standpoint. To the extent that Heidegger grappled with the problem of historical meaning, it was now in relation to ontology, and not directly to the theological motifs encountered in his early Freiburg lectures.

Heidegger's use of the word *ontology*—rather than *metaphysics*—to describe the theme of *Being and Time* signaled this difference. Ontology, he explained, traditionally the doctrine of general metaphysics (*metaphysica generalis*), analyzed Being in its universal sense; it is this sense that Heidegger sought to reinterpret. In his estimation, the differentiation of Being, such as in the concern for theology, cosmology, and psychology in the traditional discipline of special metaphysics (*metaphysica specialis*), depends on a prior analysis of the universal theme of ontology in general metaphysics.[2]

Corresponding to this shift in emphasis in *Being and Time,* the sense of the historical involved in ontology was also redefined: in its universal scope, ontology was to take precedence over any specialized theoretical discipline, including biology, anthropology—or the historical sciences. It was also to precede any general considerations of worldview (*Weltanschauung*).[3] Far from being attuned to specific systems of investigation, belief, or action, ontology sought to uncover the conditions of possibility of such systems. What notion of historical meaning might it suggest?

In important ways Heidegger's response to this question had been prepared by certain thoughts foreshadowed in his "Anmerkungen" (Annotations) and in his early Freiburg lectures, where historical meaning had arisen in a fulfillment of the sense of existence of the self, won at the expense of ready-made styles of interpretation objectified in the historical process. In *Being and Time,* historical meaning was also referred back to the self that gives meaning to finite human existence—termed *Dasein.*

Being and Time explores the ontological significance of *Dasein*'s appropriation of a sense of existence. Here the refusal to anchor a historically changing world and the ways of theoretically understanding it in stable, objective forms—whether established values, logical structures of consciousness, or objectified life coherences—gathers strength from a conviction that *Dasein*'s variable modes of interpreting existence are the fundamental source of an illumination of Being. These modes universally prefigure the world of meaning *Dasein* encounters.

A central issue regarding this claim must be raised at the outset: once the coherence of the historical world, involving the continuity of norms of judgment that arise in it, is rooted in so seemingly precarious a foundation as *Dasein*'s variable interpretation of existence and illumination of the meaning of Being, does not Heidegger's thought deliberately exacerbate the predicament of historical thinking of his times? Might one not be inclined, with Peter Gay or Georg Iggers, to see Heidegger's philosophy of existence as representing an abandonment of rational standards or as leading toward a dissolution of the "hard world of real, objective Being"?[4]

In approaching Heidegger's thought, we need to keep his own stated intentions and the intellectual context of the 1920s clearly in view. In previous chapters, we have seen that the period following the First World War proved a watershed in the broad consideration of historical styles of thinking, when the older theoretical assumptions about history faced a stiff challenge from diverse groups of German thinkers. Above all, these thinkers radically questioned the *significance* of seeking an autonomous theoretical basis for scientific historical methods, employing inductive research independent of philosophical metaphysics or naturalism.

Well before the publication of *Being and Time,* Heidegger's contemporaries spoke of a crisis of historical thinking, calling in question the capacity of historical methods to surmount "historicism [*Historismus*]," or the relativization of values and normative standards. To many, rightly or wrongly, historicism seemed an obvious legacy of the emphasis placed on historical methods in the prewar German universities. For his part, Heidegger viewed his ontology, not as a submission to relativism and historicism, but as a demonstration that the key to Germany's intellectual predicament lay in contemporary tendencies rooted in an age-old tradition that sought theoretical stability and systematic coherence on illusory grounds.[5]

Putting aside, for the time being, the question of Heidegger's contribution to relativism or irrationalism, let us first analyze the historical dimensions of his ontology. It is here that Heidegger's rebuttal of influential modern theories of history, his notion of authentic historical understanding, and his broad quest for a historical reorientation of Western intellectual traditions found their mature focus. In more specific terms, given the predicament faced by traditional ways of asking what it means to think historically, what is the significance of Heidegger's attempt to subordinate this question to another—What is the meaning of Being?

I

By the second half of the nineteenth century, metaphysics had occupied only a peripheral place in German academic life. With the advance of industry and technology and, in the universities, the unprecedented influence of the natural sciences, the metaphysical frame of mind so characteristic of the Germany of Fichte, Schelling, and Hegel gave way to more modest empirical pursuits.

As we have seen, the philosophical justification of the predominant empiricism of the humanistic disciplines found expression in the work of the critical theorists of history. Convinced of the historical contingency of human understanding, these theorists were united in their conviction that self-critical historical thinking was simply incompatible with the metaphysicians' all-encompassing statements about reality.

In the period after 1918, however, a widespread resurgence of a variety of metaphysical endeavors—far surpassing the timid "impulse to metaphysics" recorded by Heidegger in his 1915 *Habilitationsvortrag* (postdoctoral presentation; see chapter 2)—brought with it a reconsideration of the prewar critical emphasis of theory. Moving beyond what was viewed as restrictive methods of critical thought, the metaphysical orientations of the 1920s emphasized a capacity for understanding the world that was more fundamental than any gained through inductively systematizing its empirical manifestations.

As with *Lebensphilosophie* (philosophy of life) of the postwar period, metaphysics quickly became a philosophical shibboleth, often without clear definition. It generally signified a quest for meaning, not only incarnated in empirical appearances, but also in the guise of their real and necessary precondition, lying beneath them and rendering them possible. Beyond this rudimentary sense, the term "metaphysics" applied to a whole range of pursuits.

Metaphysical argumentation arose, for example, in the finely constructed work of Heidegger's Marburg colleague, Nicolai Hartmann, in *Grundzüge einer Metaphysik der Erkenntnis* (Fundamentals of a metaphysics of knowledge). Still close to the concerns of the Marburg School of Hermann Cohen and Paul Natorp, Hartmann's work, which first appeared in 1921, challenged their neo-Kantian presupposition that meaning originated entirely in the ideal faculties of consciousness. On the basis of painstaking logical argumentation, Hartmann attempted to evolve a theory of ontological inherence of meaning in the structures of real Being, one that overcame the neo-Kantian dualism between ideality and reality. In contrast to the bolder metaphysical claims of his decade, however, he insisted he was not subverting critical methods, but correcting a distortion in earlier critical perspectives.[6]

Hartmann's work carefully separated what he saw as a critically refined metaphysics from the speculative claim to attain all-encompassing truth that proponents of metaphysics had often made. Such a notion of metaphysics also inspired much Dilthey scholarship in this period, including the writings of Rudolf Unger, for which Heidegger expressed his admiration.[7] Rather than speculatively deduce an all-encompassing meaning of the real human world from closed constructions of consciousness, the metaphysical interpretations of these Dilthey scholars saw conscious life as a real and necessary precondition bringing the human world into being in the open-ended diversity of its possible manifestations.

In more popular form, the renewed preoccupation with metaphysics in the late 1920s ranged from what has already been seen as Spengler's ruminations about the history of culture to the novels of Ernst Jünger (later Heidegger's friend and correspondent), who raised the experience of soldiers on the front in World War I to a metaphysical inquiry into our cosmological destiny.[8] Moreover, metaphysics was revitalized as a subject of religious debate, as in Catholic philosopher Peter Wust's *Auferstehung der Metaphysik* (The resurrection of metaphysics).

In the course of the 1920s, the term "metaphysics" resounded so widely in Germany that Heidegger bitterly lamented: "Today, when one philosophizes so barbarically and spasmodically, as in perhaps no other period in the history of Western thought . . . one nevertheless cries out to announce the resurrection of metaphysics (*Auferstehung der Metaphysik*) on every street corner."[9] He took special pains to distinguish his own approach to ontology from the popular and theological conceptions of metaphysics of the period.[10] Moreover, despite his qualified admiration for Dilthey's presupposition of immanent conscious life as the foundation on which understanding of the human world must rest, and his willingness to see in this presupposition a step in the direction of ontology,[11] Heidegger stipulated that no modern form of thought had adequately clarified the question of Being itself.

In the first sentence of *Being and Time*, he affirmed that the sense of the ontological query that had first arisen in ancient Greek metaphysics had been forgotten in modern times, "[e]ven though in our time we deem it progressive to affirm 'metaphysics' again."[12] Heidegger believed that the ancient Greek interrogation of Being— especially in the philosophies of Plato and Aristotle—had placed the question of the meaning of Being in an originary light, which, while positing the criteria for subsequent ontological interpretation in the Western intellectual tradition, was also distorted and trivialized in its accommodation to this tradition. He sought, not to reinstate the ancient concept of Being, however, but to reinterpret the question that Greek philosophers had brought to the fore and to clarify why it had been obscured. To this end, because the question he discerned in contemporary thought had become entangled in a long-standing pattern of comprehension, he counseled "destruction" (*Destruktion*) of the traditional ways of understanding Being. Destruction would wrest from traditional understanding of the question an implicit motive for the hiddenness of the theme under investigation and a meaning in it which had been left undisclosed.

Looking over the long history of the sense attributed to Being, Heidegger noted that the concept of Being had generally been considered at once the most universal—indefinable in terms of other, more determinate concepts—and the most taken for granted. Moreover, the traditional handling of the meaning of Being had left a legacy that had not been noticed, let alone overcome, in contemporary philosophy.

This legacy expressed itself in a failure to elucidate the essential character of *Dasein* for which alone Being and the question of its sense has meaning. Against what he perceived as tradition, Heidegger insisted that, because the question of Being is oriented throughout by the possibility of *Dasein*'s understanding of it, "[i]f we are to formulate our question explicitly and transparently, we must first give a proper explication of a being [*eines Seienden*]—that of the questioner [*des Fragenden*]—with regard to its Being."[13] In avowedly circular reasoning, Heidegger thus affirmed that it is in the Being of *Dasein* that a sense of Being per se must be sought. The main point of Heidegger's statement, however, was that *Dasein* could not be reduced to a fixed metaphysical essence or to some underlying substance, nor could it be comprehended by an unclarified ontology of human life.

As we will see more clearly, in *Being and Time,* Heidegger leaves open what *Dasein*—the guiding thread through which the question of Being per se is to be pursued—is. In essence, *Dasein* is to be determined nowhere else than in its unspoken decisions about what it means *to be.* For Heidegger, no meaning, whether in everyday existence or in the most ethereal theory, can be extracted from *Dasein*'s presupposition of what it means to be, however tacit.

If, in light of understanding what it means to be, there remains a margin of indeterminacy in the way in which *Dasein* orients its Being, this orientation never arises in the abstract. At several points in the introduction to *Being and Time,* Heidegger states that *Dasein*'s ways of Being are "factically" given and, as such, are always decided in relation to circumstances of *Dasein*'s concrete past and prefigure its future choices. In this regard, he stresses that "[i]n its factical Being, any *Dasein* is as it already was, and is 'what' it already was. It *is* its past, whether explicitly or not. . . . *Dasein* 'is' its past in the way of its own *Being,* which, to put it roughly, 'historicizes' out of its future on each occasion. . . . Its own past—and this always means the past of its 'generation'—is not something that *follows along* after *Dasein,* but each time already precedes it."[14]

This statement introduces a paradox. Heidegger claims to refer to the "universal sense of Being [*Sein überhaupt*]" or, as he wrote elsewhere, to philosophy as "universal ontology [*universale Ontologie*]."[15] Yet, if this were the case, how might his presupposition that *Dasein* is its past, from which its future choices are projected, yield more that just a partial, perspectival viewpoint—which would preclude any preoccupation with Being in the universal sense that Heidegger sought to disclose?

Even earlier than Heidegger, the critical theorists of history had carefully refined a century-old historicist turn away from traditional concepts of the Being of humanity as a metaphysical substance, and had attempted to understand the meaning of humanity in terms of choices elucidated in relation to the past. In stipulating that humanity came to understand and determine itself in history, as we have seen, none of the critical theorists was ready to embrace an ontological position. For them, the potentialities of individual cultures and of individual perspectives of truth expressed in them, while held together by a tissue of universally graspable coherence, nonetheless precluded definitive knowledge both of the Being of humanity and of humanity's variable, if continuous, advent in history.

How, then, does Heidegger hope to account for the Being of *Dasein* in the universal sense he is claiming to investigate in *Being and Time*? And, once the past is founded on a universal philosophy of Being, what becomes of the national or cultural unities theretofore considered the individual bearers of historical meaning, in the context of which normative values and standards of truth emerge and are sustained from generation to generation, and on whose mediation the very possibility of history itself depends?

II

A brief recapitulation of the theme of *Dasein*'s Being-in-the-world, and then what Heidegger viewed as a laying bare of the fundamental constitution of *Dasein*'s Being, will set in relief the universal claim through which he conceived the problem of historical meaning.

Heidegger's ontology, as analyzed through *Dasein*'s Being-in-the-world, unveiled what was for the times a reorientation of philosophy: abandoning the predominant conceptions of the world as the scene of objectifications of life or of values in the context of determinate societies or cultures, Heidegger made existence in the world in its most ordinary and mundane moments the starting point of philosophy. Philosophy of life and of worldviews, phenomenology of universal structures of consciousness, and the traditional neo-Kantianism and its reinterpretation in terms of symbolic forms by Ernst Cassirer all confronted a philosophy of the most everyday and banal aspects of a world where, according to Heidegger, the analytics of *Dasein* (*Daseinsanalytik*) had to find its immediate theme.

What, according to Heidegger, does the ordinary, everyday character of the world teach us ontologically? Everydayness (*Alltäglichkeit*) describes a familiar, immediate relation between *Dasein* and the world of people and of things before any process of abstraction has distinguished *Dasein* as an observer occupied with given objects. In this relation Heidegger discerned a basis for universal coherence in everydayness as such, beyond a record of single, ordinary situations or biographies depicting everyday life: the ordinary world is given as a unity through *Dasein*'s tendency to forget what it means to be in the immediacy of its preoccupations.[16]

Exploring this context of everydayness, Heidegger developed the line of argumentation for which *Being and Time* became renowned. The sense of what it means to be is ordinarily forgotten in an everyday environment (*Umwelt*) in which *Dasein*'s self-understanding is spontaneously involved in and extracted from the useful processes of a functionally interpreted world; it is neglected under the influence of everyday collective conventionalism, conformism, and anonymity, through which *Dasein* is ordinarily led to behold itself. The predominance of the style of rapport of the everyday collectivity (*Mitwelt*)—the common opinion (*communis opinio*) that "one" has prescribed—Heidegger termed "das Man."[17] The very familiarity of everyday Being-in-the-world is the obverse side of *Dasein*'s estrangement from itself.

In the course of *Being and Time,* Heidegger elaborates on the possibility of a limited transcendence of everyday Being-in-the-world. What *Dasein* is, decided in terms of what it means to be, essentially hovers between two fundamental choices: immersion in and acceptance of spontaneous forgetfulness of what it means to be, or the attempt to recover a sense of responsibility for its own Being from the spontaneous familiarity of an everyday world.

This dualism in Heidegger's ontology pinpoints in preliminary form the fundamental assumption underlying his universal claim. In stating that "*Dasein is* its past" in deciding the possibilities of its future, Heidegger is not primarily concerned with qualitative changes in a historically evolving *Dasein* (in the sense of an unfolding of cultural or world history). His statement that *Dasein*'s Being is not given in a fixed way must be carefully distinguished from the critical theorists' claim that humanity determines itself historically. Far from focusing on the critical analysis of changes in human perspective from period to period, Heidegger presumes that, whatever the alteration in perspective, "what *Dasein is*" is ontologically prefigured by the duality of possible directions its choices must take.

In the later sections of *Being and Time,* the possibility of delineating *Dasein*'s choices is grounded in what Heidegger describes as the fundamental constitution of *Dasein*'s Being. The way in which he frames this fundamental constitution—comprising the tripartite structure of "existence," "facticity," and "fallenness"—exposes the root assumption on which his universal claim is based, and adumbrates its intention vis-à-vis the problem of historical meaning.[18]

In dealing with *Dasein*'s existence, nowhere is Heidegger concerned with the particularity of *Dasein*'s perspectival view of the world in a given historical context, and the structural differences between this perspective and that of later generations. He relegates the specific differences constituting the objective context of the choices of existence, whether analyzed as the advent of given values and the remission of others or as the ebb and flow of worldviews in the process of history, to the level of secondary, "ontic" phenomena.

More fundamental than this, for Heidegger, are the dual possibilities of ontological choice illuminated by existence's finitude. This finitude, manifested in the untransferable, unavoidable eventuality of death, universally stands before the future possibilities of all existing *Dasein* and, underlying all specific circumstances, constitutes the sense of what it means to be. In the face of this future, *Dasein* may choose to blend into the spontaneous forgetfulness offered by present modes of Being-in-the-world, which Heidegger traces to a tacit collective need to forget the distinctiveness of existence—marked by personal death—and be calmed in the face of the impending end. This is the mark, for Heidegger, of inauthentic existence. Or it may accept authentic responsibility for its existence, recognizing that its distinctiveness bears the emblem of finitude, resolving to wrest the sense of what it means to be from ordinary interpretation, and orienting this meaning in accord with the finitude of its own decisions.

When dealing with facticity, nowhere does Heidegger specifically focus on facts (*Tatsachen*) themselves.[19] Rather than deal with particular factual events, Heidegger analyzes what he views as the necessity for all *Dasein* to exist "factically" in a contingent world in which understanding finds its point of reference. Because universally entangled in given perspectives limited by *Dasein*'s own transience, this understanding allows of no absolute starting point.[20]

Fallenness, Heidegger notes, is in no way meant to be taken as a judgment of specific moral circumstances. *Dasein* is fallen because its tendency to interpret the meaning of Being in the everydayness of an immediately given world is fundamental to the facticity of existence. In this mode of Being *Dasein*'s fall into the domination of *das Man* in the everyday environment and collectivity can never be fully overcome, but only resisted. Only through the effort to recover an individual, finite sense of what it means to be can each of us oppose a flight from the anxiety of death as our death, favored by the anonymity and conventionalism of tacit collective modes of seeking security and discharging the burden of finitude in face of the exigencies of current events.

Of itself, the universal claim involved in Heidegger's vision of the fundamental structures of *Dasein*'s Being does not elicit the special importance Heidegger attributes to historical understanding, nor the grounds for his own way of conceiving of it. But this intrinsic importance of historical understanding is illuminated in the preeminent insight of *Being and Time,* through which time emerges in its structural relation to the meaning of Being. Heidegger stipulates that *Dasein*'s choice of what it is is essentially drawn from its modes of being temporal. In this qualification, the claim that *Dasein is* its past in deciding its future acquires a unique significance, laying the temporal groundwork for Heidegger's reassessment of what it means to think historically.

For Heidegger, each of the aspects of *Dasein*'s fundamental constitution refers primarily to a mode of temporal Being. As he asserts in an elaborate line of argumentation, which cannot be recapitulated in detail here, existence is primarily oriented toward the future, facticity toward the past, and fallenness toward the present. The three modes of temporal Being—or *ekstases*—are always given in a unity; they owe the style of their unification to *Dasein*'s choices concerning what it means to be.[21] As inauthentic, *Dasein* confronts the future as a mere chronological waiting for events (*gewärtigen*); a simple expectation of a foreseeable future exactly modeled on the present, in which the eventuality of death is tacitly shunned. In this mode the past, too, is overlaid with the veneer of current events, a mere retention of occurrences in which the finite sense of past *Dasein,* and of the *Dasein* that retains it, escapes notice in the immediacy of present preoccupations.

In its authentic modes of temporalization, *Dasein* strives for transcendence of spontaneous presence of everyday Being-in-the-world. Temporal *ekstases* are unified, not on the basis of a current expectation of events to be retained at a later point, where a sense of what it means to be remains hidden in the face of pressing actuality (*Wirklichkeit*); the authentic unity of temporal modes, as Heidegger saw it, reveals this hidden meaning of Being as the explicit foundation of a choice. Placed primarily in the perspective of future anticipation (*Vorlaufen*) of death, this choice pierces through the veil of everyday actuality and illuminates possibilities ontologically specific to finite *Dasein.* The past, more than a mere former presence, or weighty precedent of present actuality, discloses itself for choice in a repetition (*Wiederholung*) of possibilities it bears. These possibilities (*Möglichkeiten*), projected as an "anticipatory repetition [*vorlaufende Wiederholung*]," unify the temporal *ekstases* as the decisive moment (*Augenblick*) when authentic choice is projected.

Dasein's dual possibilities of temporalizing, and of Being, had direct ramifications for the problem of historical meaning. The major nineteenth- and early-twentieth-century conceptions of history, from Hegel to the critical theorists, conceived of it in close relation to the objective development of national cultures in world history. The sequential order of history as an objectively unfolding process comprised a collective experience, founded in the past and lending coherence to present cultural development.

Heidegger's thinking about history started from a different premise. Heidegger did not interpret *Dasein*'s historical Being—or "historicity [*Geschichtlichkeit*]"—primarily in relation to the network of cumulative experience of the past, mediated by a sequential, objective coherence of culture.[22] Any possible sense of this network was traced back to what Heidegger viewed as the more primary source of historical meaning and coherence (*Zusammenhang*) in *Dasein*'s *choice* of a mode of temporalization in the projection of possibilities.

By rooting the source of *Dasein*'s historicity in a choice of temporal modes, Heidegger underlined an important proviso: historical theorists and historians had generally sought to induce historical meaning from the processes of historical development, assuming the spontaneous coherence of these processes in what objective analysis had proved to have once been actual. Reliance on objective standards, however, and on an overarching coherence of the historical process grounding their continuity, disregarded the essential moment of the modes of Being of *Dasein*.

As Heidegger makes clear in *Being and Time*, objective reality for *Dasein* is not the only source of past meaning, but corresponds to one mode of Being as appropriated by *Dasein* from a world of events, neglectful of the finitude of interpretation grounded in a sense of Being as Being toward death. The quest for objectivity and objective coherence misplaces this finitude, but is not able to overcome it. For Heidegger, it overlooks the authentic sense of the past, which is not revealed for any possible observer, but is grounded in *Dasein*'s *own* choice of a finite sense of what it means to be.[23]

Beyond a call to decision, Heidegger's approach to historical meaning has essential bearing on the way in which the past is revealed. Neglect of *Dasein*'s sense of Being issues from subservience to the weight of what has become actual, and veils the richness of original possibility that the authentic moments of the past embodied. This original possibility is intended by *Dasein*'s authentic projection of a meaning of Being in its modes of temporalization. Only such projection can free the past, as Heidegger viewed it, from its embalmment in the traditions of the present, for which a past moment of choice is forgotten in its primordiality and is confidently taken as an objective acquisition. The projection of authentic possibilities identifies an authentic past primarily in view of what can be retrieved for resolute repetition in the authentic future.[24]

Heidegger's philosophy thus retracted the authentic ground of history from historical concatenations, such as the objective development of national cultures or world history. This should not be taken to signify, however, that *Dasein*'s authenticity is restricted to an isolated framework of action in which the individual has no ties to a larger collectivity. As a counterpart to the inauthentic collectivity characterized by *das Man,* Heidegger envisions the locus of authentic possibilities as implicit in "the people [*das Volk*]," which comprises the authentic community of individuals prepared to take upon themselves the responsibility for choice in light of the finitude of existence.

Das Volk, like *das Man,* remains empirically intangible. *Das Volk* is a community of authenticity, which has no necessary, direct counterpart in the political or cultural world. In the terse passages dealing with collective authenticity, Heidegger recounts that *Dasein*'s authentic choices, projected in a singular fate (*Schicksal*), interweaves itself into the destiny (*Geschick*) of a people. The coincident interweaving of fates finds its locus in the generation (*Generation*):

> Destiny is not something that puts itself together out of individual fates, any more than Being-with-one-another can be conceived as the occurring together of several subjects. Our fates have already been guided in advance, in our being with one another in the same world and in our resoluteness for definite possibilities. Only in communicating and in struggling (Kampf) does the power of destiny become free. *Dasein*'s fateful destiny in and with its "generation" goes to make up the full authentic historicizing of *Dasein.*[25]

From the standpoint of the problem of historical meaning (and in regard to the theme of *Being and Time* as a whole), Heidegger's elucidation of *das Volk* leaves undeniable gaps. Collective inauthenticity receives detailed description throughout the work, but the possibility of authentic community is described only in its last sections and in vague terms.

In dealing with the theme of the generation, which fills out the nexus between the authentic individual and the community of *Das Volk,* Heidegger explicitly draws on Dilthey's use of the latter concept in "Über das Studium der Geschichte der Wissenschaften vom Menschen, der Gesellschaft, und dem Staat." (On the study of the history of the sciences of man, society, and state).[26] Although he much admired Dilthey's essay, Heidegger's treatment of communal authenticity is sketchy, perhaps due to the vacuum left by his distance from pre-World War I historical theory, within which Dilthey's thought had come to expression.

In applying the concept of generation, Dilthey sought a specifically historical unit of time. He considered the purely quantitative account of temporality in hours, minutes, and seconds to be inappropriate for this purpose, choosing instead a range of time that "reaches from the demarcation line of birth to that of old age."[27] In Dilthey's thought, the concept of generation represented the individual life span and, given a certain flexibility of interpretation, might be seen to anticipate Heidegger's notion of Being-toward-death.

Yet, in envisaging the life unity of the generation, Dilthey evidently did not claim to encompass an *ontological* unity. In descriptive and inductive terms, he attempted to account for a principle of unity interweaving the lives of contemporary individuals. His conviction that the basis of such a principle lay in empirical reality had led him to reject the nominalistic conclusions of Heinrich Rickert, for whom the distance between meaning and reality itself precluded any possibility that a "generation" or "worldview [*Weltanschauung*]" might serve as the real, extraindividual context providing for meaning's preservation and transmission. For Rickert, the spirit of Goethe's generation, of the Italian Renaissance, or of any other such cultural unity might be applied as value relations only to certain great individuals. It would be erroneous to claim that the distinctive spirit of a generation or of an age might in any real sense refer to more than a few great individuals.

Dilthey's epistemology, which considered that meaning infused reality without ever exhausting its empirical plenitude, attributed the spirit of a generation to more than an atomistic collection of individuals, a conclusion Heidegger readily accepted. For Dilthey, the convictions of a generation or the spirit of an age did not touch all individuals in the same way; there nonetheless existed links between contemporary individuals, arising from the depths of a common past, through which an ideal meaning of life emerged in the limitless plenitude of a real present context. In this sense, "a generation then forms an interrelation of appearances into a whole, subject to explanatory study."[28]

It would be an oversimplification to see in Heidegger's use of the term "generation" an extrapolation from Dilthey's insights, as Heidegger's comments might lead readers of *Being and Time* to believe. Unlike Dilthey—and in complete contradistinction to the Baden neo-Kantians—Heidegger is not referring to a generation as an "interrelation of appearances,"[29] but to the ontological preconditions universally underlying appearances. With ontological constructs such as *das Man* or the generations articulated in *Das Volk*, Heidegger is referring to the conditions of possibility of interrelation between individual and community concealed beneath the empirical flux of appearances.

Heidegger's notion of generation, as of communal authenticity in general, remains undeniably vague. A year after the publication of *Being and Time*, Karl Mannheim wrote a study of the concept of generation in which both Dilthey and Heidegger were analyzed. Dilthey's achievement, as Mannheim noted, was to have clearly expressed the idea of a qualitative cohesion (*Verbundenheit*) of specific styles of life interpretation among contemporaries, which could not simply be attributed to their quantitatively considered chronology. Given the vagueness of Heidegger's application of the notion of generation, is it any wonder that Mannheim, who was by no means unsympathetic to Heidegger's work, wrote that Heidegger "deepens precisely this problem of qualitative cohesion"?[30]

The distance of his thought from pre–World War I critical theories of history becomes clearest not only in its ontological theme, but in how Heidegger defines this ontology, notwithstanding its claim to universality. Given his attempt to conceive of a community interfused with authentic purpose, the thrust of Heidegger's analysis nonetheless focuses preponderantly on the fallenness of *Dasein* into an alienated (*entfremdete*), objectified world of inauthenticity. This aspect of his thinking would hardly seem to be free of the influence of historical circumstances: Heidegger's notion of authentic community remains sketchy to the extent that *Being and Time* itself emphasizes doubt in the collective world so often characteristic of his own generation. To that extent, it is informed by the factual circumstances of the times, in which the sense of worthiness of culture came into question in a manner that had been uncommon among members of the prewar generation. In this situation, is it any surprise that, for Heidegger, the dimensions of communal authenticity could inspire only the sparsest examination?[31]

For this reason, the claim that Heidegger's philosophy denies objectivity in history misses an important point. It is misleading to claim that, for Heidegger, the "real world of objective Being is dissolved."[32] The significant point is not an alleged dissolution of real Being; it lies rather in the manner of interpreting the historical world.

World history, heretofore taken as the objective totality of developing national cultures, represented, for Hegel, the invincible progression of the consciousness of freedom; for Ranke, the opaque habitat of Divine thoughts; for Rickert, the repository of ethereal transcendent values; and for Dilthey, the unique realm of crystallization of the human spirit. Not one of these thinkers questioned world history as a primary source of normative values and meaning.

For the Heidegger of *Being and Time,* by contrast, the objective coherence of world history *exists,* yet is reinterpreted in a way that denies its primary role as a source of *Dasein*'s authenticity. It is ultimately rooted in the temporal mode of existence that, under the hidden auspices of *das Man,* dissimulates the finitude of *Dasein* in an acquired, objectified actuality:

> The transcendence of the world has a temporal foundation; and by reason of this, the world-historical is, in every case, already "objectively" there in the historicizing of existing Being-in-the-world, *without being grasped historiologically.* And because factical *Dasein,* in falling, is absorbed in that with which it concerns itself, it understands its history world-historically in the first instance. . . .
>
> Blind for possibilities, it [*das Man*] cannot repeat what has been, but only retains and receives the "actual" that is left over, the world-historical that has been, the leavings, and the information about them that is present at hand.[33]

Once authentic historical meaning is displaced from objective world history and the nations or cultures composing it to *Dasein,* and to the unity of authentic *Dasein* achieved in a generation and in *Das Volk,* there arises the problem of normative standards and values whose emergence and sustenance had previously been tied to an objective cultural context. Indeed, as we have seen, for the critical theorists of the previous generation, the objective historical process provided philosophers with material through which normative truths and the sense of human existence itself could be established. Let us therefore turn to Heidegger's reconsideration of the problem of normative truth, by way of his reformulation of the relation between philosophical truth and history.

III

In chapter 1, we examined the way in which the critical theorists— especially Windelband, Rickert, and Dilthey—attempted to establish broad principles of historical understanding in the humanistic disciplines, independent both of law-constructing methods of the natural sciences and of abstract speculation of metaphysical philosophy. Historical thinking, conceived as the study of the meaning of human existence through the comprehension of what humanity had been, proposed that elucidation of normative truths in human affairs had to depend on inductive comprehension of the development of human culture and of norms that had actually been manifested in it. As we have also seen, the cardinal significance of historical methods in the humanistic disciplines presupposed a spontaneous coherence of the cultural world, where norms emerged and were refined in a continuous, unified process of development.

Heidegger's philosophy disagreed, not only with the principles of historical understanding that had been proposed as an autonomous method for the humanistic disciplines, but, above all, with the larger assumption that culture and world-historical development were primary sources of coherence (*Zusammenhang*). The appreciation of cultures as unique individualities constituting the epochs of world history and of human understanding as intertwined with the development of norms and values of a given culture, universal in implication but particular in concrete expression, found no significant echo in Heidegger's thought.

In view of this, it is hardly surprising that Heidegger failed to acknowledge the significance of the advent of the qualitative change in human historical understanding that arose with the modern appreciation for cultural diversity and the modern insight into the uniquely historical character of human existence. For thinkers like Windelband, Rickert, Dilthey, and Troeltsch, this insight had to be counted as one of the greatest theoretical fruits nurtured and sustained by the development of Western culture, liberating theoretical norms from the dogmatism of metaphysics. If, in his early writings, Heidegger had attributed a certain importance to that qualitative change in understanding, in *Being and Time,* this theme is entirely eclipsed. Evidently, he took this change as no salient development at all: his concern is with the unrecorded history of the forgetfulness of the ontology founded in the Being of *Dasein* and lying beneath the ontic level of culture and of individual diversity that is its dynamic principle.

Heidegger's retrieval of ontology was not tantamount to a resurrection of metaphysics in any traditional sense, precisely because it tried to open ontology to *Dasein*'s fluid temporalization of Being. In this role, transferring the ground of coherence of human existence from the objective realm of culture and world history into the temporalizing modes of *Dasein*'s understanding of Being meant redefining the aim of historical thinking and of the possibility of its grasp of truth.

This redefinition brings to the fore the confrontation with the problem of historical meaning that Heidegger subtly undertakes at the end of his section on temporality and historicity. Here, and in his course lectures of the period, the significance of Heidegger's attempt to root the sense of historical thinking in the fundamental ontology of *Dasein* finds its clearest relation to the issue of philosophical truth. Heidegger's thought on this matter is closely interwoven with his explicit rebuttal of the predominant ways in which historical theory had been articulated in the nineteenth and early twentieth centuries. His critique of the historians' specialized endeavor and of critical theories of historical knowledge calls into question the larger assumptions of previous styles of historical understanding, and leads directly to the theme of history and normative truth that concerns us most closely.

In the 1928 course lecture series "Die Grundprobleme der Phänomenologie" (Fundamental problems of phenomenology),

Heidegger situated the special role of historical thinking in relation to philosophical knowledge:

> The history of philosophy is not a mere appendage to the philosophical teaching firm providing an opportunity to find oneself a comfortable and easy theme for the State examination. Nor is it there to enable one to look around and see how things once were. Rather, historical-philosophical knowledge constitutes a unity in itself, in which the specific kind of historical knowledge in philosophy, in accord with its topics, is distinct from every other kind of scientific historical knowledge.[34]

In *Being and Time,* it is obvious that Heidegger's concerns lie elsewhere than with these "other kinds of scientific, historical knowledge" claiming autonomy from philosophy. He rebuffs critical theories of history for their justification of the quest for historical meaning as it had been conceived in the historical sciences. Most explicitly, his comments touch on Heinrich Rickert's "logic with which the concepts of historiological presentation are formed" and on Simmel's "'epistemological' clarification" of historical matters; they anticipate his later, more detailed and explicit criticism of Dilthey's theory, orienting itself "toward the side of the object."[35] In opposition to these theories' quest for general validity (*Allgemeingültigkeit*) of historical meaning in the historical sciences, Heidegger counters that the place (*Ort*) of the historical problematic "is not to be sought in historiology [*Historie*] as the science of history."[36] Against any claim of an autonomous science of history, he asserts that all historical concepts presuppose an ontological interpretation of *Dasein*'s temporalizing modes, concretely expressed in its historicity: "But since the basic concepts of the historiological sciences—whether they pertain to the objects of these sciences or to the way in which these are treated—are concepts of existence, the theory of the human sciences presupposes an existential interpretation that has as its theme the *historicity* of *Dasein*."[37]

In the last section of the chapter on temporality and historicity, Heidegger investigates the contemporary claim to establish autonomous historical principles of understanding. His analysis proceeds by discussing the views of the late nineteenth-century figure Count Yorck von Wartenburg, who had remained beyond the pale of the academic institutions of his period. During the 1920s, after his death, when Yorck's correspondence with Wilhelm Dilthey was published for the first time, his letters caused a stir among the German intelligentsia, especially for the path of historical understanding he proposed as an alternative to the predominant critical ideas of his period.[38] Heidegger deftly cites passages from this extraordinary correspondence, often including Yorck's criticisms of Dilthey.

Yorck objected to the attempts to systematize the past—attempts by no means absent from Dilthey's writings—in terms of typologies. Nor could Yorck reconcile himself to Windelband's search for the crystallization of forms (*Gestalten*) in the past. Comparative typologies and the thematization of forms had been evolved in an attempt to establish methods specific to the humanistic disciplines; for Yorck, especially the latter demonstrated an illusory enterprise that, failing to achieve clarity concerning its own motives, pursued aims which it had never distinctly understood.

These aims and what Yorck—and Heidegger—viewed as their ironic outcome, can best be comprehended by recalling the *Methodenstreit* (methological debate) that preoccupied thinkers of Yorck's generation. In this period following the decline of German idealism, the problem of achieving an overarching philosophy of history had receded into the background. The debate was chiefly over whether humanistic disciplines could rely on methods specific to them or might adopt the generalizing methods of the natural sciences. Yorck's position reduced such debate to a nonproblem.[39] For him, cut loose from the moorings of a systematic philosophy of history, the methods on which autonomous historical thinking was to be based were, not an alternative, but a complement to natural scientific methods.

Questioning historical scholarship and theories of history that had been highly influential since the rise of Ranke and the Historical School, Yorck rejected Ranke's concentration on the drama of political events, Windelband's search for forms in the historical process and, to a lesser extent, Dilthey's typologies, for what he viewed as a source common to all of them. For Yorck as for Heidegger, these styles of historical thinking sought to construct history as an aesthetic picture image, where the definition of historical meaning was predisposed to "ocular" configurations accessible to the sight. They aimed primarily at that which had body (*Körperliche*) and form (*Gestalthafte*).

Far from designating a place apart from the natural scientific vision, such aesthetic construction was driven back to a starting point the natural scientific outlook had prepared. In Yorck's words: "To the natu-

ral scientist, there remains, beside his science, as a kind of human tran-
quillizer, only aesthetic enjoyment."[40] Labeling this kind of aesthetic
historical construction "antiquarian," Yorck noted wryly that "[t]he
genuine Scholar [*Philologus*] conceives of History as a cabinet of
antiquities. These gentlemen never venture were nothing is palpable—
and where one has been guided only by a living psychical transposition. At heart, they are natural scientists, and they will become skeptics
all the more because experimentation is lacking."[41]

An alternative to this, for Yorck, was the philosophical insight capable of comprehending the "virtual" character of historical appearances—the inner course of history flowing beneath the surface of
appearances constituted by political events and structural images. This
comprehension could only be achieved through a radical renewal of
the philosophy of history. As Yorck explained to Dilthey, anticipating
his incredulity on this matter: "Because to philosophize is to live, there
is, in my opinion (do not be alarmed!), a philosophy of history—but
who would be able to write it? Certainly it is not the sort of thing it has
hitherto been taken to be, or the sort that has been attempted; you have
declared yourself incontrovertibly against all that."[42]

Despite his admiration for him, Heidegger was convinced that
Yorck had failed to penetrate to the ontological basis underlying a philosophy of life. Yorck's preliminary aim, as Heidegger indicated, lay
in distinguishing between natural and historical styles of being. In this
spirit, Yorck had made his celebrated separation between the "ontic"
and the "historical"—between nature that "is" and the historical that
"lives." Yorck's attempt to base a philosophy of history on this separation was taken by Heidegger as a sign of entanglement in the same
presuppositions that ensnared the historians he criticized: the traditional neglect of the meaning of Being. This neglect obscured the ontological unity which is more fundamental than any distinction between
nature and history, both of which Heidegger deemed "ontic" to the
extent that this unity was not investigated.

Heidegger's criticism of Yorck's separating the ontic from the historical, by highlighting the broad conception of understanding
(*Verstehen*) in Heidegger's philosophy, brings us closer to the problem
of a relation between philosophical truth and its historicity. Yorck's
thinking on this matter bore a marked resemblance to Dilthey's theory
of interpretation, in which the relation between consciousness that

understands (*versteht*) other conscious life had to be sharply distinguished from any relation maintained by consciousness in its explanation (*Erklären*) of natural objects. Understanding of conscious life by other conscious life provided, for Dilthey and Yorck, a potential intimacy of apprehension that natural topics of explanation, because of their dissimilarity to consciousness, could never reveal.

Heidegger's ontology calls into question the distinction between understanding (*Verstehen*) and explanation (*Erklären*), which Heidegger views as a mere construct of the sciences.[43] For Heidegger, history and nature are both made possible by the fundamental unity constituted by *Dasein*'s modes of synthesizing time. As Heidegger points out in the concluding chapter of *Being and Time* (which follows the chapter on temporality and historicity), this synthesis of time does not have its roots in the abstract chronology of world time. Rather, world time—which *Dasein* attentively interprets in the movement of the planets—is itself made possible by *Dasein*'s finite projection of a meaning of Being. Without a projection of the meaning of Being in the structural unity of existence, facticity, and fallenness, the unification of temporal *ekstases* in any possible apprehension would have no coherence, and could be the source of no meaning.

Nowhere is the primordial unity of apprehension of nature and history in *Dasein* better illustrated than in the historicity of the most basic concepts of the natural and historical disciplines. For Heidegger, this historicity is rooted, not in a world time beyond *Dasein,* but in the temporalizing modes through which a world is approached and made meaningful. That the basic concepts of both the natural and humanistic disciplines are subject to historical modification through scientific revolutions attests to their unity in the temporalizing modes of *Dasein*'s historicity.[44] The *Dasein*-centeredness of this unity underscores the limited value of a distinction between inner understanding (*Verstehen*) and explanation (*Erklären*) of external natural objects.

Heidegger's exclusive application of the word *understanding* (*Verstehen*)—and his renunciation of the concept of explanation (*Erklären*)[45]—underlined a critical point about historicity and temporality in the ontology of *Dasein*. Natural and historical objects belong to the same synthetic structure of temporalizing and of Being, and access to them is afforded only by the finite aim toward Being that *Dasein* projects. On this basis alone, Heidegger allows for the primary historicity of normative truths serving as the criteria for all that *Dasein* understands.

Is not this fundamental grounding of the sciences in *Dasein*'s historicity tantamount to an embrace of relativism? If, for Heidegger, the historicity of *Dasein* and of the finite possibilities of understanding is undeniable, the universal claim of ontology nonetheless provides finitude with an affirmative aim.[46] As we have seen, *Dasein*'s historicity moves within the structural boundaries delimited by the fundamental constitution of its Being and its modes of temporalization. Finitude is not a mere limit to *Dasein*'s understanding but a mode of access to other finite *Dasein* and to the world it composes. In stark contrast to the absolute ground of truth that had been the legacy of traditional ontology, Heidegger is thus able to specify that "[o]ntology needs only a finite being."[47]

For Heidegger, relativism and skepticism have their source, not in a frank acknowledgement of the historicity of human existence, but in an impossible epistemological demand: "The theories of relativism and skepticism originate in a partly justified opposition against a distorted absolutism and dogmatism of the concept of truth."[48] Insofar as the historical sciences had employed this impossible epistemological demand as a theoretical buttress, it becomes clear why Heidegger in *Being and Time* can regard them as the source of "historicism."[49]

From Heidegger's perspective, the foundation of normative truths on the finitude of *Dasein* does not represent a surrender to relativism. On the contrary, this foundation leads, for Heidegger, to an interpretation of truth that genuinely transcends the temporal horizons of specific epochs and the barriers of given cultures. Beneath the criteria of truth characteristic of past epochs or foreign cultures, the existential analytic displays the universal claim of the criteria of finitude in its focus on the persistent *motives* governing *Dasein*'s quest for truth's absolute, ahistorical ground. In these motives, Heidegger discerns the tacit reiteration of *Seinsvergessenheit* (the forgetfulness of Being) amid the diversity of the criteria of truth predominant in Western intellectual traditions, from the emergence of Western metaphysics to the development of modern thought. From the vantage point provided by the broad articulation of Western intellectual traditions, the debate surrounding historicism and relativism and the related quest for stable theoretical criteria emerge in a wholly new light.

Heidegger's notion of the motives underlying the predominant Western ideas of truth informs his attempt to adumbrate, on the ground of *Seinsvergessenheit,* a transhistorical unity of Western intellectual traditions, leading up to the quest for theoretical truth capable of surmounting historicism and relativism. From the standpoint of *Being and Time,* the transhistorical unity of Western traditions finds its source in an age-old presupposition. Rather than think that the finite Being of *Dasein,* through which the question of Being emerges, is essentially implicated in the understanding of Being per se, these traditions presuppose that *Dasein,* as all Being revealed through it, *is* insofar as it can be transposed into terms foreign to its finitude—into abiding presence and subsistence (*Vorhandensein*). This "diversion from finitude [*Wegsehen von der Endlichkeit*]"[50] was not only expressed in the determination of Being in terms of the abiding idea or permanence of substance of Plato and Aristotle (and their respective medieval successors); it left its mark on the great formative influences of modernity, despite all further innovations. In each case, from the Cartesian cogito to the Kantian "I think" (*ich denke*), to the Hegelian Spirit (*Geist*), to name only the most fateful of these influences, the finite meaning of *Dasein* "each time my own [*jemeiniges*]" disappeared before conceptual structures in which consideration of finitude had been tacitly preempted.[51] Each time, rather than Being in terms of the finite Being of *Dasein,* all Being per se, including that of *Dasein,* had been posited in relation to criteria of truth residing in what remained continually present and capable of becoming a permanent acquisition of thought. Ephemerality, contingency, and finitude, rather than being viewed as essential criteria of truth, were thus excluded from its definition.

According to Heidegger's well-known thesis, the motives for this exclusion, far from a disinterested search, have their seat in *Dasein*'s forgetfulness, springing from an unspoken quest to surmount the limits of its finite Being. Forgetfulness, as an essential moment in the uncovering of the truth of Being, constitutes for Heidegger a subtle opacity at the heart of the normative criteria that have determined Western metaphysics since antiquity.

Heidegger's claim about the unity of Western intellectual traditions applies not only to traditional metaphysics but also to an essential criterion of truth characteristic of modern intellectual traditions purporting to overcome the dogmatism of metaphysics. The basis of

Heidegger's claim and its general implications for the human sciences become clearer when we (once again) consider his thought in relation to the aims of what he himself took to be the most radical critical reflection on the foundations of the human sciences—the thought of Dilthey. Precisely because Dilthey, among all the critical philosophers, most nearly anticipated Heidegger's position in *Being and Time,* this point of contrast between Dilthey and Heidegger sets in relief Heidegger's appraisal of the human sciences—and the broader debate over historicism, relativism, and stable objective standards.

Like Heidegger, Dilthey had abolished recourse to an absolute starting point outside of history; truth was bounded by impenetrable limits that no finite being could surpass. Along with other critical philosophers, Dilthey concluded that the impenetrability of these limits precluded any possible overall vision of history claiming an ontological foundation, and that the decisive break with the dogmatism of traditional metaphysics lay precisely in the emergence of critical awareness of these limits.

Heidegger's considerations emerged from a very different vantage point. Beyond the limits that historical contingency necessarily imposed on truth, Heidegger emphasizes, above all, an opacity that deepens through *Dasein*'s everyday tendency to avoid the implications of its own finitude. Indeed, because *Dasein* is continually tempted to interpret itself in terms of a communal and instrumental world that encourages it to forget the meaning of its finitude, its understanding is partial and the hidden basis of its own ideations disguised.

Nowhere is this more evident than in what might be described, from Heidegger's standpoint, as the chief "noncritical" presupposition of the critical philosophies—the normative ideal of truth embodied in the criterion of "general validity [*Allgemeingültigkeit*]," which, as we saw in chapter 1, provided Dilthey and other critical philosophers the standard of objective truth par excellence in the historical methodology of the human sciences. For Heidegger, the criterion of "general validity" assumes that only what may be leveled down to an abiding acquisition, uniformly subject to verification, may be taken as true. From Heidegger's standpoint, this idea of the uniform objectivity of norms of truth implies that the primordial source of historical meaning is not *Dasein,* but the omnipresent coherence (*Zusammenhang*) of a historical process outside of human finitude and—in the guise of permanence of an acquisition—capable of offering a measure of compensation for the contingency of finite perception. For this reason, the criterion of "general validity"—encouraged by *das Man*'s diversion of *Dasein* from its finitude—is in Heidegger's words nowhere "less applicable than in the human historical sciences."[52]

All claims about the essentially historical character of humanity notwithstanding, Heidegger believed that modern historical methodologies depended on a notion of historical meaning that neglected the radical implications of human historicity. Rooted in the idea of a spontaneous coherence of history and the uniformity imposed by the criterion of "general validity," this modern methodology masks the true character of the historicity of human understanding, whose universality arises in its orientation of a plurality of finite choices (authentic and inauthentic) through which *Dasein* decides the meaning of its finite Being and illuminates a truth specific to that decision. In this manner, he displaced the primordial source of the contingency of truth from the level of perspectival worldviews and values to the facticity of *Dasein.*

From Heidegger's standpoint, reflection on the foundation of the human sciences in the critical philosophies of history thus did not break with, but profoundly extended the predominant conception of truth that had characterized Western metaphysical traditions. Despite their explicit renunciation of metaphysical assumptions, modern critical theories of truth obscured their deep roots in the metaphysical tradition stemming from ancient philosophy and Christian theology: they unwittingly appropriated from this tradition attributes of truth derived from the traditional "ontologies of presence."

For Heidegger, these ontologies presuppose that Being manifests itself as an abiding presence in the midst of change. In critical theory as in the Western metaphysical tradition in general, the characterization of truth illustrates *Dasein*'s tacit choice of a mode of Being, in which the consequences of its finitude are obscured but never overcome. *Seinsvergessenheit,* as the forgetfulness of the finite Being of *Dasein* in the disclosure of a meaning of Being, serves as a metahistorical leitmotiv linking in a silent unity the motives of a long tradition of reflection stretching back to antiquity.

NOTES

1. "Already in the title of my *Habilitationsschrift*, 'The Doctrine of Categories and of Meaning in Duns Scotus' [Die Kategorien- und Bedeutungslehre des Duns Scotus]," Heidegger would write late in life, "two perspectives came to predominance: 'doctrine of the categories' is the usual name for the discussion of the Being of beings [*Sein des Seienden*]; 'doctrine of meaning' stands for the *grammatica speculativa*, the metaphysical consideration of language in its relation to Being. But all of these connections were still opaque to me at that time." Heidegger, *Unterwegs zur Sprache*, 91–92.

2. Heidegger, *Kant und das Problem der Metaphysik*, 18. Heidegger originally planned this work as a section of *Being and Time* (see *Sein und Zeit*, 40), but later decided to publish it separately, which he did in 1929. According to Heidegger, the possibility of overcoming traditional metaphysics presupposes analysis on the basis of "fundamental ontology" in the sense elaborated in *Being and Time*. Since the pagination of the German Niemeyer edition of *Sein und Zeit* is indicated in the margins of both the *Gesamtausgabe* edition and the 1962 English translation by John Macquarrie and Edward Robinson, I will cite only the pagination of the Niemeyer edition.

3. Heidegger, *Gesamtausgabe*, 24:3–14. The contents of *Die Grundprobleme der Phänomenologie* were originally presented as a series of course lectures at Marburg in 1927.

4. Gay, *Weimar Culture*, 82; Iggers, *German Conception*, 244.

5. Heidegger, *Sein und Zeit*, 396.

6. Hartmann, *Grundzüge einer Metaphysik der Erkenntnis*, 1–10. Heidegger would sharply attack Hartmann in *Sein und Zeit*, 208.

7. Certain contemporaries considered that Hartmann's *Grundzüge* had directly inspired the metaphysical interpretation of Dilthey's thought in the 1920s. See Degener, "Zwei Wege zu Diltheys Metaphysik," 18–19. In Degener's estimation (p. 9), the metaphysics "hidden" in Dilthey's thought came to clarity "in connection with the intensification of the metaphysical movement of the present."

Heidegger, *Gesamtausgabe*, 20:5. Heidegger referred to Unger, "Literaturgeschichte als Problemgeschichte: Zur Frage geisteshistorischer Synthese, mit besonderer Beziehung auf Wilhelm Dilthey." Unger wrote (p. 15) of a "new metaphysical consciousness" aware that the history of literature is more than a science of technique and of form, diverted into psychology or aesthetics; it had to focus its primary concern on a history of interpretation of "the atemporal ground and the temporal appearance" of real structures implied in ultimate life problems.

8. This theme became especially evident in Jünger's 1922 work *Der Krieg als inneres Erlebnis,* where he spoke of the soldier's need to reach a deeper understanding of life, a "more heartfelt enjoyment of Being" (p. 38). A concluding sentence typifies Jünger's metaphysical ruminations: "All works become nothing before the powerful and incessant swelling over [*Vorüberfluten*] into battle; all concepts become hollow against the expression of something elementary and violent that always was and always will be, even after men and wars have long ceased to exist" (p. 108).

9. Heidegger, *Gesamtausgabe,* 24:19.

10. Heidegger, *Kant,* 230.

11. Heidegger, *Gesamtausgabe,* 20:173.

12. Heidegger, *Sein und Zeit,* 2. I have modified Macquarrie and Robinson's English translation (*Being and Time*) where I have deemed it necessary.

13. Heidegger, *Sein und Zeit,* 7.

14. Ibid., 20.

15. Ibid., 15; Heidegger, *Gesamtausgabe,* 24:16.

16. Heidegger, *Sein und Zeit,* 41–110, and *Gesamtausgabe,* 20:201–15.

17. In Heidegger's estimation, *Dasein* and its fellows find themselves in a publicly defined structure of roles in relation to a world of things they commonly dispose of. This collective environment reaches beyond a functional preoccupation with the environment to encompass a public style of interpretation that unavoidably saturates collective existence per se: "We take pleasure and enjoy ourselves as *they* [*man*] take pleasure; we read, see, and judge about literature and art as they see and judge; likewise we shrink back from the 'great mass' as *they* shrink back; we find shocking what *they* find shocking. The 'they,' which is nothing definite, and which all are, though not as the sum, prescribes the kind of Being of everydayness." Heidegger, *Sein und Zeit,* 127.

18. Ibid., 301–31.

19. Heidegger, *Gesamtausgabe,* 21:233. The lecture series "Logik: Die Frage nach der Wahrheit" was originally presented in the winter of 1925–26.

20. Heidegger, *Sein und Zeit,* 348.

21. Ibid., 310–52. For a discussion of the aporias implicit in Heidegger's notion of time in relation to historicity and intratemporality in *Being and Time,* see Ricœur, *Temps et récit,* 3:90–144.

22. The translators of *Being and Time,* John Macquarrie and Edward Robinson, have translated Heidegger's "*Geschichtlichkeit*" as "historicality" and his "*Historizität*" as "historicity." Because "*Historizität*" rarely appears in the text, and the word *historicality* is by no means clear in English, I have translated Heidegger's "*Geschichtlichkeit*" as "historicity" instead. Two scholars of Heidegger's thought have confirmed this translation since the appearance of the English-language edition of *Sein und Zeit.* See Krell, "General Introduction: The Question of Being"; and Hoy, "History," 329–53.

It is curious that Heidegger hardly mentioned the theme of culture in *Being and Time*. In his 1929 debate with Ernst Cassirer at Davos, he remarked: "I can very well admit that if . . . one takes this analysis of *Dasein* in *Being and Time* as an investigation of people, and then asks the question how, on the basis of this understanding of people, it might be possible to understand culture and the realms of culture; . . . it is absolutely impossible to say anything from what is given here." Heidegger and Cassirer, "Davoser Disputation," in Heidegger, *Kant*, 256. The broader implications of Heidegger's interpretation of culture are the central theme of Barash, *Temps de l'être, temps de l'histoire: Heidegger et son siècle,*105–49.

23. Heidegger, *Sein und Zeit*, 378–97.

24. Heidegger's discussion of objectivity in historical matters and the grounding of historical meaning in the *Dasein* that seeks to grasp it bear a striking resemblance to certain aspects of Nietzsche's thought. Later in Heidegger's chapter on temporality and historicity, he explicitly uses Nietzsche's philosophy, but not in relation to this specific theme, where certain points of congruence would seem to be most striking. In the second meditation of his *Untimely Meditations,* Nietzsche wrote: "Yes, one goes so far as to suppose that he who has no relation to a moment of the past is called on to represent it . . . that is what one calls 'objectivity.' . . . Only in the strongest exertion of your most noble qualities will you discover what in the past is great and worthy of being preserved and known." Nietzsche, "Vom Nutzen und Nachteil der Historie für das Leben," in *Erkenntnistheoretische Schriften,* 56. On Heidegger's relation to Nietzsche in his critique of Dilthey, see Barash, "Über den geschichtlichen Ort der Wahrheit: Hermeneutische Perspektiven bei Wilhelm Dilthey und Martin Heidegger," 58–74.

25. Heidegger, *Sein und Zeit*, 384–85.

26. Dilthey, "Über das Studium," in *Geistige Welt*, 36–41; Heidegger, *Sein und Zeit*, 385.

27. Dilthey, "Über das Studium," in *Geistige Welt*, 37.

28. Ibid.

29. Ibid.

30. Mannheim, "Das Problem der Generationen," 164.

31. In his lectures of the late 1920s, Heidegger explicitly distanced himself from "bourgeois [*bürgerliche*]" styles of thinking, which he felt took comfort in the illusion of eternal truth. See, for example, Heidegger, *Gesamtausgabe,* 24:314, where after attacking the notion of eternal truth, he stated that "philosophical and scientific knowledge do not bother themselves at all about the consequences [of this], even if these consequences are still uncomfortable for bourgeois understanding." It was perhaps Hannah Arendt who best understood the deeper political implications of

Heidegger's emphasis on collective inauthenticity. On this theme, see Villa, *Arendt and Heidegger: The Fate of the Political*; and Barash, "The Political Dimension of the Public World: On Hannah Arendt's Interpretation of Martin Heidegger," 251–68, and "Hannah Arendt, Martin Heidegger and the Politics of Remembrance," 171–82.

32. Iggers, *German Conception*, 244.

33. Heidegger, *Sein und Zeit*, 389, 391

34. Heidegger, *Gesamtausgabe*, 24:31–32.

35. Heidegger, *Sein und Zeit*, 375.

36. Ibid., 375, 395.

37. Ibid., 397.

38. Alfons Degener, for example, noted the importance of this correspondence in highlighting the metaphysical implications of Dilthey's thought. Yorck seems to have encouraged the metaphysical tendency in Dilthey. See Degener, "Zwei Wege," 9.

39. In *Being and Time* Heidegger emphasizes past possibility and not what has actually occurred in the past as the central focus of authentic historical analysis. From this standpoint—which is closer to Nietzsche than to Yorck—Heidegger declares: "The question whether the object of historiology is just to place unique 'individual' events into a series, or whether it also has 'laws' as its objects, is one that is radically mistaken." Heidegger, *Sein und Zeit*, 395.

40. Yorck, as cited in ibid., 400.

41. Ibid.

42. Ibid., 402.

43. Heidegger, *Gesamtausgabe*, 20:2. Or, as Heidegger expressed this thought in his August 8, 1928, letter to Elisabeth Blochmann: "In the historical sciences . . . there lies a specific understanding of existence; according to my conviction, indeed, the traditional separation of natural and human sciences is in every form a superficiality. . . . From a metaphysical standpoint there is only *one* science [*Wissenschaft*]." Heidegger and Blochmann, *Briefwechsel, 1918–1969*, 25.

44. Heidegger, *Sein und Zeit*, 8–11.

45. Heidegger, *Gesamtausgabe*, 24:390.

46. Notwithstanding his argument for the primary unity of natural and historical thinking in the ontology of *Dasein*, it is difficult to see any affirmative message in Heidegger's thought for the natural sciences. However much *Dasein*'s modes of Being may apply to the human sphere, it is difficult to envision how the choices of temporalizing that underlie *Dasein*'s authenticity or inauthenticity would have anything but a negative implication for natural sciences such as physics and astronomy. Although Heidegger suggested the contrary at various points in his writings of this period, and even that authentic

science in general would be possible, when it came to defining what form authentic science would take, Heidegger sidestepped the question: "We shall not trace further how science has its source in authentic existence. It is enough now if we understand that the thematizing of entities-within-the-world presupposes Being-in-the-world as the basic state of *Dasein,* and if we understand how it does so." Heidegger, *Sein und Zeit,* 363.

47. Heidegger and Cassirer, "Davoser Disputation," in Heidegger, *Kant,* 252.

48. Heidegger, *Gesamtausgabe,* 24:316.

49. Heidegger, *Sein und Zeit,* 396.

50. Ibid., 424.

51. Ibid., 22.

52. Ibid., 395.

Part II

Toward a History of Being: 1927–1964

6

Anthropology, Metaphysics, and the Problem of Historical Meaning in Heidegger's Interpretation of the *Kehre*

IN THE DECADES following publication of *Sein und Zeit* (Being and time), Heidegger's question of Being (*Seinsfrage*) shifted its focus. In a course lecture of 1937–38, he referred to this change as a "reversal [*Kehre*]" and a "completion [*Ergänzung*]" of the questioning begun with *Being and Time.* Where he had analyzed "man in relation to Being" in *Being and Time,* after the *Kehre,* he would analyze "Being and its truth in relation in man."[1]

The theme of truth would play a pivotal role in this reversal, as Heidegger's later essays confirm. Indeed, he characterized two key essays on truth—"Vom Wesen der Wahrheit" (On the essence of truth) and "Platons Lehre von der Wahrheit" (Plato's doctrine of truth)—as having first indicated the shift in his later thought.[2] Thus we can establish in a preliminary way what will become increasingly evident as we proceed: at the heart of Heidegger's reexamination of the *Seinsfrage* stood a direct reconsideration of the basis both of truth, which in *Being and Time* referred to the fundamental ways of Being of *Dasein* (finite human existence),[3] and of coherent normative standards (*Massstäbe*), by which truth was recognized as such.

Chapter 5 has indicated how, in *Being and Time, Dasein*'s finite modes of temporal and historical existence oriented the ontological interpretation at the basis of the disclosure of truth. It was precisely the tacit elaboration of forgetfulness of *Dasein*'s finitude in the everyday mode of existence that, for Heidegger, had left its subtle mark on the theoretical quest to define truth in Western intellectual traditions: the ongoing attempt to exempt the foundation of truth from *Dasein*'s finite temporality and historicity ran throughout Western history.

This significant metahistorical claim, only adumbrated in *Being and Time,* reemerged after the *Kehre* to provide a more complete overview of the unity of Western intellectual traditions, although now in an altogether different light. Questioning the very notion of "fundamental ontology," Heidegger no longer grounded the historicity of truth in an ontology of *Dasein.* More important, his rethinking the role of ontology necessarily involved rethinking the metahistorical unity of Western ideas of truth as conceived in *Being and Time.*

In this chapter, we will analyze the implications of Heidegger's *Kehre* for the problem of historical meaning. For a more comprehensive approach to this problem in our critical analysis of Heidegger's later writings, we will focus on the significance of the *Kehre* in the first section, and directly treat this problem in later sections.

I

Our analysis must face one pressing difficulty from the outset: how to approach a shift that occurred over the period of some fifteen years and a large number of written works. In an effort sustained across a series of books, lectures, and articles—including *Kant und das Problem der Metaphysik* (Kant and the problem of metaphysics), "Was ist Metaphysik?" (What is metaphysics?), and "Vom Wesen des Grundes" (On the essence of foundation)—Heidegger gradually moved beyond the boundaries of his earlier fundamental ontology to reexamine from other vantage points the notion of ontological truth put forward in *Being and Time.*

In works written directly after *Being and Time*—above all, in *Kant and the Problem of Metaphysics*—one theme predominated, which later, in a different way, stood at the center of the *Kehre* and its shift in historical perspective: the problem of "anthropology." In relation to this problem, Heidegger's most farsighted critics, and even Heidegger himself, began to perceive the limitations of an approach to "man in relation to Being," which grounded the historicity of truth in fundamental ontology. As we will see, with his renunciation of fundamental ontology, closer investigation of this problem became ever more central to Heidegger's thought; it provides an essential clue to the later shift in his thinking on the ground of the historicity of truth as he turned toward "Being and its truth in relation to man."

Heidegger had briefly dealt with the problem of anthropology in *Being and Time* in a section entitled "Abgrenzung der Daseinsanalytik gegen Biologie, Psychologie und Anthropologie" (Demarcation of the analytics of *Dasein* with respect to biology, psychology, and anthropology). In this section, the term "anthropology" had a double sense, signifying, first, a specialized discipline, much like biology or psychology, and, second, the traditional way of thinking about humanity that had been inherited from ancient Greek and Christian sources. In accord with this second sense, Heidegger related anthropology to what he took to be the traditional neglect of the finitude of *Dasein,* the metahistorical motif by which traditional Greek and Christian conceptions of humanity predisposed a specific "diversion from finitude [*Wegsehen von der Endlichkeit*]"[4] in ideas of the "subject," the "person," and the "spirit [*Geist*]" presupposed by the modern ontic human sciences.

Ancient Greek and Christian traditions also favored a more general modern interpretation of humanity, as underscored in *Kant and the Problem of Metaphysics*, where the term "anthropology" emphasized a tendency of modern thinking in general "insofar as this always relates everything and, ultimately, the totality of beings per se, in whatever possible way, to man."[5] Such a tendency encompassed disciplines of the human sciences from sociology, psychoanalysis, and ethnology to "cultural morphology" and the "psychology of worldviews."[6] In the guise of a philosophical anthropology comprising all of the various human sciences, the claim had been advanced that philosophy grounded in the ontic sciences could replace traditional metaphysics in providing a foundation for normative standards of truth. As Heidegger wrote:

> Anthropology today has for a long time been not just the title for one discipline, but the word designates a fundamental tendency of the contemporary position of humanity in regard to itself, and amid the totality of beings. According to this fundamental position, something is known and understood only when it has found an anthropological explanation. Anthropology does not just search for truth about humanity, but now lays claim to the decision about the meaning of truth as such.[7]

The reference to anthropology as a philosophy of "today [*heute*]," with its claim "that the world is to be interpreted after the image of man,"[8] anticipated a central leitmotiv that ran throughout Heidegger's later thought and a new argument against modern historical theory that later works increasingly articulated. Insofar as modern historical theory tended to reinterpret traditional metaphysics within the sphere of human cultural existence, values, and worldviews (*Weltanschauungen*), historical reflection had been a primary constituent of the anthropological basis of modern ways of positing truth, whose predominance Heidegger came to see as the fate of Western intellectual traditions.

In these years before the *Kehre*, however, Heidegger was less concerned with the ascendant role of anthropology than with the separation from it of fundamental ontology's claim to provide the transcendental ground of truth. Consistent with this concern, Heidegger attempted to demarcate the ontological-metaphysical from the anthropological in a book on a thinker whose work had been decisive in setting the terms of the modern conception of this dichotomy: Immanuel Kant.[9] The aim of *Kant and the Problem of Metaphysics* provides salient insight into what Heidegger considered to be the transcendental parameters of his own thinking: by analyzing this aim, we will shed light on the problematic nature of Heidegger's conception of the dichotomy between anthropology and metaphysics. As I will argue, Heidegger's own shift in thinking about this dichotomy stood at the center of his reconsideration in the *Kehre* of the topic of truth—and its relation to the problem of historical meaning.

Kant's "Copernican dictum"—that knowledge does not conform to its objects; rather objects must conform to human modes of cognizance to be apprehended—prepared the way for the broad modern conception of anthropology in two respects that are of importance to our discussion. First, it centered the problem of knowledge on the constitution of a world by a human subject. This was Kant's essential contribution to philosophical anthropology, as emphasized by Max Scheler, whose work, in Heidegger's view, had provided a stronger and more fertile conception of the human being, while also indicating the "essential difficulties and complications of this task."[10] After Descartes's somewhat misguided prolongation of the classical teaching of humanity, Scheler explained, Kant set the terms of modern philosophical anthropology.[11] As Scheler put it in his *Philosophische Weltanschauung* (Philosophical worldview; 1929):

> The entire pre-Kantian metaphysics of the West had attempted to represent the absolute Being of beings from out of the *cosmos* and, in each case, in terms of its *object*—Being. This is what Kant, in his critique of reason (transcendental dialectic) demonstrated to be an *impossible*

enterprise. He justifiably thought: *all* objective Being of the inner as outer world is, above all, to be related to *man.* All forms of Being are dependent on the being of man.[12]

Second, Kant's dictum centered comprehension of "all forms of Being on the human being." This emphasis on human-centered foundations for truth was a prerequisite (albeit against Kant's own intentions) for later anthropomorphic critiques of theology, which were pushed to the extreme in the anthropologies of thinkers such as Ludwig Feuerbach. By centering his investigation on the topic of humanity, Kant intended to rescue, notably in the moral sphere, the absolute rational claim of truth that had been harmonized with theological foundations as recently as in the systems of Leibniz and Wolff—a claim, Kant recognized, that could nowhere find support in the contingent field of human experience anthropological inquiry took as its starting point.

Kant's Copernican dictum preeminently established this rescue of the absolute on the grounds of reason alone. In conceiving the world, not as a fixed entity in itself, but in relation to human modes of cognizance, Ernst Cassirer and the Marburg neo-Kantians stressed that Kant prepared the way for anthropology in the modern sense and, above all, for an appreciation of its limits. Kant moved beyond anthropology to the extent that reason, in his system, was not confined within the horizons of experience demarcated by a contingent human nature, but could deduce the limits of experience. In so doing, reason could conceive the possibility of transcendence of a contingent, experiential world of causal interaction and functional explanation, in which anthropological understanding found its basis. For Kant, this transcendental role of reason extended from a demonstration of the boundaries of causal explanation and the metaphysical possibility of freedom, to a deduction of the rational basis of all the criteria that free action had to deploy to be moral. Because grounded in the impartial rules of pure reason, rather than in contingent human affairs, such criteria could be considered not only binding for humans as anthropological beings, but absolutely valid, "for any possible rational being."[13]

Several months before Heidegger completed *Kant and the Problem of Metaphysics*—known informally as the *"Kantbuch"*—the Davos Hochschule debate between him and Ernst Cassirer announced the broad terms of the encounter between Kant's philosophy and the *Daseinsanalytik* (analytics of *Dasein*). In the series of public discussions with Cassirer that followed, Heidegger explicitly targeted Hermann Cohen, Wilhelm Windelband, Heinrich Rickert, Benno Erdmann, and Alois Riehl;[14] he aimed to reexamine the well-documented normative supremacy of reason in the interior of Kant's philosophy that the traditions of neo-Kantian scholarship, and these five thinkers in particular, had accepted as axiomatic.

Heidegger's task lay in a "radicalization of the Kantian theme of ontological knowledge to uncover the fundamental problematic of *Being and Time*,"[15] in making good his claim about the primacy of finite ontology over reason and all other possible claims regarding the basis of normative criteria. And here stood his main difficulty. Once reason had been overturned as the guarantor of an autonomous foundation of human norms and subordinated to the finitude of *Dasein,* how could he maintain the separation between anthropology and metaphysics? Insofar as the finitude of *Dasein* was taken, not as an anthropological attribute, but as the transcendental precondition of human existence and of the disclosure of Being per se, Heidegger had to convincingly argue that *Dasein*'s finitude could indeed constitute the transcendental horizon of a human world. It was incumbent on him to prove that *Dasein*'s finite approach to Being was not the ontic expression of a historical worldview, a psychological state, or a cultural disposition, but indeed defined the parameters within which a metaphysical foundation for normative truths became possible.

In this endeavor lay the significance of Heidegger's attempt to propose, from the interior of Kant's critical philosophy, an alternative to the neo-Kantian insistence on Kant's autonomy of reason. And because, for Heidegger, reason itself referred back to the *temporal* articulations of a finite *Dasein,* his reinterpretation found its leverage point in Kant's theory of reason and of the understanding in relation to time.

Heidegger's *Kantbuch* focused on the source of a difficulty that gradually emerged in the development of Kant's thought: the connection between the pure cognitive faculties of reason and understanding, on the one hand, and pure intuition in space and time, on the other. As Heidegger showed, although Kant did not foresee the scope of this difficulty in the first edition of *Kritik der reinen Vernunft* (Critique of pure reason), it was largely his awareness of it that led him to revise his text for the second edition, under the influence of a more fully elaborated moral theory. Here Kant considered that if reason, working beyond the logical categories of the understanding, could give grounds for moral action binding for any rational being, the same kind of validity could not extend to temporal intuition as a pure faculty specific to human beings alone.[16] Founding reason and logical understanding in consciousness' temporal intuition could only compromise the absolute autonomy of reason's claim to be the ultimate norm giver, independent of factors that could never assert such autonomy with regard to specifically human functions and modes of life.

Heidegger's work focused directly on a change in Kant's attitude toward the transcendental schematism, by virtue of which the pure temporal constitution of experience by consciousness related to the categorical logic of the understanding and, through this medium of understanding, to reason. The transcendental schematism enabled this relation insofar as it provided a pure, imaginative, beforehand vision of the temporal structure of experience, thus imposing a precognitive temporal order on a chaos of sense impressions and preparing them for categorical comprehension by pure understanding.

Heidegger argued that the change in Kant's position on the transcendental schematism was especially apparent in his conception of its relation to the pure intuition, on the one hand, and to the pure understanding, on the other.[17] Whereas, in the first edition, Kant had posited the transcendental imagination as an independent faculty mediating between pure intuition and pure understanding, in the second edition, he cancelled this autonomy: "[I]ts office," as Heidegger expressed it, "is transferred to the understanding."[18] Kant consistently maintained that the pure understanding worked on sense impressions made accessible by pure intuition. The incorporation of the transcendental schematism within the pure understanding thus removed any possible ambiguity from his insistence that the meaning-giving capacity of understanding, and especially the faculty of reason, stood on a foundation whose autonomy could in no way be compromised by limits imposed by pure sensuous intuition. And it was precisely this self-enclosed, absolute normative basis of reason, free from extraneous constraint, that Kant's fully developed moral philosophy required.

In a later context, the neo-Kantians appreciated the significance of this absolute normative basis as a safeguard for the universality of norms—in this case, moral standards—whose validity seemed all too readily accountable in terms of historical milieu, psychological stimuli, or other merely human circumstance. The reassertion of an absolute ground of reason independent of factors contingent on specifically human modes of apprehension (i.e., pure sensibility in time and space) reinforced the epistemological bulwark of the neo-idealist response to the problem of relativism analyzed in chapter 1.

In their treatments of reason, the understanding, and time in Kant's thought, the Marburg neo-Kantians went far beyond the master (and in a direction Heidegger's interpretation of Kant sought to reverse). Thus, responding in particular to the problem of psychologism, Hermann Cohen's *Kants Theorie der Erfahrung* (Kant's theory of experience) not only incorporated the transcendental schematism within the faculty of pure understanding, but (as indicated in chapter 1) conceived pure intuition in time and space as functions of the pure understanding.[19] On the basis of this innovation, Cohen brought into cohesive unity the theoretical and ethical dimensions of his own thinking in the philosophical system he set forth in *Logik der reinen Erkenntnis* (Logic of pure knowledge) and *Ethik des reinen Willens* (Ethics of pure will).[20]

Heidegger, on the other hand, approached Kant from the opposite standpoint, by basing his reinterpretation of Kant on what he thought to be a wholly neglected aspect of the first edition of the *Critique of Pure Reason*. Kant's original insight regarding the independence of the transcendental schematism as a faculty that viewed beforehand the structure of time meant, in Heidegger's interpretation, that the transcendental synthesis constituted by the pure temporalizing activity of consciousness stood at the root, not only of intuition in space and time, but of understanding and reason.[21] Hermann Cohen had anticipated the possibility of just such an interpretation in his *Kants Theorie der Erfahrung*: "It is in every case a remarkable misunderstanding when more recent authors direct a consideration against Kant, which comes to its deepest expression in terms of the schematism: the consideration, namely, that intuition and concept do not operate separately, but that thought, indeed knowledge, everywhere would and must be intuitive."[22]

If Cohen could find in this interpretation nothing more than a psychological betrayal of the master's intentions, Heidegger based his interpretation on a conviction reinforced by the central arguments of *Being and Time*. The rethinking of temporal intuition on the basis of finite, temporalizing modes of *Dasein* would lead—not to psychologism, historicism, or anthropologism—but to an ontological analysis that could alone provide the autonomy of normative truth from all such merely anthropological considerations (in the broadest sense of the term), the very autonomy that, for Kant, could be guaranteed by reason alone.

The problem of perspective became the cardinal point of contention regarding both Heidegger's interpretation of Kant and the philosophy of *Being and Time* as a whole. During the Davos debate and in his later review of the *Kantbuch,* Ernst Cassirer focused on this problem while defending the position of his former mentor, Hermann Cohen. Viewed from the interior of the Kantian system as a whole, Cassirer maintained, Heidegger's interpretation ignored the attempt by Kant, not only to comprehend finite temporality, but to overcome it. In leading all faculties of consciousness back to a source in *Dasein*'s finitude, Heidegger had compromised the absolute autonomy of reason and the validity of its norms regardless of time, place, or other human circumstance, and had thus removed "one of the foundational pillars upon which the whole of Kant's intellectual edifice rests." Moreover, Cassirer argued, he had failed to respect the precautions Kant had so carefully taken that "the sense of his 'transcendental' problematic . . . not be shifted into the domain of psychology—that consideration . . . not be forced into the field of mere anthropology."[23]

Edmund Husserl directed a similar objection, not so much against Heidegger's interpretation of Kant, as against his *Daseinsanalytik* per se. (Husserl had been a mentor to Heidegger, who succeeded him at Freiburg upon the elder phenomenologist's retirement in 1929.) After initially supporting Heidegger, however, he quickly became disillusioned with the direction Heidegger's phenomenology had taken in *Being and Time.* From Husserl's perspective, Heidegger's founding all truth in *Dasein*'s finitude could only compromise phenomenology's transcendental claim to reach beyond the contingency of facts to their absolute foundation in the cogito's preconceptual constitution of the essential structures of the life world. For Husserl, this foundation alone could provide normative criteria of truth necessary to the rational goals of any science. In his correspondence with Roman Ingarden, he made it clear that he considered Heidegger's renunciation of the absolute claim of phenomenology to be a retreat into anthropology.[24] Moreover, in a 1931 speech, repeated before the *Kantgesellschaften* of Halle, Frankfurt, and Berlin—which Heidegger took to be a public rejection of his thought[25]—Husserl deplored the rise of philosophical anthropology as the basic philosophical tendency of the previous decade. He then proceeded to identify this tendency with a renewal of Dilthey's thought and, conjointly, with a branch within the phenomenological movement itself (clearly including Heidegger) that sought the foundation of philosophy "in humanity alone and, indeed, in a doctrine of the essence [*Wesenslehre*] of concrete mundane human *Dasein*."[26]

Despite differences in their orientation, and despite important distinctions in their respective evaluations of the philosophy of Kant, Cassirer and Husserl each attempted to salvage the transcendental level of analysis from anthropology by reaffirming a traditional quest— what Heidegger took to be *the* traditional quest—to which Kant had given modern expression. Eschewing previous forms of theological support, which to their eyes had been discredited by the rational methods of modern science, both thinkers sought to establish absolute normative foundations. Both situated the task of philosophy in the theoretical confirmation of an absolute departure point and an infinite task for mankind. Cassirer restated this conviction in direct opposition to Heidegger in his review of the *Kantbuch*. Up until his death in 1938, Husserl never wavered in his conviction that the idea of infinity, like the idea of absolutely valid norms, constituted a revolutionary breakthrough in Western thought.[27]

Thus it would seem that the difficulty in Heidegger's thinking lay in his paradoxical attempt to place the idea of absolute, unconditioned foundations for truth in question by virtue of *Dasein*'s finitude, even while maintaining that *Dasein* transcended human historical, psychological, and cultural life contexts. Once the traditional claim to absolute foundations had been destroyed, what purpose might be served by maintaining the distinction between anthropological and metaphysical-transcendental levels of analysis that had arisen essentially to justify that claim? Was Heidegger not employing traditional terms that were now called to fulfill a role to which they no longer applied?

This paradox comes most clearly to the fore when one reflects that, in *Being and Time* and other works of this period, Heidegger's philosophy claimed to represent a new kind of scientific standard (*Wissenschaftlichkeit*), one that, beyond the focus of philosophical anthropology with its historical, psychological, or other ontically grounded methods, promised to provide an unprecedented basis for unity in the sciences as a whole.[28] Yet in view of Heidegger's separation of this standard from the criterion of general validity (*Allgemeingültikeit*) guiding the traditional notion of objectivity (even where this criterion did not claim an absolute ground), little remained to indicate precisely how this promise might be fulfilled. Even if the ontological transcendence of *Dasein* did indicate a metahistorical basis of coherence for the criteria of truth, this coherence could hardly be affirmed as a ground for *Wissenschaftlichkeit,* precisely because it arose in *Dasein*'s "diversion from finitude [*Wegsehen von der Endlichkeit*]." Indeed, its tacit identification of Being with what remained present amid change enabled *Dasein,* in applying this criterion to its own Being, to neglect the consequences of its finitude. As we have seen, the assertion of absolute or eternal truth constituted for Heidegger only the extreme form of this traditional neglect.

However complex the task might have been to establish the *Daseinsanalytik* as an alternative to the traditional absolute foundation of Western rationality—rather than simply a variant of philosophical anthropology—Heidegger nonetheless pursued this project before the *Kehre.* Moreover, he insisted that, by pushing fundamental truth beyond the confines of tradition, his *Daseinsanalytik* provided the only possible vantage point from which to call that tradition's persuasiveness in question. He was convinced that this persuasiveness arose in a dissimulation of the veritable character of the modern attempt to overcome historical, psychological, or cultural relativism, which, since Kant's Copernican turn, had presented itself as a suspension of the theological foundations of its absolute claim and its justification on purely rational grounds. Yet Heidegger considered the idea of absolute transcendental foundations as nothing more than a borrowing from the theological realm.[29] In regard to all modern thought, he had already stated in *Being and Time* that "[t]he affirmation of 'eternal truths' and the confusion of the phenomenally founded 'ideality' of *Dasein* with an absolute idealized subject belong to the residue of Christian theology, which for quite some time has not yet been radically eliminated from the problems of philosophy."[30]

Such passages questioning the validity of the absolute subject and of eternal norms only place in sharper relief Heidegger's problematic attempts to maintain a distinction between metaphysical transcendence and anthropology. The problem in his thinking now appears in the domain of theology, insofar as it was directly here that Heidegger's analysis, rather than refuting anthropology, seemed precisely to lend force to the historical movement that the anthropological standpoint had generally favored since Feuerbach: the uprooting of Christianity's truth claim per se. This becomes clear, above all, against the background of Rudolf Bultmann's attempt to apply the *Daseinsanalytik* to theological hermeneutics.

At first sight, Bultmann would seem to corroborate Heidegger's critique of traditional attempts to posit eternal values and absolute standards of truth. In harmony with his neo-orthodox inspiration, Bultmann traced the presupposition of such values and standards to what he considered to be an idealist tradition of speculation about God, which all too often was misled by an attempt to draw the Godhead into the human sphere of discourse. Thus he could write: "The being of man [is constituted] by the *logos,* reason, the eternal, and the absolute. An idealist theology believes that it speaks at the same time of God and man because it is accustomed, following an ancient and classical tradition, to think of God and the absolute together. In reality it speaks only of man."[31]

In this way, Bultmann rejected the traditional reference to terms such as "absolute" and "eternal," although he continued to refer to the "eternity of God," specifying that the *eternal* God did not belong to the domain of that which could be seen.[32] Indeed, such a notion accorded with Saint Paul's message (II Corinthians 4:18): "[F]or the things which are seen are temporal; but the things which are not seen are eternal."

In contrast to this, Heidegger's relegation in *Being and Time* of the quest for the "absolute" and "eternal" to what we have seen to be *Dasein*'s mode of inauthentic existence highlighted not only the radicalism of his finite metaphysics, but also its ambiguity.[33] Could Heidegger direct so grave a challenge to the authenticity of the quest for the absolute and the eternal, and thus bring into question traditional Christian theology, without shaking the pillars of the Christian faith itself? Did it matter from the standpoint of Christianity whether the kind of reservations Heidegger expressed were launched on the basis of a finite metaphysics of *Dasein* or of an anthropology?

For his part, Bultmann avoided this dilemma in his writings, for example, in his application of the *Daseinsanalytik* to theology in his 1928 article "Die Geschichtlichkeit des Daseins und der Glaube" (The historicity of *Dasein* and belief). In distinguishing between "*Dasein* of belief [*gläubiges Dasein*]," the theme of theology, and "natural *Dasein* [*natürliches Dasein*]," the topic of philosophy, he applied categories entirely foreign to Heidegger's concern.[34] From Bultmann's perspective, with its "transcendent" foundations on the side of belief, little remained to distinguish "natural" *Dasein* from a wholly anthropocentric range of investigation. Talk of ontology notwithstanding, the distinction between metaphysics of *Dasein* and anthropology was no longer genuinely relevant to Bultmann's theology.[35]

By appropriating Heidegger's *Daseinsanalytik* for his own purposes, Bultmann did not need to consider the dilemma Karl Löwith underscored in a key essay of 1930, "Grundzüge der Entwicklung der Phänomenologie zur Philosophie und ihr Verhältnis zur protestantischen Theologie" (Fundamentals of the development of phenomenology toward philosophy and their relation to Protestant theology). It was Löwith who provided the most profound formulation of the argument that Heidegger's thought, despite its distinction between ontology and philosophical anthropology, actually constituted a form of anthropology. Indeed, the insight it furnished into human finitude could only add to the historical momentum toward "destruction" of the "fundamental concepts of Christian theology, which the anthropology of Feuerbach had implemented and which Dilthey and Nietzsche, each in his own way, had brought to its extreme limit."[36] Löwith articulated in philosophical terms a hostile evaluation of *Being and Time* that was spreading among theologians. In a 1932 letter to Löwith, Heidegger himself disdainfully acknowledged the opposition already aroused by his attempt to relate his *Daseinsanalytik* to theology in the 1927 lecture "Phänomenologie und Theologie" (Phenomenology and theology).[37] In the years that followed, the theologians' hostility to what they perceived as Heidegger's "anthropology" only mounted. Three examples make this hostility particularly plain. In a 1928 review of *Being and Time* included in his article "Drei Richtungen der Phänomenologie" (Three directions of phenomenology), Freiburg Jesuit Erich Przywara, who would participate in the Davos debate between Heidegger and Cassirer, took Heidegger's service to Dilthey, the philosopher of "relativism, historicism, and psychologism," and Heidegger's "anthropologizing of ontology" sharply to task.[38] In a biting article of 1931, Protestant theologian Emil Brunner, a staunch partisan of dialectal theology, took issue with Heidegger's "atheistic anthropology."[39] And, in a contemporary letter to Bultmann, Karl Barth sharply criticized Heidegger's application of the *Daseinsanalytik* to theology, which, to his mind, had trapped itself in the "determination of the relation of anthropology to theology of the eighteenth and nineteenth centuries."[40]

That Heidegger was fully aware of such theological objections to his claim of fundamental ontology was made plain in his above-mentioned letter to Löwith, where he directly referred to the hostility of both Przywara and Barth.[41] Undoubtedly responding to earlier indications of such criticism, Heidegger added a note to the lecture "Vom Wesen des Grundes" (On the essence of foundation)—presented on the occasion of Husserl's seventieth birthday in 1928. He considered the "objection, eagerly passed from hand to hand," to the anthropocentric standpoint of *Being and Time,* to be a "misunderstanding." All concrete interpretations of his *Seinsfrage* had as little to do with modern "dialectical theology" as they did with "medieval Scholasticism."[42]

It remains unclear to what extent Heidegger took into account the charges that his philosophy represented a form of anthropology, nor does this question necessarily touch what is essential in the *Kehre.* Heidegger himself mentioned what he considered to be a shortcoming of the "objection, eagerly passed from hand to hand," to the anthropocentric standpoint of *Being and Time,* which stemmed from its entanglement in the conceptual language of Western philosophical traditions.[43] His relinquishing the term "ontology" to designate the *Seinsfrage* and his restricting application of the term "metaphysics" to the metaphysical tradition he sought to overcome indicated a far-reaching shift in focus that touched on the many ramifications of his new orientation. In its broadest scope, this shift marked a change in his approach to the basis of the unity of Western history. After the *Kehre,* Heidegger no longer conceived of this basis as primarily an ever-renewed expression in the Western concept of truth of *Dasein*'s *Seinsvergessenheit* (forgetfulness of Being), emerging in its tacit quest to avoid ontological finitude. Rather, he thought of this basis more as a predisposition running through the long history of Western ideas of truth since Greek antiquity, one that favored the advent of the *Seinsvergessenheit* he now conceived as the historical movement of Western metaphysics toward the unrestrained anthropomorphism of modernity.

From Heidegger's perspective, the predominance of anthropomor-phism—"the structuring and viewing of the world after the image of man"—largely explained the pervasive anthropological reading of *Being and Time*. Contemporaries accustomed to a human-centered frame of reference were unable to discern any genuine alternative.[44]

Thus the shift in Heidegger's position after the *Kehre* explicitly cleared the way for a reappraisal of the intentions of *Being and Time*. In his later writings, there could no longer be a question of considering Heidegger's untempered subversion of the traditional absolute criteria of truth as tantamount to the anthropocentrism of post-Hegelian thought, most notably advanced by the anthropologies of Feuerbach and Marx, by Dilthey and the human sciences, by the technological will to human control expressed in the natural sciences, and by the Nietzschean will to power. Well before the *Kehre*, Heidegger had claimed that the *Dasein* in humanity, in its openness to Being underly-ing the temporal and historical structures of human existence, is more fundamental than human experience itself, and is irreducible to human modes of objectification. If, after the *Kehre*, Heidegger's thought cen-tered on the metaphysical roots of modern anthropomorphism, it did so only to better demarcate its limits through a more radical distinction between Being and humanity. The shift in the basis of the unity of Western history from a historicity constituted by the temporalizing modes of *Dasein* to a historicity articulated in an anthropomorphic fate of Western metaphysical traditions reflected this distinction: anthro-pology appeared as a movement itself outside the purview of human control, one elicited through a *Seinsgeschichte* (history of Being). Ever beyond human modes of objectification, Being in Heidegger's late thought marks its distinction from humanity, evoking in humans a his-toricity expressed throughout the epochs of *Seinsgeschichte* and dis-closed in the epochal movement of truth.[45]

Granted that Heidegger always had in mind "truth" in its broad-est possible sense, presupposing a world of beings as a totality (*des Seienden im Ganzen*)[46] that tacitly orients all intellectual activity, his notion of truth is deeply perplexing. On what basis could he refer to the history of mortal humans as a historicity of truth that renders this history possible, rather than as a mere record of human concep-tions of truth, elicited in humanity in the epochal movement of *Seinsgeschichte*?

This question will guide our analysis of Heidegger's late thought and of its implications. In responding to it, we will take Heidegger at his word that the *Seinsfrage* gives itself as a *history* of Being: "The question of Being is neither the history of man nor of the history of the human relation to beings and to Being. The history of Being is Being itself and only this."[47]

The argument that *Seinsgeschichte* is other than human history and more fundamental than a mere record of human conceptions of truth operates by virtue of a key presupposition. Heidegger confronted what he considered to be the predominant assumption of contemporary intellectual life—the assertion that, in a world of human circumstances, truth is essentially determined to accord with human ends—by placing in relief what he thought to be the limitations of this assumption when illuminated by the coherent unity of *Seinsgeschichte*. As Heidegger saw it after the *Kehre,* anthropocentric criteria manifested these limitations in their essential continuity with, and dependence on, the earlier systems of traditional metaphysics in its conventional sense, even though the contemporary scientific methodologies he labeled as "anthropocentric" had expressly abjured any connection to metaphysics. In response to the question posed above, let us examine Heidegger's assertion that anthropocentrism manifested itself as a tacit continuation of the errancy (*Irre*) of metaphysics, in light of which a self-enclosed human world divulged its incapacity to account for truth. As we will see, his insight into the limits of anthropocentric criteria led Heidegger to interpret the *Kehre* as more than a simple change in his philosophical orientation, indeed, as thought elicited by the articulation of *Seinsgeschichte* itself—independent of the strictly human aspects of his own work.[48]

With intrepid brush strokes, Heidegger depicted that articulation as unifying the epochal manifestations of truth across centuries of historical change in relation to determinate philosophical perspectives. His depiction of *Seinsgeschichte* passed over broad segments of the history of Western thought in silence, especially in the centuries following classical antiquity. Although disputed on this matter by leading scholars,[49] Heidegger evidently believed that consideration of much of Stoic, neo-Platonic, early medieval, and Renaissance thought, which he largely neglected, would not have altered his account of *Seinsgeschichte*. From his perspective, it was necessary to signal what had been expressed by the greatest Western thinkers, precisely because these thinkers epitomized an essential approach to the truth of beings as a totality, an approach that served to guide whole epochs. In the coherent movement of *Seinsgeschichte,* Plato, Aristotle, Augustine, Aquinas, Suarez, Luther, Descartes, Leibniz, Kant, Hegel, and Nietzsche were anything but isolated exponents of an age or culture and its determinate productive modes. They inaugurated a historically constitutive language (*geschichteschaffende Sprache*),[50] demarcating the domain of inclusion within which the approach to the truth of beings as a totality could legitimately operate.

If Heidegger's broad reflections on Western history dispensed with the painstaking factual analysis characteristic of historical methods in the human sciences, his mode of retrieval of the meaning of the past found its essential justification in the character of his historical reflections themselves. Intrinsic to Heidegger's approach to the truth claim of Western intellectual traditions was his questioning of the rational ground of the traditions embodied in scientific principles. Such questioning could proceed only by virtue of norms that themselves were not subordinate to these principles. As he noted in a telling remark from a lecture of the 1940s: "The unscientific . . . can immediately stand under higher laws than all sciences."[51]

In the perspective of *Seinsgeschichte,* autonomy from the presuppositions of *Wissenschaftlichkeit* in general and from the historical methods of the humanistic disciplines in particular is the first precondition for grasping what Heidegger termed the "coherence [*Zusammenhang*]" underlying the articulation of history. From Heidegger's standpoint, the coherence of history (*geschichtlicher Zusammenhang*)[52] emerged through the tacit interrelation of epochal manifestations of truth. It was thinkable only when distinguished from that level of interaction for which it served as the condition of possibility: the dimension of events, or the realm of historical dependence (*historische Abhängigkeit*) made up of political, economic, or ideational objects of historical contemplation (*historische Betrachtung*).

Heidegger thus contrasted historical coherence (*geschichtlicher Zusammenhang*) and the deeper historical movement of truth grasped by historical consideration (*geschichtliche Besinnung*) to historical dependence and the historical interaction discerned by historical contemplation.[53] In his later thought, the terms "historical coherence" and "historical consideration" referred to what he understood to be the primordial source of historicity rendering possible all other forms of historical existence. The notion of an underlying coherence of history, hidden from the methods of the human sciences, enabled him to discern what he considered to be the unity of Western history amid variations in the manifestation of truth. This thought of unity emerged in his attempt to trace the sources of the end point of Western modernity (*die Neuzeit*) to distant origins in the metaphysics of Greek antiquity. Heidegger conceived of this end point as the attainment of an extreme possibility of truth that, as we will see more closely, came to light with placing humanity at the center of all things and with limiting all possibilities of truth to a wholly anthropological significance.

Our attempt to place in relief Heidegger's thought on the coherence of history will not be guided by an evaluation of his writings on their philological merits. Such an evaluation cannot by itself help us judge the meaningfulness of Heidegger's larger claim about the ground of coherence of Western history.[54] Rather, our aim in the following sections must restrict itself to Heidegger's claim itself, by way of a global analysis of his thought in relation to the issues we have indicated. We will pursue this aim in terms of two questions:

1. How could Heidegger consider *Seinsgeschichte* the nonhuman basis of the historical movement of truth, in which the errancy of traditional metaphysics, by coming to fulfillment in contemporary anthropomorphism, constituted the coherent unity of Western history?

2. How does Heidegger's view of the historicity of truth embodied in this unity call into question the autonomy of Western rationality's criteria of truth, as deployed by the contemporary sciences, and how does it bear on the problem of historical meaning?

II

Heidegger's analyses of the historical metamorphoses of truth are known to emphasize changes in language as the place where the unacknowledged traces of the errancy of metaphysics silently announced themselves. From the perspective of *Seinsgeschichte*, the emergence and development of basic words (*Grundworte*)[55] was neither gratuitous nor explicable in terms of the purposeful activity of human speakers. Heidegger embodied the unspoken history underlying the movement of truth in the history-constituting (*geschichtegründende*) capacity of language.[56]

The errancy of Western metaphysics emerged against the background of what Heidegger took to be the tacit equivocality of primordial words in early Greek antiquity.[57] As set forth in his writings between the 1930s and the 1950s, this equivocality stemmed, on the one hand, from the place these words, notably, *aletheia, logos, physis*,[58] signifying "truth" and "Being" in pre-Socratic discourse, occupied at the origin of Western thought, and, on the other, from the evocation by such words of possibilities that the errancy of Western metaphysics had left behind.

At every turn in his investigation, Heidegger sought to free the interpretation of early Greek thought from the constraint of an age-old tradition that had already become common in Roman antiquity—notably, in the writings of Cicero—and which continued to resurge with each renaissance of Greek thought, right through to what Heidegger characterized as the twilight of Western metaphysics in the speculative philosophy of Hegel.[59] Hegel had situated the genuine beginning of philosophy in the speculation of Parmenides, which he nonetheless qualified as "admittedly still dark and indistinct."[60] If Hegel admitted the importance of Heraclitus as a source for his own logic, Heidegger also recounted what Hegel considered to be the cause of a certain "obscurity [*Dunkelheit*]" in the speculations of Heraclitus: this was due not so much to his propensity for recondite phrases, as Cicero claimed, but rather to the "lack of cultivation [*Unausgebildetheit*]" his language betrayed.[61] Corresponding to the neohumanistic renewal of the Greeks by Goethe and Humboldt, and still more contemporary examples,[62] and manifesting in this instance his profound accord with a customary belief reaching back to Cicero, Hegel contrasted this primitive beginning with the apogee of the Greek intelligence attained in the philosophies of Plato and Aristotle.

Heidegger's attempt to divert understanding of the pre-Socratics away from this traditional approach was animated by a singular conviction. Accepting the presupposition that Plato and Aristotle had fulfilled the pre-Socratic questioning of Being on a higher ground, Hegel and the neohumanists shared the assumption that post-Socratic reasoning had essentially deciphered the meaning of the pre-Socratics. This assumption in turn evaluated the pre-Socratics through the criteria of the metaphysical tradition that Plato himself had inaugurated. If the pre-Socratics played an essential role in Heidegger's writings, it was because he believed their considerations to be guided by the primordial possibilities of grasping truth that the articulation of a long history of Western metaphysics since Plato had obscured. Although, in their primordial guise, these possibilities often remained implicit and could not have been grasped then as they would be in the twilight of metaphysics, they nonetheless suggested a source of criteria by virtue of which the limits of Western intellectual traditions might appear.

Where Hegel had found lack of clarity and "lack of cultivation [*Unausgebildetheit*]" in the early Greek language, Heidegger found the source of its fertility, a semantic plenitude that, though overshadowed by traditional cultivation (*Bildung*), had nonetheless left a vestige in the pre-Socratic fragments. From Heidegger's standpoint, this vestige had simply been overlooked with each expression of Western metaphysics and with each reinforcement of the criteria of Western rationality, qualified by a claim to truth that had ever more triumphantly set aside what could not be brought within the range of its determinations.[63]

In contrast, the fundamental words of the pre-Socratics—most notably, *aletheia, logos, physis*—suggested a pristine evocation of truth and of Being that had not yet been overtaken by the claim of Western metaphysics. Thus, in many works following the *Kehre*, Heidegger continually returned to the nuances of *aletheia*, on which Plato still drew in the *Republic*, which invokes *lethe*, "forgetfulness," "opacity," in whose opening the truth of beings comes to light; to *logos*, as "gathering [*Versammlung*]," which at the same time connotes the Being of beings: a collecting (*Sammeln*) or reading (*Lesen*) of what is rendered from the self-concealment of the ground of all things by virtue of which beings are drawn to their share of clarity; and to *physis*, as "Being" in the vocabulary of Heraclitus, evoking *physis kryptesthai philei*, "Being likes to hide," in an analogous reference to the opacity of Being: in the foreground of this hiddenness, the appearance of beings first emerges.[64]

Such examples, drawn from volumes of Heidegger's writings on this theme, suggest that the thought of opacity at the heart of all possible illumination of the truth of beings had not yet been cast aside by the Platonic doctrine of ideas. In its distance from pre-Socratic origins,

Hegel's positing of truth in the advent of an absolute identity of thought and Being only showed itself to be a still more conclusive unfolding of the idea of truth in the same metaphysical movement of Western rationality.

Heidegger's description of Western metaphysics as errancy identified what he claimed to be a tacit, unquestioned point of consensus—more fundamental than all points of divergence—running throughout the history of Western thought since Plato. In the vocabulary of the later Heidegger, metaphysics finds its most distinctly identifiable roots in the Platonic doctrine of truth. According to this doctrine, the truth of Being becomes accessible to humanity by virtue of the idea, which, preparing the groundwork for the traditional language of metaphysics, thinks Being from out of beings themselves, rather than as the sovereign (waltende), hidden ground of their unconcealment. It does so in relation to beings by naming the truth of Being as the "whatness [Wassein]" of beings, their quidditas, distinguished from the "thatness [dasssein]" inherent in the particularity of their presence.[65] If metaphysics successfully rethought this distinction in the great words that designate Being in the Western tradition—notably, energeia, actualitas, Wirklichkeit, reality—this manner of deciding the truth of Being also fatefully predisposed this tradition to a given approach to ontology in the continuous reference of the criteria of truth to the judgment of the one who apprehends. Following the Platonic presupposition that the idea names the ground of truth, variants of the notion of truth in terms of a correct verification of beings in relation to the normative standard of the being who apprehends (conveyed by the words hypokeimenon, cogito, subject, Geist) have not ceased their tacit domination of Western presuppositions about the character of truth. The quest for truth has thus been continually oriented toward "correctness of view and of viewpoint."[66] Indeed, the very words used to designate "verification" in the long history of this tradition—Heidegger mentioned the gradual movement from homoiosis to convenientia, assimilatio, rectitudo, and Richtigkeit[67]—are successively grounded in the presupposition that correct ideas in judgment provide an adequate criterion by virtue of which truth may be discerned.

Heidegger saw the continuity of this tacit consensus in Western intellectual traditions, above all, in the "taking for granted [Selbstverständlichkeit]" of a limited horizon within which the questioning of truth is confined. This taking for granted sets the terms for a traditional neglect of what cannot be brought within this determinate horizon, which corresponds to a gradual historical deepening of the forgetfulness of the ground of truth in its opacity to the subject's possibilities of observation. Each reassertion of the traditional criteria of truth, each reformulation of the logical canons of Western rationality governing these criteria gradually reinforced this forgetfulness.[68] Acting together, they established what Heidegger came to see as the fundamental momentum of Western thought as a whole: the ever more consequent exclusion from consideration of everything that does not correspond to the normative judgment of the idea, to the cognitive apprehension. For Heidegger, this gradual exclusion described the correlate of metaphysical errancy: "the retreat of Being" that effaces any meaningful recourse to opacity beyond the pale of human representations—the hidden source of truth these representations might reveal. This retreat elaborates the movement of *Seinsgeschichte* as the gradual, inexorable narrowing of the margin of involvement in the nonpresentable and the nonobjectifiable, which comes to expression in the language of human intellectual endeavors.

It was in the context of this retreat that the focus of the metahistorical leitmotiv in Heidegger's thinking changed perspective. We have located this motif in *Dasein*'s *Seinsvergessenheit*, imparted in its ongoing tendency to identify the Being of all beings with what remains present (*Anwesend*) amid change. *Seinsvergessenheit* tacitly enables *Dasein*, in applying the criterion of presence (*Anwesenheit*) to its own Being, to neglect the consequences of its ontological finitude. Despite changes in Heidegger's thinking after the *Kehre* (to which we will return), he continued to underline the importance of this criterion in the traditional determination of the Being of beings—right up to his final period, embodied in the essay "Das Ende der Philosophie und die Aufgabe des Denkens" (The end of philosophy and the task of thinking; 1964).[69] However, after the *Kehre*, presence as the criterion of the Being of beings was no longer a theme of ontological reflection in regard to the finite being of *Dasein*. Placed in the historical movement of *Seinsgeschichte*, it now revealed the anthropocentrism at the core of Western metaphysics—an anthropocentrism already implicit in the Platonic assumption of the adequacy of human interpretation, in light of the idea of beings, of the presence of Being.[70]

As we will see, for Heidegger, the confirmation of anthropocentrism at the heart of Western metaphysical traditions expresses itself primarily in regard to changes in the normative conception of the idea of the being through whom truth is apprehended.[71] In considering this topic, Heidegger recovered not only a central theme of *Being and Time,* but one of the earliest propositions of his thought. Transformed in the matrix of *Seinsgeschichte,* it set in relief his later identification of the relation between traditional metaphysics and anthropomorphism—and what Heidegger viewed as the limits of modern anthropomorphic norms manifested in this relation.

We have noted that, as early as the "Anmerkungen" (Annotations; 1919–21), Heidegger criticized what he identified as a continual tendency in Western intellectual traditions to reify human existence according to preconditions of the subject, cogito, spirit (*Geist*), or person. The earliest motives of the "destruction in the history of thought [*geistesgeschichtliche Destruktion*]" may be traced to a quest to bring normative criteria of truth into accord with what Heidegger defined as the historical character of existence: the movement (*Bewegtheit*) at its very core. In the language of ontology, this task of destruction aimed, by overcoming the traditional reification of *Dasein* in terms of the metaphysical criteria of presence (*Anwesenheit*), to lay bare the finite structures of its temporal and historical Being, by virtue of which truth per se becomes thinkable. Heidegger's later *Seinsfrage,* in renouncing the language of fundamental ontology, also reconsidered the notion of destruction, which had not yet been thought "in the terms of *Seinsgeschichte.*"[72]

In his later writings, Heidegger continued to think of the unity of Western intellectual traditions in relation to unfounded preconceptions of humanity, although he reappraised these preconceptions in terms of determinate traditional ways of reifying the human essence as the locus of the idea, or other normative standard of judgment.[73] In this later context, *Seinsgeschichte* offered a periodicity proper to it, independent of the plurality of authentic and inauthentic choices projected in *Dasein's* ontological quest, a periodicity in which ontological analysis gave way to global consideration of the retreat of meaningful involvement of the hidden basis of truth. This retreat tacitly insinuated itself in presuppositions of the dependence of all norms on the being through whom truth is purportedly determined, and whose character is always decided in advance. Far from the product of the modern world, anthropomorphism issued from older metaphysical presuppositions about the essential character of humanity at the center of normative determinations of truth, already implicit in the Platonic idea.

This central theme of Heidegger's *Kehre* stood at the heart of his reflections on humanism, which he took to be a necessary historical precondition for the advent of contemporary anthropocentrism. As conceived in his essays of the 1940s, "Platons Lehre von der Wahrheit" (Plato's doctrine of truth) and the "Brief über den Humanismus" (Letter on Humanism), humanism arose in the conceptions of verification predominant in late Greek antiquity, above all, in the passage of the Hellenistic heritage into the linguistic tradition of Roman and early Christian antiquity.[74] In these two essays, Heidegger referred to the Roman retrieval of the Platonic presupposition about the idea as the source of normative standards of truth, reinforced by the humanistic stress on personal cultivation (a transposition of the Greek and Platonic *paideia*), designating the matrix in which truth emerges. Far from denigrating intellection as such, Heidegger's message concerned what he took to be the survival beneath the surface of humanistic discourse of fixed presuppositions about the essence of humanity and about the revelation of truth in relation to this human essence. In the development of Western intellectual traditions, the cumulative failure to radically renew the question of the being of humanity corresponded to the precondition of the idea, taken by the human intelligence as an adequate source of truth, thus guiding comprehension of the nature of truth itself.

In light of this reflection, Heidegger interpreted what he took to be the early humanistic application of the basic words of Greek thought, whose relation to human modes of comprehension was more profoundly taken for granted as their primordial capacity to evoke the hiddenness of the ground of truth retreated irrevocably in Latin translation. By way of example: in translating *aletheia, veritas* and *convenientia* favored those connotations of truth limited to a correspondence of object and idea in the faculty of judgment; in translating *logos,* the Ciceronian *ratio* passed over the primordial connotations of Being by way of forms that originated in the qualifying and quantifying concerns of the contemporary language of commerce from which it had been appropriated; in translating *physis, natura* introduced a similar occultation by transposing Being into the realm of natural entities, conceived in harmony with the human world and with norms of human cultivation.[75]

In the "Letter on Humanism" as in *Nietzsche,* Heidegger identified what he considered to be the further elaboration of the essential direction of Roman humanism through the Roman Catholic Church.[76] In this context, the primordial Greek words found their place in the realm of created being, which, grounded in the absolute foundations of Divine providence, preestablished the nature of humanity, while reconfirming the centrality of the idea through which normative truths become accessible to it.[77] Over and again during the course of the decades following Heidegger's *Kehre,* in writings from "On the Essence of Truth" to his final seminars in Le Thor and Zähringen, Heidegger underlined the decisive importance of Christian theological support for traditional metaphysics, of how, in his apt formulation, "God intrudes into philosophy,"[78] predisposing traditional assumptions about the character of human and other created beings. In "On the Essence of Truth," he concisely described this intrusion of theological assumptions into philosophy:

> The possibility of truth of human knowledge is grounded, when all beings are "created beings," in the same manner of conformity to the idea of thing and proposition and, therefore, in their fitting one another within the unity of the Divine plan of creation. . . . *Veritas* everywhere means *convenientia,* the agreement of beings among themselves as created beings with the Creator, an "attunement" according to the determination of the order of Creation.[79]

In a brief passage in *Nietzsche,* Heidegger suggested that the synthesis of Christian dogma and Graeco-Roman metaphysics had strayed not only from the original meaning of pre-Socratic thought, but also from the primordial belief of original Christianity.[80] Unfortunately, he never pursued this parallel in his subsequent writings.

If Heidegger characterized the humanism of antiquity in terms of predominant preconceptions about the essence of humanity, these same preconceptions reemerged to his mind in each of the humanistic revivals of later centuries, from Renaissance humanism up to the neohumanism of Goethe and Humboldt. Where such revivals of antiquity understood themselves as attempts to retrieve its meaning—from Hegel's vantage point, a recollection of one decisive moment in the history of consciousness in its "cultivation toward science [*Bildung zur Wissenschaft*]"[81]— Heidegger viewed them less as a retrieval than as a break with antiquity. This break also confirmed for him a still deeper, tacit continuity at the very core of the modern world. As a change in the way of approaching the truth of beings as a totality, it brought with it a qualitatively different human self-apprehension, one that placed on a new and firmer basis the possibility of positing a determinate essence of humanity as the locus through which the truth of beings is conferred. As we will now see, this rupture with the past, which on another level reinforced the centrality of the human subject in the genesis of truth, provided the groundwork of Heidegger's thinking on the coherent continuity between traditional metaphysics and modern anthropomorphism.

III

The essence of modernity, for Heidegger, appeared as a narrowing of the domain of inclusion within which the basis of the historicity of truth could be thought. If this narrowing ultimately gave rise to the contemporary placing of humanity at the center of all things and the overlaying of all truth with an anthropological significance where, in a wholly humanized world, all extrahuman references forfeited their meaning, the possibility of this development had to be traced back to the quest that distinguished the modern character of the contemporary world. However distant the original aim of this quest might have been from a contemporary anthropocentric orientation, Heidegger argued, the preconditions of modernity required "that man set himself up by his own means and with his own capacities to render certain and secure his human being in the midst of beings as a totality."[82]

This metamorphosis in the early modern world reinforced the Platonic heritage on a different basis by rethinking the essence of the human being as subject in relation to the truth of beings as a totality.[83] Modernity signified a reinterpretation of the "idea" in terms of the constitutive activity of the subject as the foundation on which the representation of the object depends.[84] On this foundation, truth related in a different way to judgment as the locus of conformity between the idea and that which it apprehends, for the notion of conformity itself was at once conceived on a more limited basis and reinforced: the cognitive representation not only confirmed but, as its condition of possibility, constituted the objectivity of the object. In its modern guise, the role of the subject became paramount with the ascension of the language of certitude (*certum, Gewissheit*)[85]—the expression of the object in its bare relation to the representation of the subject—to the capacity of designation of the criteria of truth per se.

From the perspective of *Seinsgeschichte,* Descartes exemplified the new outlook on truth of early modernity. The Cartesian determination of the involvement of the subject in the constitution of the objectivity of the object introduced the criteria of certitude in the affirmation of truth. On the one hand, for Descartes, absolute certitude stood as the essential attribute of the thinking subject, secure in the possession of its own representations; on the other, for objects not of the order of the *res cogitans,* the sole criterion of ontological truth was the certitude of relations of extension conceivable in mathematical terms.[86]

Heidegger's thought on the coherence of history asserted the pivotal role of Descartes in predisposing the unity between traditional metaphysics and modern anthropomorphism. To grasp the thought of Descartes from the perspective of *Seinsgeschichte,* Heidegger attempted to approach him neither as an isolated thinker nor as an expression of the circumstances of European social and economic history, but as the metaphysician who inaugurated a fundamentally new attitude toward truth that defined modernity as a whole. Understood in this manner, the Cartesian metaphysics heralded the detachment of the normative basis of truth from the speculative treatment of the verities of faith in the terms of medieval Christianity toward the "representation of beings grounded in the subject, on the essential basis of which the modern predominance of man first becomes possible."[87]

On the one hand, this reorientation lent secular support both to Luther's earlier theological turning away from the speculative metaphysics of medieval theology and to his centering faith on the question of certitude of Salvation.[88] If humanity cannot ultimately possess this certitude, it is of the essence of human existence to strive for it in the security of belief. On the other hand, Descartes's vision of truth as self-certitude of the subject in its representations anticipated a second decisive secular expression of the early modern approach to truth in Leibniz's reassertion of self-certitude as its essential criterion, posited in terms of the indubitability of the universal logic of representation of a universal system of rationality (*mathesis universalis*). More important, the accommodation of truth to the self-certitude of the subject in the sure possession of its representations anticipated the resurgence of metaphysics in its contemporary anthropocentric guise. This approach to truth tacitly liberated the subject to serve as the basis of all aspects of legitimation, untrammeled by what might stand outside the field of its representations. For the criteria of self-certitude, even the Divinity—the unrepresentable par excellence for the human subject—could be conceived on the model of an ultimate subject. God and the human subjects created in His image were conceived as "beings with knowledge," the metaphysical "bearers of truth" who "thus comprise the reality of knowledge and of certitude."[89] From Heidegger's standpoint, the historical movement of modernity, defined by the gradual withdrawal of such nonhuman and unrepresentable truths as the Divine intelligence, carried Descartes's innovation to its logical end—the exaltation of the human subject in its total autonomy: "[I]n the rise of anthropologies, Descartes celebrates his ultimate triumph."[90]

For Heidegger, the successive retrenchments of the basis of truth in favor of the autonomous subject were the thread interweaving all of the epoch-making expressions of *Seinsgeschichte* in modern times.[91] In this lineage, he now situated Kant's Copernican turn. On the basis of pure reason, Kant reinforced the autonomy of the subject as the central theme of metaphysics. He did so by questioning the traditional ontotheological basis of legitimation beyond the human subject, notably, the Cartesian and Leibnizian ideas of God, which faded into the nondescript realm of the thing in itself. More decisively than ever before, the autonomous reasoning subject found its place at the center of the metaphysical universe and asserted its role in the constitution of a meaningful world.[92]

Hegel's approach to truth took Kant's metaphysics a step further by reincorporating the Divinity within the horizon of metaphysical reasoning, but in such a way that it revealed its inner identity with the subject as Spirit, in the movement of its cultivation (*Bildung*) toward possession of absolute self-certitude. For Hegel, this self-certitude constituted the true Being of beings: "True Being is absolute thought that thinks itself."[93]

From the perspective of *Seinsgeschichte*, Hegel prepared the way for the philosophy of Nietzsche, the most extreme expression of metaphysics, its culmination in the freedom of the human subject from anything beyond itself. For Nietzsche, the God of Descartes and Leibniz, the thing in itself of Kant, and the absolute spirit of Hegel all became superfluous: the Nietzschean metaphysics of the will required only the bare subject in the ultimate confirmation of itself at the source of the transcendental determination of the true Being of all beings.

For Heidegger, Nietzsche's metaphysics of the subject as the bearer of truth brought to fulfillment the inner movement of a history inaugurated by Plato and set on a modern footing by Descartes. Nietzsche's metaphysics also stood as the harbinger of the unrestrained anthropomorphism of the contemporary world. Its radical call for a transvaluation of truth—of values—delivered the coup de grâce to the possibility of truth's metaphysical provenance in the Platonic supersensible realm or in Christian Providence.

In describing the movement of Western metaphysics from Descartes to Nietzsche and in demarcating the inner coherence between traditional metaphysics and modern anthropology, Heidegger claimed to characterize, not only an abstract realm of philosophical discourse, but the language of modernity as it infuses the way of being of modern humans and the fundamental presuppositions of truth in contemporary life. As Heidegger saw it, the movement of modernity inaugurated by Descartes drew together such diverse realms as culture, religion, art, science, and technology in a single unified destiny (*Geschick*).[94]

From Heidegger's standpoint, the emergence of culture as a word and mode of human existence had roots in the humanistic conceptions of antiquity, above all, in the Roman notion of the cultivation of humanity and, more immediately in the Cartesian notion of the self-certitude of the subject as the ground of truth. Explicitly mentioning Descartes's use of the term "culture" in *Discours de la méthode*,[95] Heidegger situated the source of culture in Descartes's approach to truth; indeed, he conceived of culture as a locus of self-cultivation, whose emergence as an autonomous realm of activity corresponded to the claim to autonomy of the human subject. In the domain of culture, Heidegger wrote, "[t]he real becomes what is capable of activation through that human activity which, knowingly basing itself on itself, brings everything into the sphere of its cultivation and care."[96]

In this same contemporary articulation of *Seinsgeschichte*, Christianity moved its ultimate distance from primordial faith to assert its role in the cultural realm (*Kulturchristentum*). With the emergence of culture as an independent context constituted by the autonomous human subject, Christianity was relegated to one worldview (*Weltanschauung*) among many, competing in the claim to cultivate humanity.[97] Its status in the cultural arena corresponded to the loss of its persuasiveness as a total system of metaphysical interpretation.[98] As a cultural institution, Christianity forfeited its capacity to constitute a language of truth having the power to move history; instead, it derived its importance from the support it could rally for cultural concerns. This bare function as a cultural prop unmasked it to contemporary eyes as a mere object of anthropocentric aims, whose otherworldly reference had lost all meaning.

Art, too, in the contemporary world was divested of any possible reference to truth beyond the human sphere, its now-shrunken truth limited to transmitting a merely lived experience (*Erlebnis*).[99] Even here, Heidegger traced the precondition of a language of lived experience to the approach to truth inaugurated by Descartes.[100]

Finally, the emergence of science and of machine technology were, for Heidegger, inscribed in this same coherent movement of *Seinsgeschichte*. In their approach to truth, both shared a common root in the gradual withdrawal of any meaningful reference to the nonpresentable and the nonobjectifiable—a withdrawal that in turn marks the sphere of representation in its approach to truth as *Gestell* (enframing), the historical actualization of the calculative potentialities implicit in the *ratio* (reckoning), most notably in the methodology of the sciences and in machine technology.[101] Here again, the immediate forebear of this approach to truth was Descartes, and the Cartesian projection of the subject's self-assurance in relation to extended beings of nature in terms of the criteria of the mathematical models of the modern natural sciences.[102] It was the shift in the approach to truth exemplified by Descartes—not political, material, or social circumstances—that gave rise to the emergence of modern natural science and of machine technology:

> That the "man in the street" attributes the "Diesel motor" to Diesel's discovery is in order. Not everyone needs to know that the very essence of this inventiveness could not have made a single step had philosophy, in the historical moment when it stepped into the range of its undoing, not thought the categories of this nature and thus opened the range of inquiry and experimentation to inventors. . . .

As one-sided and in certain ways unsatisfactory as the interpretation of nature in terms of *res extensa* may be, when thought through from the standpoint of its metaphysical capacity and reckoned in relation to the breadth of its metaphysical scope, it is nonetheless that first decisive step through which modern motor-machine technology, and with it the new world and its humanity, become metaphysically possible.[103]

Heidegger's commentary on the destiny of truth embodied in culture, religion, art, science, and technology underlines the full range of what he took to be the coherent movement of history and the foundation of the unity of Western intellectual traditions. For Heidegger, this unity was characterized by a gradual deepening of the ancient occultation of the nonpresentable and nonobjectifiable ground of truth, made possible by a centuries-long process culminating in the identification of this ground with the essence of man.

The positing of the ultimate representability of the truth of beings through human modes of perception ultimately reposed on a precondition, rooted in an age-old heritage, about the nature of the human being. By virtue of an ever more intractable taking for granted of the human essence as something objectifiable, the human being becomes the source of truth, whether as *homo humanus* in ancient, Renaissance and neohumanistic doctrines, as the soul in Christianity, or as the social being in Marxism—all such concepts were, for Heidegger, synonymous with "humanism" in the broader sense.[104] Finally, in his view, even if the most extreme anthropological standpoint, namely, that of Dilthey, seemed to escape this generalization in presupposing the historicity of the human essence, this historicity was always posited in terms of preconceptions of the human being as a cultural being; thus it adapted to a philosophy of worldviews (*Weltanschauungen*) the primacy of the subject as a locus of meaning constitution that first emerged in the philosophy of Descartes.[105]

For his part, Heidegger assumed that, because the truth of beings, including the human essence itself, was *not* constituted by the human being, but was elicited by Being, the contemporary advent of metaphysics in anthropomorphism ultimately hid from humans the very character of their own essence in its relation to beings as a totality.[106] Heidegger's attempt to think beyond the horizon of contemporary anthropomorphism and the concomitant criteria of scientific rationality engaged a wholly different approach to the human being in relation to

Being. This difference is suggested by a question he asked in *Nietzsche:* "Is the distinction between Being and beings grounded in the nature of man, so that this nature can be characterized in accord with this distinction? Or is the nature of man grounded in this distinction? In the second case, this distinction itself would no longer be 'human.'"[107]

Throughout his later writings, Heidegger took seriously the proposition on the modifiability of human nature, corresponding to the involvement of the mode of being of humanity in its ways of conferring truth on the Being of beings.[108] Strange to contemporary ears, and ordinarily discounted, is Heidegger's assertion that truth is evoked independently of the human will. Far from a product of a *Volksgeist,* a romantic *génie,* a social class, or a will to power, the source of truth, for Heidegger, remains ever beyond human representation. In the period of his Nietzsche lectures (1938–44), Heidegger retained his conviction that the first Greek thinkers had an intimation of this hidden ground of truth in the evocation of truth as *aletheia*—albeit "only too vaguely"[109]—and that *Seinsgeschichte* had assumed the possibility of recollecting (*Erinnern*) it, guiding what he took to be its coherent historical movement since the Greeks. Here, in this recollection of the ground of the historical movement of truth—a historicity engendering modifications in the essential way of being of man in the midst of beings as a totality—Heidegger sought to think beyond what he took to be this heritage's confines.

IV

In *Nietzsche* and later writings,[110] Heidegger returned ever and again to Hegel's role in the final unfolding of the Western metaphysical tradition inaugurated by Plato, which would later be fulfilled, via Nietzsche, by contemporary anthropomorphism. In "Die Überwindung der Metaphysik" (The overcoming of metaphysics), he characterized contemporary thought as a whole as a "countermovement [*Gegenbewegung*]" against Hegel's metaphysics: "The countermovements against this metaphysics belong *to* it. Since Hegel's death [1831], everything is but countermovement, not only in Germany, but in Europe."[111]

Clearly, the "overcoming of metaphysics" assumed a liberty of thought, both from the influence of Hegel and neo-Hegelianism and from "countermovements" against Hegel, by virtue of which Heidegger here qualified the coherent unity of the contemporary world. This liberty suggested the possibility of a *Seinsgeschichte* outside the historical advent of metaphysics, an advent that, for Heidegger, the normative criteria of Western rationality and scientific methodologies embodied. Yet by virtue of what criteria might a thinker move beyond the historical advent of metaphysics and the normative standards it governed?

It is my conviction that Heidegger's unprecedented conception of the historicity of truth through *Seinsgeschichte,* in aiming toward recollection of truth's hidden ground, rethinks the problem of historical meaning at the very heart of its attempt to overstep the confines of metaphysics. In this section, we turn to that unprecedented conception, in which the historicity of truth lays bare the limits of metaphysics and its expression in the norms of Western rationality. We will analyze Heidegger's attempt to expose the bounds of metaphysics by examining his relation to what he characterized as essential preconditions of the contemporary world: Hegelian idealism and the attempt by post-Hegelian "countermovements" to conceive of the limits of the ideal foundations of historicity that Hegel had envisioned. Before proceeding with this analysis, however, let us turn briefly to a pertinent aspect of Heidegger's relation to his immediate historical milieu.

Among commentaries on twentieth-century philosophy, it has become a commonplace to characterize Heidegger's identification of the historicity of truth in the movement of *Seinsgeschichte,* independent of the will of human agents, as a kind of fatalism. Titles such as *Gelassenheit* (Release) have been taken to indicate Heidegger's quietude before destiny and his passivity before authority.[112] In its more extreme forms, this characterization would reduce Heidegger's claim to think beyond the norms of Western rationality to a retreat into fatalism, conveniently serving as an excuse for his own earlier political activity. Indeed, did not Heidegger himself, in *Vorträge und Aufsätze* (Lectures and essays), attribute the appearance of the *Führer* to an approach to truth elicited by the call of Being?[113]

In my opinion, nothing can justify Heidegger's shameful activity in 1933–34 when, as rector of the University of Freiburg, he lent his support to Hitler's regime. Even if Heidegger's commitment to Hitler was short-lived, nothing can explain away his willingness to adapt the terminology of the *Daseinsanalytik* to Nazi propaganda, nor his shocking attitude toward a generous and isolated mentor, Edmund Husserl, in these years, an attitude Heidegger himself later acknowledged as his "human failing."[114]

If, as we have seen, the philosophical radicalism of Heidegger's work after the First World War was deeply hostile toward "liberalism" as a worldview, in the early years of the Nazi regime, it embraced a more distinctly political outlook, targeting liberalism as a political ideology. Thus Heidegger's 1933 course lecture "Die Grundfrage der Philosophie" (The fundamental question of philosophy), which referred to the "greatness of the historical moment [*Grösse des geschichtlichen Augenblicks*]" in which the German people as a whole "finds its leadership [*findet seine Führung*],"[115] was followed in the next semester by the course "On the Essence of Truth," in which Heidegger proclaimed his opposition to liberalism, while warning that it had to be seen as only a weaker expression of more powerful actualities (*Wirklichkeiten*). The great danger, he explained, lay in a resurrection—by the so-called destroyers of liberalism themselves—of a new kind of "liberal national socialism."[116]

A 1934–35 seminar, "Hegel: 'Über den Staat'" (Hegel: "On the State"; still unpublished), held by Heidegger and the jurist Erik Wolf, points toward the central role of reflection on Hegel in Heidegger's attempts to come to grips with the political situation in Nazi Germany. Already in "The Fundamental Question of Philosophy," Heidegger had declared that, in the debate with Hegel, the entire Western intellectual tradition "speaks to us," and that only in this debate would it be possible to accede to the hidden way of future spiritual action (*die verborgene Bahn des künftigen geistigen Handelns*).[117] The Hegel seminar confirmed the central place of Hegel's thought in Heidegger's political reflection during this period. Hegel's historical metaphysics, the seminar argued, had brought together a central strand of original political thought that found its source in ancient Greece. For Hegel, the Greek polis served as the authentic origin of the political. And, even though authors such as Carl Schmitt, in his contemporary work *Der Begriff des Politischen* (The concept of the political), could designate the essence of the political as the relation between friend and foe, this relation had to be rethought in terms of the self-affirmation of the historical Being of a people rooted in the polis. Hegel's metaphysical interpretation of the Greek origin of the political in terms of the historical existence of particular peoples thus sharply contrasted with Rousseau's political theory of the general will, which, in its abstraction from the singularity of historical existence, provided the source for modern liberalism. From the perspective of historical singularity, the Nazi revolution, far from signifying the death of Hegel's philosophy, had revived it for the contemporary world.[118]

Certainly, later lectures indicate Heidegger's growing disappointment with the politics of the Nazi regime. The Nietzsche lectures and the posthumously published *Beiträge zur Philosophie* (Contributions to philosophy; 1936–38) illustrate this disillusionment and highlight, above all, Heidegger's critical attitude toward the forms of biologism that figured so prominently in the Nazi ideology. According to these writings of the late 1930s and early 1940s, such theories, in confining the interpretation of truth to the realm of human biological and racial existence, constituted so many belated expressions of the convergence of metaphysics and anthropologism that Heidegger sought to overcome.[119]

As reprehensible as Heidegger's political attitude and activity in 1933–34 might be, it in no way justifies explaining away the significance of his thought. Indeed, the attitude that would dismiss Heidegger's thought at a distance through labels such as the "irrationalism of the times" and a "destruction of reason" (Lukács) is vulnerable to the very accusations it makes—not only because Heidegger clearly came to appreciate the bankruptcy of Nazism, but, more fundamentally, because of the unwillingness of such an attitude to comprehend the seriousness of Heidegger's questioning of Western rationality and of Western intellectual traditions in general. Indeed, the objectionable character of Heidegger's actions in 1933–34 makes an immanent critique of his thought all the more urgently needed.[120]

Our next consideration follows from this same line of reflection. Heidegger's notion of truth elicited in the human subject as the ground of human historicity aroused the suspicion among his opponents that he had resuscitated a variant of the historical idealism originally espoused by Hegel, replacing the idea of the absolute with the still more inscrutable idea of Being.[121] Although Heidegger abandoned recourse to an absolute foundation, which distinguished the Hegelian phenomenology of the Spirit from all later forms of anthropology, he sought a nonanthropological basis for truth, one more primary than the material conditions of human existence. Indeed, despite his doubts about the movement of the Spirit in its retention of the essential meaning of the past, and his emphasis on the primordial significance of Greek origins, Heidegger's notion of the determining role of thought might seem to situate him among the post-Marxian epigones who have attempted to reinvigorate the idealist enterprise.

While this is one possible interpretation, it is not clear that the term "idealism," in relating Heidegger's position to the familiar philosophical terrain of the past, has the capacity to bring into focus what is unfamiliar and untimely in his distinction of *Seinsgeschichte* from the advent of anthropomorphism. A first indication of the implications of Heidegger's own questioning of the contemporary fulfillment of metaphysics lies in his application of the term "idealism" beyond what are familiarly taken to be idealist tenets. From the customary assumption that the *perceptum* or the idea is the object of knowledge,[122] he extended the term to the historicization of this assumption under the specific Hegelian premise that the idea historically encompassed the essential meaning of reality. Indeed, Heidegger broadened the familiar philosophical terminology to encompass the whole of Western metaphysical traditions, set in movement, to his mind, by the errancy of metaphysics with Plato's identifying the adequate basis of truth in the idea.[123] That Hegel can be considered as a culminating point of "idealism" in this broad sense had less to do with Hegel's own philosophical self-estimation as the all-encompassing expression of metaphysics than with the deeper significance he uncovered in this assumption. Hegel was the first philosopher to conceive of the specifically historical dimension of thought in philosophical terms and in light of the history demarcated by his own phenomenology of the Spirit.[124]

From Heidegger's perspective, questioning beyond the horizon of Western metaphysics entailed, above all, thinking beyond Hegel toward another ground for the historical fulfillment of Western intellectual traditions. It is this attempt that Heidegger termed an "eschatology of Being," within which Hegel's speculative metaphysics found its specific place. The "Phenomenology of the Spirit," Heidegger wrote, "constitutes a phase in the Eschatology of Being . . . insofar as Being, as the absolute subjecticity of the unconditioned will to willing gathers itself in the last of its hitherto existing, metaphysically configured essences."[125]

Ascribing absolute subjecticity to the movement of *Seinsgeschichte* meant not only historicizing Hegel's thought in view of the later development of Western ideas, but setting aside the absolute perspective of historical coherence in the core of its heritage for subsequent theory. For Hegel, the coherence of history emerged in an *Aufhebung* (sublation) of the estrangement of human experience of truth from its absolute source, whereas, for Heidegger, this coherence consolidated, amid the finitude of human historical experience, a conviction of the absolute underpinning of the subject as the guarantor of truth. Even where absolutes might later be disavowed, Hegel's philosophy of the subject in the sure possession of the truth that emerges in its past experience, set in place assumptions about the relation of the human subject to the truth of Being that tacitly guided the advent of the anthropocentric outlook. As choosing Hegel to be his principal interlocutor in *Identität und Differenz* (Identity and difference) makes clear, Heidegger's attempt to rethink the coherence of history beyond the advent of metaphysics in anthropomorphism involved at its center a reinterpretation of the historical dimension of the problematic relation between the human subject and the truth of Being as bequeathed by Hegel's speculative philosophy.

At issue in this key work of the 1950s is the way of engaging in a dialogue with the history of philosophy. Through his assumption of the "difference" of beings, of the human being, from Being, Heidegger demarcated his position from that of Hegel's absolute metaphysics. Because it calls in question the taking up of the truth of Being in thought, this difference sets aside the presupposition of Hegel's *Aufhebung* of the essential truth of the past. Rather than *Aufhebung,* Heidegger characterized his dialogue with the philosophy of the past as a "step backward [*Schritt zurück*] into the domain that has been previously skipped over [but] through which the essence of truth first and foremost becomes worthy of thought."[126]

That Heidegger posited, not the absolute identity of thought and the truth of Being, but the irreducible difference of this truth in regard to all beings that can be thought is less a variation on a Hegelian theme than an essential deformation of the Hegelian approach to truth and to its history. And that he described his dialogue with the philosophy of the past in terms of a "step backward" toward the omission or "skip over [*Übersprung*]" evoked by the epochal deepening of the errancy of

Being's truth, and the withdrawal of any trace of the primordial human experience of this truth, has less to do with a purported quest for origins that logically followed from Heidegger's variety of idealism[127] than with the unfamiliar perspective in which Heidegger's view of the historicity of truth placed the finite limits of human understanding.

The unfamiliarity of Heidegger's late view of the limits of human understanding is suggested by its departure, not only from the metaphysics of Hegel, but also from the diverse currents of a post-Hegelian world whose view of the limits of human understanding rendered the absolute claim of Hegel's metaphysics thoroughly questionable. On the one hand, Heidegger's *Seinsgeschichte* set in a wholly different perspective his earlier objections to the critical philosophers of history who attempted to conserve a fundamental role for ideas and the idealist legacy, while admitting a margin of opacity at the very heart of historically determined normative truths by which consciousness confers meaning on a world. On the other hand, the movement of *Seinsgeschichte* included thinkers of the contemporary world whose radical view of the limits of human ideas brought this heritage most decisively into question. This juxtaposition finds its source in Heidegger's understanding of the emergence of the human subject at the center of the universe of possible meanings. The modern "subject" in Heidegger's analysis reached beyond the Cartesian cogito, the Kantian *ich denke,* the Hegelian *Geist,* and their refinements in critical theory in view of the contingency of understanding: with his claim to account for the contemporary world as a totality, it necessarily comprehended a whole range of more hidden and impersonal functions reputedly underlying the historicity of consciousness, on which Marx, Nietzsche, and Freud, from entirely different vantage points, based their analyses.[128] Such architects of contemporary assumptions about the limits of human understanding, each in his own manner, traced the genesis of truth and its historicity to the operation of a veiled and anonymous "subject" of an order other than consciousness itself: Marx, to the process of human material self-production; Nietzsche, to the concealed work of the will to power; and Freud, to ego formation arising in the conflict between unconscious instincts and societal requirements for instinctual renunciation.

If Heidegger's later writings dealt extensively with Nietzsche's attempt to subvert Western metaphysical traditions that had arrived,

with Hegel, at a culminating point, they rarely referred to contemporary proponents of critical philosophy of history. Windelband, Rickert,
and Dilthey were simply noted in the broad epochal advent of truth that
emerged with the decline of Hegelian metaphysics,[129] while key contemporary orientations, such as historical materialism or psychoanalysis, were only touched on in scattered comments. Nonetheless, given
Heidegger's presupposition about the unitary character of truth in contemporary as in other epochs of *Seinsgeschichte,* the message of those
comments is unmistakable. Even though all these leading orientations
in the interpretation of truth embodied the contemporary advent of
Seinsgeschichte, none of them understood the essential epochal meaning of truth as profoundly as Nietzsche, whose thought, in Heidegger's
view, uncovered the fundamental tendency of truth deployed throughout the contemporary world.[130]

For Heidegger, Nietzsche alone was able to think this truth in its
essential contemporary dimensions—by conceiving its foundation
exclusively in the subject in relation to the historical movement engendered by the radical uprooting of the onto-theological underpinnings of
the idea, grounded in the ancient Platonic-Christian heritage. For
Heidegger, Nietzsche alone followed the history of truth to its ultimate
metaphysical outcome—by radically fulfilling the implicit meaning of
the idea, which he expressed in the language of values. The thought of
values fulfilled the idea by demystifying it. Values unmasked the presupposition of universal, timeless norms traditionally taken to underlie
the idea by exposing them as nothing more than particular perspectives
imposed by the subject's will, covering over the chaos of an infinite
multiplicity of real possibilities that might be placed in the service of
interpretation of a world. This conception of the foundation of possible meanings in the constitutive capacity of the human will at once
demonstrated the profound ontological limits of meaning available to
the subject and reinforced the ultimate predominance of the subject in
the creation of a meaningful world.

In this conception of the foundational role of the human subject,
which effectively excluded any extrahuman source in the explanation
of truth, Nietzsche pushed the modern approach to truth to an extreme,
anticipating the ground of Heidegger's claim about the epochal unity
evoked in contemporary intellectual orientations. Every philosophy of
the limits of modern human understanding, Heidegger maintained,

necessarily prolonged the metaphysical tradition culminating in Hegel, extending it into anthropomorphism. It did so because the thought of such limits served as an effective basis for relegating all possible attributions of truth to a man-made universe in which Being, to make sense, must be covered over by psychological, material, sociological, or historical explanations available to the human intelligence.

As Jean-Jacques Rousseau genially observed in his *Confessions:* "In complete contrast to theologians, doctors and philosophers admit as true only what they can explain, and make their intelligence the measure of the possible."[131] In the contemporary world as Heidegger saw it, theology itself, the discipline traditionally considered to be farthest removed from anthropocentrism, had slowly assimilated itself to a politico-cultural worldview paralleling the metaphysical advent of *Seinsgeschichte* through which all extrahuman forms of explanation were subject to doubt. Indeed, this complements Nietzsche's deflation of the supersensuous, ideal claim of metaphysics, ushering in that period of ontological weightlessness of values in reference to which Heidegger adopted the term "European nihilism."

Heidegger's assertion of the limit of the idea, of human conscious thought works to cast doubt on the adequacy of the subject as the foundation of truth. More directly than in his earlier notion of finitude (*Being and Time*), in his later notion of the limit of the subject, with all of its anthropomorphic ramifications,[132] the historical movement of truth designates an essence of the *Gestell,* an essence of language, an essence of humanity itself—in total independence of the subject's will. Indeed, Heidegger's all-encompassing analysis of the coherence of history advances a bold claim. On the face of it, it might seem to provide anything but an avowal of the limitations of human understanding, especially given his own description of the "step backward" as at once questioning the essence of metaphysics and claiming to grasp the foundations of Western history in its totality.[133]

The unusual character of Heidegger's thought on the limits of the human understanding of truth, however, comes into sharp focus once the level of analysis is shifted from the ground of *Seinsgeschichte* in the coherent movement of truth to the discontinuities involved in the epochal *Geschick,* according to which humanity embodies truth. We have noted that, in Heidegger's notion of historicity, the epochal distinction between Being and beings implied in the metaphysical interpretation of truth is not predisposed by a determinate human character or mode of existence, but just the reverse, with the human essence changing in relation to epochal ways of drawing this distinction. On the basis of our previous analysis, we can now see Heidegger's literal way of understanding this thought in its full implications, as a delimitation of variations in truth elicited in a given epoch, which, against the background of the errancy of metaphysics and the deepening retreat of Being, necessarily overshadow truths that guided epochs previous to it. This retreat of Being in its epochal designation of truth, as it calls forth variations in human ways of being, casts profound margins of opacity between the illumination of different epochal perspectives of human self-interpretation. Heidegger offered this insight especially in relation to modernity, where he saw a deepening forgetfulness of the veiled source of the historicity of truth accompany misunderstanding of the meaning of history per se. While the advent of modern anthropomorphic criteria of truth corresponded to a deflection of attention, more than ever before, from the shadows permeating human self-interpretation, these criteria simultaneously cast a deepening opacity between human beings across the horizons described by their historicity. The advent of anthropomorphism engendered blindness to the radical incommensurability of the ways truth emerged independently of the human subject, ways that corresponded to changes in the human essence in different epochs.

Heidegger's later perspective on the essential modifiability of humans and of the human approach to a world is highlighted by a shift in his reservations about the methodologies of the modern human sciences. According to his later thought, by defining a universe of meaning in relation to what can be made available to the human intelligence, they incorporate the modern presumption par excellence. Misconstruing the basis of the historicity of truth, they reveal less the meaning of the objects under investigation than the modern will to classify, compare, and technically dominate the past as a means of assuring a secure place for the subject in the midst of a historically changing world.[134] Three examples, taken from his later works, will illustrate the implications of Heidegger's observations.

The first concerns the term "world image [*Weltbild*]," which Heidegger examined in his essay "Die Zeit des Weltbildes" (The age of the world image). This term had indeed been in widespread use in the German human sciences since the late nineteenth century: Max Weber, for instance, referred to a "rationalization of the *Weltbild* of ancient Judaism"; Rudolf Bultmann and Ernst Troeltsch distinguished the "*Weltbild* of antiquity" from that of other epochs; Ernst Cassirer spoke of the "*Weltbild* of myth-making peoples."[135] In his early essay "On the Essence of Foundation," Heidegger himself qualified *Dasein*—without regard to historical epoch—as "*Weltbildend.*"[136]

Heidegger's understanding of the meaning of the term "*Weltbild*" changed in relation to the more radical approach to the historicity of truth characteristic of his later thinking. From the standpoint of the essay "The Age of the World Image," the application of "*Weltbild*" to the whole of human history said little about truth in its historical dimension, but much about the modern way of representing truth. Like its sister term "*Weltanschauung,*" the term "*Weltbild,*" for Heidegger, drew its meaning from the modern epoch, in which the world could be conceived of in the human image, as a pure object of human representation. The "time [*Zeit*]" of the *Weltbild* corresponds to the period in which "[b]eings as a totality . . . first become and only are beings insofar as they are conveyed by the representations and productions of humanity."[137]

In contrast to this, references to an "ancient Greek *Weltbild*" or to a "medieval Catholic *Weltanschauung*" are more than just anachronisms; deaf to the resonance of "*Weltbild*" and "*Weltanschauung*" as applied to contemporary subjects' distinct ways of being, they tacitly reduce to a uniform standard what are in fact incommensurable ways in which truth reveals itself to humans in different epochs of history. The same was true, for Heidegger, with regard to the contemporary resonance of the word *culture,* our second example. If culture had deep roots in the humanism of Roman and Christian antiquity, its function as a context of cultivation of the subject was essentially modern in origin. As Heidegger wrote in "Parmenides": "There has been 'culture' only since the beginning of modern times. It began in the moment when *veritas* became *certitudo,* as man through his own 'cultivation'—*cultura*—through his own creation, made himself the 'creator,' that is to say a *génie.* The Greeks knew neither anything comparable to 'culture' nor anything like 'génie.'"[138]

In Heidegger's view, the Greeks defined their collective existence in relation, not to culture, but to *mythos, logos,* and *epos.* Reference to a Greek "culture," on the other hand, rather than simply a heuristic device of the historian, tacitly conveys uniformity in the nature of human existence, while hiding the different ways in which truth emerges out of the opacity of its ground to evoke changes in the most basic approaches to truth characteristic of different ages. Even the man considered by Heidegger to be the greatest of modern historical thinkers, Jacob Burckhardt, fell prey to this methodological conflation of the modern human sciences, as betrayed in the title of his work on Greek antiquity, *Griechische Kulturgeschichte* (The history of Greek culture).[139]

For Heidegger, the leveling of distinctions among human ways of being evoked in the epochal grasp of truth manifested itself most directly in the psychologist's claim to universality, our third example. In contrast to this claim, Heidegger insisted on the character of psychology itself as a historically determined appearance,[140] corresponding to the anthropocentric quest for security in the certitude of the human subject. Such a quest, to his mind, was entirely foreign to the ancient Greek attitude toward truth. Derived from modern propositions about the universality of meaning, such a methodology remained wholly blind to the fundamental epochal divergence of truth, for instance, in the variable historical ground of dream interpretation. In this light, Heidegger asked in relation to Pindar's evocation of the dream in the eighth of the *Pythian Odes* "whether the interpretation of the human essence in regard to consciousness does not correspond to a wholly particular self-experience of man, namely of modern humanity and only of this humanity; whether one could at all explain the dream from the character of human psychic life, or whether, conversely, the dream is not more fit to first provide a glimpse at the essence of man."[141] In his interpretation of the Greeks, Heidegger made it clear that, to his mind, the dream had to be thought in its relation to the historicity of the human essence.[142]

These examples indicate the basis of Heidegger's designation of the unhistorical (*ungeschichtliche*) character of the contemporary world,[143] grounded in a misapprehension of the human subject which, far from the master of truth, was essentially evoked in the historical movement of truth. From Heidegger's standpoint, this unhistorical character of contemporary humans persisted despite mounting eagerness for historical knowledge. In *Being and Time,* Heidegger had already distinguished the historical character of an age from its knowledge of history: "Ages not oriented toward historical knowledge," he wrote, "are not just for that reason also unhistorical."[144] In his later works, this distinction was rephrased in the context of *Seinsgeschichte* to interpret the present age: despite all historical knowledge, its unhistorical character unwittingly closed off the past to what did not correspond to present standards.[145] Even more markedly than the earlier Heidegger in the *Daseinsanalytik* of *Being and Time,* the later Heidegger, in view of the movement of *Seinsgeschichte,* withdrew any guarantee that the demand for transhistorical certitude on the basis of modern standards of objectivity and of general validity (*Allgemeingültigkeit*) could make contact with what is meaningful in the past. Indeed, coupling together the aims of natural scientific and historical knowledge under the heading of a "technical-historical consciousness [*technisch-historisches Bewusstsein*]," Heidegger considered that historical analysis complemented a technological quest for mastery of the present in the face of historical change by means of the criteria of certitude, asserted in an unbridled objectification (*Vergegenständlichung*) of the material under investigation.[146] As he had in *Being and Time,* Heidegger later believed that such objectification had led to the endemic modern problem of historicism, which he defined as a confusion (*Ratlosigkeit*) of historical existence, and as a straying among previous historical forms with the anthropocentric aim, imposed on the basis of calculative reckoning, of ensuring the security of the present.[147]

If, by calculative reckoning,[148] Heidegger did not primarily have in mind the specific quantitative methods that have come to occupy a central role in the methodologies of the human sciences since his time, his attention was drawn to a more general characterization of the historicism of the criteria of the human sciences in their explanation of history as a universal process of cause and effect relations (*Wirkungszusammenhang*). Such explanations might subject world history as a whole to psychological, political, or sociological assumptions about the foundation underlying events. In each case, it was here, for Heidegger, that the historicism of these disciplines most precisely betrayed their technological character, like that of the natural sciences. By admitting as true only what could be explained on the basis of cause and effect relations, the criteria of calculative certitude closed historicist explanation to what did not conform to human modes of representation. Similarly, the natural disciplines undertook a thoroughgoing objectification of nature in conformity with the criteria of certitude, which confined the subject within the realm of its representations and separated it from its earthly habitat. This separation was evidenced by the subject's approach to the earth which, instead of its thoughtful habitation, led to its calculated devastation (*Verwüstung*).[149]

Although in his book *Schellings Abhandlung über das Wesen der menschlichen Freiheit* (Schelling's treatise on the essence of human freedom), Heidegger wrote that "mere relativizing (*Relativieren*) does not comprise the essence of historicism," he also believed that the relativism of standards accompanies their entanglement in a current historicist approach to truth and follows logically from the theoretical methods of the historical sciences.[150] At the same time, Heidegger's vision of an "overcoming of metaphysics [*Überwindung der Metaphysik*]" involved what he took to be an overcoming of relativism in this sense. In his later writings, this overcoming depended on an essential encounter with earlier thought that, even though it could not claim to capture the past "in itself"[151]—and outside the movement of *Seinsgeschichte*—nonetheless delineated an essential contact with what has been (*das Gewesene*) through a further articulation of its implicit possibilities. Nietzsche, for example, in the period of the fulfillment of Western metaphysics, recapitulated past Platonic thought of truth in his philosophy of values. The Nietzschean interpretation of values by no means encompassed the idea in its "original" meaning, for this would have been impossible; in terms evoked by the historical movement of Being, Nietzsche conveyed the essential meaning of the idea more conclusively than Plato himself could have done, ultimately fulfilling the possibility of truth implicit in Plato's writings. According to Heidegger, only in the context of such an essential dialogue on the thought of truth elicited by Being's history would it be possible to speak of an encounter with "what has been," reaching beyond the representational confines of historical theory (*überhistorisch*).[152]

Heidegger's hope of encountering the truth of earlier thought (*von der Wahrheit eines Denkens betroffen zu werden*)[153] should not conceal the pervasiveness of the problem of historical understanding that his thinking involves in a broader sense. The thought of the opacity of the foundations of truth—"This veil vanishing unto itself [*Dieser zu sich selbst entschwindende Schleier*]"[154]—and of the conveyance of this opacity in the differentiation of truth as it emerges in different epochs, leaves little room for the possibility—in *any* given age—of a meaningful approach to essential thought of truth "as it actually has been [*wie es eigentlich gewesen*]." Nowhere is this recondite character of truth more graphically illustrated than in the interior of Heidegger's own course of thought. Whereas, in "Parmenides," *Nietzsche,* and other writings of the 1930s and 1940s, Heidegger asserted that the experience of *aletheia,* "truth as disclosedness," stood at the origins of Western notions of truth, in his 1964 essay "The End of Philosophy and the Task of Thinking," he retracted this assertion, knocking down one of the central supports of his speculation since the *Kehre.* Because the Greek word for "disclosedness"—however implicit in the Greek term for "truth"—could never have been experienced as truth by ancient Greek thinkers or poets, Heidegger explained, "the assertion of an essential metamorphosis of truth, that is, from disclosedness to correctness [is therefore] not tenable."[155]

This perplexing development in Heidegger's course of thinking perhaps only confirms his own earlier statements about the difficulty of interpreting the basic texts of Greek antiquity. Indeed, in "Parmenides," he had gone so far as to declare:

> Yet how seldom and to what a small extent has man understood the essence of the true, that is, truth. But even were we today in the happy situation of knowing the essence of truth, there would still be no guarantee that we also would be able to rethink what was experienced as the essence of truth in the early thought of the Greeks. This is because, not only the essence of truth, but the essence of all that is essential has its own allotted domain out of which a given historical age can only create a small share corresponding to it.[156]

Heidegger's retraction of his previous interpretation of the pre-Socratic approach to truth in "The End of Philosophy" renders such statements thoroughly problematic. It also casts a doubtful light on his earlier assumption of a possible encounter with the truth of earlier epochs, of which each given historical age "can only create a small allotted share." Given the final turn in his path of thought (*Denkweg*), to what extent might his now-retracted interpretation support the charge that Heidegger had imposed standards on the Greek thinkers irrelevant to them? More generally stated, in light of his original interpretation of pre-Socratic thought, to what extent could Heidegger still have justified his claim that the tie of historical consideration (*geschichtliche Besinnung*) to what has been (*das Gewesene*) remained essentially stronger than the link to former times (*das Vergangene*) of historical contemplation (*historische Betrachtung*)?[157]

These questions identify a serious difficulty confronting Heidegger's later *Seinsfrage,* revealed, above all, by his telling retraction in "The End of Philosophy." As early as his works of the 1930s and 1940s, however, Heidegger's own orientation could little admit such a difficulty. He made clear that, in retrieving what has been—most notably, the meaning of ancient Greek texts—the task of thinking and of historical scholarship guided by it, far from fixing the primary goal at a "correct [*richtige*]" recapitulation of what the Greeks themselves understood, must aim toward comprehension of what, in the essential character of truth indicated by their language, remained unthinkable, both to them and to subsequent Western intellectual traditions.

> For that which in essential historical moments did not come to pass—and what would be more essential than an origin—must for the first time still come to pass, not as a simple recapitulation, but in the sense of those thrusts, leaps, and plunges, of that which is momentary and elementary, in terms of which we conceive ourselves and must be conceived, when otherwise we expect something essential from future history.[158]

As suggested in this passage and in similar passages of *Nietzsche,*[159] Heidegger's later interpretation of the significance of historical understanding underscored the unthought dimension of the past in light of its anticipation of a future—in this case of *another* origin (*Anfang*).[160] Although this thought of the future may seem reminiscent of *Being and Time,* where futurity (*Zukünftigkeit*) constitutes the predominant mode of *Dasein*'s temporal existence with which the question of authenticity of historicity and historical understanding has to reckon, the notion of the predominance of the future in *Being and Time* was closely tied to Heidegger's ontological analysis of *Dasein*'s modes of approaching Being-toward-death. After his shift away from ontology, Heidegger returned to the theme of temporality in one of his last essays, "Zeit und Sein" (Time and being; 1962), where he considered time from the standpoint, not of *Dasein*'s ontological mode of temporalization, but of how time is given to humanity.[161] Here Heidegger accentuated the difference between human responsibility—which was grounded in a mode of existence of *Dasein*—and the movement of truth through which a possible grasp of the past might be directed toward opening the horizon of a future. The later Heidegger emphasized that the decisions (*Entscheidungen*) orienting the advent (*Ereignis*) of truth that was to come "do not fall within the well-tended garden of our inclinations, wishes, and intentions."[162]

The premise of the opacity of the past that pervades Heidegger's later thought corresponds to this notion of the historicity of a truth whose movement stands entirely outside the bounds of human choice and whose hidden depths, unseen by limited human vision, remain beyond the range of human production and human representation. For Heidegger, however, it was outside this range that essential thought itself emerged: thinkers did not choose their thought in any conventional sense, but were "those isolated ones who have no choice, who rather must put into words what beings in the history of Being respectively *are*."[163] From this perspective, thought designated human freedom in its capacity to open a horizon of the future in its essential contact with the truth of what has been. The hermeneutic problem of establishing a methodology of encounter was entirely absorbed by the quest for coherence (*Zusammenhang*) of the history of Being in relation to which an epochal thought of truth and a corresponding epochal way of deploying freedom announced itself. Despite serious difficulties in Heidegger's manner of interpretation, difficulties only exacerbated by changes in its course, Heidegger's analyses ultimately stand on a level of inquiry radically different from that of the human sciences by carrying the freedom to establish standards of inquiry outside the field of human discretion. This freedom remained all the more invisible to modern man and to the methodologies of the human sciences because of its dependence on Being's epochal advent. "To search for dependence and influence between thinkers," wrote Heidegger, "is a misunderstanding of thought. Every thinker is dependent, namely on the call of Being. The breadth of this dependence decides the freedom from influences that lead astray. The broader the dependence, so much the more powerful is the freedom of thought."[164]

This interpretation of freedom underlines the full range of distance that the later Heidegger's historical thinking had covered since *Being and Time,* which conceived the problem of freedom in terms of finite decisions of *Dasein* orienting its possible ways of being, and of revealing truth. It was in the freedom (or unfreedom) of these decisions that the historicity of *Dasein*—its way of rendering history coherent—found its roots. The later Heidegger, on the other hand, conceived freedom in terms of its dependence on Being, in the fullness of its distinction from the modes of being of finite *Dasein.* Freedom became possible epochally, through its concrete delineation in the historical movement of truth. From this vantage point, *Seinsgeschichte* recapitulated a history of interpretations of freedom in light of a given epochal expression of truth.[165] Freedom was defined in a necessary epochal way, called forth by Being, of thinking the truth of beings and, notably, the essence of the human being in particular.[166]

This depiction of freedom in terms of necessary epochal ways of thinking the truth of Being furthermore brings into its clearest perspective Heidegger's later considerations of his *own* thinking. It was consistent with his later turn from the analysis of finite, singular *Dasein* to the epochal articulations of *Seinsgeschichte* that Heidegger portrayed the *Kehre* itself in terms, not of decision primarily characteristic of his individual path of thought, but of the epochal possibility of overcoming metaphysics.[167] Conceived of as a possibility of thinking beyond metaphysical criteria of truth and beyond the fulfillment of these criteria in Western scientific rationality, the *Kehre* could thus itself appear as an elucidation of the truth of beings—and of the freedom corresponding to that truth—called forth by the coherent movement of *Seinsgeschichte.*

The distance that Heidegger had taken from *Being and Time* in this interpretation of freedom lays bare a paradox in his later historical thought, one that may be clearly expressed in two related questions. Does not the later Heidegger's attempt to reconcile human freedom with the movement of a history whose source is neither human nor derivable from finite ontology of *Dasein* ultimately identify historical meaning with an overarching principle of historical coherence? Does not this attempted reconciliation resolve the problem of historical meaning in much the same way as the traditional philosophies of history that *Being and Time* had sought to undermine?

V

Heidegger marked his distance from earlier approaches to the coherence of history, above all, in his thought of the peril (*Gefahr*) facing contemporary humanity.[168] The history of Being evoked the historicity of the limits within which the truth of beings, hence the truth of the human essence itself, could be thought. But this movement also required a response from humans, a preparedness to listen to the truth that elicited the epochal horizons delimiting the meaningfulness of human existence in terms of which freedom became thinkable.[169] That humanity could remain blind and deaf to the source of truth beyond the pale of human representation, was, to Heidegger's mind, an alienation of the human essence that threatened it with annihilation (*Vernichtung*).[170] For Heidegger, this peril announced itself, not only in the devastation of the earth or in the shutting off of human existence from the essential meaning of the past, but also in the "flight of the Gods" and the subsequent extinguishing of the sacred in contemporary life.[171]

In *Nietzsche,* Heidegger traced the impelling source of this peril to a freedom delineated in an unprecedented approach to truth in the history of Being. He thought of modern human freedom essentially as liberation, as freedom from the ties to the biblical-Christian faith in the truth of Revelation to pursue the quest for certitude that constituted the modern approach to truth.[172] Impelled by the advent (*Ereignis*) of truth elicited by Being, however, freedom from faith in Revelation, far from simply liberating humanity from a given set of dogmas, set in place a radically new way of interpreting beings as a whole, touching the essence of humanity in how it conceived of its freedom. And herein lay the peril. Into his broad understanding of the meaning of the sacred, Heidegger introduced the notion of desacralization (*Entgötterung*), which he characterized as the departure of the sacred before the technical-historical consciousness of contemporary humanity. This understanding marked the depths of Heidegger's separation from traditional presuppositions of an intelligible course of human history within which human freedom was circumscribed, whether sustained by Divine Providence or an Absolute Subject, or whether constituted by human praxis. It is here, I will argue, that Heidegger's ultimate presuppositions with regard to the problem of historical meaning come to light.

The distinctiveness of Heidegger's historical thought stands in his willingness both to conceive of a nonhuman foundation for the historicity of truth, a foundation that involved, in the contemporary epoch, freedom in face of the retreat of Being and the departure of the sacred, and, at the same time, to affirm the truth of the sacred per se, in want of which humanity confronted its profound peril. For Heidegger, the problem of historical meaning made no concessions either to a reassertion of eternal foundations underlying the flux of truth or to an assumption that the sacred beliefs of the past could be reconciled with the historicity of truth, whether as an ultimate philosophical vision of historical coherence or as a process of demystification of outmoded credences. Heidegger faced his contemporary readers with the untimely resolve not to place in doubt the truth of the sacred in its originary embodiment, even as he told them that the opacity of the historicity of truth blinded contemporary vision to the originary meaning of what had been held sacred in the past. By way of consolation, Heidegger quoted the poet Hölderlin: "Only at times can man bear the fullness of the sacred."[173]

In this vision of the historicity of sacred truth, Heidegger provided his ultimate answer to the anthropocentric standpoint of contemporary humanity, for which the advent of a totally humanized world placed in question the meaningfulness of any dimension of human experience that could not be explained in human terms. Moreover, without retracting his earlier rejection of the anthropocentric view of liberal theology toward cultural manifestations of religion, Heidegger radicalized his historicization of the sacred to such an extent that Christianity itself fell under the shadow of historical opacity, and Christ did not embody the only or even the ultimate religious truth. Paraphrasing Hölderlin in the essay "Wozu Dichter?" (What are poets for?), Heidegger held that Christ was the most recent incarnation of the sacred, whose disappearance was imminent after the extinction of his brothers Dionysus and Heracles.[174]

Thus Heidegger's thoroughgoing historicization of sacred truth cast doubt, not only on the methodology of liberal Christian theology, but on the hermeneutic task of Christian theology per se.[175] Christian theology depended on the possibility of a continuity between historical epochs enabling the retrieval of a message, a kerygma, latent in a sacred source. But what if this kerygma remained as mute to us as the message of the gods of Greek antiquity?

In "Phänomenologie und Theologie" (Phenomenology and theology; 1927), Heidegger had assumed that the fundamental continuity and hidden constitutive influence of the Christian kerygma underlay the radical historicity of human existence. By contrast, Heidegger's later portent of desacralization and of the want of God (*Fehl Gottes*)—of the eclipse of the sacred before the modern *Weltbild*—emphasized an aspect of his presupposition of an articulated historical coherence to which his earlier philosophy could have accorded no place.

The exact terrain Heidegger relinquished with his later approach to the problem of historical meaning may be placed in sharpest relief by reconsidering, in light of its theological implications, Heidegger's use of the term "*Weltbild*." In writings roughly contemporaneous with *Being and Time,* as we have seen, Heidegger asserted that *Dasein* was "*weltbildend*"—a term Heidegger then employed irrespective of historical epoch. Common in German usage, this same term was adopted by Rudolf Bultmann, who continued to use it in its more usual sense in later years, and well after the *Kehre,* when Heidegger had abandoned its application to all but the modern epoch of *Seinsgeschichte.* Bultmann, however, insisted on this usage for a precise motive, consistent with his faithfulness to the thought of a fundamental historical continuity of the Christian kerygma. If the later Bultmann continued to refer to an ancient as well as to a modern *Weltbild,* this was not to deny the "historicity" of finite human existence (understood in a sense more in tune with the early Heidegger). Rather, it was in conformity with Bultmann's later conviction of a profound historical *similarity* in the finitude of human representations of the world—not only as couched in the language of modern science, but also of primitive Christianity—manifested in human attempts to grasp the ever present sacred truth underlying human existence and rendering it coherent.[176] Indeed, it was in relation to the concealed, ongoing presence of sacred truth, which continually had to be reappropriated beneath the distortions of ancient and modern world constructions that the later Bultmann conceived of Christian eschatology: "The meaning of history lies always in the present, and when the present is conceived as the eschatological present by Christian faith, the meaning of history is realized."[177]

Heidegger's emphasis on the *absence* of the sacred signaled an aspect of his later historical reflection that remained farthest removed, not only from a possible Christian theology—in this case, that of Bultmann—but also from *Being and Time*: the notion of *mediation* of the truth of faith by an epochally articulated coherence that *Seinsgeschichte* described.[178] While hidden to human capacities of representation, this mediation expressed itself as a dependence of the emergence of the sacred on the epochal articulations of a history of Being. To be sure, Heidegger never intended to place in question the validity of faith of an individual Christian, and went so far as to assert that the philosopher must remain silent in matters of faith.[179] Nothing, however, can hide the equivocal nature of such statements in view of Heidegger's comments on the dependence of the sacred, indeed of God, on Being. "Whether God is God," he pronounced in one of his last talks, "comes to pass through and within the constellation of Being."[180]

Where, for the Heidegger of "Phenomenology and Theology," the Christian kerygma was beheld from the standpoint of an unmediated source of historicity, for the later Heidegger, this kerygma faced imminent eclipse through the mediation of the history of Being, which was to decide Christianity's ultimate fate. Like the owl of Minerva, Heidegger's notion of an eschatology of Being took flight just before the night to evoke a bygone possibility of the sacred illuminated by the epochal incarnation of truth. If the ultimate aim of this eschatology was the end of metaphysics that had been interwoven with the Christian message, Christianity itself was to be principally approached in terms of the loss of its "history-constituting force" (*geschichte-bildende Kraft*).[181] Here the ultimate darkening of the Christian kerygma embodied Heidegger's definitive and most extreme expression of the straying of Christianity from primitive Christian devotion (a theme he adopted from Overbeck). That this disappearance of the sacred promised a future return, however (albeit not necessarily in Christian incarnation), is suggested in Heidegger's "Ein Brief an einem jungen Studenten" (Letter to a young student; 1950):

> The want of God and of the sacred is absence. But absence is not nothing. It is directly the presence of the hidden fullness of what has been which is yet to be assimilated. As such, it gathers the essential: the sacred in Greek antiquity, in the prophetic-Judaic, in the Gospel of Jesus. This no-longer is in itself a not-yet of the hidden advent of its inexhaustible essence.[182]

NOTES

1. Heidegger, "Letter to W. J. Richardson" (1962), printed as the introduction to Richardson, *Heidegger,* xx.

2. Although not published until 1943, "Vom Wesen der Wahrheit" and "Platons Lehre von der Wahrheit" were first presented as lectures in 1930 and 1930–31, respectively. See Heidegger, vol. 34 of *Gesamtausgabe.*

3. Heidegger, *Sein und Zeit,* 227.

4. Ibid., 424.

5. Heidegger, *Kant,* 203; see also Heidegger, "Die Aufhellung der Tendenz zur Anthropologie" (1929), in *Gesamtausgabe,* 28:9–21.

6. Heidegger, *Kant,* 202.

7. Ibid., 203.

8. Heidegger, *Nietzsche,* 2:129.

9. Besides *Kant and the Problem of Metaphysics,* other Heidegger works focusing on Kant in this period include his Marburg lectures of 1927–28, "Phänomenologische Interpretation von Kants Kritik der reinen Vernunft," published as vol. 25 of *Gesamtausgabe,* and the second half of Heidegger's 1930 Freiburg lectures, "Vom Wesen der menschlichen Freiheit: Einleitung in die Philosophie," published as vol. 31 of *Gesamtausgabe.*

10. Heidegger, *Kant,* 204.

11. Scheler, "Die Stellung des Menschen im Kosmos" (1928), in *Späte Schriften,* 56. *Kant and the Problem of Metaphysics* was dedicated to the memory of Max Scheler, who died in 1928. Most of Heidegger's references to Scheler in relation to philosophical anthropology quote from "Die Stellung des Menschen im Kosmos."

12. Scheler, "Philosophische Weltanschauung," in *Späte Schriften,* 82.

13. Kant, *Grundlegung zur Metaphysik der Sitten,* 265.

14. Heidegger and Cassirer, "Davoser Disputation," in Heidegger, *Kant,* 246.

15. Heidegger, *Gesamtausgabe,* 25:426.

16. Pure intuition, in the words of the second edition, could be considered valid "at least for us humans." Kant, *Kritik der reinen Vernunft,* as cited in Heidegger, *Kant,* 163.

17. Objecting to Heidegger's claim that Kant essentially modified the role of the schematism between the first and second editions of the *Critique of Pure Reason,* Alexis Philonenko noted that "in the two editions the only text that remained identical is that of the transcendental schematism." Philonenko, *Études kantiennes,* 13. Heidegger, however, had explicitly stated that his description of changes in Kant's treatment of the transcendental schematism referred, not to the (unchanged) chapter specifically devoted to this faculty,

but to the (revised) preceding section on transcendental deduction, where transcendental schematism figures as the "constitutive center of pure knowledge." Heidegger, *Kant,* 154.

18. Ibid., 159.

19. For the Marburg neo-Kantians, as Heidegger observed: "Space and time are comprehended as categories in the logical sense." Ibid., 140.

20. See Cohen, *System der Philosophie,* parts 1 and 2.

21. For Heidegger, the first edition of the *Critique of Pure Reason* seemed to open interpretation of Kant to the possibility that even the rational foundation of morals could be rooted, through the "feeling of respect [*Gefühl der Achtung*]," in the temporal synthesis achieved by the pure schematism. Heidegger, *Kant,* 150–54. Cassirer, however, maintained that Kant's statements in this regard related to psychological factors of the *Gefühl,* factors that might act as *incentives* to moral action, but which had no authority regarding an ontological basis of moral laws. Cassirer, *"Kant und das Problem der Metaphysik"* (review), 14–15.

22. Cohen, *Kants Theorie der Erfahrung,* 491.

23. Cassirer, *"Kant,"* 15–16.

24. See, in this regard, Husserl's letter to Ingarden, April 19, 1931, in Husserl, *Briefe an Roman Ingarden,* 67: "I will speak in Berlin . . . in Halle and Frankfurt on 'Phenomenology and Anthropology' . . . and must devote a precise reading to my antipodes, Scheler and Heidegger."

25. Heidegger, "Nur noch ein Gott kann uns retten: *Spiegel*-Gespräch mit Martin Heidegger [on September 23, 1966]," 59.

26. Husserl, "Phänomenologie und Anthropologie" (1931), 1.

27. Husserl, "Die Krisis des europäischen Menschentums und die Philosophie" (1935), in *Die Krisis der europäischen Wissenschaften und die transcendentale Phänomenologie,* 325.

28. After referring to the fragmentation of the university disciplines and to what he considered to be a contemporary dying off of their essential roots, Heidegger wrote in 1929: "Only when science exists from out of metaphysics [*aus der Metaphysik*] is it able to regain its essential task ever anew." Heidegger, "Was ist Metaphysik?" in *Wegmarken,* 18. On the problematic relation between science and metaphysics in this lecture, see Courtine, "Phénoménologie et science de l'être," 211–24.

29. For an exposition of this problem in relation to Kant, see Heidegger, *Gesamtausgabe,* 26:205–8.

30. Heidegger, *Sein und Zeit,* 229.

31. Bultmann, "Die Bedeutung der 'dialektischen Theologie' für die neutestamentliche Wissenschaft" (1928), in *Glauben und Verstehen,* 1:118.

32. Bultmann, "Die Krisis des Glaubens" (1931) and "Die Eschatologie des Johannes-Evangeliums" (1928), in *Glauben und Verstehen*, 2:8 and 1:143, respectively.

33. Heidegger considered this theme in a footnote in *Sein und Zeit*, 427: "That the traditional concept of eternity, grasped in the sense of the abiding now [*nunc stans*], is produced by an everyday comprehension of time and is circumscribed by the orientation toward an 'abiding' presence requires no detailed commentary. If the eternity of *God* can be philosophically 'constructed,' then this could only be understood as a more primary and 'infinite' temporality." However, these comments do not in any way lessen the ambiguity of *Being and Time* with regard to Christianity because Heidegger had also written (p. 424): "Inauthentic temporality of fallen-everyday *Dasein* must, as distraction from finitude [*Wegsehen von der Endlichkeit*], mistake authentic futurity and, with it, temporality as such. And when, indeed, everyday understanding of *Dasein* is oriented by *das Man,* then the self-forgetful 'representation' of 'infinity' of public time can first gain hold."

34. Bultmann, "Geschichtlichkeit," 72–94.

35. Eberhard Jüngel would therefore seem entirely justified when he observes in this respect: "Yet Bultmann always conceived the *Daseinsanalytik* in *Sein und Zeit* as a fundamental anthropology, while ignoring Heidegger's fundamental-ontological interpretation in its preparation of the ground for the question of Being." Jüngel, *Glauben und Verstehen: Zum Theologiebegriff Rudolf Bultmanns*, 20–25.

36. Löwith, "Grundzüge der Entwicklung der Phänomenologie zur Philosophie und ihr Verhältnis zur protestantischen Theologie," 340 (*Wissen, Glaube und Skepsis,*75–76).

37. Heidegger, unpublished letter to Karl Löwith, April 19, 1932.

38. Przywara, "Drei Richtungen der Phänomenologie," 252, 263.

39. Brunner, "Theologie und Ontologie—oder die Theologie am Scheidewege" (1931), in *Heidegger und die Theologie*, 125–35.

40. Barth and Bultmann, *Briefwechsel,*118.

41. Heidegger, unpublished letter to Karl Löwith, April 19, 1932.

42. Heidegger, "Vom Wesen des Grundes," in *Wegmarken*, 58n.

43. Heidegger, "Brief über den Humanismus," in *Wegmarken,* 187–88; see also, in this regard, Heidegger, *Gesamtausgabe*, 65:87–88.

44. Heidegger, *Nietzsche*, 2:127, 194. In keeping with Heidegger's usage, I will employ the terms "anthropology," "anthropomorphism," and "anthropocentrism" interchangeably.

45. Ibid., 489.

46. Heidegger's thinking on the metaphysical interpretation of "beings as a totality" is reflected in the following passage from *Nietzsche*, 2:273:

"Beings [*das Seiende*] as such are conceived as a totality [*im Ganzen*] in regard to the supersensuous, and these beings are at the same time recognized as true, whether as the supersensuous God of Creation and Salvation of Christianity, as the supersensuous moral imperative, the authority of reason, progress, the happiness of the majority. In every case, immediately present sensuous beings are reckoned in terms of an aspired ideal."

47. Heidegger, *Nietzsche,* 2:489.

48. See, in this regard, Heidegger's essay "Die Kehre," in *Die Technik und die Kehre.* Note also, for example, Heidegger's insistence, in 1946, that the truth of Being by no means related to the "unique discovery of an individual." Heidegger, *Die Grundfrage nach dem Sein selbst: Dicté,* 33.

49. Beierwaltes's analysis of Neoplatonism led him to question Heidegger's claim about the unity of Western metaphysical traditions as expressed in the continuing Western interpretations of Being in terms of beings. Beierwaltes, *Identität und Differenz,* 131–43.

50. Heidegger, *Gesamtausgabe,* 45:156.

51. Heidegger, *Gesamtausgabe,* 52:107.

52. Heidegger, *Nietzsche,*1:497 and 2:173.

53. Ibid., 2:92; Heidegger, *Gesamtausgabe,* 65:5–6. On Heidegger's use of "*geschichtliche Besinnung*" and "*historische Betrachtung,*" see Heidegger, *Gesamtausgabe,* 45:49–50.

54. In this regard, Heidegger's changes in orientation in the final period of his writing on the pre-Socratic interpretation of truth, to which we will have occasion to refer, leave open the question whether the comprehension of pre-Socratic fragments is not subject to the same aporia that no less an author than Jacob Burckhardt distinguished in the interpretation of Heraclitus: "From his fragments," wrote Burckhardt, "which are ever and again a source of inspiration, the most diverse conclusions can be drawn even today." Burckhardt, *Griechische Kulturgeschichte III,* 297.

55. Heidegger *Gesamtausgabe,* 55:85–97, and *Nietzsche,* 1:169.

56. Heidegger, *Nietzsche,* 1:169, and *Gesamtausgabe,* 45:156.

57. See, for example, Heidegger's treatment of this theme in regard to *aletheia* in *Gesamtausgabe,* 45:108–18.

58. See, in this regard, the analyses of Schürmann, *Le principe d'anarchie: Heidegger et la question* (English translation: *Heidegger on Being and Acting: From Principles to Anarchy*); and Zarader, *Heidegger et les paroles de l'origine.*

59. Heidegger, "Hegel und die Griechen," in *Wegmarken,* 267, and *Gesamtausgabe,* 55:21.

60. Hegel, *Vorlesungen über die Geschichte der Philosophie, Werke,* 18:290; Heidegger, "Hegel und die Griechen," in *Wegmarken,* 264.

61. Hegel, *Vorlesungen, Werke,*18:320, 322; Heidegger, *Gesamtausgabe,* 55:21.

62. Heidegger, "Die Zeit des Weltbildes," in *Holzwege,* 95.

63. See, for example, Heidegger, *Gesamtausgabe,* 45:105–6.

64. Heidegger, "Platons Lehre," in *Wegmarken,* 109–44, "*Aletheia:* Heraklit, Fragment 16," in *Vorträge und Aufsätze,* 257–82, "Vom Wesen der Wahrheit" (1933–34), in *Gesamtausgabe,* 36/37:224–29, *Einführung, in die Metaphysik,* 87, 97–104, "*Logos:* Heraklit, Fragment 50," in *Vorträge und Aufsätze,* 207–29, and "Vom Wesen und Begriff der *Physis:* Aristoteles *Physik* B, 1," in *Wegmarken,* 309–71.

65. Heidegger, *Nietzsche,* 2:400.

66. Heidegger, "Platons Lehre," in *Wegmarken,* 140, and "Vom Wesen der Wahrheit" (1933–34), in *Gesamtausgabe,* 36/37:121–23.

67. Heidegger, *Gesamtausgabe,* 45:15–16.

68. In regard to the principle of sufficient ground (*Satz vom Grund*), for example, Heidegger wrote that the "power of this principle is ever more exclusively and ever more quickly obeyed." Heidegger, *Der Satz vom Grund,* 197.

69. Heidegger, "Platons Lehre," in *Wegmarken,* 139, *Nietzsche,* 2:229, and "Das Ende der Philosophie und die Aufgabe des Denkens," 62.

70. Heidegger, "Platons Lehre," in *Wegmarken,* 131.

71. See, for example, Heidegger, *Gesamtausgabe,* 45:149 and 65:83–84.

72. Heidegger, *Nietzsche,* 2:415, and "Seminar in Zähringen" (1973), in *Vier Seminare,*133.

73. Heidegger, "Brief über den Humanismus," in *Wegmarken,* 145–94.

74. Heidegger, *Gesamtausgabe,* 45:68 and 54:62.

75. Heidegger, *Gesamtausgabe,* 45:105, *Satz vom Grund,* 210, and "Vom Wesen und Begriff der *Physis,*" in *Wegmarken,* 309–71.

76. Heidegger, "Brief über den Humanismus," in *Wegmarken,*151–52, and *Nietzsche,* 2:412–13.

77. See, for example, Heidegger, "Vom Wesen der Wahrheit," in *Wegmarken,* 76–77, *Gesamtausgabe,* 54:75, and *Einführung in die Metaphysik,* 97, 147.

78. Heidegger, *Identität und Differenz,* 52. On the relation between theology and metaphysics in Heidegger's thought during the earlier period of the *Kehre,* see Heidegger, "Die Grundfrage der Philosophie" (1933), in *Gesamtausgabe,* 36/37:51–80.

79. Heidegger, "Vom Wesen der Wahrheit," in *Wegmarken,* 76–77.

80. Heidegger, *Nietzsche,* 2:427.

81. Hegel, *Phänomenologie des Geistes, Werke,* 3:73.

82. Heidegger, *Nietzsche,* 2:133.

83. Heidegger distinguished between subjecticity (*Subiectität*), which referred to the unity of the history of Being inaugurated with the identification of Being and idea, and subjectivity (*Subjektivität*), which referred to the modern epoch of subjecticity, and which conceived of the essence of reality in relation to the self-certainty of consciousness. See ibid., 450–54. See also Heidegger, *Nietzsche,* trans. Capuzzi, 300.

84. Heidegger, "Zeit des Weltbildes," in *Holzwege,* 84.

85. Heidegger, *Nietzsche,* 1:550.

86. Ibid., 2:155, 164–65.

87. Ibid., 187–88.

88. Heidegger, *Gesamtausgabe,* 54:75, and "Seminar Le Thor" (1968), in *Vier Seminare,* 30.

89. Heidegger, *Nietzsche,* 2:422.

90. Heidegger, "Zeit des Weltbildes," in *Holzwege,* 92.

91. From Heidegger's standpoint, Locke and Hume represented nothing more than a coarser version of the philosophy of Descartes. See Heidegger, *Nietzsche,* 2:180.

92. Ibid., 1:584–85.

93. Heidegger, "Hegel und die Griechen," in *Wegmarken,* 258.

94. Heidegger, "Zeit des Weltbildes," in *Holzwege,* 69–70.

95. Heidegger, *Nietzsche,* 2:423–24.

96. Ibid., 423.

97. Ibid., 424–29.

98. Heidegger, "Zeit des Weltbildes," in *Holzwege,* 70.

99. Ibid., 69.

100. Heidegger, *Gesamtausgabe,* 45:149.

101. Heidegger, "Die Frage nach der Technik" and "Wissenschaft und Besinnung," in *Vorträge und Aufsätze,* 13–70.

102. Heidegger, *Nietzsche,* 2:164–65.

103. Ibid., 76, 165.

104. Heidegger, "Brief über den Humanismus," in *Wegmarken,* 152–53. How closely Heidegger linked Marxism with a tradition inherited—via Hegelian idealism—from the Platonic conception of the human being as the deployer of the idea is demonstrated as early as the key 1933–34 course lecture "Vom Wesen der Wahrheit," where Heidegger wrote: "Marxism can only be definitively overcome, when we first enter into debate with the doctrine of ideas and with its two-thousand-year-old history." Heidegger, *Gesamtausgabe,* 36/37:151–57.

105. Heidegger, "Zeit des Weltbildes," in *Holzwege,* 92.

106. Heidegger, "Frage nach der Technik," in *Vorträge und Aufsätze,* 35.

107. Heidegger, *Nietzsche,* 2:245.

108. Heidegger, *Gesamtausgabe,* 45:139.

109. See, for example, Heidegger, *Nietzsche,* 2:138.

110. Heidegger, "Überwindung der Metaphysik," "Hegel und die Griechen," *Vier Seminare, Identität und Differenz,* "Der Spruch des Anaximander," *Holzwege.*

111. Heidegger, "Überwindung der Metaphysik," in *Vorträge und Aufsätze,* 76.

112. See, for example, Habermas, *Der philosophische Diskurs der Moderne,* 168 (English translation: *The Philosophical Discourse of Modernity: Twelve Lectures*).

113. Heidegger, "Überwindung der Metaphysik," in *Vorträge und Aufsätze,* 93. For a balanced discussion of the political dimension of Heidegger's thought, see Pöggeler, *Philosophie und Politik bei Heidegger.*

114. Heidegger, "Nur noch ein Gott," 61. For a critique of Heidegger's claims in this interview, see Schuhmann, "Zu Heideggers *Spiegel*-Gespräch über Husserl," 591–612. See also Arendt's letter to Karl Jaspers, July 9, 1946, in Arendt and Jaspers, *Briefwechsel: 1926–1969,* 83–87. On Heidegger's willingness to adapt the terminology of *Daseinsanalytik* to Nazi propaganda, see documents gathered in Heidegger, *Reden und andere Zeugnisse eines Lebensweges: 1910–1976,* in *Gesamtausgabe,* 16:70, 366; Schneeberger, *Nachlese zu Heidegger: Dokumente zu seinem Leben und Denken;* and Martin, *Martin Heidegger und das "Dritte Reich": Ein Kompendium.*

115. Heidegger "Die Grundfrage der Philosophie," in *Gesamtausgabe,* 36/37:3.

116. Heidegger, "Vom Wesen der Wahrheit," in *Gesamtausgabe,* 36/37:119.

117. Heidegger, "Die Grundfrage der Philosophie," in *Gesamtausgabe,* 36/37:13.

118. Heidegger and Wolf, "Hegel: 'Über den Staat.'" I would like to thank Dr. Hermann Heidegger for permission to read and to quote from the written transcription of this seminar. For more complete details on its contents, see Barash, *Heidegger et son siècle: Temps de l'être, temps de l'histoire,* and "Martin Heidegger in the Perspective of the Twentieth Century," 52–78.

119. See also Heidegger, *Gesamtausgabe,* 47:58–93 and 65:18–19, 53–54. This does not signify that the only forms of racism are biological in character, nor that, by extension, Heidegger's manner of exaltation of the German *Volk* during this period was free of "racist" implications. On this point, see Rockmore, *On Heidegger's Nazism and Philosophy,* 296–98.

120. On Heidegger's own contemporary political statements, which are hardly without contradiction, see Heidegger, letter to Hannah Arendt, winter 1932–33, in Arendt and Heidegger, *Briefe, 1925–1975,* 68–69; Heidegger,

letters to Elisabeth Blochmann, March 30, June 10, August 30, and September 19, 1933, in Heidegger and Blochmann, *Briefwechsel, 1918–1969,* 60–74; see also Heidegger's 1929 letter on what he took to be the increasing *"Verjudung"* of the German Universities, in Sieg, "Die Verjudung des deutschen Geistes," 52, and Heidegger's report for the University of Munich in 1933 on Richard Hönigswald in Schorcht, *Die Philosophie an den bayerischen Universitäten, 1933–45,* 161. An important investigation of Heidegger's relation to the Nazi worldview may be found in Löwith, *Mein Leben;* see also Bourdieu, *The Political Ontology of Martin Heidegger.* Since the publication of Victor Farías's *Heidegger et le nazisme,* a large number of works have been published on the theme of Heidegger's political ideology. See, for example, Derrida, *De l'esprit; Heidegger et la question*; Fédier, *Heidegger: Anatomie d'un scandale*; Ferry and Renaut, *Heidegger and Modernity*; Janicaud, *L'ombre de cette pensée: Heidegger et la question politique* (English translation: *The Shadow of that Thought: Heidegger and the Question of the Political*); Ott, *Martin Heidegger: Unterwegs zu seiner Biographie;* Fritsche, *Historical Destiny and National Socialism in Heidegger's* Being and Time; Lacoue-Labarthe, *Heidegger, Art and Politics*; Safranski, *Ein Meister aus Deutschland: Martin Heidegger und seine Zeit*; Pöggeler, *Neue Wege mit Heidegger*; Rockmore, *On Heidegger's Nazism and Philosophy*; Rorty, *Essays on Heidegger and Others*; Sluga, *Heidegger's Crisis: Philosophy and Politics in Nazi Germany*; Wolin, *The Heidegger Controversy: A Critical Reader,* and *The Politics of Being: The Political Thought of Martin Heidegger*; Young, *Heidegger, Philosophy, Nazism.* For my own reflections on this question, see Barash, "Martin Heidegger in the Perspective of the Twentieth Century," 52–78.

121. After dealing with the theme of what he takes to be similarities between Hegel and Heidegger, Jürgen Habermas refers to Heidegger's "idealist optic." Habermas, *Der philosophische Diskurs der Moderne,* 159.

122. Heidegger, *Gesamtausgabe,* 45:17.

123. Heidegger, *Nietzsche,* 2:220.

124. Heidegger, "Hegel und die Griechen," in *Wegmarken,* 256–57.

125. Heidegger, "Der Spruch des Anaximander" (1938), in *Holzwege,* 302. On "subjecticity," see also note 83.

126. Heidegger, *Identität und Differenz,* 45.

127. Habermas, *Philosophische Diskurs,* 180.

128. Heidegger, "Brief über den Humanismus," in *Wegmarken,* 151–53, "Seminar in Zähringen" (1973), in *Vier Seminare,* 110–38, *Kant,* 202, *Was heisst Denken?,* 25, and *Gesamtausgabe,* 55:311–13.

129. Heidegger, *Nietzsche,* 2:99, and "Zeit des Weltbildes," in *Holzwege,* 92.

130. Heidegger, *Nietzsche,* 2:48, and "Nietzsches Wort 'Gott ist tot'" (1943), in *Holzwege,* 209–10.

131. Rousseau, *Les Confessions,* 258.

132. Heidegger, *Satz vom Grund,* 185; for Heidegger's use of "limit [*Grenze*]," see, for example, "Protokoll zu einem Seminar über den Vortrag 'Zeit und Sein'" (1962), in *Zur Sache des Denkens,* 58.

133. Heidegger, *Identität und Differenz,* 46.

134. Heidegger, "Zeit des Weltbildes," in *Holzwege,* 69–104, and *Satz vom Grund,* 138.

135. Weber, *Gesammelte Aufsätze zur Religionssoziologie,* 240; Troeltsch, *Absolutheit,* 131; Bultmann, *Mythos und Mythologie IV: Im neuen Testament,*1278–82; Cassirer, *Das mythische Denken, Philosophie der symbolischen Formen,* 2:78.

136. Heidegger, "Vom Wesen des Grundes," in *Wegmarken,* 55.

137. Heidegger, "Zeit des Weltbildes," in *Holzwege,* 89.

138. Heidegger, *Gesamtausgabe,* 45:103; see also ibid., 161: "For this reason . . . access to . . . everything Greek—above all, to the origin—is so difficult for us, since we search right away for 'lived experiences' [*Erlebnisse*], 'personalities' [*Persönlichkeiten*], and 'culture,' which never existed in that time, as great as it was short."

139. Ibid., 134.

140. Heidegger, *Gesamtausgabe,* 55:311 and 45:161.

141. Heidegger, *Gesamtausgabe,* 52:107.

142. Ibid., 126.

143. Heidegger, *Nietzsche,* 2:385.

144. Heidegger, *Sein und Zeit,* 396.

145. See, for example, Heidegger, *Gesamtausgabe,* 45:134: "We infer from this [the opacity of the origin] that history itself is not only many-layered . . . that there are not only in it ages that follow one another and intersect, but that we know almost nothing of their authentic reality, above all, because the demands of our knowledge remain insufficient and become more and more so."

146. Heidegger, *Gesamtausgabe,* 55:188, *Nietzsche,* 1:173 and 2:385, and "Überwindung der Metaphysik," in *Vorträge und Aufsätze,* 80.

147. Heidegger, *Schellings Abhandlung über das Wesen der menschlichen Freiheit (1809),* 204.

148. I use the term "calculative reckoning" to suggest the different nuances of Heidegger's terms "*rechnen,*" "*nachrechnen,*" and "*rechnendes Denken.*"

149. Heidegger, "Überwindung der Metaphysik," in *Vorträge und Aufsätze,* 99. I note, in passing, that in one of his last essays, *Zur Frage nach der Bestimmung der Sache des Denkens,* Heidegger claimed that industrial

society had attained a level of autonomy that pushed it beyond the modern configuration of subject-object relations.

150. Heidegger, *Schellings Abhandlung,* 204, and "Überwindung der Metaphysik," in *Vorträge und Aufsätze,* 80.

151. Heidegger, "ALETHEIA," in *Vorträge und Aufsätze,* 261, and *Satz vom Grund,* 160.

152. Heidegger, *Vorträge und Aufsätze,* 80.

153. Heidegger, "ALETHEIA," in *Vorträge und Aufsätze,* 261.

154. Heidegger, *Nietzsche,* 2:353.

155. Heidegger, "Das Ende der Philosophie," in *Zur Sache des Denkens,* 77–78.

156. Heidegger, *Gesamtausgabe,* 54:15.

157. Heidegger, *Gesamtausgabe,* 45:49 and 65:5–6.

158. Heidegger, *Gesamtausgabe,* 45:123, and "Das Ende der Philosophie," in *Zur Sache des Denkens,* 80.

159. Heidegger, *Nietzsche,* 2:487.

160. Ibid., 481; Heidegger, *Identität und Differenz,* 34.

161. Heidegger, "Zeit und Sein," 16–17.

162. Heidegger, *Gesamtausgabe,* 45:124, and *Gelassenheit,* 20–23.

163. Heidegger, *Nietzsche,* 2:37.

164. Heidegger, "Der Spruch des Anaximander," in *Holzwege,* 340–41; on the topic of freedom in Heidegger, see Guilead, *Être et liberté: Une étude sur le dernier Heidegger;* see also Figal, *Martin Heidegger: Phänomenologie der Freiheit.*

165. Heidegger, *Nietzsche,* 2:142–43.

166. Ibid., 143–44; Heidegger, "Frage nach der Technik," in *Vorträge und Aufsätze,* 32.

167. Heidegger, "Die Kehre," in *Die Technik und Kehre,* 40–41.

168. Heidegger, "Frage nach der Technik," in *Vorträge und Aufsätze,* 40–44.

169. Heidegger, "Die Kehre," in *Technik und die Kehre,* 38–39, *Nietzsche,* 2:481–90, and *Gelassenheit,* 11–28.

170. Heidegger, *Nietzsche,* 2:391–94.

171. Martin Heidegger, "Wozu Dichter?" (1946), in *Holzwege,* 248, and *Nietzsche,* 2:394–95.

172. Heidegger, *Nietzsche,* 2:143–44.

173. Heidegger, *Gesamtausgabe,* 4:48 and 65:23–29. On the theme of Heidegger and the sacred, see also Birault, "De l'être, du Divin, des dieux chez Heidegger." On the problematic relation between the question of God and the *Seinsfrage,* see also Marion, *Dieu sans l'être;* and Kearney, *The God Who May Be.*

174. Heidegger, "Wozu Dichter?" in *Holzwege,* 248.

175. "Wherever theology emerges, there has God already begun His flight." Heidegger, *Gesamtausgabe,* 52:132–33.

176. See, in regard to this theme, Bultmann, *Jesus Christus und die Mythologie;* Ricœur, "Préface à Bultmann," in *Le conflit des interprétations Essais d'herméneutique,*373–92; Johnson, *The Origins of Demythologizing: Philosophy and Historiography in the Theology of R. Bultmann.*

177. Bultmann, *History and Eschatology,* 154.

178. See, in this regard, Krüger, "Martin Heidegger und der Humanismus," 157.

179. Heidegger, *Identität und Differenz,* 51.

180. Heidegger, "Die Kehre," in *Technik und Kehre,* 46. On this theme, see ibid., 23–29, and the illuminating interpretation in *Gesamtausgabe,* 65:424–41. See also Capelle, *Philosophie et théologie dans la pensée de Martin Heidegger;* Jäger, *Gott, nochmals Martin Heidegger!;* Jung, *Das Denken des Seins und der Glaube an Gott: Zum Verhältnis von Philosophie und Theologie bei Martin Heidegger.*

181. Heidegger, *Nietzsche,* 2:144, 255.

182. Heidegger, "Ein Brief an einen jungen Studenten," in *Vorträge und Aufsätze,* 183.

CONCLUSION

In part I of this study, we analyzed the implications for historical thought of Heidegger's philosophy, up to and including the period of *Being and Time*. We focused on his reassessment of the complex articulation of historical principles of understanding that came to full expression in the critical theories of history of the late nineteenth and early twentieth centuries. Critical theorists had approached historical reflection as a unique way of comprehending the human world. They shared an idea in common that all understanding, as part of the human world, participated in its historical development. Because all understanding was tied to the historical context in which it arose, it was unable to reach beyond this context to grasp the world as a metaphysical totality.

This critical view of human understanding presupposed that historical meaning had its basis in the objective development of history, in which divergent collective outlooks, whether defined in terms of cultures, nations, or worldviews, served as a coherent medium in which meaning becomes manifest. Because the diversity of human historical collectivities could not themselves provide an irrefutable ground for continuity and coherence, the problem of assuring such a ground, and of providing for the general validity of normative standards beyond the particular contexts in which they came to expression, became an important theoretical consideration for each of the critical thinkers before World War I.

As we have seen, Heidegger's philosophy in *Being and Time* approached the problem of historical meaning from an entirely different standpoint, finding the primary source of historical meaning, not in continuity and coherence of an objective historical process, but in the ontological structures of *Dasein* (finite human existence). Here understanding of humanity's past was a key to understanding of humanity, not primarily because of the objective manifestations of meaning in history, but through *Dasein*'s way of appropriating the past, and of making possibilities implicit in it the basis of a choice concerning the meaning of Being. Repeating these possibilities and projecting them in the decisive moment toward what Heidegger viewed as the authentic future was the ultimate aim of historical understanding.

In reorienting historical thought along ontological lines, Heidegger contributed two special insights. First, he directed attention away from the diversity of development in the course of history and toward individual *Dasein*. Here Heidegger introduced a notion of universal ontology into historical thinking which situated *Dasein*'s Being-toward-death as the universal precondition underlying all that is historical and making it accessible to understanding. Although this universal ontology never exhausted the ontic diversity of *Dasein*'s Being-in-the-world, it nonetheless constituted the fundamental criterion making history possible. Second, Heidegger identified the source of what he saw as the traditional neglect of this universal ontological ground of history in *Dasein*'s collective flight from responsibility for the meaning of Being. Because of this flight, the unveiling of the philosophical foundation of Western history had to proceed by deconstruction (*Abbau*) of the masks that had been accumulated from the past to serve the traditions of the present. According to this perspective, the quest for objective coherence uniting the epochs of history was no authentic source of historical meaning, but only served an inauthentic attempt to deny the implications of human finitude in the creation of intellectual systems in which finitude could be hidden by an alleged participation in objective forces beyond it.

To be sure, there were instances of authenticity in history, and a locus of authentic community that, in this period, Heidegger vaguely referred to as the generations of *das Volk*. As we seen, however, he directed most of his attention to excoriating collective inauthenticity and expressing profound doubt about the soundness of Western intellectual traditions. As we have seen, this doubt contributed to a widespread challenge, expounded in different ways by a number of the most influential thinkers of Heidegger's own generation, to assumptions of coherence and continuity of a historical heritage as the primary source of meaning in the human world.

It is surely no accident that this challenge emerged after World War I, which played a significant, if never discretely discernible, role in directing attention to the shortcomings of the intellectual traditions of modern culture. Mounting discontent, especially among members of the younger generation, expressed itself most prominently in the radical rejection of traditional German historical styles of thought, whose affirmation of historical culture had exercised an enormous influence before the war. That this radical rejection could be supported by such different thinkers as Heidegger, neo-orthodox theologians, and Spengler, all of whom were widely acclaimed in the 1920s, attests to the important shift in attitude among diverse groups of young thinkers after the war. Here the problem of historical meaning arose not as an issue that could be overcome with the proper theoretical approach, but as a predicament deeply situated in the texture of the modern world.

II

In dealing with Heidegger's reversal (*Kehre*) in the 1930s and 1940s, part II of this study highlighted a shift in the ground of his historical thinking. From this time, Heidegger's interpretation of the basis of historical coherence changed in relation to the turn in his *Seinsfrage* from the finite ontology of *Dasein* to the history of Being (*Seinsgeschichte*). In the movement of *Seinsgeschichte,* the aim of all ontology appeared shortsighted, because not radical enough in its separation from the tradition of metaphysics, now rethought as the epochally articulated advent of the forgetfulness of Being (*Seinsvergessenheit*) implicit in the modern age's forgetting the hiddenness of the ground of truth. This advent of *Seinsvergessenheit* culminated, for the later Heidegger, in the identification of the human subject itself with this ground, and truth with what could become a possible object of human representation.

Heidegger's attempt to recollect the hidden ground of truth as *Seinsgeschichte* questioned what he identified as the tradition of metaphysics. It did so by seeking a foothold for thought beyond the pale of the logical norms of reasoning that had emerged in that tradition and had accompanied it to its anthropocentric culmination. This attempt proceeded by contesting the anthropocentric terms of interpretation of the development of Western rationality since Plato. Here Heidegger sought to expose what, to his mind, had been concealed on the obverse side of the victory of rationalization: the progressive diminution of the possible margins of any truth claim founded outside the sphere of human intelligence. In evoking a recollection of the hiddenness of the ground of truth, Heidegger's contestation anticipated an unprecedented advent (*Ereignis*) of truth, conceived of, not as a mode of human intelligence, but as prior to that intelligence and, indeed, as a condition of possibility of the variable human essence itself. If Heidegger thus rethought the ground of the historicity of truth, the unique character of this feat lay, above all, in the uncompromising presupposition that the *Ereignis,* which "announces itself directly as a metamorphosis in the essence of truth,"[1] and from which the meaningfulness of human history proceeded, stood entirely outside the range of human representation and of human influence.

On the basis of the analysis in this second part, I have argued that Heidegger's characterization of the historicity of truth does not, because of its exteriority to the methods of contemporary theoretical science, invalidate its implications for theory. Far from a groundless meditation that, in effect, would tacitly complement the technical aim of the sciences by leaving the way open to a more intensive rationalization of experience, Heidegger's *Seinsgeschichte* ultimately sought to lay bare the "true" historical significance of rationalization, which necessarily remained opaque to the rational methods of the sciences themselves. One need not be a disciple of Heidegger, nor deny what we have considered to be the internal inconsistencies of his thought, to recognize the serious implications for the problem of historical meaning of this untimely claim to truth. In its light, modernity appears as the epoch of convergence of the rational heritage of Western intellectual traditions with a will to technical domination and as one of confusion of truth in its profoundest sense with the immediacy of human experience.

NOTE

1. Heidegger, *Nietzsche,* 2:489.

SELECTED BIBLIOGRAPHY

WORKS BY HEIDEGGER

"Anmerkungen zu Karl Jaspers" *Psychologie der Weltanschauungen,*" In H. Saner, ed., *Karl Jaspers in der Diskussion.* Munich: Piper, 1973. (Reprinted in *Wegmarken*; vol. 9 of *Gesamtausgabe.*)

Being and Time. Translated by John Macquarrie and Edward Robinson. New York: Harper and Row, 1967.

Einführung in die Metaphysik. 4th ed. Tübingen: Niemeyer, 1976.

Die Frage nach dem Ding: Zu Kants Lehre von den transzendentalen Grundsätzen. Tübingen: Niemeyer, 1962.

Frühe Schriften. Frankfurt am Main: Klostermann, 1972.

Gelassenheit. Pfullingen: Neske, 1959.

Gesamtausgabe. Frankfurt am Main: Klostermann, 1975–.

Vol. 3: *Kant und das Problem der Metaphysik.*

Vol. 4: *Hölderlin und das Wesen der Dichtung.*

Vol. 9: *Wegmarken.*

Vol. 16: *Reden und andere Zeugnisse eines Lebensweges: 1910–76.*

Vol. 17: *Einführung in die phänomenologische Forschung.*

Vol. 18: *Grundbegriffe der aristotelischen Philosophie.*

Vol. 19: *Platon: Sophistes.*

Vol. 20: *Prolegomena zur Geschichte des Zeitbegriffs.*

Vol. 21: *Logik: Die Frage nach der Wahrheit.*

Vol. 22: *Grundbegriffe der antiken Philosophie.*

Vol. 24: *Die Grundprobleme der Phänomenologie.*

Vol. 25: *Phänomenologische Interpretation von Kants Kritik der reinen Vernunft.*

Vol. 26: *Metaphysische Anfangsgründe der Logik im Ausgang von Leibniz.*

Vol. 27: *Einleitung in die Philosophie.*

Vol. 28: *Der deutsche Idealismus (Fichte, Schelling, Hegel) und die philosophische Problemlage der Gegenwart.*

Vol. 29/30: *Die Grundbegriffe der Metaphysik: Welt, Endlichkeit, Einsamkeit.*

Vol. 31: *Vom Wesen der menschlichen Freiheit: Einleitung in die Philosophie.*

Vol. 32: *Hegels Phänomenologie des Geistes.*

Vol. 33: *Aristoteles: Metaphysik IX.*

Vol. 34: *Vom Wesen der Wahrheit: Zu Platons Höhlengleichnis und Theätet.*

Vol. 36/37: *Sein und Wahrheit:* 1. "Die Grundfrage der Philosophie." 2. "Vom Wesen der Wahrheit."

Vol. 38: *Logik als die Frage nach dem Wesen der Sprache.*

Vol. 39: *Hölderlins Hymnen "Germanien" und "Der Rhein."*

Vol. 40: *Einführung in die Metaphysik.*

Vol. 43: *Nietzsche: Der Wille zur Macht als Kunst.*

Vol. 44: *Nietzsches metaphysische Grundstellung im abendländischen Denken: Die ewige Wiederkehr des Gleichen.*

Vol. 45: *Grundfragen der Philosophie: Ausgewählte "Probleme" der "Logik."*

Vol. 47: *Nietzsches Lehre vom Willen zur Macht als Erkenntnis.*

Vol. 48: *Nietzsche: Der europäische Nihilismus.*

Vol. 49: *Die Metaphysik des deutschen Idealismus: Zur erneuten Auslegung von Schelling: Philosophische Untersuchungen über das Wesen der menschlichen Freiheit und die damit zusammenhängenden Gegenstände (1809).*

Vol. 50: *Nietzsches Metaphysik: Einleitung in die Philosophie.*

Vol. 51: *Grundbegriffe.*

Vol. 52: *Hölderlins Hymne "Andenken."*

Vol. 53: *Hölderlins Hymne "Der Ister."*

Vol. 54: *Parmenides.*

Vol. 55: *Heraklit:* 1. "Der Anfang des abendländischen Denkens." 2. "Logik: Heraklits Lehre vom Logos."

Vol. 56/57: *Zur Bestimmung der Philosophie:* 1. "Die Idee der Philosophie und das Weltanschauungsproblem." 2. "Phänomenologie und transzendentale Wertphilosophie." 3. Anhang: "Über das Wesen der Universität und des akademischen Studiums."

Vol. 58: *Grundprobleme der Phänomenologie (1919–20).*

Vol. 59: *Phänomenologie der Anschauung und des Ausdrucks: Theorie der philosophischen Begriffsbildung.*

Vol. 60: *Phänomenologie des religiösen Lebens:* 1. "Einleitung in die Phänomenologie der Religion." 2. "Augustinus und der Neuplatonismus." 3. "Die philosophischen Grundlagen der mittelalterlichen Mystik."

Vol. 61: *Phänomenologische Interpretationen zu Aristoteles: Einführung in die phänomenologische Forschung.*

Vol. 63: *Ontologie: Hermeneutik der Faktizität.*

Vol. 65: *Beiträge zur Philosophie: Vom Ereignis.*

Vol. 67: *Metaphysik und Nihilismus:* 1. "Die Überwindung der Metaphysik." 2. "Das Wesen des Nihilismus."

Vol. 68: *Hegel:* 1. Die Negativität. 2. Erläuterung der "Einleitung" zu Hegels "Phänomenologie des Geistes."

Die Grundfrage nach dem Sein selbst: Dicté. Bilingual ed. Paris: Aux Editions de l'Abîme en Effet, 1985.

Holzwege. Frankfurt am Main: Klostermann, 1972.

Identität und Differenz. Pfullingen: Neske, 1957.

Introduction to W. Richardson, *Heidegger: Through Phenomenology to Thought.* Hague: Nijhoff, 1963. Reprinted New York: Fordham University Press, 2003.

Kant und das Problem der Metaphysik. Frankfurt am Main: Klostermann, 1951.

Letter to Karl Löwith, June 30, 1925. Unpublished. Karl Löwith Estate.

Letter to Karl Löwith, August 24, 1925. Unpublished. Karl Löwith Estate.

Letter to Karl Löwith, April 19, 1932. Unpublished. Karl Löwith Estate.

"M. Heidegger: A Recollection." Translated by H. Siegfried. *Man and Word* 3, no. 1 (1979).

Nietzsche. 2 vols. Pfullingen: Neske, 1961.

Nietzsche. Vol. 4: *Nihilism.* Translated by F. A. Capuzzi. Edited by D. F. Krell. San Francisco: Harper and Row, 1982.

"Nur noch ein Gott kann uns retten: *Spiegel*-Gespräch mit Martin Heidegger am [September 23, 1966]." In *Die Logoslehre: Hegels Logik heute, Augstein/Heidegger-Interview.* Duisburg: Braun, 1980.

Phänomenologie und Theologie. Frankfurt am Main: Klostermann, 1970.

"Phänomenologische Interpretationen zu Aristoteles: Anzeige der hermeneutischen Situation." Edited by Hans-Ulrich Lessing. *Dilthey-Jahrbuch für Philosophie und Geschichte der Geisteswissenschaften*, 6 (1989): 235–74.

"Das Realitätsproblem in der modernen Philosophie." *Philosophisches Jahrbuch* 25 (1912): 353–63.

Der Satz vom Grund. Pfullingen: Neske, 1957.

Schellings Abhandlung: Über das Wesen der menschlichen Freiheit. Tübingen: Niemeyer, 1971.

Sein und Zeit. 12th ed. Tübingen: Niemeyer, 1972.

Die Technik und die Kehre. Pfullingen: Neske, 1962.

Unterwegs zur Sprache. Pfullingen: Neske, 1959.

Vier Seminare. Frankfurt am Main: Klostermann, 1977.

"Vom Geheimnis des Glockenturms." In *Martin Heidegger: Zum 80. Geburtstag von seiner Heimatstadt Messkirch.* Frankfurt am Main: Klostermann, 1969.

Vorträge und Aufsätze. Pfullingen: Neske, 1978.

Was heisst Denken? Tübingen: Niemeyer, 1961.

Wegmarken. Frankfurt am Main: Klostermann, 1967.

What Is a Thing? Translated by W. B. Barton and V. Deutsch. Chicago: Gateway Press, 1967.

"Wilhelm Diltheys Forschungsarbeit und der gegenwärtige Kampf um eine historische Weltanschauung" (Kasseler Vorträge). *Dilthey-Jahrbuch für Philosophie und Geschichte der Geisteswissenschaften,* vol. 8 (1992–93): 143–80.

Zur Frage nach der Bestimmung der Sache des Denkens. St.-Gallen: Erker, 1984.

Zur Sache des Denkens. Tübingen: Max Niemeyer, 1976.

With Arendt, Arendt. *Briefe, 1925–1975.* Frankfurt am Main: Klostermann, 1998.

With Blochman, Elisabeth. *Martin Heidegger–Elisabeth Blochmann, Briefwechsel, 1918–1969.* Edited by Joachim Storck. Marbach am Neckar: Deutsches Literaturarchiv, 1990.

With Fink, E. *Heraklit.* Frankfurt am Main: Klostermann, 1970.

With Jaspers, Karl. *Martin Heidegger–Karl Jaspers, Briefwechsel, 1920–1963.* Frankfurt am Main: Klostermann/Munich: Piper, 1990.

With Rickert, Heinrich. *Martin Heidegger–Heinrich Rickert. Briefe 1912–33.* Frankfurt am Main: Klostermann, 2002.

With Wolf, Eric. *Hegel: "Über den Staat."* Unpublished seminar, University of Freiburg im Breisgau, 1934–35. Transcribed by Wilhelm Hallwachs and Siegfried Bröse. Heidegger Estate. Deutsches Literaturarchiv, Marbach am Neckar.

WORKS BY OTHER AUTHORS

Adorno, Theodor W. *Negative Dialektik.* Frankfurt am Main: Suhrkamp, 1975.

Arendt, Hannah. *The Life of the Mind.* 2 vols. New York: Harcourt-Brace, 1975.

_____. "Martin Heidegger ist achtzig Jahre alt." *Merkur* 23, no. 10 (October 1969): 893–902.

Arendt, Hannah, and Karl Jaspers. *Briefwechsel, 1926–1969.* Munich: Piper, 1985.

Aron, Raymond. *La philosophie critique de l'histoire.* Paris: Vrin, 1936.

Aschheim, Steven E. *The Nietzsche Legacy in Germany, 1890–1990.* Berkeley: University of California Press, 1992.

Avenarius, Richard. *Kritik der reinen Erfahrung.* 2 vols. 2d ed. Leipzig: O. R. Reisland, 1907–08.

Bambach, Charles. *Heidegger, Dilthey and the Crisis of Historicism.* Ithaca, N.Y.: Cornell University Press, 1995.

Barash, Jeffrey Andrew, "Hannah Arendt, Martin Heidegger and the Politics of Remembrance," *International Journal of Philosophical Studies* 10, no. 2 (May 2002): 171–82.

_____. *Heidegger et son siècle: Temps de l'être, temps de l'histoire.* Paris: Presses Universitaires de France, 1995.

_____. "Martin Heidegger in the Perspective of the 20th Century," *Journal of Modern History* 64, no. 1 (March 1992): 52–78.

_____. "The Political Dimension of the Public World: On Hannah Arendt's Interpretation of Martin Heidegger." In Larry May and Jerome Kohn, eds., *On Hannah Arendt: Twenty Years Later.* Cambridge, Mass.: MIT Press, 1996.

_____. "Les temps de la mémoire: A propos de la lecture heideggerienne de saint Augustin." *Transversalités: Revue de l'Institut Catholique de Paris* 60 (October–December 1996): 103–12.

_____. "Über den geschichtlichen Ort der Wahrheit. Hermeneutische Perspektiven bei Wilhelm Dilthey und Martin Heidegger." In *Martin Heidegger: Innen- und Aussenansichten.* Frankfurt am Main: Suhrkamp, 1989.

Barth, Karl. *Die protestantische Theologie im 19. Jahrhundert. Ihre Vorgeschichte und ihre Geschichte.* Zollikon/Zurich: Evangelischer Verlag, 1947.

_____. *Der Römerbrief.* Munich: Kaiser, 1922.

_____. *La théologie protestante au 19ᵉ siècle.* Geneva: Labor et Fides, 1969.

_____. *Die Theologie und die Kirche.* 2 vols. Munich: Kaiser, 1928.

Barth, Karl , and Rudolf Bultmann. *Briefwechsel.* Zurich: Theologischer Verlag, 1971.

Barth, Karl, Rudolf Bultmann, Friedrich Gogarten, and Ernst Troeltsch. *Anfänge der dialektischen Theologie.* 2 vols. Edited by Jürgen Moltmann. Munich: Kaiser, 1967.

Beierwaltes, W. *Identität und Differenz.* Frankfurt am Main: Klostermann, 1980.

Beyer, Wilhelm R. *Vier Kritiken: Heidegger, Sartre, Adorno, Lukácz.* Cologne: Pahl-Rugenstein, 1970.

Birault, H. "De l'être, du Divin, des dieux chez Heidegger." In *L'existence de Dieu, Cahiers de l'actualité religieuse.* Paris: Casterman, 1961.

_____. *Heidegger et l'expérience de la pensée.* Paris: Gallimard, 1978.

Bourdieu, Pierre. *The Political Ontology of Martin Heidegger.* Stanford, Calif.: Stanford University Press, 1996.

Boyce-Gibson, W. R. "Excerpts from a 1928 Freiburg Diary." *Journal of the British Society for Phenomenology* 2, no. 1 (January 1971): 52–81.

Braig, Carl. *Der Modernismus und die Freiheit der Wissenschaft.* Freiburg im Breisgau: Herder, 1911.

_____. *Über Geist und Wesen des Christentums.* Freiburg im Breisgau: Wagner, 1902.

_____. *Vom Sein: Abriss der Ontologie.* Freiburg im Breisgau: Herder, 1896.

Brandner, Rudolf. *Heideggers Begriff der Geschichte und das neuzeitliche Geschichtsdenken.* Vienna: Passagen-Verlag, 1994.

Brentano, Franz. *On the Several Sense of Being in Aristotle.* Translated by R. George. Berkeley: University of California Press, 1967.

_____. *Vom Ursprung sittlicher Erkenntnis.* 2d ed. Leipzig: Meiner, 1921.

_____. *Von der mannigfachen Bedeutung des Seienden nach Aristoteles.* Freiburg im Breisgau: Herdersche Verlagshandlung, 1862.

Brunner, Emil. "Theologie und Ontologie—oder die Theologie am Scheidewege." In G. Noller, ed., *Heidegger und die Theologie.* Munich: Kaiser, 1967.

Bultmann, Rudolf. "Die Geschichtlichkeit des Daseins und der Glaube." In G. Noller, ed., *Heidegger und die Theologie.* Munich: Kaiser, 1967, p. 72–94.

_____. *Glauben und Verstehen.* 2 vols. Tübingen: Mohr, 1933 and 1952.

_____. *History and Eschatology.* 1955. Reprint, Edinburgh: University Press, 1957.

_____. *Jesus Christus und die Mythologie.* Hamburg: Furche, 1964.

_____. Letter to Friedrich Gogarten, October 19, 1924. Unpublished.

_____. Letter to Hans von Soden, December 23, 1923. In Bernd Jaspert, ed., *Rudolf Bultmanns Werk und Wirkung.* Darmstadt: Wissenschaftliche Buchgesellschaft, 1984.

_____. *Mythos und Mythologie IV: Im neuen Testament.* Vol. 4 of *Die Religion in Geschichte und Gegenwart.* 3d ed. Tübingen: Mohr, 1960.

Burckhardt, J. *Griechische Kulturgeschichte III.* Vol. 10 of *Gesamtausgabe.* Stuttgart: Deutsche Verlags-Anstalt, 1931.

Cacciatore, Giuseppe. *Scienza e filosofia in Dilthey,* 2 vols. Naples: Guida Editori, 1976.

_____. *Storicismo problematico e metodo critico.* Naples: Guida Editori, 1993.

Capelle, Philippe. *Philosophie et théologie dans la pensée de Martin Heidegger.* Paris: Éditions du Cerf, 1998.

Caputo, John D. *Heidegger and Aquinas: An Essay on Overcoming Metaphysics.* New York: Fordham University Press, 1982.

_____. *The Mystical Element in Heidegger's Thought.* Athens: Ohio University Press, 1978.

_____. "Phenomenology, Mysticism, and the 'Grammatica Speculativa': A Study of Heidegger's 'Habilitationsschrift.'" *Journal of the British Society of Phenomenology* 5, no. 2 (May 1974): 101–17.

Cassinari, Flavio. *Definizione e rappresentazione. Antropologia e metafisica nell'interpretazione heideggeriana di Kant.* Milan: Guerini, 1994.

Cassirer, E. *Das Erkenntnisproblem in der Philosophie und Wissenschaft der neueren Zeit.* Vol. 4: *Von Hegels Tod bis zur Gegenwart (1832–1932).* Stuttgart: Kohlhammer, 1957.

_____. "*Kant und das Problem der Metaphysik*" (review). *Kantstudien* 36 (1931): 1–26.

_____. *Philosophie der symbolischen Formen.* 3 vols. 5th ed. Darmstadt: Wissenschaftliche Buchgesellschaft, 1969.

_____. *The Problem of Knowledge: Philosophy, Science, and History since Hegel.* Translated by William H. Woglom and Charles W. Hendel. New Haven, Conn.: Yale University Press, 1974.

Cecchi Duso, Gianna de. *L'interpretazione heideggeriana dei Presocratici.* Padua: CEDAM, 1970.

Cicero. *Gespräche in Tusculum.* Munich: Hermann, 1951.

Cohen, Hermann.Introduction to Friedrich Lange, *Geschichte des Materialismus und Kritik seiner Bedeutung in der Gegenwart.* 2 vols. Leipzig: Baedeker, 1896.

_____. *Kants Theorie der Erfahrung.* 3d ed. Berlin: B. Cassirer, 1918.

_____. *System der Philosophie.* Part 1: *Logik der reinen Erkenntnis.* Berlin: B. Cassirer, 1902.

_____. *System der Philosophie.* Part 2: *Ethik des reinen Willens.* Berlin: B. Cassirer, 1904.

Courtine, Jean-François. *Heidegger et la phénoménologie.* Paris: Vrin, 1990.

_____. "Phénoménologie et science de l'être." In *Les Cahiers de l'Herne, Martin Heidegger.* Paris: Éditions de l'Herne, 1983.

Croce, Benedetto. *Histoire de l'Europe au 19ᵉ siècle.* Translated by H. Bedarida. Paris: Gallimard, 1959.

Degener, Alfons. "Zwei Wege zu Diltheys Metaphysik." Ph.D. diss., University of Münster, 1927.

Derrida, Jacques. *De l'Esprit, Heidegger et la question.* Paris: Éditions Galilée, 1987.

_____. *Marges de la philosophie.* Paris: Éditions de Minuit, 1972.

_____. *Of Spirit: Heidegger and the Question.* Chicago: University of Chicago Press, 1991.

Dilthey, Wilhelm. *Der Aufbau der geschichtlichen Welt in den Geisteswissenschaften.* Vol. 7 of *Gesammelte Schriften.* 6th ed. Stuttgart: Teubner, 1973.

_____. *Einleitung in die Geisteswissenschaften.* Vol. 1 of *Gesammelte Schriften.* 7th ed. Stuttgart: Teubner, 1973.

_____. *Die geistige Welt, Einleitung in die Philosophie des Lebens.* Vol. 5 of *Gesammelte Schriften.* 6th ed. Stuttgart: Teubner, 1974.

_____. *Weltanschauungslehre: Abhandlungen zur Philosophie der Philosophie.* Vol. 8 of *Gesammelte Schriften.* Stuttgart: Teubner, 1931.

Dyroff, Adolf. "Review of M. Heidegger, 'Die Kategorien- und Bedeutungslehre des Duns Scotus.'" *Historische Zeitschrift* 119 (1919): 497–9.

Ebbinghaus, Julius, et al. *Philosophie in Selbstdarstellungen.* Vol. 3. Hamburg: Meiner, 1977.

Ermarth, Michael. *Wilhelm Dilthey: The Critique of Historical Reason.* Chicago: University of Chicago Press, 1978.

Farías, Victor. *Heidegger and Nazism.* Philadelphia: Temple University Press, 1991.

_____. *Heidegger et le nazisme.* Paris: Verdier, 1987.

Fédier, François. *Heidegger: Anatomie d'un scandale.* Paris: Robert Laffont, 1988.

Ferry, Luc, and Alain Renaut. *Heidegger and Modernity.* Chicago: University of Chicago Press, 1990.

Figal, Günter. *Martin Heidegger: Phänomenologie der Freiheit.* Frankfurt am Main: Anton Hain, 1991.

Fräntzki, Ekkehard. *Die Kehre: Heideggers Schrift "Vom Wesen der Wahrheit."* Pfaffenweiler: Centaurus-Verlagsgesellschaft, 1987.

Franzen, Winfred. *Martin Heidegger.* Stuttgart: Metzler, 1976.

Frede, Dorothea. "Die Einheit des Seins: Heidegger in Davos— Kritische Überlegungen," In D. Kaegi and E. Rudolph, eds., *Cassirer-Heidegger: 70 Jahre Davoser Disputation.* Hamburg: Meiner, 2002.

Fried, Gregory. *Heidegger's Polemos: From Being to Politics.* New Haven, Conn.: Yale University Press, 2000.

Fritsche, Johannes. *Historical Destiny and National Socialism in Heidegger's* Being and Time. Berkeley: University of California Press, 1999.

Fuchs, Ernst. "Aus der Marburger Zeit." In G. Neske, ed., *Erinnerung an M. Heidegger.* Pfullingen: Neske, 1979.

Fynsk, Christopher. *Heidegger: Thought and Historicity.* Ithaca, N.Y: Cornell University Press, 1986.

Gadamer, Hans-Georg. Afterword to J. G. Herder, *Auch eine Philosophie der Geschichte zur Bildung der Menschheit.* Frankfurt am Main: Suhrkamp, 1967.

_____. Introduction to Martin Heidegger, *Der Ursprung des Kunstwerkes.* Stuttgart: Reclam, 1977.

_____. *Heideggers Wege: Studien zum Spätwerk.* Tübingen: Mohr, 1983.

_____. *Kleine Schriften.* 3 vols. Tübingen: Mohr, 1972.

_____. *Philosophische Lehrjahre.* Frankfurt am Main: Klostermann, 1977.

_____. *Truth and Method.* Translated by G. Barden and J. Cumming. New York: Seabury Press, 1975.

_____. *Wahrheit und Methode: Grundzüge einer philosophischen Hermeneutik.* Vol. 1 of Gesammelte Werke. Tübingen: Mohr, 1986.

Gay, Peter. *Weimar Culture: The Outsider as Insider.* New York: Harper and Row, 1968.

Gethmann-Siefert, Annemarie. *Das Verhältnis von Philosophie und Theologie im Denken Martin Heideggers.* Freiburg und Munich: Karl Alber, 1974.

Giugliano, Antonello. "Intorno al concetto di Weltanschauung nel primo Heidegger." *Atti dell'Accademia di Scienze Morali e Politiche* 107 (1996).

_____. *Nietzsche, Rickert, Heidegger (ed altre allegorie filosfiche).* Naples: Liguri, 1999.

Glockner, Hermann. *Heidelberger Bilderbuch.* Bonn: Bouvier, 1969.

Gogarten, Friedrich. "Karl Barths Dogmatik." *Theologische Rundschau,* n.s. 1 (1929): 68–81.

_____. "Zwischen den Zeiten." In J. Moltmann, ed., *Anfänge der dialektischen Theologie,* vol. 2. Munich: Kaiser, 1967.

Görland, Ingtraud. *Die Kantkritik des jungen Hegel.* Frankfurt am Main: Klostermann, 1966.

Grabmann, Martin. *Mittelalterliches Geistesleben.* 3 vols. Munich: Heubner, 1926–56.

Greisch, Jean. *Ontologie et temporalité. Esquisse d'une interprétation intégrale de* Sein und Zeit. Paris: Presses Universitaires de France, 1994.

Greisch, Jean. *La Parole Heureuse. Martin Heidegger entre les choses et les mots.* Paris: Beauchesne, 1987.

Grondin, Jean. *Hans-Georg Gadamer. Eine Biographie.* Tübingen: Mohr-Siebeck, 1999.

_____. *Le tournant dans la pensée de Martin Heidegger.* Paris: Presses Universitaires de France, 1987.

Guignon, Charles B. *Heidegger and the Problem of Knowledge.* Indianapolis: Hackett, 1983.

Guilead, R. *Être et liberté: Une étude sur le dernier Heidegger.* Louvain: Éditions Nauwelaerts, 1965.

Guzzoni, Alfredo. "Rezension zu Otto Pöggeler, 'Der Denkweg Martin Heideggers.'" *Philosophisches Jahrbuch* 71, no. 2 (1964): 397–401.

Haar, Michel. *La fracture de l'Histoire. Douze essais sur Heidegger.* Grenoble: Jérôme Millon, 1994.

Habermas, Jürgen. *Der philosophische Diskurs der Moderne.* Frankfurt am Main: Suhrkamp, 1985.

_____. *The Philosophical Discourse of Modernity: Twelve Lectures.* Translated by F. Lawrence. Cambridge, Mass.: MIT Press, 1987.

Harnack, Adolf von. *Das Wesen des Christentums.* Gütersloh: Gütersloher Verlagshaus, 1977.

Hartmann, Nicolai. *Grundzüge einer Metaphysik der Erkenntnis.* Berlin: de Gruyter, 1921.

Hegel, G. W. F. *Werke.* 20 vols. *Theorie-Werkausgabe.* Frankfurt am Main: Suhrkamp, 1971.

Herder, J. G. *Auch eine Philosophie der Geschichte zur Bildung der Menschheit.* Frankfurt am Main: Suhrkamp, 1967.

_____. *Briefe.* Vol. 5 of *Gesamtausgabe.* Edited by W. Dobbek and G. Arnold. Weimar: H. Böhlaus Nachfolger, 1979.

_____. *Vernunft und Sprache: Eine Metakritik zur Kritik der reinen Vernunft: Mit einer Zugabe, betreffend ein kritisches Tribunal aller Facultäten, Regierungen und Geschäfte.* Part 2. 1799. Vol. 21 of *Sämtliche Werke.* Berlin: Weidmannsche Buchhandlung, 1881.

Herrmann, Wilhelm. *Die Wirklichkeit Gottes.* Tübingen: Mohr, 1914.

Heussi, Karl. *Die Krisis des Historismus.* Tübingen: Mohr, 1932.

Hoy, David Couzens. "History, Historicity, and Historiography in *Being and Time.*" In M. Murray, ed., *Heidegger and Modern Philosophy: Critical Essays.* New Haven, Conn.: Yale University Press, 1978.

Hühnerfeld, Paul. *In Sachen Heidegger: Versuch über ein deutsches Genie.* Hamburg: Hoffmann und Campe, 1959.

Humboldt, Wilhelm von. *Schriften zur Anthropologie und Geschichte.* Vol. 1 of *Werke.* Stuttgart: H. G. Cotta, 1969.

Hume, David. *An Enquiry Concerning Human Understanding.* Vol. 2 of *Essays: Moral, Political and Literary.* Edited by T. H. Green and T. H. Grose. London: Longmans, Green, 1875.

_____. *An Enquiry Concerning the Principles of Morals.* Vol. 3 of *Essays and Treatises on Several Subjects.* London: A. Millar, 1753.

Husserl, E. *Aufsätze und Vorträge (1911–1921).* Edited by Thomas Nenon and Hans Rainer Sepp. Dordrecht: Nijhoff, 1987.

_____. *Briefe an Roman Ingarden.* Hague: Nijhoff, 1968.

_____. *Ideen zu einer reinen Phänomenologie und phänomenologischen Philosophie.* Edited by Herman L. van Breda, Samuel Ijsseling, Karl Schuhmann. The Hague: Nijhoff, 1950.

_____. *Die Krisis der europäischen Wissenschaften und die transzendentale Phänomenologie.* Edited by Walter Biemel. The Hague: Nijhoff, 1962.

_____. *Logical Investigations.* Translated by J. N. Findlay. London: Routledge and Kegan Paul, 1970.

_____. *Logische Untersuchungen.* 2 vols. Edited by Elmar Holenstein, Ursula Panzer. Hague: Nijhoff, 1975 and 1984.

_____. "Phänomenologie und Anthropologie." *Philosophy and Phenomenological Research* 2 (1941): 1–14.

_____. "Philosophie als strenge Wissenschaft." *Logos* 1 (1910): 289–341.

_____. "Philosophy as a Rigorous Science." In *Phenomenology and the Crisis of Philosophy: Philosophy as a Rigorous Science, and Philosophy and the Crisis of European Man.* Translated with notes and an introduction by Q. Lauer. New York: Harper and Row, 1965.

Iggers, Georg. *The German Conception of History.* Middletown, Conn.: Wesleyan University Press, 1968.

Iselin, Isaac. *Über die Geschichte der Menschheit.* Zurich: Orell, Gessner, Fuesslin, 1770.

Jäger, Alfred. *Gott: Nochmals Martin Heidegger!* Tübingen: Mohr, 1978.

Janicaud, Dominique. *Heidegger en France.* 2 vols. Paris: Albin Michel, 2001.

―――. *L'ombre de cette pensée. Heidegger et la question politique.* Grenoble: Millon, 1990.

―――. *The Shadow of That Thought: Heidegger and the Question of the Political.* Translated by M. Gendre. Evanston, Ill.: Northwestern University Press, 1996.

Jaspers, Karl. *Philosophische Autobiographie.* 2d ed. Munich: Piper, 1977.

―――. *Psychologie der Weltanschauungen.* 6th ed. Munich: Springer, 1971.

Jaspert, Bernd, ed. *Rudolf Bultmanns Werk und Wirkung.* Darmstadt: Wissenschaftliche Buchgesellschaft, 1984.

Johnson, R. A. *The Origins of Demythologizing: Philosophy and Historiography in the Theology of Rudolf Bultmann.* Leiden: Brill, 1974.

Jung, M. *Das Denken des Seins und der Glaube an Gott: Zum Verhältnis von Philosophie und Theologie bei Martin Heidegger.* Würzburg: Königshausen und Neumann, 1990.

Jüngel, Eberhard. *Glauben und Verstehen: Zum Theologiebegriff Rudolf Bultmanns.* Heidelberg: Winter, 1985.

Jünger, Ernst. *Der Kampf als inneres Erlebnis.* Vol. 5 of *Werke.* Stuttgart: Klett, 1960.

Kant, Immanuel. *Critique of Pure Reason.* Translated by N. K. Smith. New York: St. Martin's Press, 1965.

―――. *Grundlegung zur Metaphysik der Sitten.* Vol. 4 of *Werke.* Edited by E. Cassirer. Berlin: B. Cassirer, 1913.

―――. *Kritik der reinen Vernunft.* Vol. 3 of *Werke.* 2nd ed. Berlin: B. Cassirer, 1913.

―――. *Werke.* 12 vols. *Theorie-Werkausgabe.* Frankfurt am Main: Suhrkamp, 1977.

Kearney, Richard. *The God Who May Be.* Bloomington: Indiana University Press, 2002.

Kisiel, Theodore J. *The Genesis of Heidegger's* Being and Time. Berkeley: University of California Press, 1993.

Kolakowski, Leszek. *Die Philosophie des Positivismus.* Munich: Piper, 1977.

Koselleck, Reinhart. *Vergangene Zukunft. Zur Semantik geschichtlicher Zeiten.* Frankfurt: Suhrkamp, 1979.

Krell, David Farrell. *Daimon Life. Heidegger and Life Philosophy.* Bloomington: Indiana University Press, 1992.

———. "General Introduction: 'The Question of Being.'" In *Martin Heidegger: Basic Writings: From* Being and Time *(1927) to* The Task of Thinking *(1964).* New York: Harper and Row, 1977.

———. *Intimations of Mortality. Time, Truth and Finitude in Heidegger's Thinking of Being.* University Park: Pennsylvania State University Press, 1986.

Krieger, Leonard. *Ranke: The Meaning of History.* Chicago: University of Chicago Press, 1977.

Krokow, Graf Christian von. *Die Entscheidung: Eine Untersuchung über E. Jünger, C. Schmitt, M. Heidegger.* Stuttgart: F. Enke, 1958.

Krüger, G. "Martin Heidegger und der Humanismus." *Theologische Rundschau,* n.s. 18 (1950).

Külpe, Oswald. *Einleitung in die Philosophie.* 5th ed. Leipzig: Hirzel, 1910.

Kuschbert-Tölle, Helga. *Heidegger—der letzte Metaphysiker?* Königstein i. Ts.: Hain, 1979.

Lacoue-Labarthe, Philippe. *La fiction du politique.* Paris: Bourgois, 1987.

———. *Heidegger, Art and Politics.* Oxford: Blackwell, 1990.

Langan, Thomas. *The Meaning of Heidegger.* New York: Columbia University Press, 1961.

Lask, Emil. *Gesammelte Schriften.* 3 vols. Tübingen: Mohr, 1923.

Lehmann, Karl. "Christliche Geschichtserfahrung und ontologische Frage beim jungen Heidegger." *Philosophisches Jahrbuch* 74 (1966): 126–54.

Lévinas, Emmanuel. *En découvrant l'existence avec Husserl et Heidegger.* Paris: Vrin, 1949.

———. *Le temps et l'autre,* 3d ed. Paris: Presses Universitaires de France, 1989.

Löwith, Karl. *European Nihilism.* Translated by Gary Steiner. Edited by Richard Wolin. New York: Columbia University Press, 1995.

———. *Gesammelte Abhandlungen: Zur Kritik der geschichtlichen Existenz.* Stuttgart: Kohlhammer, 1960.

_____. "Grundzüge der Entwicklung der Phänomenologie zur Philosophie und ihr Verhältnis zur protestantischen Theologie." *Theologische Rundschau,* Neue Folge 2 (1930): 26–64, 333–61.

_____. *Heidegger—Denker in dürftiger Zeit. Sämtliche Schriften,* vol. 8. Stuttgart: Metzler, 1984.

_____. "Les implications politiques de la philosophie de l'existence chez Heidegger." *Les Temps Modernes* 2 (1946): 343–60.

_____. *Mein Leben in Deutschland vor und nach 1933. Ein Bericht.* Stuttgart: Metzler, 1986.

_____. *My Life in Germany before and after 1933: A Report.* Champaign: University of Illinois Press, 1994.

_____. *Von Hegel zu Nietzsche. Sämtliche Schriften,* vol. 4. Stuttgart: Metzler, 1988.

_____. *Weltgeschichte und Heilsgeschehen. Sämtliche Schriften,* vol. 2. Stuttgart: Metzler, 1983.

_____. *Wissen, Glaube und Skepsis. Sämtliche Schriften,* vol. 3. Stuttgart: Metzler, 1985.

Löwith, Karl, et al. *Martin Heidegger im Gespräch.* Edited by R. Wisser. Munich: Alber, 1970.

Mach, Ernst. *Beiträge zur Analyse der Empfindungen.* Jena: G. Fischer, 1886.

_____. *Erkenntnis und Irrtum: Skizzen zur Psychologie der Forschung.* Leipzig: Barth, 1905.

Makkreel, Rudolf A. *Dilthey: Philosopher of the Human Sciences.* Princeton, N.J.: Princeton University Press, 1975.

Mandelbaum, Maurice. *History, Man and Reason: A Study in Nineteenth-Century Thought.* Baltimore: Johns Hopkins University Press, 1971.

_____. *The Problem of Historical Knowledge.* New York: Harper and Row, 1967.

Mannheim, Karl. "Das Problem der Generationen." *Kölner Vierteljahreshefte* 7, nos. 2–3 (1928–29): 157–85, 309–30.

Marcuse, Herbert. "Beiträge zu einer Phänomenologie des historischen Materialismus." *Philosophische Hefte* 1 (1928): 45–68. Reprinted in *Schriften.* Vol. 1: *Der deutsche Künstlerroman: Frühe Aufsätze.* Frankfurt am Main: Suhrkamp, 1978.

Marcuse, Ludwig. *Mein zwanzigstes Jahrhundert: Auf dem Weg zu einer Autobiographie.* Hamburg: Fischer, 1968.

Marion, J. L. *Dieu sans l'être*. Paris: Communio/Fayard, 1982.

Marrou, Henri-Irénée. *De la connaissance historique*. Paris: Éditions du Seuil, 1954.

Martin, Bernd, ed. *Martin Heidegger und das "Dritte Reich": Ein Kompendium*. Darmstadt: Wissenschaftliche Buchgesellschaft, 1989.

Martin, G. M. "Dezisionismus in der Theologie Rudolf Bultmanns?" Ph.D. diss., University of Tübingen, 1973.

Mazzarella, Eugenio. *Ermeneutica dell'effettività: Prospettive ontiche dell'ontologia heideggeriana*. Naples: Guida, 1993.

Meinecke, Friedrich. *Autobiographische Schriften*. Vol. 8 of *Werke*. Stuttgart: Koehler, 1969.

_____. *Die Entstehung des Historismus*. 2d ed. Munich: Leibniz, 1946.

Mesure, Sylvie. *Dilthey et la fondation des sciences historiques*. Paris: Presses Universitaires de France, 1990.

Mink, Louis O. *Historical Understanding*. Edited by Brian Fay, Eugene O. Golob, and Richard T. Vann. Ithaca, N.Y.: Cornell University Press, 1987.

Motzkin, Gabriel. *Time and Transcendence: Secular History, the Catholic Reaction, and the Rediscovery of the Future*. Dordrecht: Kluwer, 1992.

Muller, Jerry Z. *The Other God that Failed: Hans Freyer and the Deradicalization of German Conservatism*. Princeton, N.J.: Princeton University Press, 1987.

Murray, Michael, ed. *Modern Philosophy of History: Its Origin and Destination*. Hague: Nijhoff, 1970.

Nietzsche, Friedrich. *Friedrich Nietzsche: Erkenntnistheoretische Schriften*. Edited by J. Habermas et al. Frankfurt am Main: Suhrkamp, 1968.

_____. *Vom Nutzen und Nachteil der Historie für das Leben*. Vol. 1 of *Werke*. Edited by Frankfurt am Main: Ullstein, 1980.

Nolte, Ernst. *Martin Heidegger. Politik und Geschichte im Leben und Denken*. Berlin: Propyläen Verlag, 1992.

Ott, Hugo. *Martin Heidegger: A Political Life*. London: HarperCollins, 1993.

_____. *Martin Heidegger: Unterwegs zu seiner Biographie*. Frankfurt am Main: Campus, 1988.

Overbeck, Franz. *Über die Christlichkeit unserer heutigen Theologie.* 2d ed. Darmstadt: Wissenschaftliche Buchgesellschaft, 1974.

Palmier, Jean-Michel. *Les écrits politiques de Heidegger.* Paris: L'Herne, 1968.

Pereira, Miguel Baptista. *Tradição e crise no pensamento do jovem Heidegger.* Coimbra, Portugal: Biblos, LXV, 1989.

Philolenko, A. *Études kantiennes.* Paris: Vrin, 1982.

Pöggeler, Otto. *Der Denkweg Martin Heideggers.* Pfullingen: Neske, 1963.

_____. *Neue Wege mit Heidegger.* Freiburg im Breisgau: Alber, 1992.

_____. *Philosophie und Politik bei Heidegger.* Freiburg im Breisgau: Alber, 1972.

Przywara, Erich. "Drei Richtungen der Phänomenologie." *Stimmen der Zeit* 115 (1928): 252–64.

Ranke, Leopold von. "Idee der Universalhistorie." In Eberhard Kessel, "Rankes Idee der Universalhistorie." *Historische Zeitschrift* 178 (1954): 269–308.

_____. "Über die Epochen der neueren Geschichte." *Geschichte und Politik: Ausgewählte Aufsätze und Meisterschriften.* Edited by H. Hofmann. Stuttgart: Kröner, 1940.

Renthe-Fink, Leonhard von. "Geschichtlichkeit." In *Historisches Wörterbuch der Philosophie,* vol. 3. Basel: Schwabe, 1974.

_____. *Geschichtlichkeit: Ihr terminologischer und begrifflicher Ursprung bei Hegel, Haym, Dilthey und Yorck.* 2d ed. Göttingen: Vandenhoeck and Ruprecht, 1968.

Rickert, Heinrich. "Geschichtsphilosophie." In W. Windelband, ed., *Philosophie im Beginn des 20. Jahrhunderts: Festschrift für Kuno Fischer.* Heidelberg: Winter, 1907.

_____. *Die Grenzen der naturwissenschaftlichen Begriffsbildung.* 3d and 4th eds. Tübingen: Mohr, 1921.

_____. *Wilhelm Windelband.* Tübingen: Mohr, 1915.

Ricœur, Paul. *Temps et récit.* 3 vols. Paris: Éditions du Seuil, 1983–85.

_____. "Preface à Bultmann." In *Le conflit des interprétations: Essais d'herméneutique.* Paris: Éditions du Seuil, 1969.

_____. *Time and Narrative,* 3 vols. Translated by K. Blamey and D. Pellauer. Chicago: University of Chicago Press, 1984–88.

Ritschl, Albrecht. *Die christliche Lehre von der Rechtfertigung und Versöhnung.* 3 vols. 3d ed. Bonn: Marcus, 1888–89.
_____. *Theologie und Metaphysik.* Bonn: Marcus, 1881.
Rockmore, Tom. *On Heidegger's Nazism and Philosophy.* Berkeley: University of California Press, 1992.
Rodi, F. "Die Bedeutung Diltheys für die Konzeption von 'Sein und Zeit': Zum Umfeld von Heideggers Kasseler Vorträgen (1925)." *Dilthey-Jahrbuch für Philosophie und Geschichte der Geisteswissenschaften* 4 (1986–87): 161–77.
Rollin, Bernard E. "Heidegger's Philosophy of History in *Being and Time.*" *Modern Schoolman* 49 (January 1972): 97–113.
Rorty, Richard. *Essays on Heidegger and Others.* Cambridge: Cambridge University Press, 1991.
Rousseau, J.-J. *Les Confessions.* Vol. 1 of *Oeuvres Complètes. Édition de la Pléiade.* Paris: Gallimard, 1959.
Ruin, Hans. *Enigmatic Origins: Tracing the Theme of Historicity through Heidegger's Works.* Stockholm: Almquist and Wiksell International, 1994.
Safranski, Rüdiger. *Martin Heidegger: Between Good and Evil.* Cambridge, Mass.: Harvard University Press, 1999.
_____. *Ein Meister aus Deutschland: Heidegger und seine Zeit.* Munich: Hanser, 1994.
Scheler, Max. *Die deutsche Philosophie der Gegenwart.* Vol. 7 of *Gesammelte Werke.* Bern: Francke, 1973.
_____. *Späte Schriften.* Vol. 9 of *Gesammelte Werke.* Edited by Manfred S. Frings. Bern: Francke, 1976.
Schleiermacher, F. *Über die Religion: Reden an die Gebildeten unter ihren Verächtern.* Hamburg: Meiner, 1958.
Schnabel, Franz. *Deutsche Geschichte im 19. Jahrhundert.* 4 vols. Freiburg im Breisgau: Herder, 1950.
Schnädelbach, Herbert. *Geschichtsphilosophie nach Hegel: Die Probleme des Historismus.* Freiburg im Breisgau: Alber, 1974.
Schneeberger, Guido, ed. *Nachlese zu Heidegger: Dokumente zu seinem Leben und Denken.* Bern: Suhr, 1962.
Schorcht, Claudia. *Die Philosophie an den bayerischen Universitäten, 1933–45.* Erlangen: H. Fischer, 1990.
Schuhmann, K. "Zu Heideggers *Spiegel*-Gespräch über Husserl." *Zeitschrift für philosophische Forschung* 32 (1978): 591–612.

Schürmann, Rainer. *Heidegger on Being and Acting: From Principles to Anarchy.* Bloomington: Indiana University Press, 1987.
_____. *Le Principe d'anarchie. Heidegger et la question de l'agir.* Paris: Éditions du Seuil, 1982.
Schütte, Hans-Walter. *Religion und Christentum in der Theologie Rudolf Ottos.* Berlin: de Gruyter, 1969.
Sheehan, Thomas. "Heidegger's Early Years: Fragments for a Philosophical Biography." *Listening: Journal of Religion and Culture* 12, no. 3 (1977): 3–20.
_____. "Heidegger's 'Introduction to the Phenomenology of Religion,' 1920–1921." *Personalist* 55 (1979–80): 312–24.
Sieg, Ulrich. "Die Verjudung des deutschen Geistes." *Zeit* 52 (December 22, 1989).
Simmel, Georg. *Lebensanschauung: Vier metaphysische Kapitel.* Munich: Duncker and Humblot, 1918.
_____. *Philosophie des Geldes.* Vol. 6 of *Gesamtausgabe.* Frankfurt am Main: Suhrkamp, 1989.
_____. *The Philosophy of Money.* Translated by T. Bottomore and D. Frisby. London: Routledge and Kegan Paul, 1978.
_____. "The Problem of Sociology." Translated by K. H. Wolff. In D. Levine, ed., *On Individuality and Social Forms: Selected Writings.* Chicago: University of Chicago Press, 1971.
_____. *Die Probleme der Geschichtsphilosophie: Eine erkenntnistheoretische Studie.* 4th ed. Munich: Duncker and Humblot, 1922.
_____. *Soziologie: Untersuchungen über die Formen der Vergesellschaftung.* 5th ed. Berlin: Duncker and Humblot, 1968.
Simon, M. W. *European Positivism in the Nineteenth Century.* Port Washington, N.Y.: Kennikat Press, 1963.
Sluga, Hans. *Heidegger's Crisis: Philosophy and Politics in Nazi Germany.* Cambridge, Mass.: Harvard University Press, 1993.
Spengler, Oswald. *Der Untergang des Abendlandes.* 2 vols. Munich: Beck, 1920.
Staudenmaier, F. A. *Johannes Scotus Erigena und die Wissenschaft seiner Zeit.* 2d ed. Frankfurt am Main: Minerva, 1966. (Photoreproduction of 1834 edition.)
Steiner, George. *Martin Heidegger: Eine Einführung.* Translated by M. Pfeiffer. Munich: Hanser, 1989.

Strohm, Theodor. *Theologie im Schatten politischer Romantik: Eine wissenschaftssoziologische Anfrage an die Theologie F. Gogartens.* Mainz: Grünewald, 1970.

Taminiaux, J. *La nostalgie de la Grèce à l'aube de l'idéalisme allemand: Kant et les Grecs dans l'itinéraire de Schiller, de Hölderlin et de Hegel.* Hague: Nijhoff, 1967.

Tillich, Paul. *Vorlesungen über die Geschichte des christlichen Denkens.* Stuttgart: Evangelisches Verlagswerk, 1967.

Troeltsch, Ernst. *Die Absolutheit des Christentums und die Religionsgeschichte und zwei Schriften zur Theologie.* Munich: Siebenstern Taschenbuch Verlag, 1969.

————. *Die Bedeutung des Protestantismus für die Entstehung der Modernen Welt.* Munich: Oldenburg, 1911.

————. "Christentum und Kultur von Franz Overbeck." *Historische Zeitschrift* 122 (1920): 279–87.

————. *Gesammelte Schriften.* 4 vols. Tübingen: Mohr, 1912–25.

————. "Geschichte und Metaphysik." *Zeitschrift für Theologie und Kirche.* Edited by D. Gottschick 8 (1898): 1–70.

————. *Die Soziallehren der christlichen Kirchen und Gruppen.* Tübingen: Mohr, 1912.

Unger, Rudolf. "Literaturgeschichte als Problemgeschichte: Zur Frage geisteshistorischer Synthese, mit besonderer Beziehung auf Wilhelm Dilthey." *Schriften der Königsberger Gelehrten Gesellschaft: Geisteswissenschaftliche Klasse* 1, no. 1 (1924): 1–30.

Van Buren, John. *The Young Heidegger: Rumor of the Hidden King.* Bloomington: Indiana University Press, 1994.

Vattimo, Gianni. *Avventure della Differenza.* Milan: Garzanti, 1980.

Verra, Valerio. *Letture Hegeliane. Idea, Natura e Storia.* Bologna: Il Mulino, 1992.

Villa, Dana R. *Arendt and Heidegger. The Fate of the Political.* Princeton, N.J.: Princeton University Press, 1996.

Weber, Max. *Gesammelte Aufsätze zur Religionssoziologie.* Tübingen: Mohr, 1921.

————. *Gesammelte Aufsätze zur Wissenschaftslehre.* 4th ed. Edited by J. Winckelmann. Tübingen: Mohr, 1973.

————. *The Methodology of the Social Sciences.* Translated by E. Shils and H. Finch. New York: Free Press, 1969.

_____. *Die protestantische Ethik und der "Geist" des Kapitalismus.* 2d ed. Edited by Klaus Lichtblau. Weinheim: Beltz, 1996.

Wenzel, Uwe. *Die Problematik des Grundes beim späten Heidegger: Gründen in einer weltlichen Bezughaftigkeit als "anderes Gründen."* Rheinfelden: Schäuble, 1986.

Windelband, Wilhelm. *Die Philosophie im deutschen Geistesleben des 19. Jahrhunderts.* Tübingen: Mohr, 1909.

_____. *Präludien.* 9th ed. Tübingen: Mohr, 1924.

Wohl, Robert. *The Generation of 1914.* Cambridge, Mass.: Harvard University Press, 1979.

Wolin, Richard. *The Politics of Being: The Political Thought of Martin Heidegger.* New York: Columbia University Press, 1990.

Wolin, Richard, ed. *The Heidegger Controversy: A Critical Reader.* Cambridge, Mass.: MIT Press, 1992.

Wren, T. "Heidegger's Philosophy of History." *Journal of the British Society for Phenomenology* 3, no. 2 (May 1972): 111–26.

Young, Julian. *Heidegger, philosophy, Nazism.* Cambridge: Cambridge University Press, 1997.

Zarader, Marlène. *Heidegger et les paroles de l'origine.* Paris: Vrin, 1986.

INDEX

Adorno, Theodor W., xxviii
d'Alembert, Jean le Rond, 5
Anaximander, 249, 251
Arendt, Hannah, xxiii, xxviii,
    100–101, 126, 186, 248
Aristotle, xxiv, 33, 65–69, 72–74,
    84, 93, 127, 142, 162, 180, 205,
    207–208, 246
Aron, Raymond, 61
Augustine, Saint, xiii, 40, 80, 132,
    135, 142–43, 145, 147, 151, 154,
    205
Avenarius, Richard, 17–19, 34, 59

Bambach, Charles, xxvii–xxviii
Barash, Jeffrey Andrew, 185–86,
    248–49
Barth, Karl, xii, 113–14, 129–30,
    133, 137–40, 145–46, 148–53,
    155–56, 202, 244
Beierwaltes, Werner, 245
Bergson, Henri, 129
Beyer, W. R., xxviii, 92
Blochmann, Elisabeth, 186, 249
Birault, Henri, xxvii, 251
Bonaparte, Napoleon, 27–29
Boudieu, Pierre, 249
Bousset, Wilhelm, 136
Boyce Gibson, W. R., 152
Braig, Carl, 73–77, 83, 91, 93–94
Brandner, Rudolf, xxvii
Brentano, Franz, 33–34, 67–69, 78,
    86, 93
Breysig, Kurt, 130

Brunner, Emil, 201–202, 244
Büchner, Ludwig, 17
Bultmann, Marianne, 155
Bultmann, Rudolf, xii, xiii, xxiii,
    xxviii, 114–15, 129–30, 133,
    138–40, 144–49, 151, 153–56,
    200–202, 230, 240, 243–44, 250,
    252
Burckhardt, Jacob, 231, 245

Cacciatore, Giuseppe, 61
Capelle, Philippe, 252
Caputo, John D., 94, 97
Cassirer, Ernst, xv, 56, 129–30, 164,
    185, 187, 193–94, 197–98, 201,
    230, 243, 250
Catholic Church, 65, 67–68, 74–76,
    79, 94, 132, 136, 213
Catholicism, modernist movement,
    51, 75–76, 94
Christianity, primitive, xiii, 142–43,
    150–51, 213, 217
Cicero, 207, 212
Cohen, Hermann, xi, 21–25, 60,
    160, 194, 196–97, 243
Comte, Auguste, 16, 31, 47, 59–60
Courtine, Jean-François, 243
critical philosophy of history, x, xii,
    xiv, xvi, xvii–xix, xxvi, xxviii,
    2–4, 12, 14, 20, 22, 43–54,
    61–62, 120,124, 160, 163, 165,
    168, 171, 173–75, 181–82,
    226–27, 253
Croce, Benedetto, 94, 96

Darwin, Charles, 17, 19
deconstruction (*Abbau*): *see* destruction
Degener, Alfons, 183, 186
Derrida, Jacques, xxvii, 249
Descartes, René, 180, 192, 205, 215–19, 226, 247
destruction, deconstruction, ix, 98–100, 103, 110, 113, 115–16, 125–26, 132, 143, 151, 154, 162, 198, 201, 211, 254
Dilthey, Wilhelm, xi–xii, xiv, xviii–xix, xxiii–xxiv, xxvi, xxiii–xxiv, 2–4, 16, 20, 32–34, 37–42, 44–48, 52–54, 56, 59, 61–62, 72–73, 78, 90–91, 93, 97, 101–102, 107–109, 113–14, 117, 119–20, 122, 124–26, 128–29, 131, 135, 143, 161, 170–78, 181, 183, 185–86, 198, 201, 203, 219, 227
Dostoyevsky, Fyodor, 78
Droysen, Johann Gustav, 80
Duns Scotus, John, 75, 81–82, 84–88, 90, 95–97, 99–100, 132, 183
Dyroff, Adolf, 97

Enlightenment, the, 5–7, 58
Ebbinghaus, Julius, 78–79, 95
empiricism, 7, 16–17, 71–72, 160
empiriocriticism, 17–18, 59, 69–70
Erdmann, Benno, 194
Erigena, John Scotus, 94
Ermarth, Michael, 61
existentialism, x, xxii

Farías, Victor, 92, 249
Fédier, François, 249
Ferry, Luc, 249
Feuerbach, Ludwig, 193, 200–201, 203

Fichte, Johann Gottlieb, 1, 160
Figal, Günter, 251
Finke, Heinrich, 78
Fischer, Kuno, 20
Franzen, Winfried, 92
Freud, Sigmund, 226
Fritsche, Johannes, 249
Fuchs, Ernst, 152
Fynsk, Christopher, xxvii

Gadamer, Hans-Georg, xxiii, xxv, xxvii, xxix, 56, 100–101, 112–14, 126, 129, 151,156
Gay, Peter, xxviii, 159, 183
German idealism, xxvi, 1–2, 11–14, 31, 52, 65, 74, 160, 176
Geyser, Joseph, 69
Giugliano, Antonello, 92
Glockner, Hermann, 95
Görland, Ingtraud, 58
Goethe, Johann Wolfgang von, 170, 207, 213
Gogarten, Friedrich, xii, 114–15, 129–30, 133, 138–40,145–49, 151–56
Grabmann, Martin, 95
Greece, ancient, 9–10, 45, 58, 72, 117–18, 143, 151, 162, 180, 182, 191, 202, 204, 206–207, 212–13, 220, 222–23, 230–31, 234–35, 239, 241
Grimm, Jakob, 94
Gröber, Konrad, 67
Guilead, Reuben, 251

Habermas, Jürgen, 248–49
Haeckel, Ernst, 17, 135
Harnack, Adolf von, xii, 51, 77, 135–39, 143–44, 150, 153
Hartmann, Nicolai, 160–61, 183
Haym, Rudolf, 56

Hegel, Georg Wilhelm Friedrich,
xviii, xx, 1, 4, 7–14, 16–18, 31,
36–37, 41–42, 53, 55–59, 65, 74,
78, 82, 91–92, 154, 156, 160,
168, 172, 180, 203, 205,
207–209, 213, 216–17, 220–28,
245–49
Heidegger, Elfriede Petri, 132
Heidegger, Friedrich, 64
Heidegger, Hermann, 248
Heidegger, Martin, ix–xvi,
xvii–xxix, 1, 3, 6–7, 11–12,
15–18, 20, 22–23, 32–33, 35–36,
38, 40, 47, 49–50, 56–62,
chapters 2–6, conclusion
Heraclitus, 207–208, 245–46
Herder, Johann Gottfried, 4–6,
56–58
Hermelink, Heinrich, 133
Herrmann, Wilhelm, 129, 133, 138,
153
Heussi, Karl, xxii, xxvii–xxviii, 130
historicism, x–xi, xiii, xvii, xxi,
xxvii–xxviii, 5, 32, 36–37, 49,
52–53, 63, 77, 107, 126–27, 153,
159, 163, 179–81, 196, 201,
232–33
history of Being, (Seinsgeschichte),
x, xv, xxvii–xxviii, 203–11,
215–16, 218, 220–21, 224–27,
232–33, 237, 240–41, 255–56
Hitler, Adolf, xxiv, 221
Hölderlin, Friedrich, 239
Hönigswald, Richard, 249
Hoy, David C., xxvii, 184
Hühnerfeld, Paul, xxix, 92
Humboldt, Wilhelm von, 12–14, 24,
32, 41, 58, 96, 109, 124, 207, 213
Hume, David, 5, 7–8, 17–18, 57, 59,
66, 70–72, 247

Husserl, Edmund, xi, xii, xxiii, xxvi,
xxviii, xxvi, 20, 32–39, 42,
54–55, 59–61, 68, 78, 83, 86, 88,
92–93, 96–97, 99, 102–106,
112–13, 126–29, 132–33, 152,
197–98, 202, 222, 243

Iggers, Georg, xxviii, 63, 130, 153,
159, 183, 186
Ingarden, Roman, 197, 243
irrationalism, x
Iselin, Isaac, 5, 57

Jäger, Alfred, 252
Janicaud, Dominique, 249
Jaspers, Karl, xii, 96, 98, 101–102,
106–9, 111–12, 117, 128–29,
152, 248
Jaspert, Bernd, 129
Jesus Christ, 136, 139–40, 143–44,
239, 241
Jewish prophets, 241
John, Saint, 148, 155
Johnson, Robert A., 252
Jülicher, Adolf, 139, 145
Jung, M., 252
Jüngel, Eberhard, 244
Jünger, Ernst, 155, 161, 184

Kant, Immanuel, xxiv, 2, 7–9,
20–22, 24, 32, 43, 45, 47, 49,
57–58, 62, 66, 69–72, 78, 121,
135, 142, 180, 190–99, 205,
216–17, 226, 242–43, 249
Kearney, Richard, 251
Kessel, Eberhard, 58
Kierkegaard, Sören, 78, 129, 133,
138, 150, 152
Kisiel, Theodor, xxix, 92
Kolakowski, Leszek, 59
Krell, David Farrell, 184

Krieger, Leonard, 59
Krokow, Christian Graf von, 155
Krüger, Gerhard, 252
Külpe, Oswald, 69–72, 93, 95–96

Lacoue-Labarthe, Philippe, 249
Lagarde, Paul de, 139
Lamprecht, Karl, 130–31
Lange, Friedrich A., 20, 60
Lask, Emil, 96, 112
Lebensphilosophie (philosophy of
    life), 101–102, 121–22, 126, 160,
    164, 177
Leibniz, Gottfried Wilhelm, 114,
    193, 205, 215–16
Leo XIII, Pope, 65, 68
Liebmann, Otto, 20
Locke, John, 7, 247
Löwith, Ada, 130
Löwith, Karl, 98–101, 113, 125,
    129–30, 152–53, 155–56,
    201–202, 244, 249
Lotze, Hermann, 20, 24, 87, 135
Lukács, Georg, 223
Luther, Martin, xiii, 133–34,
    142–43, 145, 147, 151, 205, 215

Mach, Ernst, 17–19, 34, 60
Machiavelli, Niccolo, 40
Macquarrie, John, xxix, 126, 183–84
Makkreel, Rudolf, 61
Mandelbaum, Maurice, 62
Mannheim, Karl, 171
Marcus Aurelius, 40
Marcuse, Herbert, xxiii, xxviii
Marcuse, Ludwig, 96
Marion, Jean-Luc, 251
Marrou, Henri I., 62
Martin, Bernd, 248
Martin, G. M., 155
Marx, Karl, 203, 226

marxism, 219, 224, 247
Meinecke, Friedrich, 78, 93–94
Messer, August, 69
Möhler, Johann Adam, 74, 94
Moleschott, Jacob, 17
Montaigne, Michel E. de, 40
Motzkin, Gabriel, xxvii, 94
Murray, Michael, xxvii

Natorp, Paul, xi, 96, 160
naturalism, naturalistic worldview,
    2, 15–21, 23, 31, 34–37, 40, 42,
    44, 47–48, 50–51, 53–54, 60,
    124–25
Nazism, xxviii–xxix, 221–23
neo-Kantianism, xii, 20–21, 24–25,
    31–36, 38, 48–50, 52–53, 59, 77,
    79, 96, 99, 102–103, 105, 112,
    114, 117, 129, 134–35, 142, 148,
    152, 160–61, 164, 194–96
  Baden School, xi, xii, 20–25, 37,
    42, 44–48, 104, 124, 171
  Marburg School, xi, 21–22,
    160–61, 193, 196, 243
neo-Platonism, 72, 132, 135,
    142–43, 145, 147, 204, 245
neo-Scholasticism, neo-Thomism,
    65–66, 68–69, 72, 76, 84, 132,
    157
Niebuhr, Barthold Georg, 13, 94
Nietzsche, Friedrich, xiii, xx, 55–56,
    63, 78, 91, 97, 101, 119–21, 131,
    148–50, 156, 185–86, 201, 203,
    205, 213, 215–17, 220, 223,
    226–28, 233–35, 242, 244,
    247–52, 256
nihilism, xiii, 228

Ott, Hugo, xxix, 92, 95, 152, 249
Otto, Rudolf, 132, 152
Overbeck, Franz, xiii, 133, 149–51,
    153, 156, 241

Palmier, Jean-Michel, xxix, 92
pantheism, 74, 146
Parmenides, 207, 230, 234
Pascal, Blaise, 40
Paul, Saint, 138–41, 143, 148, 153, 200
Pereira, Miguel Baptista, 92
Philonenko, Alexis, 242
Pindar, 231
Pius IX, Pope, 68, 76
Plato, 38, 121–23, 142, 162, 180, 205, 207–10, 212, 214, 217, 224, 233, 242, 246–47, 255
Pöggeler, Otto, xxvii, 74, 91, 94, 97, 152, 154, 248–49
Portalis, Jean Etienne Marie, 29
positivism, 11, 16, 22, 31, 59–60
presocratics, xv, 207–208, 213, 234–35, 245
Protestantism
    liberal, 51, 76–77, 115, 129, 133–40, 142, 146,151–52, 239
    neo-orthodox (dialectical theology), xii, 51, 114–15, 129, 133, 136, 138–40, 145–50, 200, 202, 255
Protestant Reformation, 137, 142
Przywara, Erich, 201–202, 244
psychoanalysis, 191, 226–27

Ranke, Leopold von, xviii, 13–14, 24, 32, 41–42, 58–59, 81, 94, 109, 124, 172, 176
realism, critical, 71–72, 84, 93, 95–96
relativism, x–xi, 32, 37, 52, 55, 83, 103, 118,126–27, 137, 159, 179–81, 196, 199, 201, 233
Renaissance, Italian, 29, 170, 219
Renaut, Alain, 249
Renthe-Fink, Leonhard von, 56
Richardson, William, 93, 242

Rickert, Heinrich, xi, xviii, xxi, xxiii, xxvi–xxvii, xxvi, 2, 20–32, 34–35, 38–45, 47, 49–51, 54, 60–63, 77–79, 81, 83, 85, 88, 90, 92, 95–97, 99, 102–103, 105–106, 112–13, 116, 119–22,124–25, 126–31, 154, 170, 172–75, 194, 227
Ricœur, Paul, xxvii, 184, 252
Riehl, Alois, 194
Rilke, Rainer Maria, 78
Ritschl, Albrecht, 63, 134–36, 139, 152
Robertson, William, 5
Robinson, Edward, xxix, 126, 183–84
Rockmore, Tom, 248–49
Rodi, F., 131
Rollin, Bernhard E., xxvii
Rorty, Richard, 249
Rousseau, Jean-Jacques, 223, 228, 250

Safranski, Rüdiger, xxix, 92, 249
Saner, Hans, 128
Savigny, Friedrich von, 94
Scheler, Max, 130, 192–93, 242
Schelling, Friedrich W., 1, 16, 74, 78, 160, 233, 250–51
Schleiermacher, Friedrich, 4–6, 56–57, 94, 135–36, 139, 152
Schmitt, Carl, 155, 222
Schnabel, Franz, 59, 94
Schneeberger, Guido, 248
scholasticism, medieval, 34, 45, 68, 72, 74–76, 84–86, 88–91, 94, 133, 142–43, 202, 215
Schorcht, Claudia, 249
Schürmann, Rainer, 245
Schütte, Hans-Walter, 132
Schuhmann, Karl, 248
Seneca, 40
Sheehan, Thomas, 92–93, 95–97, 152

Sieg, Ulrich, 249
Siegfried, H., 92
Simmel, Georg, xviii, xxvi, 2, 31,
    47–49, 62, 90–91, 101, 113–14,
    119–20, 122, 124–25, 175
Simon, M. W., 59
Sluga, Hans, 249
Soden, Hans von, 129, 133, 152
Spengler, Oswald, xii, 113–20,
    122–25, 129–30, 161, 255
Spiegelberg, H., 152
Staudenmaier, F. A., 74–76, 94
Stichweh, Klaus, 130
Strohm, Theodor, 155
Suarez, Francisco, 73, 205

Taminiaux, Jacques, 58
Thomas Aquinas, Saint, 65–68,
    73–74, 205
Thomas of Erfurt, 87–88, 95
Tillich, Paul, 152–53
Trakl, Georg, 78
Trendelenburg, Adolf, 33, 69
Troeltsch, Ernst, xii, xviii, xxi,
    xxvi–xxvii, 2, 31, 50–52, 54–55,
    63, 80, 83, 113–16, 119–20, 122,
    124–25, 129–30, 134–39,143–44,
    146, 150, 152–54, 156, 174, 230,
    250
Tübingen Speculative School,
    74–76, 91
Turneysen, Eduard, 114

Unger, Rudolf, 161, 183

Van Buren, John, xxix, 92
Villa, Dana, 186
Vattimo, Gianni, xxvii
Voltaire, François Marie Arouet, 5, 7

Vossler, Karl, 96

Weber, Max, xxiii, 31, 49–50, 63,
    112, 137, 230, 250
Weimar Republic, xxiv, xxviii
Weiss, Johannes, 136
Wieland, Christoph Martin, 58
Windelband, Wilhelm, xi, xviii, 2,
    16–17, 20–26, 34, 38–39, 42–43,
    45–47, 50, 54–55, 59–60, 62, 83,
    92, 113, 119–22, 124–25, 126,
    131, 142, 173–74, 176, 194, 227

Wolf, Erik, 222, 248
Wolff, Christian, 193
Wolin, Richard, 249
Wrede, Wilhelm, 136, 139
Wren, Thomas E., xxvii
Wust, Peter, 161

Yorck von Wartenburg, Count Paul,
    xiv, 3, 56, 61, 175–78, 186
Young, Julian, 249

Zarader, Marlène, 245

PERSPECTIVES IN CONTINENTAL PHILOSOPHY SERIES
John D. Caputo, series editor

1. John D. Caputo, ed., *Deconstruction in a Nutshell: A Conversation with Jacques Derrida.*
2. Michael Strawser, *Both/And: Reading Kierkegaard—From Irony to Edification.*
3. Michael D. Barber, *Ethical Hermeneutics: Rationality in Enrique Dussel's Philosophy of Liberation.*
4. James H. Olthuis, ed., *Knowing* Other-*wise: Philosophy at the Threshold of Spirituality.*
5. James Swindal, *Reflection Revisited: Jürgen Habermas's Discursive Theory of Truth.*
6. Richard Kearney, *Poetics of Imagining: Modern and Postmodern.* Second edition.
7. Thomas W. Busch, *Circulating Being: From Embodiment to Incorporation—Essays on Late Existentialism.*
8. Edith Wyschogrod, *Emmanuel Levinas: The Problem of Ethical Metaphysics.* Second edition.
9. Francis J. Ambrosio, ed., *The Question of Christian Philosophy Today.*
10. Jeffrey Bloechl, ed., *The Face of the Other and the Trace of God: Essays on the Philosophy of Emmanuel Levinas.*
11. Ilse N. Bulhof and Laurens ten Kate, eds., *Flight of the Gods: Philosophical Perspectives on Negative Theology.*
12. Trish Glazebrook, *Heidegger's Philosophy of Science.*
13. Kevin Hart, *The Trespass of the Sign: Deconstruction, Theology, and Philosophy.*
14. Mark C. Taylor, *Journeys to Selfhood: Hegel and Kierkegaard.* Second edition.
15. Dominique Janicaud, Jean-François Courtine, Jean-Louis Chrétien, Michel Henry, Jean-Luc Marion, and Paul Ricœur, *Phenemenology and the "Theological Turn": The French Debate.*
16. Karl Jaspers, *The Question of German Guilt.* Introduction by Joseph W. Koterski, S.J.
17. Jean-Luc Marion, *The Idol and Distance: Five Studies.* Translated with an introduction by Thomas A. Carlson.
18. Jeffrey Dudiak, *The Intrigue of Ethics: A Reading of the Idea of Discourse in the Thought of Emmanuel Levinas.*
19. Robyn Horner, *Rethinking God As Gift: Marion, Derrida, and the Limits of Phenomenology.*

20. Mark Dooley, *The Politics of Exodus: Søren Keirkegaard's Ethics of Responsibility*.
21. Merold Westphal, *Toward a Postmodern Christian Faith: Overcoming Onto-Theology*.
22. Edith Wyschogrod, Jean-Joseph Goux and Eric Boynton, eds., *The Enigma of Gift and Sacrifice*.
23. Stanislas Breton, *The Word and the Cross*. Translated with an introduction by Jacquelyn Porter.
24. Jean-Luc Marion, *Prolegomena to Charity*. Translated by Stephen E. Lewis and Jeffrey L. Kosky.
25. Peter H. Spader, *Scheler's Ethical Personalism: Its Logic, Development, and Promise*.
26. Jean-Louis Chrétien, *The Unforgettable and the Unhoped For*. Translated by Jeffrey Bloechl.
27. Don Cupitt, *Is Nothing Sacred? The Non-Realist Philosophy of Religion: Selected Essays*.
28. Jean-Luc Marion, *In Excess: Studies of Saturated Phenomena*. Translated by Robyn Horner and Vincent Berraud.
29. Phillip Goodchild, *Rethinking Philosophy of Religion: Approaches from Continental Philosophy*.
30. William J. Richardson, S.J., *Heidegger: Through Phenomenology to Thought*.